UFOs and Related Subjects:
An Annotated Bibliography

by
Lynn E. Catoe

Prepared by the Library of Congress
Science and Technology Division

for the

Air Force Office of Scientific Research
Office of Aerospace Research, USAF
Arlington, Virginia   22209

1969

Supplemented by

Unidentified Flying Objects

by

Kay Rodgers

Reference Section
Science and Technology Division
Library of Congress
Washington, D.C.

1976

---

*WITH AN INTRODUCTION BY
LESLIE SHEPARD*

Republished by
Gale Research Company
Book Tower
Detroit, Michigan   48226

1978

UFOs and Related Subjects: An Annotated Bibliography
was prepared under Air Force Office of Scientific
Research Project Orders 67-0002 and 68-0003
(Publication Number AFOSR 68-1656)

Library of Congress Card Catalog No. 68-62196

A Hawksbill Press Book

U.S. Government Printing Office, Washington: 1969

Library of Congress Cataloging in Publication Data

Catoe, Lynn E
  UFOs and related subjects.

  Includes index.
  1. Flying saucers--Bibliography. I. United
States. Library of Congress. Science and Tech-
nology Division. II. United States. Air Force.
Office of Scientific Research. III. Rodgers,
Kay. Unidentified flying objects. 1978.
IV. Title.
Z5064.F5C373 [TL789]   016.0019'42   78-26124
ISBN 0-8103-2021-5

NEW INTRODUCTION

This is the most comprehensive bibliography of Unidentified Flying Objects ever compiled.

This monumental work with over 1,600 items was the result of a two-year survey initiated by the U.S. Air Force Office of Scientific Research. Every major aspect of the subject has been covered, ranging from scientific discussion to mythology and occultism. There are forty-five main headings and various sub-sections. Publications relevant to more than one heading are entered more than once under each appropriate heading. Many items have valuable annotations, clarifying the contents or the approach of individual writers. The book includes an appendix on Mirages and an Author Index.

Originally published by the Library of Congress Science and Technology Division, this key bibliography has been out of print for some years, and nothing has since been attempted on the same scale. It was partially supplemented in 1976 by *Unidentified Flying Objects; A Selected Bibliography* compiled by Kay Rodgers, containing some two hundred additional items published in the succeeding seven years.

Because of the ever increasing public interest in the subject of Unidentified Flying Objects, the present publishers decided to reprint Ms. Lynn E. Catoe's great bibliography in full, together with *Unidentified Flying Objects; A Selected Bibliography* as an additional appendix. This combined reprint constitutes an authoritative bibliographical guide to UFO reports, speculations and discussions at all levels, popular and scientific. In addition, the present publishers are also preparing a comprehensive bibliographical supplement intended to cover other publications on the subject subsequent to the present two works.

'Unidentified Flying Object' is a general term covering a wide range of mysterious celestial phenomena, including what are popularly known as 'flying saucers', i.e. mysterious aerial objects of a saucer-like shape, apparently intelligently guided. In spite of widespread and persistent reports of sightings over many centuries, the subject remains a baffling mystery.

Strange objects have been seen in the skies for thousands of years, and the mythologies of ancient India described *vimanas* or aerial chariots used by gods and demons. For many centuries, reports of celestial phenomena (comets, bright stars, fire-balls) as well as mysterious figures and objects in the skies have been interpreted as happy auguries or portents of doom. Much of this supernatural quality is still present in modern reports of UFO sightings, although this period reflects the technological approach of the last two hundred years and the recent era of space travel.

In relatively modern times, sightings have tended to occur in waves, in line with the mass media society of improved communications and public preoccupation with common topics of the day. Widespread reports and discussions have consciously and unconsciously stimulated new sightings, real or imaginary. Usually such reports are stereotyped to the outlook of their time.

For example, the first mass wave of UFO sightings occurred in the U.S. between 1896 and 1897, with thousands of reports of cigar-shaped airships, at a time when heavier-than-air rigid dirigibles were being discussed as a technological possibility. During World War II, many pilots reported strange balls of light which followed them in their missions over Germany and Japan. These 'foo-fighters' were in line with ideas of possible secret weapons, but dismissed as 'mass hallucination' by the U.S. Eighth Army, although still an unsolved mystery. From 1946-48, there were many reports from Scandinavia of mysterious cigar-shaped objects in the sky which became known as 'ghost rockets'. At that time, secret rocket research and weaponry was well advanced.

On June 24, 1947, U.S. pilot Kenneth Arnold saw nine bright disc-shaped flying objects, moving in close formation at an estimated speed of 1,700 m.p.h. between the peaks of Mount Rainier and Mount Adams, Washington. Arnold described the movement of the objects as like 'a saucer skipping over water' and a reporter coined the term 'flying saucers', which has stuck ever since. Subsequently 'flying saucers' of disc-like shape were reported in many thousands of sightings all over the world.

After half a century of science-fiction stories of other planets, anticipating modern space travel, the concept of visitors from outer space in flying objects has now become firmly embedded in Ufology.

In 1953, George Adamski, co-author with Desmond Leslie of the book *Flying Saucers Have Landed*, claimed to have contacted the occupant of a flying saucer which landed in the Arizona desert, and produced as proof a photograph of a mysterious footprint. Soon afterwards there was a spate of reports of contact with flying saucer occupants on Adamski lines, some even involving abductions and journeys in flying saucers.

This pattern of waves of reports and claims, involving various stereotyped appearances and explanations has a curiously ambiguous quality, which has been interpreted in two ways. The skeptic says that it reflects the same collective myth-making activity as the creation of folklore and mass hysteria; the advocate for the reality of UFOs suggests that public discussion of phenomena stimulates awareness and observations, and that certain themes are characteristic of particular moments in history.

The latter point was emphasized by the iconoclastic writer Charles Fort (1874-1932), who was the first modern writer to classify unidentified flying objects reported throughout history. His famous books *The Book of the Damned* (1919), *New Lands* (1923), *Lo!* (1931) and *Wild Talents* (1932) listed and discussed all kinds of anomalous phenomena (the 'damned' were the data ignored or explained away by orthodox scientists). Fort was aware of the curious synchronicity of certain ideas and events, which he formulated in the whimsical concept that human beings 'steam-engine' when 'steam-engine time' comes, just as plants bud and blossom in their seasons. It is a formulation that has particular relevance to the strange coincidence of many inventions such as aviation, the internal-combustion engine or photography, when pioneer inventors had similar ideas or worked on comparable lines without knowledge of other work in the field. Certain ideas and developments are 'in the air' at a given time. And whilst it is true that many claims of contact with visitors in spacecraft from other planets may have been stimulated by science-fiction stories on this theme, who is to say where the imaginative writers drew their inspiration? It may be that both fact and fiction emanate from a common source.

Again, paranormal appearances in literature and life favor particular conventionalizations at different periods in history. Where some sensitive souls once saw angels, ghosts and fairies, modern folk now see shining visitors from Mars and Venus in technologically advanced spacecraft. And if space probes have not so far disclosed Martian and Venusian residents or their vessels, there are also contemporary theories of perception which posit alternative realities, multi-dimensional universes and other concepts in which scientific speculation and the occult revival find curious synchronicities.

This collective conventionalization of UFO sightings and concepts is a formidable obstacle in trying to evaluate the reality of the phenomenon, as various official inquiries and Government agencies have found out to their cost. Although normal scientific method favors quantitative evaluation, a thousand reports of contact with a flying saucer entity do not necessarily validate such claims and indeed are more likely to generate new mythologies. In their nature, official investigations are often unsatisfactory ways of dealing with bizarre and controversial subjects, and it is easy to imagine the pitfalls and shortfalls of a U.S. Government investigation into (for example) the phenomena of Uri Geller. So far no method of official investigation of UFOs has yet been devised which can deal adequately with the many complexities of the subject without setting in train near paranoid accusations of secret conspiracies to 'hide the facts'. The basic problem remains, that every claimed sighting and report must be considered on its own merits, and often individual cases are too subjective to be amenable to positive verification or dismissal.

A comparable problem has always existed in the field of psychic and occult phenomena. Spontaneous paranormal events carry conviction only to those immediately involved. After the event, these individuals may be accused of malobservation, hoaxing or downright fraud. And even the carefully monitored experiments in parapsychological laboratories tend to inhibit paranormal phenomena and culminate in antiseptic jargon reports, heavily decorated with higher mathematics which might mean one thing and again might mean another. In the laboratory the Spiritualist marvels of materialization and contact with other worlds dwindle to ambiguities of card-guessing and shape visualization on a relatively trivial scale that would be little help to a professional gambler.

All this indicates the need for comprehensive bibliography in controversial and treacherous fields of research where rumor and exaggeration are special hazards. UFOs have generated a vast literature, as well as myriad sightings, theories, new mythologies and esoteric cults. It is impossible to evaluate claimed phenomena without a detailed knowledge and study of pre-existing publications.

It has to be said that in spite of official and unofficial studies and reports, nobody has yet decisively proved or disproved the claimed extraterrestrial nature of UFOs or physical and telepathic contact with them. There have been known frauds and hoaxes, as well as some malobservation of natural phenomena (stars, ball lightning, air inversion, etc.) and meteorological objects like sky balloons. There has certainly been some self-deception and romanticization, fuelled by science-fiction and popular occult literature. But clearly there is also a solid core of so far inexplicable phenomena (some of it photographed or filmed) involving reliable witnesses, which cannot be explained away under any of these headings.

In 1973, while campaigning for the presidency of the United States, Governor Jimmy Carter of Georgia reported seeing a UFO. He promised that if elected he would ensure that there was no official secrecy on the subject of UFOs. In 1978, NASA rejected a White House suggestion to reopen government investigation into UFOs, claiming that it would be 'wasteful and probably unproductive.' However,

NASA expressed willingness to analyze substantive material on UFOs that was 'bona fide physical evidence from credible sources.'

Meanwhile bibliographies like the present work are enormously helpful in identifying individual aspects of this vast and confusing subject, as well as providing data for evaluation. Even if individual books are sometimes dubious or even suspect, comparison of different accounts can assist correlation, and a survey of the whole field of UFO phenomena is essential in order to grasp the scope and complexity of the subject.

This reissue of Lynn E. Catoe's monumental bibliography, together with the Kay Rodgers supplement, comes at a time when public fascination with UFOs has received a powerful stimulus through the Steven Spielberg movie "Close Encounters of the Third Kind" (released in 1977), inaugurating a new wave of UFO movies and public interest in the theme. Sightings continue and new books pour off the paperback presses, some of them thoughtful, others cashing in on a popular trend. Intelligent and responsible analyses of the UFO phenomenon rub shoulders with wild speculations and romantic myths.

More than ever, it is essential for the serious investigator or the informed member of the public to be aware of the scope of earlier publications and materials in this controversial field.

This present bibliography stands as an essential reference work on a subject of continuing public and official concern.

LESLIE SHEPARD

FOREWORD

The subject of unidentified flying objects is a popular phenomenon of the period from 1947, evoking widespread speculation, and producing a literature of great variety and scope. This body of literature and documentation is source material for readers seeking better understanding of this question, which has involved the U.S. Air Force as well as other official groups.

This is believed to be the most comprehensive bibliography published to date on the subject, and includes the extensive UFO collection of the Library of Congress, as well as related material useful in understanding the nature of the question.

The bibliography was produced by the Library's Division of Science and Technology with support provided by the Air Force Office of Scientific Research, a unit of the Office of Aerospace Research, the research agency of the U.S. Air Force.

The bibliographer is Miss Lynn E. Catoe, who also collected the books, journal articles, pamphlets, conference proceedings, tapes, original manuscripts, and other material listed here, a total of more than 1,600 items.

This literature survey was requested by AFOSR to assist a scientific research project at the University of Colorado under the direction of Dr. Edward U. Condon on unidentified flying objects. The research began 1 November 1966, and has been carried out with support provided by AFOSR at the direction of the Secretary of the Air Force under contract F44620-67-C-0035. The preparation of the bibliography was accomplished under AFOSR project orders 67-0002 and 68-0003.

i

Material collected by the Library of Congress and cited in this bibliography was made available in its entirety, with the exception of the addenda, to the University of Colorado project in the form of microfilm. The bibliography itself was provided the university in card form. While much of this material is protected by copyright, photocopies of some items are available for sale to the public. Inquiries on their purchase may be directed to the Library of Congress, Photoduplication Service, Washington, D.C. 20540.

In keeping with its policy of making widely available the results of projects it supports, AFOSR has undertaken publication of the bibliography, and its expected sale through the Superintendent of Documents of the U.S. Government Printing Office. This publication in no way constitutes an endorsement by the Department of the Air Force of any material cited, or of any views expressed in any of the material. Responsibility for editorial content remains that of the bibliographer. Inquiries on this publication may be directed to the Staff Information Officer, AFOSR, Arlington, Virginia 22209.

Cartoons have developed as a distinct art form reflecting public opinions of our time. Appreciation is expressed here to the artists who have permitted the use of their work, and to their publications holding copyright.

AFOSR was fortunate to avail itself of the resources of the Science and Technology Division, and especially the dedicated and highly skillful services of Miss Catoe. The material she developed will assist those seeking to understand not only these and related phenomena but also their various implications for a wide range of inquiry.

July 1969

PREFACE

This bibliography will indicate to many that the subject of unidentified flying objects is far broader and more complicated than has been recognized by the adherents to any one theory or solution. There are deep historical roots, involved social and psychological implications, and a complex overlapping of many disparate subject fields.

It would seem that the whole must be studied to understand the significance of the parts, and the phenomenon would seem to be multiple in case and diffuse in source. There is no simple, single explanation of the UFO phenomenon that can be applied to all cases described in the literature.

In historical perspective, UFO literature, especially during the last two decades, indicates a pattern of brief but voluminous "waves." These are made up of books, magazine articles and newspaper stories devoted to detailed descriptions of unidentified flying objects, including controversial accounts of people who claim to have had direct personal experience with these objects and their occupants.

Each new wave of literature is a rediscovery of an old subject, for the tales of marvelous flying machines piloted by unearthly beings can be traced even beyond their mention in the ancient Hindu scriptures. Also, it should be noted that the folklore and mythology of many countries and the legends of many aboriginal tribes seem to be integrally related -- if not completely bound -- to the belief that this planet's skies are occupied, perhaps even populated, by entities superior to man.

Thousands of books and pamphlets on the UFO phenomenon have appeared, offering a wide range of speculation and explanation. Some of these works were first published in the 19th century. An appreciable wave of "flying saucer" literature appeared in the 1920's, simultaneously with astronomers' growing interest in other planets. The most popular thesis has always been that the UFOs and their occupants are visitors from another planet or from a distant star system. However, in 1818, some individuals became convinced that the earth is hollow and that another and alien race occupies its interior. Since 1944, much material has been published to support this "inner earth" theory and the hypothesis that UFOs originate there.

iii

A large part of the available UFO literature is closely linked with mysticism and the metaphysical. It deals with subjects like mental telepathy, automatic writing, and invisible entities as well as phenomena like poltergeist manifestations and "possession." One school of thought holds that flying saucers are Biblical "signs in the sky" that portend the Second Coming. Another believes that an invisible fourth- or other-dimensional world is involved. Some groups have concluded that mankind is being, and may have always been, manipulated by extraterrestrial forces -- the UFO occupants. Others detail the endless battle between "good" and "evil" believing that the UFOs play an integral part in this "war." Unearthly "police forces" are described and explained.

Many of the UFO reports now being published in the popular press recount alleged incidents that are strikingly similar to demoniac possession and psychic phenomena which have long been known to theologians and parapsychologists. Therefore, references to these subjects have been included as well as references to occult works which have similarities to the general tone and content of the UFO literature.

A major objective of this bibliography was to gather material from the physical sciences which related to the UFO phenomenon. The results of this intensive effort were a collection of articles which appeared in scientific and technical journals. Some discussed UFOs in general terms in light of the limitations of present physical theories, and others explore peripheral areas, such as ball lightning and interstellar travel, which relate to certain theories regarding UFOs. Admittedly the number of such "hard science" references is small, but they fill an important place in this collection.

For his very useful contribution, the section on mirages, I wish to thank Lt. Col. Daniel H. Lufkin, USAF, Chief of the Aerospace Sciences Division of the Environmental Technical Applications Center, Military Airlift Command, U.S. Air Force. The references are the best treatments, theoretical and practical, of this classical subject. Because of its special nature, I have incorporated his bibliography separately as appendix 1. These items are not included in the author index, nor are others in the addenda.

This two-year survey of the growing UFO literature reveals many publications that are the result of painstaking research, yet in its entirety, contradictions are far more common than consistencies. It is also noteworthy that points of view are taken up by factions, each of which seems convinced that its answer to the UFO riddle is the right one and the only one.

I have sought to include items of scholarly interest and intent, and to make the bibliography as useful as possible for both scholars and general readers interested in the subject. The principal difficulties in achieving completeness are the great volume of UFO and UFO-related literature, and the fact that much of it is privately published and of limited distribution.

Scientific theory of today often becomes fact tomorrow. The line between the possible and the impossible is arbitrary. Many misconceptions pass for information. One day, perhaps within our time, out of all the contradictions surrounding the UFO phenomenon, man may discover to his complete satisfaction its exact nature and origin.

July 1969   LYNN E. CATOE

ACKNOWLEDGEMENTS

Much of the "flying saucer" literature of the past twenty years was privately printed and poorly distributed and would have quickly and permanently disappeared if it had not been carefully preserved by individual collectors and students of the phenomenon. This bibliography could not have been compiled without the full and selfless cooperation of such collectors throughout the world. Many of these people gave most freely of their time, and their assistance and enthusiasm was of inestimable value. I am particularly grateful to the following individuals who located rare items or, in some cases, even lent their entire collections to this project for copying. Others painstakingly supplied information which made it possible to locate obscure items, and offered practical suggestions and lists of books which they felt should be included.

Jan Aldrich
Hulvio Brant Aleixo
Hernani Ebecken de Araujo
Gray Barker
William Don Barnes
Lionel Beer
Otto O. Binder
Ted Bloecher
Charles Bowen
Eileen L. Buckle
Edwardo Buelta
C. Maxwell Cade
Robert J. Childerhouse
Leonard G. Cramp
Gordon Creighton
Leon Davidson
Isabel Davis
W. Raymond Drake
H. C. Dudley
Gene Duplantier
P. M. H. Edwards
Lucius Farish
Zindermans Forlag
Rene Fouere
Wolfram Fragner

Stanton T. Friedman
Oscar A. Galindez
Richard C. Gerdes
Gabriel Green
Richard Hall
Carol Halford-Watkins
James A. Harder
Rene J. Hardy
Joanna Hugill
Philipp Human
J. Allen Hynek
George Isuis
Sushil K. Jain
Ebbe Johansson
Kurt Kauffmann
Aleksandr Kazantsev
Lars Kim-Nicklason
John A. Keel
Elizabeth Klarer
Eugene B. Konecci
Kenneth Larson
June Larson
L. Gerald Laufer
John D. Llewellyn
Ernest Linder

L. James Lorenzen
Walter F. Luna
Sven Magnusson
Mario Maioli
James E. McDonald
Donald H. Menzel
Aime Michel
Modern Space Flight Association
James W. Mosely
Stewart Nixon
Peter E. Norris
Hermann Oberth
Frank Pedersen
Roberto Pinotti
Hector Quintanilla
K. Gosta Rehn
Philip Rodgers
Mary F. Romig
Margaret Rose

Frank B. Salisbury
Ivan T. Sanderson
Philip Seff
Gianni Settimo
Benjamin Simon
Edgar Simons
Leo Sprinkle
Fred P. Stone
Ivy Sutton
Egerton Sykes
Howard Timmins
Brinsley Le Poer Trench
M. R. Veillith
M. Jean Vuillequez
Joseph A. Webb
William B. Weitzel
Alice K. Wells
Paul J. Willis
Lou Zinsstag

Deep appreciation is expressed to Arthur G. Renstrom, Head of the Aeronautics Section, Science and Technology Division, Library of Congress, who generously assisted production of this volume in such matters as research, translations and preparation of the manuscript.

LYNN E. CATOE

CONTENTS

Unidentified Flying Objects

GENERAL REFERENCES

<u>Books and Pamphlets</u>

Adamski, George. Flying saucers farewell. London, New York, Abelard-Schuman, 1961. 190 p.

Adamski discusses the reasons spacecraft from other planets are visiting earth and man's place in the universe as reportedly revealed to him through contact with beings from Venus, Mars, and Saturn.

-----Inside the spaceships. New York, Abelard-Schuman, 1955. 256 p.

Account of alleged physical contact and communication with beings from Venus, Mars, and Saturn. Descriptions of trips in extraterrestrial spacecraft. Photographs and diagrammatic drawings.

Adler, Billy, comp. Letters to the Air Force on UFOs. New York, Dell Pub. Co., 1967. 157 p.

"From the files of the U.S. Air Force 'Project Blue Book'."

Aleman Velasco, Miguel. Los secretos y las leyes del espacio. México, D. F., 1962. 258 p.

Allingham, Cedric. Flying saucer from Mars. New York, British Book Center, 1955. 153 p.

Report of alleged UFO landing Feb. 18, 1954, near Lossiemouth, North Scotland, and author's contact with a Martian.

1

Angelucci, Orfeo M. The secret of the saucers. Amherst, Wis., Amherst Press, 1955. 167 p.

Account of author's alleged ride in extraterrestrial spacecraft and contact with extraterrestrial beings associated with the objects. Propulsion of spacecraft explained as converted magnetic energy "inherent in all the universe."

Arnold, Kenneth A. The flying saucer as I saw it. Boise, Idaho, The Author, 1950. 16 p.

Author's account of UFO sighting June 24, 1947, near Mt. Rainier, Washington.

Arnold, Kenneth A. and Ray Palmer. The coming of the saucers. Boise, Idaho, The Authors, 1952. 192 p.

Detailed account of Arnold's sighting on June 24, 1947, of chain of nine saucer-like objects flying in formation near Mt. Rainier and of June 21, 1947, reported sighting of six disc-shaped UFOs off Maury Island, Wash., by Harold A. Dahl. Photographs.

Babcock, Edward J. and Timothy G. Beckley, eds. UFOs around the world. [n.p] Interplanetary News Service, 1966. 64 p.

Selected articles by UFO researchers, including Jacques Vallée, Antonio Ribera, Frank Edwards, and Henry R. Gallart.

Baker, Robert M.L. Investigations of anomalistic observational phenomena. El Segundo, Calif., The Author, 1968. 23 p.

In his statement, the author (1) presents a summary of analyses that have lead him to believe that anomalistic phenomena [UFOs] exist; (2) explains the probable inadequacy of current terrestrial sensors in observing and/or defining characteristics of the anomalistic phenomena; (3) suggests a number of tentative hypothetical sources for the phenomenon and the justification for their scientific study; and (4) makes specific recommendations for new observational and study programs. Presented at Symposium on Unidentified Flying Objects, Committee on Science and Astronautics, House of Representatives, July 29, 1968.

Barker, Gray. Gray Barker's book of saucers. Clarksburg, W. Va., Saucerian Books, 1965. 77 p.

Book catalogues UFO sightings in all parts of the world, 1962-1963. Saucer landings, communication between saucer crews and humans, seizure of terrestrials by saucer crews, mating of extraterrestrials with terrestrials, and "the men in black" are discussed.

----- They knew too much about flying saucers. New York, University Books, 1956. 256 p.

Instances are cited in which flying saucer investigators have allegedly been frightened into silence by various visitors, including "three men in black."

2

Beer, Lionel. An introduction to flying saucers. London, The Author, 1964. 44p.

Typescript. A five-part series of articles: (1) How, What and Where?; (2) The Historical Aspect; (3) UFO Research Today; (4) Friendly and Hostile?; (5) The Visitors Themselves.

Bender, Albert K. Flying saucers and the three men. Annotated and with introd. and epilogue by Gray Barker. Clarksburg, W. Va., Saucerian Books, 1962. 194 p.

Discussion of activities of and reports of UFO sightings made to International Flying Saucer Bureau, organized by Bender in April 1952 in Bridgeport, Conn., and of Bender's contact with extraterrestrial beings which he claimed resulted in his dissolving IFSB in November 1953.

Bray, Arthur. Science, the public, and the UFO: a philosophical study. Ottawa, Canada, Bray Book Service, 1967. 193 p.

State-of-the-art summary of available facts on unidentified flying objects in world perspective. Includes history of the UFO phenomenon; possible existence of extraterrestrial life; contact stories; and possible modes of propulsion for extraterrestrial spacecraft.

Buckle, Eileen. The Scoriton mystery. London, Neville Spearman, 1967. 303 p.

Full details of investigation by British Unidentified Flying Object Research Association (BUFORA) of E. A. Bryant's claim that on April 24, 1965, near Scoriton, England, he encountered three individuals from a landed extraterrestrial spacecraft, one of whom told him, "My name is Yamski." (George Adamski had died on April 23.)

Bull, F. Malcolm. UFO handbook 2. London, British UFO Research Assn., [1964] 31 p.

Details are given of the various natural and man-made phenomena that could be misinterpreted as unidentified flying objects.

Calvillo Madrigal, Salvador. Plativología, ensayo nesciente. México, 1954. 21 p.

Listing of worldwide sightings of UFOs from 1947 with emphasis on those viewed throughout Mexico in 1952.

Campione, Michael J. Reality of UFOs, their danger, their hope. Cinnaminson, N. J., The Author, 1965. 16 p.

General discussion of the UFO phenomenon, including recognizable characteristics, physiological effects on humans, statistics on sightings and landings, theories on their origin, and USAF policy.

Chambers, Howard V. UFOs for the millions. Los Angeles, Sherbourne Press, Inc., 1967. 158 p.

Book discusses UFO sightings, the persons who made them, the persons who made evaluations of the sightings, and what people who think they've made actual contacts with aliens think these sightings mean.

Chartrand, Robert L. and William F. Brown. Facts about unidentified flying objects. Washington, Library of Congress, Legislative Reference Service, 1966. 29 p.

Includes the following: description of various types of UFOs; trends in UFO activity; historical sightings of aerial phenomena; identification of flying objects (versus UFOs); U.S. Government monitoring of UFO activity; special studies of UFOs; special briefings on UFO activity; public reaction to UFOs; Air Force Regulation 200-2.

Coelho Netto, Paulo. A realidade dos discos voadores. Rio de Janeiro, Editora Minerva, 1966. 59 p.

Cohen, Daniel. Myths of the space age. New York, Dodd, Mead & Co., 1967. 278 p.

Author discusses "myths" -- including flying saucers -- that have persisted into modern times "although mankind should by now know better." In his discussion of UFOs, he cites and offers explanations for several classic sightings.

Cox, Donald W., ed. America's explorers of space, including a special report on UFOs. Maplewood, N.J., Hammond, 1967. 93 p.

Special report on unidentified flying objects gives brief overview of the UFO controversy. Possible UFO sightings by Gemini astronauts Young and Collins in mid-1966 are discussed as well as attempts made to contact other worlds under Project Ozma.

Cremaschi, Inisero and Guiseppe Pederiali. Dischi volanti: benvenuti. Bologna, Carroccio, 1967. 157 p.

Summary of evidence in support of theory of extraterrestrial origin of UFOs. UFO photographs from many parts of the world are analyzed and discussed as are contactee reports.

Da Silva, Renato I. No espaco nao estamos sós. São Paulo, Edart, 1966. 213 p.

Theories relating to possibility of life on the moon and other planets are summarized. Parapsychological phenomena of mental telepathy precognition, ESP, premonition, and astral projection are discussed as they might relate to contact with extraterrestrial entities or intelligences.

David, Jay. The flying saucer reader. New York, New American Library, 1967. 244 p.

4

An anthology of material on various aspects of the UFO phenomenon. Authors include Brinsley le Poer Trench, Paul Thomas, Edward J. Ruppelt, Jacques Vallée, Brad Steiger, W. Gordon Allen, George Adamski, George Hunt Williamson, Albert K. Bender, Donald Keyhoe, Gavin Gibbons, Raymond Bernard, Donald H. Menzel and Lyle G. Boyd, Aimé Michel, and Harold Wilkins.

Earley, George W. Unidentified flying objects: an historical perspective. Bloomfield, Conn., The Author, 1967. 14 p.

Paper presented at ASME Design Engineering Conference in New York City, May 15-18, 1967. Examines overall UFO scene from 1947; summarizes several representative unsolved sightings reported in U. S.; discusses global nature of sighting reports; suggests that some UFOs may be extraterrestrial spacecraft; advances general suggestions for more effective study of UFO phenomenon.

Edwards, Frank. Flying saucers, serious business. New York, Lyle Stuart, Inc., 1966. 319 p.

Report on worldwide sightings of UFOs and attack on veil of secrecy that governments of the world have drawn around the matter. Data cited authenticated by NICAP.

Erskine, Allen L. Why are they watching us? New York, Tower Books, 1967. 124 p.

Author expresses his personal opinions on the UFO phenomenon.

Feryer, R. Fliegende untertassen. UFO's -- Greifen Ausserirdische machte imunsere verhaltnisse ein? Wohor kommen sie? Wer sind ihre piloten? Was bezwecken sie? Boniswil/Aargau, Schiftenverlich, 1954. 32 p.

The flying saucer menace. New York and London, Universal Publishing and Distributing Corp., 1967. 64 p.

Facts and photographs that would seem to indicate UFO hostility.

Flying saucer review. World roundup of UFO sightings and events. Introd. by Brinsley le Poer Trench. New York, Citadel Press, 1958. 224 p.

Chronological listing of UFO sightings between late 1955 and December 1957 as reported to Flying Saucer Review.

Flying saucers and UFOs 1968. New York, K. M. R. Publications, 1968. 73 p.

Contents includes: The South Hill Scare in Virginia; A Strange Feud: Animals and Flying Saucers; The Millerton Bowling Ball; Russia Begins a Search for UFOs; Who are those Mysterious Men in Black?; The Secret of Deception Island's Volcano.

Flying saucers illustrated. Studio City, Calif., Kling House, Ltd., 1967. 80 p.

UFO phenomenon is treated from several points of view by different authors:
"Contact Outer Space, " by John Otto; "Lies in the Skies, " by Frank Edwards;
"The World's Strangest Convention, " by Jacob Konrath; "George Adamski the
First Ambassador to Outer Space?, " by Bob Grant; "The UFO and Anti-Gravity,"
by Bud Pecaro; "Does He Talk to Flying Saucers?, " by Michael X. Barton;
"The Case for Flying Saucers, " by Bill Hughes; "Mysteries of the Deep, " by
Jacob Konrath; "Flying Saucers and their Occupants, " by Jacob Konrath; "First
Authentic Flying Saucer Photo, " by Kenneth Larson. Many UFO photos are
included.

Flying saucers pictorial. Tucson, Ariz., Arizill Realty and Pub. Co., 1967.

Flying saucers: UFO reports -- No. 1. New York, Dell Publishing Co., 1967.
67 p.

Compilation of speculation and theories relating to UFO phenomena. Flying
saucer photos taken during IGY mission, reports of alleged encounters with
humanoids, and discussion of life on other planets are included. Sighting of
mysterious object by Hillsdale College (Mich.) coeds on March 14, 1966, and
incident in which Betty and Barney Hill were allegedly taken aboard a flying
saucer for physical examination are detailed.

Flying saucers: UFO report -- No. 2. New York, Dell Publishing Co., 1967. 64p.

Summary of the "sense and nonsense, speculation and theories" relating to the
UFO phenomenon. Includes information on landings, saucer occupants, the
Michigan "flap, " commonly report UFO types, and UFO research organizations.
Details are given of sighting at Wanaque Reservoir (N.J.) on Jan. 13, 1966,
and mysterious glowing particles seen by John Glenn while in orbit around the
earth Feb. 20, 1962.

Flying saucers: UFO reports -- No. 3. New York, Dell Publishing Co., 1967. 64p.

Coverage on UFO controversy, theories, hoaxes, and photographs.

Flying saucers: UFO reports -- No. 4. New York, Dell Publishing Co., 1967.
64 p.

Fact and theory on the UFO phenomenon. Features reports on UFOs seen in
outer space by U. S. astronauts; a ring-shaped UFO that gradually became engulfed in and hidden by a vapor cloud; "outer space grass"; historical evidence
that space ships from alien worlds provided the life power for ancient stone-
works that baffle archeologists.

Fry, Daniel W. The White Sands incident. Los Angeles, New Age Publishing Co.,
1954. 66 p.

Author describes how on July 4, 1950, he was taken in remote-controlled extraterrestrial spacecraft on a ride from White Sands Missile Range, N. Mex.,
to New York City and back in approximately 30 minutes, and claims he conversed telepathically with extraterrestrial being in UFO's base ship 900 miles
above earth's surface.

----- The White Sands incident. Louisville, Ky., Best Books, Inc., 1966. 120 p.

Account of 20-minute roundtrip ride to New York in unmanned, extraterrestrial
spacecraft which allegedly landed near White Sands Proving Grounds, New
Mexico, and report of subsequent conversations with an extraterrestrial on
science, technology, and philosophy.

Fuller, John G. Incident at Exeter; the story of unidentified flying objects over
America today. New York, Putnam, 1966. 251 p.

Report of Sept. 3, 1965, sighting of UFO at Exeter, N.H., with testimony of
60 persons who allegedly viewed the object.

Girvan, Ian Waveney. Flying saucers and common sense. London, Frederick
Muller, Ltd., 1955. 160 p.

Discusses mental processes by which author came to accept validity of theory
that UFOs emanate from somewhere outside earth's atmosphere and that they
are piloted or remotely controlled by intelligent beings. Also writes of the
impact of the subject of UFOs on the public mind. Published also in American
edition (New York, Citadel Press, 1956).

Goodwin, Harold. The science book of space travel. New York, Franklin Watts,
Inc., 1954. 213 p.

Popular discussion of the technical problems inherent in space travel. Chapter
18 summarizes current fact and theory regarding the UFO phenomenon.

Green, Gabriel and Warren Smith. Let's face the facts about flying saucers. New
York, Popular Library, 1967. 127 p.

Reports from research members of the Amalgamated Flying Saucer Clubs of
America (AFSCA) that would seem to indicate that UFOs are vehicles from
other planets and are piloted by extraterrestrials.

Greenbank, Anthony. Creatures from outer space (stepping from flying saucer).
In The book of survival. New York and Evanston, Harper & Row, 1967. p. 34.

Advice on what to do in the event of encounter with crew disembarking from
landed flying saucer: (1) avoid rapid forceful movement; (2) use no shrill
sounds; (3) breathe quietly; (4) avoid giving a direct menacing gaze.

Greenfield, Irving A. The UFO report. New York, Lancer Books, 1967. 141 p.

Summary of the author's personal investigations into the numerous UFO sighting reports on Long Island, N.Y., in the spring of 1966, including many first-
hand accounts and a review of the history of the phenomenon. Supports the
extraterrestrial thesis and the "Air Force conspiracy" allegations.

----- Why are they watching us? by Allen L. Erskine [pseud]. New York, Tower
Publications, 1967. 124 p.

Concise review of the UFO "classics, " with emphasis on the Air Force "conspiracy" and the extraterrestrial thesis.

Hall, Richard H., ed. The UFO evidence. Washington, National Investigations
Committee on Aerial Phenomena, 1964. 184 p.

Documented report containing 746 UFO sighting cases selected from NICAP
files and covering NICAP's investigations from early 1957 to the end of 1963.
Sightings are listed and analyzed by observer categories. Historical development of phenomenon and Congressional attitudes and activity are treated. Evidence is presented to support hypothesis that UFOs are under intelligent control and that some of them might therefore be of extraterrestrial origin.

Heard, Gerald. The riddle of the flying saucers. Is another world watching?
London, Carroll & Nicholson, 1950. 157 p.

Lists in chronological order the UFO phenomena reported throughout the world
between Midsummer 1947 and early Autumn 1950. Revised edition with new
material published in New York in 1953 by Bantam Books with title Is Another
World Watching? The Riddle of the Flying Saucers.

Herrmann, Joachim. Das falsche Weltbild; Astronomie und Aberglaube. Stuttgart,
Kosmos Verlag, Franckh' sche Verlagshandlung, 1962. 162 p. (Die Orion-
Bücher)

Fact and fiction relating to UFO phenomenon are discussed.

Hynek, J. Allen. The scientific problem posed by unidentified flying objects.
Evanston, Ill., The Author, 1968. 15 p.

Author makes the following recommendations: (1) that a mechanism be set up
whereby the problem posed by the reports from all over the world, but expe-
cially in the U.S., from people of high credibility, can be adequately studied,
using all methods available to modern science; and (2) that the U.S. seek the
cooperation of the United Nations in establishing a means for the impartial and
free interchange among nations of information about unidentified flying objects.
Statement made at the Symposium on Unidentified Flying Objects, Committee
on Science and Astronautics, House of Representatives, July 29, 1968.

James, Trevor. They live in the sky. Los Angeles, New Age Publishing Co.,
1958. 270 p.

Author postulates that reevaluation of the UFO phenomenon is needed: "Blanket terms, such as the 'space people' need to be eliminated, and careful attention paid not only to the invisible animals that fly in our air, but to the various orders of beings who either visit us or who have their natural habitat in invisible domains surrounding and interpenetrating our own. "

Jessup, Morris K. The case for the UFO, unidentified flying objects. Introd. by Frank Edwards. New York, Citadel Press, 1955. 239 p.

Author analyzes and correlates many paranormal phenomena of scientific record and theorizes that objects such as stones, ice, water, colored rain, organic matter, living organisms, and vegatable matter that have fallen to earth from the heavens come from intelligently operated extraterrestrial spacecraft or are in some way formed, guided, or influenced by the operators of such spacecraft.

----- The expanding case for the UFO. New York, Citadel Press, 1957. 253 p.

In this sequel to The Case for the UFO, the author further develops the theory that paranormal phenomena, when collated and analyzed, support belief in the existence of intelligence functioning in space. He suggests that UFOs may be a sentient animal life form that originated on earth aeons ago but which now lives naturally in open space.

Johnson, DeW. B. Flying saucers, fact or fiction? Los Angeles, 1950. 339 p.

Master of Arts thesis in journalism at UCLA.

Keyhoe, Donald E. The flying saucer conspiracy. New York, Holt, 1955. 315 p.

Covers important developments 1953-55 in UFO sightings and events. Reports paraphrased from official USAF records and cleared through USAF Press Office, DOD.

----- The flying saucers are real. New York, Fawcett Publications, 1950. 175 p.

Author states his conclusions about the UFO phenomenon: (1) the earth has been under periodic observation from another planet, or other planets, for at least two centuries; (2) this observation suddenly increased in 1947 following the series of A-bomb explosions begun in 1945; (3) the observation, now intermittent, is part of a long-range survey and will continue indefinitely.

----- Flying saucers from outer space. New York, Holt, 1953. 276 p.

Reports USAF information on UFOs leading to alleged Intelligence admission that they are extraterrestrial and under intelligent control.

----- Flying saucers: top secret. New York, Putnam, 1960, 283 p.

Evidence on UFO sightings presented by NICAP to individual congressmen and committee chairmen in attempt to secure open Congressional hearings on subject. Details of NICAP's behind-the-scenes battle against USAF censorship. Main points are backed by documents available at NICAP office in Washington, D. C.

Knaggs, Oliver. Let the people know. Cape Town, South Africa, Howard Timmins, 1966. 113 p.

References to flying saucers that go back as far as the 14th century are cited to "prove" that flying saucers are not something of the present generation. Author concludes that there are definite grounds for believing military authorities are keeping details of UFO activities from the public to avoid possible panic since there are so many factors they cannot explain themselves.

Kraspedon, Dino. My contact with flying saucers. Translated from the Portuguese by J. B. Wood. London, Neville Spearman, 1959. 205 p.

Discusses in detailed technical terms the forces that UFOs use to navigate in earth's atmosphere and to travel through space on interplanetary voyages. Presented in question-and-answer form, information synthesizes series of five alleged meetings between author and captain of an extraterrestrial spacecraft.

Le Poer Trench, Hon. Brinsley. The flying saucer story. London, Neville Spearman, 1966. 208 p.

Author presents evidence to support his belief that UFOs are extraterrestrial and that they have visited earth for millenia.

Leslie, Desmond and George Adamski. Flying saucers have landed. London, Werner Laurie, 1953. 232 p.

Account of alleged contact by Adamski with a landed extraterrestrial spacecraft and a meeting with a man from Venus on Nov 20, 1952, near Desert Center, Calif. Photographs of spacecraft. Review by Leslie of material from old manuscripts referring to sightings of unidentified objects flying through the air from earliest times.

Loftin, Robert. Identified flying saucers. New York, David McKay Co., 1968.

General summary of the various aspects of the UFO controversy. Author states that although evidence he has gathered over a fifteen year period would tend to support the extraterrestrial hypothesis, it is still an hypothesis.

Lore, Gordon and Harold H. Deneault. Mysteries of the skies: UFOs in perspective. Englewood Cliffs, N. J., Prentice-Hall, 1968. 237 p.

Historical aspects of the UFO phenomenon are presented. The 1897 "airship" reports are treated in detail.

Lorenzen, Coral E. The great flying saucer hoax; the UFO facts and their interpretation. New York, William-Frederick Press, for the Aerial Phenomena Research Organization of Tucson, Ariz., 1962. 257 p.

Author, director of Aerial Phenomena Research Organization, presents documented information to support theory that UFOs are not only real, but are extraterrestrial and unfriendly and that visitations follow a pattern indicating military reconnaissance and biological and ecological survey.

Lorenzen, Coral and Jim Lorenzen. UFOs over the Americas. New York, Signet Books, The New American Library, 1968. 254 p.

Authors report that 1967 brought an unprecedented number of UFO landings, low-level hovering maneuvers, and landings with occupants visible. They suggest that the almost constant UFO activity from 1965 to the present indicates that close approaches of the planet to Mars to earth is no longer a necessary factor there are no longer cyclical recurrences of UFO activity peaks. An interpretation of this might be that UFOs are interplanetary in origin and the occupants have established bases close enough to earth so that long journeys are no longer necessary, the authors say.

McDonald, James E. Are UFOs extraterrestrial surveillance craft? Tucson, Ariz., The Author, 1968. 4 p.

Stressing the need for establishment of a vigorous investigation program of the UFO phenomenon, the author noted that close-range sightings of machine-like objects of unconventional nature and unconventional performance characteristics, seen at low altitudes, appeared to be occurring all over the globe, possibly with increasing frequency. Suggestions that such observations can be explained away in terms of meteorological optics or in terms of atmospheric plasmas cannot be supported with cogent scientific arguments, he said. Talk given Mar. 26, 1968, before the American Institute of Aeronautics and Astronautics, Los Angeles, Calif.

----- Science, technology, and UFOs. Tucson, Arizona, The Author, 1968. 14 p.

Noting that throughout the entire world only a small handful of scientists have taken the trouble to attempt direct checks on the puzzling and recurrent reports of UFO phenomena, author presents evidence, based on personal investigation, to support his hypothesis that UFOs are extraterrestrial probes or vehicles -- products of some technology other than our own. He also reviews competitive hypotheses. Speech presented Jan. 26, 1968, at a General Seminar of the United Aircraft Research Laboratories, East Hartford, Conn.

----- Statement on unidentified flying objects. Tucson, Arizona, The Author, 1968. 39 p.

In his statement, the author reviews his experiences in interviewing UFO witnesses in the U.S. and abroad and discusses ways in which his professional experience in the field of atmospheric physics and meteorology assisted past and present attempts to account for UFO phenomena. Presented at the Symposium on Unidentified Flying Objects, Committee on Science and Astronautics, House of Representatives, July 29, 1968.

----- U FOs--an international scientific problem. Tucson, Ariz., The Author, 1968. 40 p.

Summarizing his position, the author states: (1) the UFO problem seems to be a matter of great scientific interest; (2) machine-like objects--possibly extraterrestrial in origin--have been repeatedly seen, often by observers of very high credibility; (3) UFO observations are being made on a global scale indicating an international scientific problem; (4) there has never been a thorough scientific investigation of UFOs; (5) there is no convincing evidence of U.S. cover-up conspiracy operating to conceal true nature of UFO problem; (6) Condon Committee's lack of scientific vigor in conducting USAF-sponsored UFO study is disappointing; (7) UFO study programs by scientific groups are needed throughout the world to systematically appraise conceivable hypotheses to account for UFO phenomena. Speech given Mar. 12, 1968, at the Canadian Aeronautics and Space Institute Astronautics Symposium, Montreal, Canada.

Maney, Charles A. and Richard Hall. The challenge of unidentified flying objects. Washington, The Authors, 1961. 208 p.

Book is a series of separate articles by authors in which each presents his own version and interpretation of UFO phenomena.

Michel, Aimé. The truth about flying saucers. New York, Criterion Books, 1956. 255 p.

Author presents and comments on UFO sightings reported throughout the world from 1947. Sources include: Project Saucer records; communiques or records of the air forces in U.S.A., U.K., Canada, South Africa, France, and Sweden; USAF's Air Technical Intelligence Center; National Meteorological Office (France and the French Union); French and foreign technical periodicals; personal inquiries; and information in the files of NICAP. Summarizes current theories and explanations of UFO phenomena. Translation of Lueurs sur les soucoupes volantes. Published also in paperback edition by Pyramid Pubns. (T1647), New York.

Miller, Robert W. and Rick R. Hilberg. The saucer enigma. Cleveland, Ohio, UFO Magazine Publications, 1968. 23 p.

In "A Brief History of the Saucers," UFO sightings 1619-1897 are listed; a general summary of the UFO controversy follows.

Moseley, James W., ed. Jim Moseley's book of saucer news. Clarksburg, W. Va., Saucerian Books, 1967. 118p.

Selected articles from back issues of Saucer News: Why are They Here?, Justin Case; Florida's Coral Castle, James W. Moseley; The Antiquity of Civilized Man, M.K. Jessup; Message From Mars Sent to Earth Fifty Years Ago?, news item; The Case of the Crashed UFO, Bob Barry; Nexus Staff Demonstrates Reality of ESP, Nexus Staff; UFO Spotter Taken to Washington (The Olden Moore Story), by C.W. Fitch; California Newsboy Attacked by Saucer, news item; The Legends of Mt. Shasta, Richard Cohen; Scully Breaks a Long Silence, Frank Scully; Connecticut Teacher Reports Saucer with Three Little Men Inside, news item; Humanoids and the Mars Saucer Cycle, Lonzo Dove; Figure of Christ on Wall, news item; A Reporter's Report, Ivan

Sanderson; The Death of Captain Mantell, Kenneth H. Ford; Are Spacemen Living Among Us?, unscheduled newsletter; Glass Pitting at Saucer News Headquarters, news item; The Air Force Position on Flying Saucers, Maj. Lawrence J. Tacker, USAF; The Red Plague, news item; The UFO Coloring Book, Patricia A. Jones; Flying Saucers and the United Nations, Michael G. Mann; Outstanding Sightings from the year 1881; The Electromagnetic Effects of Flying Saucers, John J. Robinson; Twenty Minutes of Terror, Jeanne Stevens; Do Flying Saucers Come From Mars?, Justin Case; The Mysterious Fate of Clipper 944, Max B. Miller; Mystic Barber's "Doomsday Demonstration," photo newsstory; Flying Saucer Research on Trial, Thomas M. Comella; Astronaut Photographs UFO, news item; Detailed Sighting from Pennsylvania, news item; Who is Fooling Donald Keyhoe?, Michael G. Mann; Weird Sighting in Oregon, news item; Howard Menger, the New Adamski, James W. Moseley; How to Build A Saucer, Y. N. Ibn Aharon; An Open Letter to Saucer Researchers, Dr. Leon Davidson; Open Letter of Reply to Dr. Leon Davidson, Brinsley le Poer Trench; Dr. Leon Davidson and the Secret Weapon Theory, Richard Hall; Three Men in Black--the Al Bender Story, James W. Moseley; Saucer with Hieroglyphics Found in England, news item.

National Investigations Committee on Aerial Phenomena. [NICAP Headquarters UFO Newspaper Clipping File, 1947-1966]. Washington, D.C., 1967. 37 v. (looseleaf) 35 mm.

Material constituted the newspaper clippings file of Civilian Saucer Intelligence (CSI), New York, now defunct. Microfilm made by the Science and Technology Division, Library of Congress, 1967.

Nebel, Long John. The flying saucer story. New York, American Music Library, 1966. Matrix no. AML-201. 2s. 12 in. 33 1/3 rpm microgroove.

Interviews by the author of individuals involved in UFO controversy.

The new report on flying saucers. Greenwich, Conn., Fawcett Publications, Inc., 1967. 80 p.

Contains UFO sighting reports and photographs; interviews with Project Blue Book Chief Maj. Hector Quintanilla and broadcaster Long John Nebel; and statements by Wernher von Braun, Dr. J. Allen Hynek, John Fuller, and Maj. George W. Ogles.

Olsen, Thomas M. The reference for outstanding UFO sighting reports. Riderwood, Md., UFO Information Retrieval Center, Inc., 1967. 1 v. (various pagings) (UFORIC - 6661)

Collection of 160 outstanding UFO reports as originally published. A numerical value of reliability is formulated for each case: the reports are presented in chronological order and cross-indexed by date, geographical location, and source.

Pereira, Flavio A. O livro vermelho dos discos voadores. São Paulo, Edicoes Florenca Ltda., 1967. 486 p.

Handbook containing summary tables of information on all aspects of the UFO phenomenon worldwide: sightings, occupants, electromagnetic effects, radar detection, professions of witnesses, physiological effects, geographical distribution, and statements by prominent individuals.

Rehn, K. Gösta. De flygande tefaten; dokument och teori. Göteborg, Zindermann; Stockholm, Seelig, 1966. 174 p.

State-of-the-art survey on fact and theory about the UFO phenomenon.

Ribera, Antonio. El gran enigma de los platillos volantes. Santiago de Chile, Buenos Aires, Mexico, Barcelona, Editorial Pomaire, 1966. 431 p.

Author summarizes worldwide reports of unexplained aerial phenomena (1800s-1960s) with emphasis on U.S. accounts and on the 1954 wave of UFO sightings in France. Current theories on the possibility of life in other worlds are discussed. Hypotheses attempting to explain the UFO phenomenon are surveyed.

Ruppelt, Edward J. The report on unidentified flying objects. Garden City, New York, 1956. 315 p.

Author, a former chief of USAF's Project Blue Book, writes a factual account of Air Force investigation of UFO sighting reports and discusses all aspects of the UFO controversy. Published also in paperback edition by Ace Books (G537), New York.

Sanderson, Ivan T. Uninvited visitors. New York, Cowles Education Corp., 1967.

Author, a biologist, speculates on the nature of the UFO phenomenon. Chapter headings: What Could UFOs Be?; Things in the Sky; A Thing on the Ground; The Shape and Substance of UFOs and UAOs; What Do They Do?; Could UFOs or UAOs Be Alive?; Other Strange Things Come Down From the Sky; Our Uninvited Visitors; And More Uninvited Visitors!; Where Do They Come From? How?; When Did They Start Coming and Why?; A Concept of Cosmic Evolution.

Scully, Frank. Behind the flying saucers. New York, Henry Holt, 1950. 230 p.

Presents information to support position that UFOs are real and that official disclaimers of their existence by DOD are calculated to deceive the public.

Simões, Auriphebo Berrance. Os discos voadores; fantasia e realidade. São Paulo, Edart Livraria Editora Ltda., 1959. 390 p.

Survey of world literature on UFO phenomena with emphasis on contactee claims. Current theories on possibility of life on other planets are evaluated.

Stanford, Rex G. Brev från Rex Stanford. Sökaren, v. 5, no. 3, 1968: 16.

Author's response to questions submitted to him by the editor, Sven Magnusson. He states his belief that flying saucers come from and are controlled by beings from outer space. The author's book, Look Up, was translated into Swedish with title Kontaktimed Rymdmänniskor (Halsingborg, Parthenon, 1959). Also discussed is Project Starlight International, organized by his brother, Ray Stanford, Corpus Christi, Tex., to collect physical proof of the existence of UFOs.

Soule, Gardner. UFOs & IFOs: a factual report on flying saucers. New York, G. P. Putnam's Sons, 1967. 189 p.

Surveys UFO sighting reports and discusses current explanatory hypotheses. Includes a chapter on "What to Do If You See a UFO. "

Sprinkle, R. Leo. Personal and scientific attitudes: a survey of persons interested in UFO reports. Laramie, Wyoming, The Author, 1968. 11 p.

A questionaire survey was conducted among three groups: 26 Ph.D faculty and graduate students in a university Psychology Department; 59 graduate students enrolled in an NDEA Guidance Institute; and 259 members of the National Investigations Committee on Aerial Phenomena (NICAP). It was hypothesized that there would be no differences between the scores of the three groups on the Personal Attitude Survey (Form D, Dogmatism Scale, Rokeach, 1960) and the Scientific Attitude Survey (Sprinkle, 1962). Results showed significant differences (P < .001) between the three groups with respect to their mean scores on both inventories, with the NICAP group scoring higher on both "dogmatic" and "scientific" inventories, followed by the guidance group and the psychology group, respectively. Investigation was supported by Grants-in-Aid Committee, Society for the Psychological Study of Social Issues (a division of the American Psychological Association).

Stanton, L. Jerome. Flying saucers: hoax or reality? New York, Belmont Books, 1966. 157 p.

Attempts to answer certain questions relating to the UFO problem: (1) what is happening, how did it begin, what do we know up to the moment?; (2) are we being studied by non-earthly visitors, or are all UFOs natural phenomena we don't understand?; (3) is there really a conspiracy to conceal the truth from the public, and if so, who is responsible, and what is the motive for the concealment?; (4) what reasons are there for thinking intelligent life may exist elsewhere in our solar system, or in other similar systems nearby in our galaxy?; (5) if other intelligent life does exist, what are the chances of their contacting us, or vice versa?; (6) will a real scientific attack on the UFO problem provide us with a definite solution?

Stanway, R. H. and A. R. Pace. Flying saucers. Stoke-on-Trent, Eng., Newchapel Observatory, 1968. 85 p.

Steiger, Brad. Strangers from the skies. New York, Award Books, 1966. 158 p.

Author cites cases (1897 to date) on a worldwide scale involving sightings of flying saucers and their crews by humans.

Stranges, Frank E. Flying saucerama. New York, Vantage Press, 1959. 115 p.

Catalogue of worldwide UFO sightings to support thesis that problem demands international investigation and worldwide interest.

Stringfield, Leonard H. Inside saucer post...3-0 blue. Cincinnati, Civilian Research, Interplanetary Flying Objects, 1957. 94 p.

"Inside story" of CRIFO (Civilian Research, Interplanetary Flying Objects) operations from September 1955 when the Air Defense Command designated the author's home a "UFO reporting post, " and CRIFO was known internationally as a "civilian clearinghouse for saucer information. " Author concludes that UFOs are interplanetary vehicles and that the world governments with technical know-how also believe this to be the answer.

Tacker, Lawrence J. Flying saucers and the U.S. Air Force. Princeton, N.J., Van Nostrand, 1960. 164 p.

Author, a former USAF public information officer on UFOs, discusses UFO sightings reported to Aerospace Technical Intelligence Center (Project Blue Book), Wright Patterson Air Force Base, from Summer 1947 through Summer 1960 in attempt to demonstrate that, in general, they were misinterpretations of known objects. He also gives history of USAF's research effort into UFO phenomena, including Project Saucer and Project Grudge.

The True report on flying saucers. Greenwich, Conn., Fawcett Publications, 1967. 96 p.

Reprint of articles on UFO controversy for True by Donald E. Keyhoe, John A. Keel, Edward Ruppelt, William B. Nash and William H. Fortenberry, and Lloyd Mallan.

Twitchell, Cleve. The UFO saga. Lakemont, Ga., CSA Press, 1966. 94 p.

Summary of experiences of individuals who claim to have seen UFOs, or ridden in them, or communicated with their crews.

Tyler, Steven. Are the invaders coming? New York, Tower Publications, 1968. 139 p.

Survey of basic UFO literature such as Edward Ruppelt's writings, and extracts from the publications of NICAP and APRO. Supports the "Air Force conspiracy" hypothesis.

UFO: flying saucers. Poughkeepsie, N.Y., Western Publishing Co., 1968. 64 p.

Comic book. Accounts of UFOs in ancient history, UFO kidnappings, and "classic" sightings and landing cases, including those where occupants were allegedly seen.

Unidentified Flying Objects Research Committee. Report on unidentified objects observed Feb. 24, 1959, by American and United Airlines pilots. Akron, Ohio, 1960. 22 p.

Report includes statements reporting simultaneous UFO sightings by ground observers.

United Press International. Flying saucers; a Look special by the editors of United Press International and Cowles Communications, Inc. [New York, 1967] 65 p.

State-of-the-art review of the flying saucer controversy. Chapter headings are: Scientific fact? Or science fiction?; The Man Who started it All (Kenneth Arnold); First Man Killed in a Saucer Incident (Capt. Thomas Mantell); Mystery of the Lubbock Lights; The Day the Saucers Visited Washington, D.C.; Olha o disco! (UFO Photographed off Trinidade by Brazilian ship on IGY mission); Lonnie Zamora's Big White Egg; The Thing at Exeter; It Looked Like a Football Field! (200-ft.-wide UFO seen by Texas Police Officers); Case of the Crashing Russian Satellite; Four Nights of UFOs Rock Michigan; Now do you believe me? (UFO Photographs); Saucer Jokes and UFO Hoaxes; Man-made Flying Saucers; Believers, unite!; Have no fear, we mean you no harm (Contactee stories); What do the psychologists think?; What are we doing about UFOs?; What to do if you see a UFO. Published also in paperback edition (New York, Cowles Education Corporation, 1968, 157 p.).

U.S. Congress. House. Committee on Armed Services. Unidentified flying objects. [Washington, U.S. Govt. Print. Off., 1966] 84 p. (89th Cong., 2d sess. House. Report no. 55)

Information concerning U.S. Air Force activities in the area of reported unidentified flying objects.

Uriondo, Oscar A. Objetos aereos no identificados: un enigma actual. Buenos Aires, The Author, 1965. 155 p.

State-of-the-art report on theories and research relating to the UFO phenomenon. Author concludes that at present it is impossible to either prove or disprove the reality of flying saucers. He urges international cooperation in a program to resolve the problem.

Vallee, Jacques. Anatomy of a phenomenon: unidentified objects in space--a scientific appraisal. Chicago, H. Regnery Co., 1965. 210 p.

Analyzes and collates selected UFO sighting reports to support proposition that the phenomenon can be studied with the greatest degree of scientific accuracy only in terms of classes--not as a collection of individual oddities. Summarizes current theories on UFO phenomenon.

Vallée, Jacques and Janine Vallée. Challenge to science; the UFO enigma. Chicago, H. Regnery Co., 1966. 268 p.

Scientific study of UFO sightings reported throughout world from 1951. Book emphasizes global nature of phenomenon, showing how European sightings illuminate observations in U. S. and other parts of the world. Sightings in France are treated in detail and the methods developed for studying them are suggested as applicable to the phenomenon as a whole. Published also in paperback edition by Ace Books (H28), New York.

Vallée, Jacques and Janine Vallée. Les phenomenes insolites de l'espace; le dossier des mystérieux objets célestes   Paris, La Table Rond, 1966. 321 p.

Part I (Chapters 3-5) is devoted to a discussion of whether the location of sightings follows a precise law; Part II (Chapters 7-10) discusses variations in the frequency of sighting reports and their possible correlation with known phenomena; Part III (Chapters 11-13) is an attempt to establish as accurate classification categories as possible for different types of sighting reports and descriptions of physical characteristics of objects sighted.

Vogt, Cristian. El misterio de los platos voladores. Buenos Aires, Editorial "La Mandragora" [1956] 190 p.

Contains general discussion of UFO phenomenon and summaries of explanatory hypotheses relating to it. Activities of governmental and private research projects and contactee claims are also reported.

Weor, Samael. Los platillos voladores. San Salvador, The Author, 1966. 28 p.

Overview of the UFO controversy with emphasis on the plausibility of the extraterrestrial hypothesis.

Wilkins, Harold T. Flying saucers uncensored. New York, Citadel Press, 1955. 255 p.

Author catalogues UFO sightings and incidents over U. S., Western Europe, U. S., and Australia from 1947 through 1955 and speculates that extraterrestrial visitants are possibly established in bases on moon and other planets; a cosmic general staff may receive reports on terrestrial affairs as well as biological and ecological samples from earth for purposes of study and experimentation. Published also in British edition (London, Arco, 1956), and in paperback edition by Pyramid Pubns., Inc. (T1651), New York.

Williamson, George Hunt and John McCoy. UFOs confidential!; the meaning behind the most closely guarded secret of all time. Corpus Christi, Tex., Essene Press, 1958. 100 p.

Zeñabi, J. El misterio de los discos voladores. Santiago de Chile, The Author, 1953. 77 p.

Account of author's alleged contact with landed flying saucer and its Martian crew and trip to Mars aboard spacecraft. He describes in detail physical features of Mars, its science, culture, and political institutions. Experience reportedly took place in September 1952.

Periodical Articles

"Apparaissaient des soucoupes volantes." France illustration, v. 8, Oct. 4, 1952: 363-372.

Barker, Gray. Chasing the flying saucers. Flying saucers from other worlds, June 1957: 28-38.

General summary of activities of UFO research groups and reports of UFO sightings.

----- Chasing the flying saucers. Flying saucers from other worlds, Aug. 1957: 29-40.

General summary of reported UFO sightings during March 1966 and activities of UFO researchers.

----- Chasing the flying saucers. Flying saucers, July-Aug. 1958: 20-35.

General report of activities of UFO researchers. Mentions messages from extraterrestrial beings allegedly received by John Otto of Chicago, beginning November 28, 1954.

----- Chasing the flying saucers. Flying saucers, Dec. 1958: 43-56.

Summary of UFO sightings and activities of UFO researchers during summer 1958.

----- Chasing the flying saucers. Flying saucers, Feb. 1959: 24-34.

Report on high incidence of UFO sightings in 1958.

Benard, Paul C. Who believes in flying saucers? Bluebook, v. 101, July 1955: 20, 110-113.

Results of author's inquiry into 123 UFO sightings reported during 1952-1955 near Blythe and Desert Center, Calif.

Binder, Otto O. "Oddball" saucers that fit no pattern. Fate, v. 21, Feb. 1968: 54-62.

Report of rarities in UFO sightings.

Bowman, Norman J. The need for critical analysis of flying disc reports. Journal of spaceflight, v. 5, Nov. 1953: 11.

UFO data that have been gathered by Government and civilian research groups should be analyzed statistically to indicate what is probably unreliable, determine averages, etc., the author suggests. He feels that this is the only way the UFO problem can be approached to yield conclusions of significance.

Bowman, Norman J. A scientific analysis of the flying disk reports. The rocket news letter, v. 3, June 1950: 2-7.

Reprint of an address given before the Chicago Assn. of News Broadcasters on Apr. 16, 1950. Author states belief that flying disks are real. If best authenticated reports are correct, performance characteristics are beyond current earth aircraft technology and one must conclude they are of extraterrestrial origin. But if reports have been exaggerated, disks may be a new type of U.S. aircraft. Instrument observations of disks would settle question.

BUFORA research officer's annual report - 27th Nov. 1965. BUFORA journal and bulletin, v. 1, Spring 1966: 9-12.

Survey and summary of 1,200 reports of UFO sightings in the United Kingdom; summary of 20 worldwide UFO landing reports.

Caputo, Livio. Anche gli astronauti hanno visto i dischi volanti. Epoca, v. LXIV, Aug. 28, 1966: 16-23.

Report on UFO sightings, chiefly in the U.S., from 1897 to date and on investigation of phenomenon by Project Blue Book. Research programs of NICAP and APRO are mentioned.

----- Rapporto sui dischi volanti-2: stanno per invaderci? Epoca, v. LXIV, Sept. 4, 1966: 32-37.

Report of UFO sightings, chiefly in the U.S., during 1965-1966. Summary of various theories explaining UFO phenomenon.

Cheerio there, earthlings! America, v. 113, Aug. 21, 1965: 177.

Commentary on increase in reported UFO sightings during August 1965.

Clark, Jerome. The roots of skepticism. Flying saucers, Apr. 1968: 19-21.

Historical and modern reasons for widespread disbelief in the reality of UFOs are discussed.

Cohen, Daniel. The return of flying saucers. The nation, v. 201, Sept. 13, 1965: 212-124.

Overall survey of UFO events in the U.S. from 1947 and of the personalities and organizations involved.

Comella, Thomas M. Why the real saucer is interplanetary. Fate, v. 8, Dec. 1955: 17-23.

Postulating that the maneuvers and speeds of the "saucers" reported by reliable witnesses are proof that they operate "by some totally revolutionary process which outdates rocket and jet propulsion," the author reviews "evidence" in support of the extraterrestrial-origin hypothesis.

Confusion in the sky. Fate, v. 8, Mar. 1955: 24-29.

Article asserts that contradictory statements of the "experts" are responsible for confusion in the public's mind about the UFO phenomenon.

Cort, David. Saucery and flying saucers. The nation, v. 189, Nov. 7, 1959: 331-332, 340.

Compares practice of alchemy with belief in flying saucers, postulating that both are based on "the event for which there are no data."

Crum, Norman J. Flying saucers and book selection. Library journal, v. 79, Oct. 1, 1954: 1719-1722.

Survey of library experiences and policies in adding flying saucer books to the collections.

Current comment: What goes on up there? America, v. 87, Aug. 23, 1952: 489.

Article states reported USAF position on flying saucers: they are not spacecraft from distant planets; they are not secret enemy weapons.

Dagenis, Arleigh J. Do you believe in flying saucers? Michigan technic, Jan. 1960: 16-17, 50-51.

Author summarizes details of June 1947 sighting by Kenneth Arnold of flying disc-shaped objects; the January 1958 crash of Capt. Mantell while chasing a UFO; and the June 1952 appearance of mysterious objects over the White House and Capitol. He reviews the various explanatory theories.

Daniel-Rops. Une enigme sous nos yeux. France illustration, v. 7, May 5, 1951: 490.

Day, Langston. Flying saucers: fact or fiction? Chambers's journal, Nov. 1950: 688-670.

Edwards, Frank. An astronomer reports on UFOs. Fate, v. 12, Mar. 1959: 34-41.

Astronomer Frank Halstead, former curator of Darling Observatory, University of Minnesota, states his belief that UFOs are extraterrestrial spacecraft and describes circumstances under which he personally made a sighting.

Edwards, Frank. Are our satellites hunting the saucers? Fate, v. 16, May 1963:
29-35.

Within the 24-month period following 1947-1948 appearance of UFOs in the region of the South Pole, Argentina, Chile, Australia, France, Great Britain,
the United States, Sweden, and the Soviet Union sent expeditions to the Antarctic. Tangible developments were (1) motion and still pictures of disc-shaped
objects that circled ships under Chilean commander Orrego; and (2) realization
that objects presumably entered earth's atmosphere at polar regions for a reason. On March 2, 1958, telemetry from Explorer satellites confirmed existence
of zone of intense radiation - Van Allen belt - encircling earth about 600 miles
out from equator. There is no such belt above either of the polar regions.

----- Frank Edwards' report: authorities who believe in flying saucers. Fate,
v. 14, Jan. 1961: 29-35.

Astronomers said to   have seen and/or photographed unidentified flying objects are Sr. Jose Bonilla, director of observatory at Zacatecas, Mexico;
Dr. H. Percy Wilkins; Dr. James Bartlett, Jr.; Frank Halstead, curator of
the University of Minnesota observatory; and Clyde Tombaugh.

----- Frank Edwards' report: an open forum on UFOs. Fate, v. 11, Aug. 1958:
75-81.

Author lists and gives answers to questions which he thinks indicate what the
average person wants to know about UFOs: (1) What are flying saucers? (2)
Have they landed? (3) What do they want? (4) Where do they come from? (5)
Why don't they contact us? (6) Why does the Air Force persist in ridiculing
those who report unidentified flying objects?

----- Frank Edwards' report: science heads for outer space. Fate, v. 11, Jan.
1958: 33-40.

Discussion of the influence that the UFO phenomenon has had on the direction
of scientific research.

----- Frank Edwards' report: scientists and satellites. Fate, v. 11, Feb. 1958:
69-76.

Author says that the scientific community which, in 1957, "derided, denounced
and dismissed" the possibility of a Soviet-launched earth satellite, is probably
just as misguided currently in negative attitude regarding the reality of flying
saucers.

------ Frank Edwards' report: ten years of UFOs. Fate, v. 10, Oct. 1957: 65-
69.

Summarizes government research into the attitudes of the public concerning
UFO phenomena during 1947-1957.

Edwards, Frank. Frank Edwards' report: why shoot the moon? Fate, v. 11, May 1958: 41-47.

Cites evidence of unusual UFO activity near both polar regions, with numerous reports of UFOs moving north and south at considerable altitude, presumably in transit from one pole to the other. Suggests that "unknowns" may have established a base on the moon.

----- The plot to silence me. Fate, v. 10, June 1957: 17-23.

Author claims that in August 1954 he was fired from his job as news commentator for the Mutual Broadcasting System because the president of the sponsoring organization (AFL) said he "talked too much about flying saucers." He says he was later offered a well-paid job by the Pentagon" to silence him. "

----- To see or not to see flying saucers. Fate, v. 10, May 1957: 17-32.

Instance of near-collisions between aircraft and UFOs (1954-1955) are noted. Other sightings by credible observers are reported. Author suggests that rather than insist that the objects do not exist, the Air Force should keep the public informed of findings in investigations underway. Excerpted from author's book, My First 10,000,000 Sponsors (New York, Ballantine Books, 1956).

Everson, Vincent. The fowls that fly in mid-heaven. Fate, v. 11, Feb. 1958: 62-68.

Author describes mysterious objects apparently fluttering near the sun and the telescopic rig he developed to watch them.

Fawcett, George D. Current UFO status. Flying saucers, June 1968: 18-19.

During 1967, 93 UFO landings, 81 UFO car chases, 62 UFO photographs, 36 UFO plane encounters, 30 UFO occupant reports, 11 radar trackings of UFOs, and 9 power failures related to UFO appearances were reported worldwide.

----- Flying saucers: explosive situation for 1968. Flying saucers, Apr. 1968: 22-25.

Study of 1967 reports of UFO incidents from 40 states and 20 foreign countries. Included are 75 landings, 56 photographs, 52 car chases, 30 pilot pursuits, 14 "occupant" reports, 11 radar trackings, and 7 UFO-related power failures. Many of these incidents occured in North Carolina, Pennsylvania, New England, Florida, California, Ohio, England, Canada, Argentina, Australia, Peru, and Mexico.

----- 1966--the year of saucers. Flying saucers, Aug. 1967: 6-11.

Postulating that the subject of flying saucers "has finally taken on respectability, " author lists significant "breakthroughs" and analyzes major occurrences during 1966.

23

Fawcett, George D. UFO repetitions. Flying saucers, Aug. 1966: 28.

Lists aspects of UFO sightings that are repeatedly reported.

Flick, David. Tripe for the public. Library journal, v. 80, Feb. 1, 1955: 202, 204.

Commenting on the "thought processes and the strange logic" employed by librarians responsible for book selection, the author says that no amount of rationalizing about "future historical importance," "balanced collections," and "public demand" can justify their expenditure of tax dollars for books about flying saucers "whose purpose seems to satisfy a jaded taste for the bizarre and the sensational."

Flying saucers. Journal of the British Interplanetary Society, v. 11, Sept. 1952: 224-226.

Conclusions in April 7, 1952, Life magazine feature on the UFO phenomenon tending to support the reality of flying saucers are summarized. British Interplanetary Society states its position of remaining unconvinced that earth is already in contact with extraterrestrial forces and gives the reasons.

Flying saucers. Public opinion quarterly, v. 14, Fall 1950: 597-598.

Results of poll in which question was asked: What do you think flying saucers are? Asked of 94% of a national sample who had heard or read of UFOs. 23% believed they were Army or Navy experiments or new weapons; 16% thought them to be an optical illusion or hoax; 5% said they were comets, shooting stars, or something from another planet.

Fontes, Olavo T. Project Argus and the "anonymous" satellite. Flying saucers, Oct. 1959: 8-12.

Author suggests that the mission of nuclear missile launching Project Argus may have been to destroy an unidentified satellite that circled the earth from Aug. 16, 1959, until Argus' warheads were exploded in space Aug. 27, Aug. 30, and Sept. 6. Satellite may have been associated with UFOs, author speculates.

----- A suggested scientific investigation of the UFO phenomenon. Flying saucer review, v. 13, Nov.-Dec. 1967: 22-24.

In setting up a scientific investigation into the UFO phenomenon, it is suggested that the following steps be taken: (1) cancellation of unnecessary security restrictions; (2) a systematic rather than haphazard search for UFO appearances; (3) use of the most effective detection methods available; (4) determination of the best locations to set up detection instruments; (5) use of a convergent procedure to alert given areas of a possible UFO sighting; (6) distribution of available equipment and trained observers in reasonable proportions in different areas (7) consideration of effect the search procedure might have on the searched object.

Fouéré, René. Méteors à hublots. Phénomènes spatiaux, Feb. 1965: 7-9.

Meteors and atmospheric phenomena have often been mistaken for flying saucers. Plasmas resembling flying saucers have been synthesized in the laboratory. However, none of these phenomena have features that even remotely resemble the "portholes" described in many alleged sightings. Presence of portholes would then preclude a meteoric or other "natural" explanation for a UFO sighting.

----- Observations d' un astronome argentin. Phénomènes spatiaux, June 1966: 3-11.

On Nov. 14, 1964, the Reverend Father Benito Reyna of the Society of Jesus, saw and photographed a "flotilla" of flying saucers from the Adhara Observatory, San Miguel, Buenos Aires, Argentina. Incident is reported in detail and newspaper accounts quoted.

----- Sommes-nous à un tournant? Phénomènes spatiaux, Dec. 1966: 6-12.

Author postulates that UFO research seems to have reached a crucial turning point and cites as indications of this the fact that (1) USAF has begun to make its Project Blue Book files more accessible to researchers, and (2) establishment of the Condon Project at the University of Colorado to study UFO phenomena.

Fuller, Curtis. The saucers are flying. Fate, v. 8, Aug. 1955: 6-16.

Postulates five possible explanations of flying saucers: (1) they are space ships piloted by intelligent beings from somewhere else in the universe; (2) they are space animals which live in space; (3) they are natural phenomena such as aggregations of electrons, or some other kind of energy which we do not understand; (4) they originate on earth and are man-made; (5) they are hallucinations.

Fuller, Jean. The Exeter incidents. Flying saucer review, v. 13, Sept.-Oct. 1967: 25-27.

Summary of the 21 UFO sighting cases described in detail by John Fuller in his book, Incident at Exeter.

Fuller, John G. A communication concerning the UFOs. Saturday review, v. 50, Feb. 4, 1967: 70-72.

In SR's science sections for August 6, September 3, and October 1, John Lear, SR's science editor, discussed various aspects of the UFO controversy. Among several books from which he took excerpts was John Fuller's Incident at Exeter. Fuller takes exception to Lear's articles and defends his own position.

Gearhart, Livingston. Bombed by meteors. Fate, v. 18, Mar. 1965: 80-82.

On November 5, 1906, SS St. Andrew was caught in an apparent meteor shower; fall included a saucer-shaped meteor 10-15 feet in diameter.

Gibbs-Smith, Charles H. Flying saucers. The queen, v. 202, Nov. 17, 1954: 64.

A discussion by the well-known aeronautical historian of the UFO phenomenon. He states that one can rule out UFOs as being foreign aircraft and secret weapons and speculates that techniques may have been achieved in some other civilization in the universe that surmount matter and time as we know them-- techniques no more startling for such a civilization than flying and radio appear to our civilization on earth.

Goble, H. C. Did Jones chart an unknown world? Fate, v. 10, Apr. 1957: 68-70.

Analysis of the 700-page observations of Zodiacal Light made Apr. 4, 1853 to Feb. 3, 1855, by Rev. Jones, Chaplain of Commodore Perry's expedition to Japan, seems to indicate that some components of the "light" were artificially-propelled luminous objects with behavior identical to that of UFOs.

Gray, Grattan. The town that believes in flying saucers. Maclean's, v. 80, Mar. 1967: 4.

Describes projected $14,000 landing pad for flying saucers to be erected for centennial celebration of St. Paul, Alberta, Canada.

A hard look at "flying saucers." U.S. news & world report, v. 60, Apr. 11, 1966: 14-15.

Summary of opinion about the reality of the UFO phenomenon.

Harney, John and Alan W. Sharp. Report on a visit to Warminster. Flying saucer review, v. 13, Sept. -Oct. 1967: 3-4.

Report in investigation of alleged UFO incidents at Warminster, England. Reprinted from July 1967 MUFORG Bulletin of the Merseyside UFO Research Group.

Heavenly bogies. Time, v. 88, Sept. 2, 1966: 81-82.

Reviews of Frank Edwards' Flying Saucers -- Serious Business and John G. Fuller's Incident at Exeter.

Hynek, J. Allen. Are flying saucers real? The Saturday evening post, v. 239, Dec. 17, 1966: 17-21.

Hynek, chairman of the department of astronomy at Northwestern Univ. and consultant to USAF's Project Blue Book, states that of the 15,000 cases of UFO sightings that have come to his attention, "several hundred are puzzling, and some of the puzzling incidents, perhaps one in 25 are bewildering." He cites illustrative examples and urges a serious inquiry into the nature of the phenomenon.

----- The UFO gap. Playboy, v. 14, Dec. 1967: 144-146, 267, 269-271.

Author says that from what "hard" information he has, the U.S.S.R. may have been studying the UFO phenomenon with dispassionate thoroughness for years; the U.S. is only now beginning to consider treating the problem seriously. He outlines what he believes to be a thorough and efficient way to obtain scientific knowledge of UFOs.

Hynek, J. Allen. UFOs merit scientific study. Science, Oct. 21, 1966: 329.

In an open letter, the author states that he "cannot dismiss the UFO phenomenon with a shrug" and urges that the Air Force "ask physical and social scientists of stature to make a respectable, scholarly study of the UFO phenomenon."

----- Unusual aerial phenomena. Journal of the Optical Society of America, v. 43, Apr. 1953: 311-314.

Author reports that several hundred serious reports of "unidentified aerial objects" have been studied in detail in an attempt to get a pattern classification. It appears to him that reported phenomena which do not admit of a ready and obvious explanation exhibit fairly well-defined patterns and that these are worthy of further study. One pattern in particular, that of a hovering nocturnal light, does not appear to him to be readily explainable on an astronomical basis or by mirages, balloons, or by conventional aircraft.

Is the U.S. Government expecting invaders from space? Flying saucers from other worlds, Aug. 1957: 16-21.

Presents "factual" though circumstantial evidence to support theory that USAF knows that some of the unidentified objects observed are from other worlds and is taking measures to repulse an extraterrestrial invasion force.

Jones, Harold S. The flying saucer myth. The spectator, Dec. 15, 1950: 686-687.

Author, the British astronomer royal, says that flying saucers are "improbable" and the extraterrestrial hypothesis "the strongest possible demonstration that the whole thing is a myth."

Jones, R. V. The natural philosophy of flying saucers. Physics bulletin, July 1968: 225-230.

Prominent British physicist examines the UFO evidence. Although commending genuine scientific inquiry into the subject, he retains his skepticism of flying saucers.

Kaempffert, Waldemar. Expert sees flying object--saucer or balloon. Science digest, v. 31, Feb. 1952: 74.

Account of Charles B. Moore's sighting of UFO while tracking a Skyhook balloon with a theodolite. Moore was project engineer for Project Skyhook; UFO sightings have often been explained as Skyhook balloons.

Keel, John A. Secret UFO bases across the U.S. Saga, v. 36, Apr. 1968: 30-33, 86, 89-90, 92-94, 96.

Author suggests that "while everyone has been studying the skies, searching for a clue to the origin of the UFOs, the objects and their occupants may have been happily nesting almost in our very midst, quietly preparing for their 'D-Day'!"

Keel, John A. UFOs--the statistical problem. Flying saucers, Aug. 1968: 18-19.

Author states that random UFO sighting reports do not provide data of sufficient depth or "keys to the many hidden factors" of the phenomenon. He suggests that UFO researchers revise their approach to the subject and "search for new and possibly illogical (by our standards) clues buried in the more controversial cases."

Keyhoe, Donald E. Flying saucers--fact or fancy? The air line pilot, v. 22, Oct. 1953: 9-10.

Major Keyhoe describes official statements from USAF's Air Technical Intelligence Center to refute Dr. Donald Menzel's explanations that UFO sightings are attributable to natural atmospheric phenomena. He also cites "an official Air Force document" which states that an increasing number of officials linked with the investigation are convinced "that the saucers are interplanetary."

----- Flying saucers: menace or myth? Argosy, v. 350, June 1960: 17, 80-83.

Author states that for 13 years, USAF has maintained officially that reports of UFOs are the result of delusions and hoaxes, with no solid basis whatsoever. He purports to expose this cover-up policy by making public official USAF documents, including Regulation 200-2 and a directive referring to UFOs as "serious business."

Klemin, Alexander. The flying saucer. Aero digest, v. 32, Mar. 1950: 129-130.

Author examines "flying saucer stories" from point of view of aerodynamic feasibility and practicality and concludes there is "nothing in them."

Kor, Peter. Perspective: flying saucers--physical or psychic? Saucer news, v. 13, Fall 1966: 10-12.

Inquiry into the language and concepts that have been used to determine the nature of the UFO phenomenon.

----- UFOs from the critic's corner: the myth of the flying saucer mystery. Flying saucers, Dec. 1959: 48-53.

Author, a non-believer in UFOs, gives reasons for his non-belief and critically analyzes current UFO "research."

Lang, Daniel. Ils livrent combat aux soucoupes volantes. Constellation, v. 79, Nov. 1954: 133-154.

Review of UFO sighting reports, especially in the U.S.A., and of theories advanced by members of the scientific community to explain the phenomenon.

----- A reporter at large: something in the sky. The New Yorker, v. 28, Sept. 6, 1952: 68-89.

Discussion of USAF's Project Saucer investigation into reports of "strange celestial objects."

Lear, John. A reply. Saturday review, Feb. 4, 1967: 73.

SR's science editor restates his position in the UFO controversy and answers John Fuller's criticisms of him for publishing excerpts from Incident at Exeter (New York, G.P. Putnam's Sons, 1966) without permission and out of context.

Le Poer Trench, Brinsley. The three W's. Saucer news, v. 11, Dec. 1964: 7-10.

Discusses three questions important in UFO research: (1) where do they come from? (2) who crews them? (3) why are they coming?

Lyustiberg, Villen. "Letaiushchie tarelki"? Mif! [Are flying saucers a myth?] Pravda ukrainy, no. 40, Feb. 17, 1968: 2.

Flying saucers are described as a well camouflaged means of misinforming masses of people: "whenever magazine or newspaper circulation lags, whenever the reader gets sated with economics and politics, whenever he has to be distracted from asking embarrassing questions, then Western businessmen use one of three sure-fire perennial sensations--flying saucers, sea serpents (sometimes the Loch Ness monster), and Abominable Snowmen."

McDonald, James E. A need for an international study of UFOs. Flying saucer review, v. 14, Mar.-Apr. 1968: 11.

Author writes an endorsement to Soviet scientist Zigel's plea for "a joint effort of all the scientists of the world" to determine the nature of UFOs. From a Dec. 10, 1967, New York Times story by Henry Kamm.

----- UFOer - det største videnskabelige problem i vor tid? Randers, Denmark, UFO-NYTs Forlag, 1967. 64 p.

Translation of "UFOs: the greatest scientific problem of our times," delivered at the convention of the American Society of Newspaper Editors, Washington, D.C., April 22, 1967.

Mallan, Lloyd. What we are doing about UFOs. Science & mechanics, v. 38, Jan. 1967: 38-43, 62-67, 76.

Survey of activities of official and private organizations engaged in UFO research.

Mandel, Siegfried. The great saucer hunt. The Saturday review, v. 38, Aug. 6, 1955: 28-29.

Ten books dealing with flying saucers are reviewed: Flying Saucers have Landed, Desmond Leslie and George Adamski; Inside the Space Ships, George Adamski; Flying Saucers from Mars, Cedric Allingham; Space, Gravity, and the Flying Saucers, Leonard G. Cramp; Flying Saucers on the Attack, Harold T. Wilkins; The Case for the UFO, M.K. Jessup; Roundtrip to Hell in a Flying Saucer, Cecil Michael; The Saucers Speak, George H. Williamson and Alfred C. Bailey; Flying Saucers from Outer Space, Donald E. Keyhoe; Flying Saucers, Donald H. Menzel.

Maney, Charles A. Scientific aspects of UFO research. Flying saucer review, v. 4, Sept-Oct. 1958: 10-12, 30.

Maney discusses role of scientific method in UFO research in speech at opening of Planetary Center, Detroit, Mich., June 14, 1958.

Marais, D. Are we being watched? Personality, v. 1410, Jan. 1, 1954: 26-28.

Margolis, Howard. The UFO phenomenon. Bulletin of the atomic scientists, v. 23, June 1967: 40-42.

Problems and difficulties inherent in the University of Colorado study of unidentified flying objects are discussed by the author. He concludes that it is unlikely that the final report will resolve the issue and speculates that it may "add more fuel to the controversy."

Markowitz, William. The physics and metaphysics of unidentified flying objects. Science, v. 157, Sept. 15, 1967: 1274-1279.

Reported UFOs cannot be under extraterrestrial control if the laws of physics are valid, the author asserts. He adds that the data published do not justify the holding of investigations of the phenomenon.

Miller, Max B. Report on the UFO. Fate, v. 9, Dec. 1956: 31-34.

Review of Edward J. Ruppelt's book about the U.S. Air Force's UFO investigations, The Report on Unidentified Flying Objects (New York, Doubleday, 1956).

----- Scientists track space radio signals. Fate, v. 12, June 1959: 57-58.

Mysterious radio signals whose source may be moving in a direction away from the earth were monitored on frequencies of 20 and 40 megacycles for three hours in late November 1958, from an Air Force Missile Test Center installation at Cape Canaveral.

Miller, Stewart. On scientific dogma. Flying saucer review, v. 13, Mar.-Apr. 1967: 26-27.

Speculation about UFOs must be expressed within a coherent and consistent framework, the author postulates; otherwise UFO researchers must not level accusations of narrow-mindedness at those who point out mistakes.

Moorehouse, Frederick G.   The case of the flying saucers.   Argosy, v. 329, July 1949: 22-24, 92.

Author states that: (1) there are flying saucers; (2) they represent the most advanced form of guided missile yet to appear; (3) they use a new source of propulsion which derives from a compact "soft fission" atomic powerplant that affords amazing performance in terms of range and speed; (4) they use a new scheme for guidance and control that gives a never-before-reached degree of precision. He documents his claims.

The mysterious chunk of hardware at Ottawa.   Topside, Spring 1968: 1-4.

On June 12, 1960, a sonic boom was heard in Quebec City, Canada. At about the same time, a fiery object fell out of the sky, splitting into two pieces, both of which fell into the St. Lawrence River about 20 mi. upriver from Quebec City and were later recovered. X-ray diffraction analysis indicated the un-identified objects consisted of a metallic face-centered cubic compound, with a unit-cell dimension agreeing with those of austenitic steel and meteoric iron. The semi-quantitative spectrographic analysis showed there was insufficient nickel present for the material to be of meteoric origin; the subject was con-sidered to be of terrestrial origin. Subsequent laboratory experiments on the metal by Wilbur B. Smith and co-workers resulted in a number of unusual re-actions not consistent with the normal behavior of terrestrial metal.

The new saucer epidemic.   New republic, v. 127, Aug. 18, 1952: 7.

Commentary on increased reports of UFO sightings. Opinions are given of scientists (including Donald H. Menzel and Noel Scott) who believe it unlikely that flying saucers come from another planet.

Nollet, A. R.   Flying saucers..a hard look.   Marine corps gazette, v. 43, Dec. 1959: 20-25.

States that hope for a U.S. scientific "saucer" breakthrough based on April 29, 1959, article in U.S. News and World Report entitled "Flying Saucer Age for the U.S. -- It's Getting Nearer" were misplaced since the "saucers" turned out to be ground effect vehicles. Describes the different types of GEVs worldwide and suggests military uses.

Oberth, Hermann.   Dr. Hermann Oberth discusses UFOs.   Fate, v. 15, May 1962: 36-43.

Author says that in the absence of a more plausible explanation, one might assume that UFOs are "flying machines" that (1) are not built by humans; (2) fly by means of artificial gravity fields; and (3) produce high-tension electric charges to push the air out of their paths so that it does not start glowing, and strong magnetic fields to interact with ionized air.

Transitions of UFOs from half-transparent to invisible state might be related
to creation of artificial gravity fields. Oberth "would bet 100 to one that some
of the contact persons are normal and have seen and experienced something."

Oberth, Hermann. Warum Ufoforschung? In Mitteilungen der Gesellschaft für
  Interplanetarik. Wien, Europäischer-Verlag, 1961. p. 1-7.

After summarizing hypotheses that might explain the UFO phenomenon, the
author predicts that scientific institutions will enter seriously into UFO research once the field has been more clearly defined so that it can be assigned
to the appropriate specialists and when enough evidence has been collected so
that the facts can no longer be denied or ridiculed.

----- Wir werden beobachtet. Deutsche illustrierte, Sept. 11, 1954: 10-11, 24-28.

Discussion of UFOs, their behavior and characteristics is followed by examples
of UFO sightings. It is concluded that in the light of current scientific and
technological knowledge and research, they are too advanced to have been built
by man and must have been constructed by extraterrestrial beings especially
adapted biologically to space travel. Author urges serious research by the
scientific community and that official agencies make available all records in
their possession.

Official Air Force statements on unidentified flying objects. The UFO investigator,
  v. 1, Jan. 1958: 25-26.

Period 1947-1952 is covered.

Ogles, George W. What does the Air Force really know about flying saucers?
  Washington, D.C., The Airman, 1967. 8 p. Reprinted from The Airman,
  v. 11, July 1967, p. 4-9; Aug. 1967, p. 26-31.

Survey of the UFO controversy and statement of the Air Force position: the
Air Force has never denied the possibility of life on other planets; what it does
say is that no evidence has been received nor discovered which proves the existence and intraspace mobility of extraterrestrial life. Some widely publicized
"sightings" are also discussed.

Ormond, Ron. Is Siam a secret base for flying saucers? Flying saucers, May
  1959: 51-56.

Story is told of big fiery wheels that come out of the sky and land near the village
of the Lahus, an aboriginal tribe inhabiting the northern sector of Thailand.

Out-of-the-blue believers. The New Yorker, v. 35, Apr. 18, 1959: 36-37.

Commentary on a symposium relating to UFO phenomena sponsored by Civilian
Saucer Intelligence of New York.

Pack, Warren E. Interview with Donald Keyhoe. Fate, v. 12, Aug. 1959: 86-90.

Keyhoe discusses UFO sightings by reliable observers and states the determination of NICAP (National Investigations Committee on Aerial Phenomena) to obtain public Congressional hearings on the phenomenon.

Palmer, Ray. New report on the flying saucers. Fate, v. 4, Jan. 1951: 63-81.

Excerpts from article entitled "The Flying Saucers--Fact or Fiction" printed in July 1950 Flying. Reports alleged UFO sightings on March 31, 1950, by Chicago and Southern Air Lines pilots Capt. Jack Adams and G.W. Anderson, Jr., near Little Rock, Ark.; in July 1948 by Eastern Air Lines pilots Capt. Clarence S. Chiles and John B. Whitted southwest of Mongomery, Ala.; on April 27, 1950, by Trans-World Air Lines pilots Capt. Robert Adickes and Robert Manning near South Bend, Ind.; and on May 29, 1950, by American Airlines pilot Capt. William T. Sperry near Washington, D.C.

Pastorino, Luiz P. The flying discs and the U.S.S.R. BUFORA journal and bulletin, v. 1, Spring 1967: 4-6.

The people who see "flying saucers." The UFO investigator, v. 1, Jan. 1958: 23-24.

Listing of witnesses to UFO sightings; professions are given.

Posin, Dan Q. An eye on space. Popular mechanics, v. 113, Feb. 1960: 103.

Commentary on reports of "hair-raising sights in the sky." Unnamed scientist is quoted as saying that while it is not probable that extraterrestrial spacecraft have visited earth, "they can come and they might come--any day."

Pravda i vynsysel ob UFO [Truth and fantasy about UFOs]. Tekhnika molodezhi, No. 8, 1967: 23-27.

A series of articles by Alexander Kazantsev and Jacques Vallée, Yu Makerov, and George Campbell.

Priestly, Lee. Inside APRO...a saucer fan club. Fate, v. 12, Jan. 1959: 59-65.

Account of the activities of the Aerial Phenomena Research Organization (APRO) of Tucson, Arizona.

Prytz, John. The Air Force opinion on UFOs. Flying saucers, Oct. 1966: 26-27.

Author states that although officially USAF disclaims the reality of flying saucers, a high percentage of USAF personnel believe in the seriousness of phenomenon.

Rankow, Ralph. The disc with the domed top. Fate, v. 19, Aug. 1966: 54-61.

Highway inspector describes encounter with soundless aerial object that he was able to photograph.

Ross, John C. What were the doughnuts? Fate, Spring 1948: 12-14.

In an analysis of military aircraft and weaponry, author states it would be difficult to confuse them with the flying disks reportedly seen by Kenneth Arnold. He suggests extraterrestrial origin.

Ruppelt, Edward J. Inside story of the saucers. Science digest, v. 39, Apr. 1956. 35-41.

Condensed from a chapter of the book, The Report on Unidentified Flying Objects, published in New York by Doubleday, 1956. Author describes his activities as head of USAF's Project Blue Book, 1951-1953. He states that while balloons, airplanes, stars, and many other common objects have been reported as UFOs, there are hundreds of other UFO reports which carry the verdict, "Conclusion Unknown."

----- What our Air Force found out about flying saucers. True, May 1954: 19-20, 22, 24, 26, 30, 124-134.

Ruppelt, in charge of USAF's Project Blue Book from 1951 to 1953, reports what he learned about flying saucers during this period. He states his opinion that the saucers are either inter planetary or do not exist.

Sagan, Carl. Unidentified flying object. In Encyclopedia Americana, v. 27, New York, Americana Corp., 1967. p. 368-369.

"Unidentified flying object" is defined and then discussed in terms of investigations, hypotheses of extraterrestrial origin, and psychological factors.

Salisbury, Frank B. The scientist and the UFO. Bioscience, Jan. 1967: 15-24.

Five hypotheses purporting to explain the UFO phenomenon are discussed and a few representative sightings considered.

Sharp, Peter F. An appraisal of the present UFO position. Flying saucer review, v. 7, 1961: 19-22.

Analysis of current hypotheses which attempt to explain UFO phenomena.

Simons, Rodger L. The space ship hokum. The Catholic world, v. 140, Nov. 1934: 164-170.

Arguments on the improbability of there ever being travel to and from other planets.

Situation report: What is the unidentified flying object situation these days? American engineer, Mar. 1967: 55.

Two new developments relating to the UFO phenomenon are cited: (1) Dr. J. Allen Hynek's open letter to Science urging serious scientific investigation of the problem; and (2) the USAF-sponsored, 15-month study at the University of Colorado, headed by Dr. Edward U. Condon.

Smith, E.R. UFOs and artificial satellites. Flying saucer review, v. 7, Sept-Oct. 1961: 6-11.

Some conventional methods of observing things seen in the sky are discussed for benefit of UFO researchers. Possibility of confusing satellites with UFOs-- and vice versa--is treated.

Snova "Letaiushchie tarelki"? [!'Flying saucers" again?] Pravda, Feb. 29, 1968: 8.

In answer to letters from readers claiming to have seen flying saucers, article on the subject by several scientists was published. It is postulated that "no one has in his possession any new facts that would substantiate the reality of flying saucers. They are not encountered by scientists who study the state and conditions of earth's atmosphere. This therefore means there are no grounds for reviving the nonsensical, long-buried rumors about secret trips to our planet by Martians or Venusians." Article signed by E. Mustel, D. Martynov, and V. Leshkovtsev.

Stanford, Rex G. Brev från Rex Stanford. Sökaren, v. 5, no. 3, 1968: 16.

Author's response to questions submitted to him by the editor, Sven Magnusson. He states his belief that flying saucers come from and are controlled by beings from outer space. The author's book, Look Up, was translated into Swedish with title Kontakt med Rymdmänniskor (Hälsingborg, Parthenon, 1959). Also discussed is Project Starlight International, organized by his brother, Ray Stanford, Corpus Christi, Tex., to collect physical proof of the existence of UFOs.

Stevens, Stuart. Sighting peaks and planetary oppositions. Flying saucers, Aug. 1966: 20-21.

Author suggests the UFO sighting peaks between the Martian oppositions might mean there is also an opposition wave for other planets in our solar system. Reprinted from Orbit, journal of the Tyneside, England, U.F.O. Society.

The strange intruder. Newsweek, v. 56, July 4, 1960: 83.

Radio astronomer Ronald Bracewell comments on possibility that an unidentified satellite from an extraterrestrial civilization is orbiting the sun.

Szachnowski, Antoni. The necessity of a global international federation of UFO groups. BUFORA journal and bulletin, v. 1, Spring 1965: 5-9.

Lecture at the Southern Region UFO Research Groups Conference, Oxford, England, May 8, 1965.

The truth about the book "The report on unidentified flying objects" by Edward J. Ruppelt. Flying saucers, Dec. 1958: 35-42, 56.

Ruppelt's "report" is challenged, specifically his statement that the Maury Island incident was "the dirtiest book in UFO history" and was perpetrated by Ray Palmer.

UFO: an objective look at unidentified flying objects. Science & mechanics, v. 37, Dec. 1966: 30-39, 57-58, 62-76.

Illustrated directory of all major sightings through December 1966. Detailed case histories of the 12 most mysterious UFO sightings.

Vallée, Jacques. How to classify and codify saucer sightings. Flying saucer review, v. 9, Sept.-Oct. 1963: 9-12.

Article sets forth briefly principles which can be used in the classification and coding of flying saucer sightings.

----- How to select significant UFO reports. Flying saucer review, v. 11, Sept.-Oct. 1965: 15-18.

Author believes that the scientific way to process UFO data is to divide the problem into two parts: (1) consider all the reports from all available sources, trying to explain them in terms of conventional objects; (2) when all identified cases have been eliminated, the residue must contain reference to the UFO phenomenon if it exists as an unconventional, objective agent in the generation of reports.

----- UFO research in the U.S.A. Flying saucer review, v. 12, Jan.-Feb. 1966: 6-11.

Author reports on his impressions of trends--motivations and theories--in American ufology.

Vallée, Jacques, and Aleksandr Kasantsev. What is it that is flying in our skies? Flying saucer review, v. 13, Nov.-Dec. 1967: 11-12.

General discussion of theories relating to the UFO phenomenon. "Classic" UFO sighting cases are cited.

Vallée, Jacques and Janine Vallée. Astronomers' verdict: flying saucers are real. Fate, v. 20, Apr. 1967: 62-72.

An objective review of major hypotheses on origin of UFOs leads author to conclude that (1) all sightings cannot be attributed to conventional causes; (2) existence of alien intelligence must be considered; (3) extreme caution must be used in developing latter hypothesis because of phenomenon's complexity. Excerpted from Challenge to Science: UFO Enigma, published in Chicago by H. Regnery Co., 1966.

Vallée, Jacques and Janine Vallee. Mars and the flying saucers. Flying saucer review, v. 8, Sept.-Oct. 1962: 5-11.

Study of the periodicity of the flying saucer phenomenon in its correlation with the oppositions of Mars.

Veit, Karl. Mainzer Weltkongres der UFO-Forscher. UFO-nachrichten, Dec. 1967: 1, 3.

Proceedings of the 7th International UFO Congress, Mainz, Germany, Nov. 3-6, 1967.

Vonkeviczky e gli UFO all'UNU. Centro unico nazionale per lo studio del fenomeni ritenuti di natura extraterrestre. Notiziario, no. 5, 1967: 8-14.

Because of his interest in UFOs and letters to the Secretary General of the United Nations urging an international study of the phenomenon, Colman Vonkeviczky, a U.N. photo technician, allegedly lost his job and was subsequently denied employment at the U.N. when a vacancy occurred.

Waithman, Robert. These flying saucers. The spectator, v. 184, Apr. 14, 1950: 489-490.

Commentary on the flying saucer controversy.

What were the flying saucers? Popular science, v. 159, Aug. 1951: 74-75, 228.

Results of an unofficial Popular Science survey in which eye-witnesses to UFO phenomena were asked to choose the explanation that seemed most plausible to them: 52% believe they saw "man-made aircraft"; 16% believe they saw "something commonplace"; 4 % believe they saw a "visitor from afar"; 28% are still uncertain, but more than half of them think they saw either man-made aircraft or visitors from afar.

Wilkins, Harold T. Flying saucers. The contemporary review, July 1950: 49-53.

Well-corroborated UFO incidents are cited by author as proof that the phenomenon cannot be dismissed as misinterpretation of natural objects.

Willems, Louis. De lieve invasie. A.B.C., Oct. 8, 1966: 14-16.

Speculation on whether increasing reports of worldwide sightings of UFOs harbinger an invasion by extraterrestrial beings.

Wilson, Harvey. Found: flying saucer base in outer space. The National police gazette, v. 173, Aug. 1968: 14, 24.

It is speculated that pulsating signals from the region of the star Vega are indicative of a flying saucer base there.

The wind is up in Kansas. Time, v. 60, Sept. 8, 1952: 86.

Wichita Beacon issues a state-wide call for a flying saucer watch.

Zigel, Felix. The UFO problem -- a challenge to science. Flying saucers, June 1968: 25-26.

The joint effort of all scientists in the world should be applied to discovering the nature of the UFO phenomenon, the author says. Details given of sightings in the U.S.S.R., 1965-1967.

Zinsstag, Lou. Conversations with Dr. Jung. Flying saucer review, v. 9, July-Aug. 1963: 14-16.

Author, a relative of Dr. Jung, gives details of informal talks about various aspects of the flying saucer controversy.

ABDUCTIONS

The Brazilian abduction. Flying saucer review, v. 8, Nov.-Dec. 1962: 10-12. Dec. 1962: 10-12.

Description by Raimundo Mafra of the disappearance of his father, Rivalino Mafra da Silva, from Duas Pontes, Diamantina, Brazil, and concomitant events that might indicate abduction by UFO.

Comella, Tom. Have UFOs "swallowed" our aircraft? Fate, v. 14, May 1961: 32-37.

Master/Sergeant O. D. Hill of Project Blue Book allegedly related instances where aircraft being tracked on radar mysteriously disappeared after "merging" with UFOs also being tracked.

Creighton, Gordon. Attempted abduction by UFO entity? Flying saucer review, v. 13, Mar.-Apr. 1967: 23-24.

Translation of newspaper account (Ettala'at Teheran, Iran , Oct. 15, 1954) of an apparent attempted abduction by UFO.

----- Even more amazing. Flying saucer review, v. 12, July-Aug. 1966: 23-27; Sept.-Oct. 1966: 22-25; Nov.-Dec. 1966: 14-16; v. 13, Jan.-Feb. 1967: 25-27; v. 14, Jan.-Feb. 1968: 18-20.

English version of original declaration made by Antonio Villas Boas that on the night of October 15-16, 1957, he was abducted by helmeted, uniformed creatures from his farm near Francisco de Sales, Brazil, onto a landed spacecraft of apparently extraterrestrial origin; there, he was seduced by a naked, fair-skinned, red-haired woman with slanting eyes in what may have been a biological experiment. A translation of the medical report confirms the possibility of the alleged experience.

----- The most amazing case of all: Part 1--a Brazilian farmer's story. Flying saucer review, v. 11, Jan.-Feb. 1965: 13-17.

On Dec. 15, 1957, Antonio Villas Boas, a Brazilian farmer, was allegedly taken aboard a flying saucer and seduced by a white-skinned, red-haired woman with "slanted" eyes. Based on account in the April/July 1962 bulletin of the Sociedad Brasileira de Estudos Sobre Discos Voadores.

----- The most amazing case of all. Part II--Analysis of the Brazilian farmer's story. Flying saucer review, v. 11, Mar.-Apr. 1965: 5-8.

Author analyses details of Antonio Villas Boas story that he was taken aboard a landed flying saucer and seduced by a white-skinned, red-haired, slant-eyed woman. He speculates that the mission of some extraterrestrial visitors might be to breed a mixed race--a new race which would have inherited some of our characteristics, including our ability to live in a mixture of 80% nitrogen and 20% oxygen.

Gaddis, Vincent H. Survey of mysterious disappearances. In his Invisible horizons. Philadelphia, Chilton Co., 1965. p. 161-225.

Describes disappearances of men and aircraft under circumstances that would suggest kidnapping by extraterrestrials.

Important discoveries. Flying saucer review, v. 12, Nov.-Dec. 1966: 17.

Comparison of case of Barney and Betty Hill who, on the night of Sept. 19, 1961, were allegedly captured by beings from a flying saucer and taken aboard the spacecraft for physical examination and that of Antonio Villas Boas who was allegedly abducted by extraterrestrial beings for sexual experiment aboard their landed spacecraft on Oct. 15/16, 1957.

Keel, John A. More from my Ohio Valley notebook. Flying saucer review, v. 13, July-Aug. 1967: 20-21.

During a visit to Sistersville, Ohio, for information about the 1897 UFO sighting there, author learns there have been numerous UFO sightings 1966-1967 and is told of an abortive attempt by a UFO to kidnap a bloodmobile in March 1967.

----- The UFO kidnappers. Saga, v. 33, Feb. 1967: 10-14, 50, 52-54, 56-60, 62.

Documents instances where UFOs have tracked and sometimes kidnapped humans. Reports cases where airborne planes have been engulfed by UFOs.

Lorenzen, Coral. The disappearance of Rivalino da Silva: kidnapped by a UFO? Fate, v. 16, June 1963: 26-33.

A 12 year-old boy told police that on August 20, 1962, two strange, globe-shaped objects had visited his home and taken away his terrified father. Alleged incident occurred in Diamantino, Brazil.

Spraggett, Allen. Kidnapped by a UFO. Fate, v. 20, Jan. 1967: 34-41.

Account of UFO's abduction of Barney and Betty Hill on Sept. 19, 1961, near Franconia Notch, N. H.

Steiger, Brad and Joan Whritenour. Flying saucers are hostile. New York, Award Books, 1967. 160 p.

Documented cases in which UFOs have allegedly been involved in murders, kidnappings, auto crashes, destruction of airplanes, and other acts of aggression.

Wells, Leslie E. They disappeared into the unknown. Fate, v. 9, July 1956: 63-67.

Cases are detailed which suggest that men, both singly and in numbers, have been spirited from the earth. It is speculated that they might have entered worlds that coexist with ours.

Wolk, George. The terror above us, by Malcolm Kent [pseud.] New York, Tower Publications, 1967. 124 p.

A fiction novel presented as fact, representing the story of two young men who are abducted by a flying saucer and subjected to a form of "brain washing. "

AIR FORCE

Adler, B. , comp. Letters to the Air Force on UFO's. New York, Dell Pub. Co. , 1967. 157 p.

Binder, Otto O. Exposed: why the Air Force sits on UFOs. Bluebook, v. 106, Dec. 1967: 16-19, 74-76, 78-79.

Speculation on reason that USAF does not declare that UFOs are real: "the USAF cannot admit that they are unable to protect America from UFO surveillance or they would be 'out of business' in short order for having failed in their main mission. "

Booth, Leon. Flying saucers. Ordnance, v. 51, July-Aug. 1966: 30-31.

USAF role in investigating UFO sighting reports is discussed.

Bryant, Larry W. The UFO cover-up at Langley Air Force Base. Flying saucers, June 1968: 11-14.

Author gives details of UFO sighting at Langley Air Force Base on Jan. 28, 1965, by responsible witnesses and of Air Force failure to investigate the incident and subsequent misrepresentation of the facts.

Cahn, J. P. Flying saucers and the mysterious little men. True, v. 32, Sept. 1952: 17-19, 102-112.

Report of investigation into allegations in Frank Scully's book, Behind the Flying Saucers (New York, Henry Holt, 1950), that a crashed flying saucer and corpses of its three-foot-tall crew had been taken into custody by the U. S. Air Force. Claims prove untrue and the book a hoax.

Chartrand, Robert L. and William F. Brown. Facts about unidentified flying objects. Washington, D. C., Library of Congress, Legislative Reference Service, 1966. 29 p.

Includes the following: description of various types of UFOs; trends in UFO activity; historical sightings of aerial phenomena; identification of flying objects (versus UFOs); U. S. Government monitoring of UFO activity; special studies of UFOs; special briefings on UFO activity; public reaction to UFOs; Air Force Regulation 200-2.

Cohen, Daniel. UFOs--what a new investigation may reveal. Science digest, v. 60, Dec. 1966: 54-56, 58, 60-63.

Reviews USAF's Project Blue Book investigation of UFO reports and summarizes aims of independent 15-month study by University of Colorado.

Current comment: What goes on up there? America, v. 87, Aug. 23, 1952: 489.

Article states reported USAF position on flying saucers: they are not spacecraft from distant planets; they are not secret enemy weapons.

Davidson, Leon. Flying saucers: an analysis of the Air Force Project Blue Book Special Report No. 14. [3rd ed., rev. and enl.] Ramsey, N. J., Ramsey-Wallace Corp., 1966. 84 p.

Author states that throughout its investigation of UFO phenomena, USAF has withheld information, photographs, and other evidence it has amassed. He suggests that full text of Project Blue Book Special Report No. 14 (analysis of reports of unidentified aerial objects)--an offset copy dated May 5, 1955 is in the appendix--probably was not made readily available to the public because in 20% to 30% of cases in main study, origin of objects sighted was declared unknown. He also points out that the report did not discuss whether or not there was evidence to prove or disprove that UFOs might be extraterrestrial objects or devices. First and second editions published by author (White Plains, 1956, 1957).

Edwards, Frank. Frank Edwards' report: some answers to the saucers. Fate, v. 11, July 1958: 45-51.

Author outlines several possible reasons that the Air Force has remained silent on the question of the reality of UFO activity. He postulates that there is official recognition of the phenomenon although such recognition is denied publicly.

Greenfield, Irving A. Why are they watching us? by Allen L. Erskine [pseud]. New York, Tower Publications, 1967. 124 p.

Concise review of the UFO "classics," with emphasis on the Air Force "conspiracy" and the extraterrestrial theses.

Hall, Richard. Is there a veil of secrecy around the flying saucers? Flying saucers from other worlds, June 1957: 51-56.

Author postulates that although individuals continue to sight UFOs, the press remains silent and the Air Force tries to convince the public it is all imagination.

Keyhoe, Donald F. Flying saucers: menace or myth? Argosy, v. 350, June 1960: 17, 80-83.

Author states that for 13 years, USAF has maintained officially that reports of UFOs are the result of delusions and hoaxes, with no solid basis whatsoever. He purports to expose this coverup policy by making public official USAF documents, including Regulation 200-2 and a directive referring to UFOs as "serious business."

Lee, Ben S. AF vs. saucers. Aviation week, v. 56, June 23, 1952: 16.

Article reports that under USAF Air Technical Intelligence Command direction, physicist at the Univ. of California is developing and testing special photographic equipment that may enable scientists to determine the composition of light phenomena, including "flying saucers."

Maney, Charles A. Why the Air Force cannot investigate UFOs. Flying saucer review, v. 9, July-Aug. 1963: 29, 33.

Author suggests that USAF resists publicizing evidence of real navigating space travel by intelligences from outer space in deference to the protection of capital investment: if the U.S. government were unhampered in its study and investigation of the scientific means by which space travel is accomplished, those means could in time be determined; the resultant scientific breakthrough might upset orthodox conceptions and result in financial disaster for certain vested interests.

----- Why the Air Force can't investigate UFOs. Fate, v. 16, May 1963: 26-28.

Author postulates that there is sufficient proof to establish the actuality of real, navigating space travel by intelligence from outer space.

Miller, Max B. Report on the UFO. Fate, v. 9, Dec. 1956: 31-34.

Review of Edward J. Ruppelt's book about the U.S. Air Force's UFO investigations, The Report on Unidentified Flying Objects (New York, Doubleday, 1956).

Ogles, George W. What does the Air Force really know about flying saucers? Washington, D.C., The Airman, 1967. 8 p.

Survey of the UFO controversy and statement of the Air Force position: the Air Force has never denied the possibility of life on other planets; what it does say is that no evidence has been received nor discovered which proves the existence and intraspace mobility of extraterrestrial life. Some widely publicized "sightings" are also discussed. (Reprinted from The Airman v. 11, July 1967, p. 4-9; Aug. 1967, p. 26-31.)

Prytz, John. The Air Force opinion on UFOs. Flying saucers, Oct. 1966: 26-27.

Author states that although officially USAF disclaims the reality of flying saucers, a high percentage of USAF personnel believe in the seriousness of the phenomenon.

Quintanilla, Hector. Unidentified flying objects. Dayton, Ohio, The Author, [196-] 37 p.

Summary of USAF investigation of the UFO phenomenon.

Ruppelt, Edward J. Inside story of the saucers. Science digest, v. 39, Apr. 1956: 35-41.

Condensed from a chapter of the book, The Report on Unidentified Flying Objects, published in New York by Doubleday, 1956. Author describes his activities as head of USAF's Project Blue Book, 1951-1953. He states that while balloons, airplanes, stars, and many other common objects have been reported as UFOs, there are hundreds of other UFO reports which carry the verdict, "Conclusion Unknown."

----- The report on unidentified flying objects. Garden City, New York, 1956. 315 p.

Author, a former chief of USAF's Project Blue Book, writes a factual account of Air Force investigation of UFO sighting reports and discusses all aspects of the UFO controversy. Published also in paperback edition by Ace Books (G537), New York.

----- Report on unidentified flying objects. Fate, v. 10, Apr. 1957: 27-43.

An Air Force F-86 jet pilot, paced by a flying saucer during summer 1952, opened fire on it. Account excerpted from author's book, The Report on Unidentified Flying Objects (Garden City, N.Y., Doubleday, 1956).

----- What our Air Force found out about flying saucers. True, May 1954: 19-20, 22, 24, 26, 30, 124-134.

Ruppelt, in charge of USAF's Project Blue Book from 1951 to 1953, reports what he learned about flying saucers during this period. He states his opinion that the saucers are either interplanetary or do not exist.

Scientific Advisory Panel on Unidentified Flying Objects. Report of meetings of Scientific Advisory Panel on Unidentified Flying Objects, January 14-18, 1953. Washington, D.C., 1963. 24 p.

Report of the scientific panel on unidentified flying objects, under the chairmanship of H.P. Robertson. Conclusions were: (1) that the evidence presented on unidentified flying objects showed no indication that these phenomena constitute a direct physical threat to national security; and (2) that the continued emphasis on the reporting of these phenomena results in a threat to the orderly functioning of the protective organs of the body politic. It recommended: (1) that the national security agencies take immediate steps to strip the unidentified flying objects of the special status they have been given and the aura of mystery they have unfortunately acquired; and (2) that the national security agencies institute policies on intelligence, training and public education designed to prepare the material defenses and the morale of the country to recognize most promptly and to react most effectively to true indications of hostile UFO intent or action.

Serious flaws in AF Special Report 14 revealed by NICAP analysis. The UFO investigator, v. 1, Jan. 1958: 16-18.

Analysis of the main points of USAF Project Blue Book report.

Shalett, Sidney. What you can believe about flying saucers. Part I. Saturday evening post, v. 221, Apr. 30, 1949: 20-21, 136-139.

Reports on USAF probe of 250 reports on unidentified flying objects and concludes that "if there is a scrap of bona fide evidence to support the notion that our inventive geniuses or any potential enemy, on this or any other planet, is spewing saucers over America, the Air Force has been unable to locate it."

Stringfield, Leonard H. Inside saucer post... 3-0 blue. Cincinnati, Civilian Research, Interplanetary Flying Objects, 1957. 94 p.

"Inside story" of CRIFO (Civilian Research, Interplanetary Flying Objects) operations from September 1955 when the Air Defense Command designated the author's home a "UFO reporting post," and CRIFO was known internationally as a "civilian clearinghouse for saucer information." Author concludes that UFOs are interplanetary vehicles and that the world governments with technical know-how also believe this to be the answer.

Tacker, Lawrence J. Flying saucers and the U.S. Air Force. Princeton, N.J.,
Van Nostrand, 1960. 164 p.

Author, a former USAF public information officer on UFOs, discusses UFO
sightings reported to Aerospace Technical Intelligence Center (Project Blue
Book), Wright Patterson Air Force Base, from Summer 1947 through Summer
1960 in attempt to demonstrate that, in general, they were misinterpretations
of known objects. He also gives history of USAF's research effort into UFO
phenomena, including Project Saucer and Project Grudge.

Tyler, Steven. Are the invaders coming? New York, Tower Publications, 1968.
139 p.

Survey of basic UFO literature such as Edward Ruppelt's writings, and
extracts from the publications of NICAP and APRO. Supports the "Air Force
conspiracy" hypothesis.

"UFOs"--they're back in new sizes, shapes, colors. U.S. news & world report,
v. 61, Aug. 22, 1966: 59-60.

Of 1966 UFO sightings, USAF officials say: (1) more variety in sizes and shapes
is reported; (2) there are lights of all kinds concomitant with sightings; (3)
UFOs seem to be noisier than in the past; (4) appearance of objects allegedly
seen during daylight hours is invariably that of some light-colored metal;
(5) movement of reported UFOs continues to be erratic; (6) no "little green
men" have appeared; (7) sightings have been concentrated more in the
northeastern U.S. than in the past; and (8) objects exhibit apparent tendency
to follow power lines.

U.S. Air Force. Aids to identification of flying objects. Washington, D.C., U.S.
Govt. Print. Off., 1968. 35 p.

Introduction is a brief history of UFO reports and studies and provides some
information on scientific observations and analyses; the section "Aids to
Identification of Flying Objects" gives in-depth information on flying objects
and natural phenomena; the "Questions and Answers" section responds to
many of the questions commonly asked about UFOs.

U.S. Air Force. Air Materiel Command. Unidentified aerial objects; Project
Sign. Dayton, Ohio, Wright-Patterson Air Force Base, 1949. 35 p.
(Its Technical Report No. F-TR-2274-IA)

Descriptive and analytical study of 243 domestic and 30 foreign reported UFO
sightings between 1947 and 1948. Individual cases are described in brief
form as an appendix. Methods and reasoning applied in evaluating data are
presented. Project Sign was initiated by the Technical Intelligence Division,
Air Materiel Command, on January 22, 1948.

----- Unidentified flying objects; Project Grudge. Dayton, Ohio, Wright-Patterson
Air Force Base, 1949. 366 p. (Its Technical Report No. 102-AC 49/15100)

Report discusses in full the history of Project Grudge, the problems encountered, and the procedures followed in the investigation and evaluation of reports of unidentified flying objects through January 1949.

U.S. Air Force. Air Technical Intelligence Center. Special report no. 14. (Analysis of reports of unidentified aerial objects.) Dayton, Ohio, Wright-Patterson Air Force Base, 1955. 308 p. Project no. 10073.

Results of 1953 study of UFOs by committee chaired by H. P. Robertson, theoretical physicist at California Institute of Technology. Examination of distributions of important characteristics of sightings and study of sightings evaluated as "unknown" led to conclusion that a combination of factors, principally the reported maneuvers of the objects and the unavailability of supplemental data such as aircraft flight plans or balloon-launching records, resulted in failure to identify as "knowns" most of the reports of objects classified as "unknowns. "

U.S. Air Force. Scientific Advisory Board. Ad Hoc (O'Brien) Committee to review Project Blue Book. Special report. Washington, D.C., 1966. 10 p.

In order that the present USAF UFO investigation program be strengthened to provide opportunity for scientific investigation of selected sightings in greater depth and detail than had been possible to date, it was recommended that: (A) contracts be negotiated with a few selected universities to provide scientific teams to investigate promptly and in depth certain selected UFO sightings; (B) at each AFSC base, an officer skilled in investigation should be designated to work with the corresponding university team for that geographical section; (C) one university or one not-for-profit organization should be selected to coordinate the work of the teams mentioned under (A) above, and also to make certain of close communication and coordination with Project Blue Book.

U.S. Congress. House. Committee on Armed Services. Unidentified flying objects. Washington, U.S. Govt. Print. Off., 1966. 84 p. (89th Cong., 2d sess. House. Report no. 55)

Information concerning U.S. Air Force activities in the area of reported unidentified flying objects.

Webster, Robert N., and John C. Ross. Air Force report on UFOs. Fate, v. 12, Feb. 1959: 54-66.

Critique of USAF's Special Report No. 14, originally issued on May 5, 1955, summarizing its investigations of unidentified flying objects through July 31, 1958.

What the Air Force believes about flying saucers. Fate, v. 2, Nov. 1949: 69-83.

Digest of official report of studies made by Project Saucer of the Air Materiel Command, Wright-Patterson Air Force Base, Ohio. Incidents involving Kenneth Arnold (June 24, 1947), Capt. Thomas F. Mantell (Jan. 7, 1948), Eastern Air Lines pilots Capt. C. S. Chiles and John B. Whitted(July 1948), and North Dakota National Guard Lt. George F. Gorman (Oct. 1, 1948) are discussed.

Adamski's hieroglyphics. Flying saucer review, v. 8, Jan.-Feb. 1962: 7-8.

Report of discovery by Prof. Marcel F. Homet in northern Brazil of boulder with engraved symbols bearing a striking resemblance to those allegedly given Adamski on a photographic plate by a Venusian.

Allen, W. Gordon. Spacecraft over Mexico. Flying saucer review, v. 5, Mar.-Apr. 1959: 16-19.

Author postulates that one of the reasons Cortez had such an easy victory over Montezuma in the conquest of Mexico was the ruler's preoccupation with the predicted return of Quetzalcoatl--an extraterrestrial. He also quotes writings from the archives of the Aztec priesthood on early cataclysms and on phenomena that may have been UFO appearances.

Ancient records of UFO in Japan. Australian saucer record, v. 2, June 1962: 15-17.

Material in ancient Japanese history books that may be interpreted as meaning that earth has had extraterrestrial visitors from the very earliest times is listed in chronological order from 637-1714 A. D. Reprinted from Flying Saucer News of Japan published by the Cosmic Brotherhood Association.

Belgische UFO-Waarnemingen. Het interplanetair nieuwsbulletin, v. 2, Oct.-Nov.-Dec. 1967: 3-7.

List of UFO sightings over Belgium 1575-1967. City where sighting occurred and description of object are included.

Boncompagni, Solas. Attualita' del mito di Osiris. Clypeus, v. 5, Feb. 1968: 9-12.

According to legend, the Egyptian god Osiris came to earth from the heavens in a vehicle whose description was similar to that of the "flying saucer."

Creighton, Gordon. A Russian wallpainting and other "spacemen." Flying saucer review, v. 11, July-Aug. 1965: 11-14.

Discussion of artifacts, drawings, and images which are said by some to portray extraterrestrial visitors who landed on earth long ago.

Dikshitar, V. R. Ramachandra. Aerial and naval warfare. In War in ancient India. Madras, Bombay, Calcutta, and London, Macmillan and Co., 1944. p. 275-298.

The "Samarangana Sutradhara" (circa 11th century) is quoted, where some 230 stanzas are devoted to the various types of space equipment then in use. "It is said that in an aerial car one can mount up to the Suryamondala or solar region and to the Naksatra mandala or stellar region. They are said to move so fast as to make a noise that could be heard from the ground."

Drake, W. Raymond. Did UFOs stop a war? Flying saucer review, v. 9, Mar.-Apr. 1963: 13-14.

In 776 A.D., an event that may be interpreted as intervention by UFOs was chronicled by an unknown French monk in the Annales Laurissenses and paralleled by the Annales Eginhardi compiled by Abbot Einhard, biographer of Charlemagne: during the siege of Sigiburg by the Saxons, two large shields, reddish in color, appeared above the church causing the Saxons to flee in panic.

----- Gods or spacemen? Amherst, Wis., Amherst Press, 1964. 176 p.

Author suggests that present theology may be based on false premises since the experiences and visions of saints are phenomena that might be associated with UFOs and their extraterrestrial crews. He reviews the mythological and religious traditions of the countries of the world to demonstrate worldwide "race memories" of spacemen visiting earth. He suggests that terrestrial destruction in ages past may have been caused by interplanetary warfare rather than by collision of celestial bodies with earth.

----- Space gods of ancient Britain. Flying saucer review, v. 11, July-Aug. 1965: 15-17.

Examination of the history and mythology of the ancient Britons for indications of visitations from extraterrestrial beings.

----- Spacemen in antiquity. Sunderland, England, The Author, 196- 1 v.

Typescript is composed of the following monographs: Spacemen in Antiquity; UFOs over Ancient Rome; Space Gods of Ancient Britain; Spacemen in Saxon Times; UFOs Fought for Charlemagne; Spacemen in Norman Times; A Bride from Space; Spacemen in the Middle Ages; Spacemen in Ancient India; Spacemen in Old Tibet; Spacemen in Old China; Spacemen in Old Japan; Semiramis, Space-Queen of Babylon.

----- Spacemen in the Middle Ages. Flying saucer review, v. 10, May-June 1964: 11-13.

Chronicles from the Middle Ages are cited and reveal that throughout that period the belief persisted in beings from the skies who were keeping earth under surveillance.

----- Spacemen in Norman times. Flying saucer review, v. 12, Mar.-Apr. 1966: 17-19.

Ancient historical writings in France are interpreted in terms of UFO phenomena.

----- Spacemen in Saxon times. Flying saucer review, v. 10, Sept.-Oct. 1964: 10-12.

References in Anglo-Saxon literature to phenomena that might correspond to appearances of UFOs and their extraterrestrial crews are listed.

----- Spacemen in the ancient East. London, Neville Spearman, 1968.

Traditions are cited which tell of "supermen" from the skies, "Divine Dynasties," who ruled on earth in India, Tibet, China, Japan, and Babylonia.

----- UFOs over ancient Rome. Flying saucer review, v. 9, Jan.-Feb. 1963: 11-13.

Passages from the works of classical historians that may record visits to earth of extraterrestrial spacecraft are cited.

Drury, Neville. Flying ships in "Oahspe." Australian flying saucer review, no. 9, Nov. 1966: 40-41.
    Passages from Oahspe are cited that would seem to describe spacecraft of extraterrestrial origin.
Enoch and other cosmonauts; Soviet theories. Time, v. 75, Feb. 22, 1960: 26.

Evans, Gordon H. UFOs in history and myth. Science and mechanics, v. 38, Feb. 1967: 52-55, 86, 88, 90.

Survey of references to unexplained aerial phenomena from Biblical times through the 19th century. Similarities between ancient and modern accounts are noted. Author suggests that mythology and the literature of the supernatural (including the Irish leprechaun) may have been derived from contact between human and extraterrestrial beings.

Farish, Lucius. Myths, legends, and UFOs. Flying saucer review, v. 11, Nov.-Dec. 1965: 19-21.

Author cites possible references to the UFO phenomenon found in Rushton M. Dorman's treatise on American Indian mythology and folklore, The Origin of Primitive Superstitions, published in 1881.

Hansen, L. Taylor. He walked the Americas. Amherst, Wisc., Amherst Press, 1963. 256 p.

A collection of American Indian legends that refer to a saintly teacher who performed miracles of healing, and who may have been an extraterrestrial.

Helland, Albert E. They caught a spaceman. Fate, v. 11, Mar. 1958: 62.

Author quotes from ancient manuscript to cite instance when an apparently extraterrestrial being was captured and released during the 13th century.

Homet, Marcel. Sons of the sun. London, Neville Spearman, 1963. 239 p.

Chiefly reporting on an archeological expedition to the Amazon, the book describes 10,000-year-old symbols discovered there that are deeply-engraved in rock and almost identical to the symbols on the photographic plate allegedly dropped by a Venusian scoutship over George Adamski's home in California on December 13, 1952.

Kazantsev, Aleksandr. Vizitnye kartochi s stru. (Calling cards from other planets?) Tekhnika molodezhi, no. 1, 1967: 22-25.

Author suggests there are traces on earth of the passage of extraterrestrial beings in the form of paintings on rocks, with special note of the Dogu statuettes that were found in northern Japan; these are discussed in detail. It is suggested that they represent visitors from outer space dressed in their space suits.

Knaggs, Oliver. Let the people know. Cape Town, South Africa, Howard Timmins, 1966. 113 p.

References to flying saucers that go back as far as the 14th century are cited to "prove" that flying saucers are not something of the present generation. Author concludes that there are definite grounds for believing military authorities are keeping details of UFO activities from the public to avoid possible panic since there are so many factors they cannot themselves explain.

Lambert, Richard S. Flying saucers--their lurid past. Saturday night, v. 67, May 10, 1952: 9, 18.

Historical records of UFO manifestations from 1662 are surveyed.

Larson, Kenneth. The discovery of the graphic message of Goodhue. Los Angeles, The Author, 1968. 30 p.

The Great Pyramid architect incorporated geometrical and engineering designs seemingly concerned with the coming of the space age and increasing UFO activity, the author suggests. He gives a detailed explanation of how he reached this conclusion.

----- The Great Pyramid a UFO beacon? Flying saucers, Oct. 1966: 31-33.

Author cites passages in the Royal Annals of Pharoah Thutmose III (1483-1450 B.C.) that record the visit of a fleet of unidentified flying objects to Egypt. Since the Great Pyramid was in existence at that time, he speculates on whether it was built as a monument or to reflect beams of sunlight into space to attract the attention of extraterrestrial visitors.

Ledger, Joseph R. Saucers or ghosts? Flying saucer review, v. 8, Sept.-Oct. 1962: 19-20.

Article suggests that in the days before flying machines were considered possible, the rationalization employed to accomodate the inexplicable took an occult form. Old legends are examined to determine whether the form in which they now appear is really the result of such a fanciful embroidery of an actual UFO sighting in the remote past.

Leslie, Desmond and George Adamski. Flying saucers have landed. London, Werner Laurie, 1953. 232 p.

Account of contact by Adamski with a landed extraterrestrial spacecraft and a meeting with a man from Venus on Nov. 20, 1952, near Desert Center, Calif. Photographs of spacecraft. Review of material from old manuscripts referring to sightings of unidentified objects flying through the air.

Lovitch, A. UFOs--science or sorcery? Engineering digest, v. 61, Feb. 1967: 29-34.

Historical reports of strange aerial phenomena from 45,000 B.C. to 1952 are cited. Postulating that centuries of recorded reports must reflect response to unknown phenomena that deserve scientific study, the author discusses feasibility of flying saucers from propulsion, structural, and biological tolerance points of view.

Michell, John F. The flying saucer vision: the holy grail restored. London, Sidgewick & Jackson, 1967. 176 p.

Establishes the existence in the past of a flying saucer cult and examines its origins. Suggests some of the ways in which the current revival of our belief in these objects is likely to affect us in the years to come. Postulates that it is essential that the true basis of mythology be recognized and the origins of our civilization examined in the light of what we can now suspect of extraterrestrial influences in the past.

Miller, Max B. Flying saucers, fact or fiction? Los Angeles, Trend Books, 1957. 128 p.

Survey of references to UFOs in literature from earliest written records to 1957 and state-of-the-art review of research relating to subject. Non-technical.

Misraki, Paul. Les extraterrestres, par Paul Thomas [pseud.]. Paris, Plon, 1962. 224 p.

Develops hypothesis that from earliest antiquity to modern times, extraterrestrial beings have kept earth under surveillance, have at times visited this planet, and have frequently modified the course of history by means of spectacular appearances. Cites biblical passages and ancient manuscripts. First English edition translated by Gavin Gibbons and published under title Flying Saucers Through the Ages (London, Neville Spearman, 1965).

Moseley, James W. Peruvian desert: map for saucers? Fate, v. 8, Oct. 1955:
28-33.

Describes complex markings recently discovered on the desert near Nasca,
Peru, by airliners passing over the area. Markings may be 1,000 years old
and are clearly visible and meaningful only from the air. It is speculated
that they may have been constructed as signals to interplanetary visitors or
to some advanced earth race that occasionally visited the peoples of the
region in an aircraft.

The official guide to UFOs: a special Science & Mechanics news book. New York,
Science & Mechanics Publishing Co., 1968. 96 p.

Contents: UFO: Theories of Flight; The Mysterious 12 [most unusual
sightings of a decade]; The Scientist and the UFO; Ithaca's Terrifying UFO
Epidemic; What Happened at Wanaque, N.J.?; Complete Directory of
UFOs; UFOs in History and Myth.

Oge-Make. Tribal memories of the flying saucers. Fate, v. 2, Sept. 1949:
17-21.

Navajo Indian legend of city built in caverns of Panamint Mountains (Calif.)
by beings who arrived in silver spacecraft centuries before the coming of the
white man and who are believed to still dwell there.

Pinotti, Roberto. Space visitors in ancient Egypt. Flying saucer review, v. 12,
May-June 1966: 16-18.

Author suggests that ancient records such as the Tulli papyrus (part of the
royal annals of Pharoah Thutmose III, 1483-1450 B.C.) seem to indicate
that extraterrestrial creatures visited earth in the past and that most of
our religions and mythologies were originated by deification of these
space visitors.

-----. Space visitors in ancient Egypt. Flying saucers, Aug. 1966: 18-19.

Author quotes excerpts from the papers of Professor Alberto Tulli, former
director of the museum of the Vatican. Tulli says the Royal Annals of the
Pharoah Thutmose III (1483-1450 B.C.) reveal that unknown objects with the
same characteristics as the so-called flying saucers of today were often seen
in the skies of Egypt in those days.

Voorname Kronologie. Het interplanetair nieuwsbulletin, June 1966: 1-6.

Chronology of UFO sightings 83,000 B.C. - 1966.

Wilkins, Harold T. Flying saucers on the attack. New York, Citadel Press,
1954. 329 p.

Author traces reports of cosmic visitors to earth's skies as far back as 729 A.D. Conjectures that sinister or hostile forces of unknown interplanetary origin may act to keep space explorers from earth well within limits of substratosphere. London ed. has title: Flying Saucers from the Moon.

Wilkins, Harold T. 1,000 years of flying saucers. Fate, v. 4, Apr. 1951: 23-30.

Accounts are reported from archives of the British Royal Society, medieval chroniclers, 17th century astronomers' ephemerides, and from rare volumes in Latin of strange lights and flying objects seen in the sky for the past 1,250 years.

Williamson, George Hunt. Other tongues--other flesh. Amherst, Wis., Amherst Press, 1952. 448 p.

Author affirms that extraterrestrial visitors have been coming to earth in spacecraft for several millenia and quotes references to them in the Bible, ancient mythology, and old documents. He relates technological and sociological progress on earth to influence of space intelligences and cites references from latest authenticated UFO sightings to support theory that visitors from space are now making themselves known to the world as a whole to lead mankind to a new, enlightened age.

-----. Road in the sky. London, N. Spearman, 1959. 243 p.

Develops hypothesis that there is a connection between the flying saucers of the past and present and the legends of mankind that attempt to explain God and the supernatural. Cites instances of past extraterrestrial visitations recorded in legends and myths of ancient civilizations and the American Indians.

Zaitsev, Vyacheslav. Visitors from outer space. Sputnik, v. 1, Jan. 1967: 162-179.

Author reports on thirty years of research to substantiate theory that intelligent beings from outer space have had contact with earth. Among evidence cited are hieroglyphics deciphered by Chinese archeologist revealing that extraterrestrial spacecraft landed on earth 12,000 years ago; legends supporting information in the hieroglyphics and vestiges of graves and skeletons that seem to confirm the legends; myths, biblical passages, and apocryphal legends; and frescoes dating from 1350 at Dechaney Monastery, Yugoslavia.

ANGEL HAIR

Pottage, Barrie. Ring clouds and angel hair. Flying saucer review, v. 10, May-June 1964: 14-16.

Listing of unusual cloud formation sightings that may have a connection with UFO phenomenon. An instance of the fall of "angel hair" is cited.

Sharp, Peter F. Angel hair. Flying saucer review, v. 10, Jan-Feb. 1964: 14-15.

Reports of appearance of "angel hair"--often accompanying UFO phenomena--are examined for evidence of a connection with the life cycle of the spider.

Webster, Robert N. Things that fall from UFOs. Fate, v. 11, Oct. 1958: 25-31.

Discussion of falls from the sky of cobweb-like material called "angel hair," and speculation on its origin.

BASES

Fouere, Rene. Existe-t-il des bases sous-marines de soucoupes volantes? Phénomènes spatiaux, Feb. 1965: 16-25.

Lists instances 1845-1960 where disc-like or wheel-like glowing objects were seen entering the ocean, in or on the oceans, or leaving the oceans. Gives reasons the ocean depths would be ideal flying saucer bases.

Ormond, Ron. Is Siam a secret base for flying saucers? Flying saucers, May 1959: 51-56.

Story is told of big fiery wheels that come out of the sky and land near the village of the Lahus, an aboriginal tribe inhabiting the northern sector of Thailand.

Ribera, Antonio. More about UFOs and the sea. Flying saucer review, v. 11, Nov.-Dec. 1965: 17-18.

Author summarizes events which may indicate underwater reconnaissance by UFOs of submarine bases.

-----. UFOs and the sea. Flying saucer review, v. 10, Nov.-Dec. 1964: 8-10.

Account of strange happenings at sea that might support hypothesis that the bodies of water covering three-quarters of earth's surface are providing a hiding place for UFOs.

Steiger, Brad and Joan Whritenour. Unidentified underwater saucers. Saga, v. 36, June 1968: 34-37, 54-57.

Instances are cited in which UFOs seen hovering over oceans, lakes, and rivers have submerged in the water. It is suggested that the objects may have underwater "bases."

Binder, Otto O. Our space age. New York, Bell-McClure Syndicate, 1965-1968.

Series of cartoons and illustrations of worldwide UFO reports, both current and past, covering the period September 27, 1965-May 13, 1968.

Farris, Joseph. UFO--ho ho! New York, Popular Library, 1968. 90 p.

Selected UFO cartoons by Joseph Farris.

Menzel, Donald H. Meet the Martians. n. p. , 1965· p. 220-223.

Doodles, in color, of "creatures and their associates" representing "some form of extraterrestrial life, most probably from Mars. " Reprinted from The graduate journal, v. 7, Winter 1965: 220-233.

CENSORSHIP

Barker, Gray. Chasing the flying saucers. Flying saucers, Dec. 1959: 22-29.

Tells how Long John Nebel Show in New York was ordered cut off the air during discussion of flying saucers by Gray Barker, James Moseley, and Jonah ibn Aharon.

Bryant, Larry W. A hard look at UFO news management. Fate, v. 17, Feb. 1964: 41-44.

Author asserts that "paper curtain" around UFO news includes the local as well as national level.

----- The UFO cover-up at Langley Air Force Base. Flying saucers, June 1968: 11-14.

Author describes UFO sighting at Langley AFB on Jan. 28, 1965, by responsible witnesses and alleged Air Force failure to investigate the incident, and subsequent alleged misrepresentations.

Edwards, Frank. Censorship and UFOs. Fate, v. 12, Sept. 1959: 47-52.

Author gives examples of "latest techniques" for suppressing UFO reports: (1) numerous conflicting solutions are offered to cases which have been given widespread publicity, thereby confusing the public; (2) pressure is applied to officials of the agency employing an alleged witness to ask the witness to keep quiet about UFO sighting; (3) Congressmen requesting available information about the UFO phenomenon are given "a brush-off to the effect that everything adds up to nothing. "

Edwards, Frank. Flying saucers, serious business. New York, Lyle Stuart, Inc., 1966. 319 p.

Report on worldwide sightings of UFOs and attack on "veil of secrecy" that governments of the world have drawn around the matter. Data cited authenticated by NICAP.

----- Frank Edwards' report: Do you still believe in flying saucers? Fate, v. 13, June 1960: 27-34.

Author cites instances where military and scientific authorities attempted to discredit the subject of UFOs through ridicule.

----- Frank Edwards' report: is the UFO "curtain" lifting? Fate, v. 11, June 1958: 47-54.

Cites instances of apparent suppression of UFO news by the Air Force and analyzes current official actions that seem to indicate a change in policy.

----- Frank Edwards' report: some answers to the saucer. Fate, v. 11, July 1958: 45-51.

Author outlines several possible reasons that the Air Force has remained silent on the question of the reality of UFO activity. He postulates that there is official recognition of the phenomenon although such recognition is denied publicly.

----- The plot to silence me. Fate, v. 10, June 1957: 17-23.

Author claims that in August 1954 he was fired from his job as news commentator for the Mutual Broadcasting System because the president of the sponsoring organization (AFL) said he "talked too much about flying saucers." He says he was later offered a well-paid job by the Pentagon "to silence him."

----- The spies from outer space. Real, v. 5, Nov. 1954: 20-21, 58-60.

Evidence is given by the author to support his belief that a "blanket of silence" imposed by the Government is preventing the public from getting all the facts about unidentified flying objects. He also suggests that flying saucers are extraterrestrial and engaged in reconnaissance activities.

----- To see or not to see. In his My first 10,000,000 sponsors. New York, Ballantine Books, 1956. p. 110-125.

Reports are given of UFO sightings 1947-1954 by apparently reliable witnesses, especially airlines pilots, and subsequent apparent "muzzling" of witnesses and suppression of news stories ostensibly by a Government agency.

Fitch, C.W. UFOs and Governmental secrecy. Saucer news, v. 11, Dec. 1964: 16-18.

Postulates that it is not the U.S. Air Force but "a small group very high up in the government" that is keeping UFO information from the public.

Hall, Richard. Is there a veil of secrecy around the flying saucers? Flying saucers from other worlds, June 1957: 51-56.

Author postulates that although individuals continue to sight UFOs, the press remains silent and the Air Force tries to convince the public it is all imagination.

Keel, John A. The "silencers" at work. Flying saucer review, v. 13, Mar.-Apr. 1967: 10.

Col. George P. Freeman, Pentagon spokesman for Project Blue Book, is alleged to have said in a press interview that "mysterious men dressed in Air Force uniforms or bearing impressive credentials from government agencies have been 'silencing' UFO witnesses." Similar mystery men have reportedly turned up and confronted UFO witnesses in the states of Washington, Texas, Connecticut, and on Long Island, N.Y.

Keyhoe, Donald F. Flying saucers: menace or myth? Argosy, v. 350, June 1960: 17, 80-83.

Author states that for 13 years, USAF has maintained officially that reports of UFOs are the result of delusions and hoaxes, with no solid basis whatsoever. He purports to expose this cover-up policy by making public official USAF documents, including Regulation 200-2 and a directive referring to UFOs as "serious business."

----- Flying saucers: top secret. New York, Putnam, 1960: 283 p.

Evidence on UFO sightings presented by NICAP to individual Congressmen and committee chairmen in attempt to secure open Congressional hearings on subject. Details of NICAP efforts to expose alleged Air Force censorship of information on subject. NICAP documents cited in support of these views.

Lasco, Jack. Has the Air Force captured a flying saucer? Saga, Apr. 1967: 18-19, 67-68, 70-74.

Available information on alleged sighting of landed oval-shaped UFO by policeman Lonnie Zamora near Socorro, New Mexico, on April 24, 1964; alleged sighting of oval-shaped UFO near La Madera, New Mexico, by Orlando Gallegos on April 26; and radio message from an RB-57 bomber pilot from Stallion Site on April 30 reporting a landed egg-shaped UFO is detailed. Author suggests that USAF censorship has prevented release of full and accurate descriptions of incidents.

Lear, John. The disputed CIA document on UFOs. Saturday review, Sept. 3, 1966: 45-50.

Discussion of questions raised by CIA editing of the Robertson panel minutes before the document was declassified. It is suggested that vital information of long-range significance regarding possible visits to earth by extraterrestrial spacecraft may have been withheld for strategic reasons.

Scully, Frank. Behind the flying saucers. New York, Henry Holt, 1950. 230 p.

Presents information to support position that UFOs are real and that official disclaimers of their existence by DOD are calculated to deceive the public. Published also in British edition (London, Gollancz, 1950).

Steiger, Brad. What price silence? Flying saucers, June 1968: 31.

A private citizen investigates an alleged UFO landing and is given a piece of metal that supposedly fell from the machine. The metal sample is taken away from him during a visit by what seemed to be representatives of "the men in black."

Steiger, Brad and Joan Whritenour. Flying saucers panic U.S. airlines. Saga, v. 36, Aug. 1968: 33-35, 82-84, 86, 88-90.

Newark Star-Ledger reporter John Lester quotes a pilot as saying that any pilot who did not maintain maximum secrecy after sighting a UFO was subject to a possible 10 years in prison and a fine of $10,000. Organization of the Volunteer Flight Officer's Network which includes 68 airlines, 50 of which are outside the U.S., is mentioned; member crewmen would attempt to amass photographic evidence of UFOs.

White House is hiding the truth about flying saucers. Midnight, v. 14, May 20, 1968: 14-15.

Unnamed "UFO expert" states that the flying saucer mystery has been solved but that the U.N. and world heads of state have entered a conspiracy of silence, releasing as little information to the public as possible.

Young, Mort. UFO: top secret. New York [Essandess Special Editions] 1967. 156 p.

Author relies heavily on official documents to present "a convincing account of how for two decades the United States Government caused you and me to believe that people who saw unidentified flying objects were mistaken or were fools or were charlatans."

Davidson, Leon. ECM + CIA = UFO. Flying saucer review, v. 6, Mar. Apr. 1960: 9-12.

Author postulates that UFO phenomena are created by the CIA as part of the cold war and explains techniques that could be used to produce "authentic" radar sightings of UFOs.

----- An open letter to saucer researchers. Flying saucers, no. FS-24, Mar. 1962: 36-51.

Author states what he believes to be the true explanation of the UFO phenomenon: "The Central Intelligence Agency... took over the public image of the 'flying saucer' created by secret flights of U.S. aircraft and artificial meteor research, etc. , during the period 1947-48. By 1950, the CIA had set in motion a plan encouraging public belief in interplanetary travel through a psychological technique of guiding the release of planted information, ordering secret tests of authentic military developments which gave misleading impressions to observers, etc. CIA delegated the Air Force to act as the official "investigator" to stave off public inquiry. It secretly sponsored the formation of saucer study groups and contact clubs, including NICAP... The CIA set up many saucer publishers, sponsored the publicizing of Adamski's books and others, and sponsored the wave of saucer articles in 1952 in 'Life' and 'Look,' etc. The CIA also conducted the hoaxes played upon Adamski and Fry, including Adamski's desert contacts, his 'train disappearance,' etc. , in addition to other activities of this nature.

----- Why I believe Adamski. Flying saucers, Feb. 1959: 38-46.

Author postulates that the C. I. A. or its subsidiaries were involved in "causing" the Adamski contacts, and that the extraterrestrial "Brothers" were agents or operatives of these agencies. Adamski, subject of a CIA-engineered hoax, was honestly and sincerely reporting what he was told, the author believes.

----- Why I believe Adamski. Flying saucer review, v. 6, Jan. - Feb. 1960: 3-8.

Author suggests that Adamski was sincere in his reports of contact with extraterrestrial spacecraft and their crews but was victim of deception perpetrated by CIA as a move in the cold war.

Lear, John. The disputed CIA document on UFOs. Saturday review, Sept. 3, 1966: 45-50.

Discussion of questions raised by CIA editing of the Robertson panel minutes before the document was declassified. It is suggested that vital information of long-range significance regarding possible visits to earth by extraterrestrial spacecraft may have been withheld for strategic reasons.

Adamski. Centro unico nazionale per lo studio del fenomeni ritenuti di natura
extraterrestre. Notiziario, no. 5, 1967: 2-7.

Summary of the claims made by George Adamski regarding his encounter with
flying saucers and their crews and of the controversy surrounding the truth
of his allegations.

Adamski, George. Flying saucers farewell. London, New York, Abelard-
Schuman, 1961. 190 p.

Adamski discusses the reasons spacecraft from other planets are visiting
earth and man's place in the universe as allegedly revealed to him
through contact with beings from Venus, Mars, and Saturn. Published also
with title Behind the Flying Saucer Mystery by Paperback Library (53-439),
New York.

----- Inside the spaceships. New York, Abelard-Schuman, 1955. 256 p.

Account of alleged physical contact and communication with beings from Venus,
Mars, and Saturn. Descriptions of trips in extraterrestrial spacecraft. Photographs and diagrammatic drawings.

Albanesi, Renato. The Italian scene: Signor Siragusa's message. Flying
saucer review, v. 9, Jan.-Feb. 1963: 3-5.

Report of alleged contact by Eugenio Siragusa with extraterrestrial beings from
UFO on Apr. 30, 1962, and Sept. 5, 1962, in Catania, Sicily. Communication
was by mental telepathy. Information in article first appeared in Oct. 28, 1962,
issue of Domenica del Corriere.

Allingham, Cedric. Flying saucer from Mars. New York, British Book Center,
1955. 153 p.

Report of UFO landing Feb. 18, 1954, near Lossiemouth, North Scotland,
and author's alleged contact with a Martian.

Angelucci, Orfeo M. The secret of the saucers. Amherst, Wis., Amherst Press,
1955. 167 p.

Account of author's ride in extraterrestrial spacecraft and alleged contact with
extraterrestrial beings associated with the objects. Propulsion of spacecraft explained as converted magnetic energy "inherent in all the universe."

----- Son of the sun. Los Angeles, DeVorss & Co., 1959. 211 p.

Account of alleged experiences among Alpha Centaurians spiritually, morally, and technologically superior to earthmen and of trip into sun's interior on one of their spacecraft.

Another speech by Wilbert B. Smith. Flying saucer review, v. 9, Nov.-Dec. 1963: 11-14.

Author, head of Canada's Project Magnet, imparts information allegedly obtained from extraterrestrial sources that casts serious doubt on validity of some basic concepts of our science and on our ideas of time. He mentions having made "hardware that works" from information given him by extraterrestrial intelligences. Extracts from speech delivered to Vancouver (Canada) Flying Saucer Club in March 1961.

Barker, Gray. Chasing the flying saucers. Flying saucers from other worlds, May 1958: 20-35, 80.

Includes radio interview by Gene Lasson, station KGFW, Kearney, Nebraska, of California grain dealer Reinhold Schmidt who claimed that on Nov. 5, 1957, he came upon a flying saucer landed in a river bed and conversed with the crew members.

----- Chasing the flying saucers. Flying saucers, July-Aug. 1958: 2035.

General report of activities of UFO researchers. Mentions messages from extraterrestrial beings allegedly received by John Otto of Chicago, beginning November 28, 1954.

----- Chasing the flying saucers. Flying saucers, May 1959: 19-43.

General discussion of activities of UFO researchers and alleged contactees. Claims made by "Prince Neosom of the Planet Tythian" are mentioned.

----- ed. Gray Barker's book of Adamski. Clarksburg, W. Va., Saucerian Books, 1967, 78 p.

Summary articles relating to George Adamski's alleged contact with Venusians and rides in their spacecraft. Reprints of the following monographs by Adamski: (1) My Fight with the Silence Group; (2) Questions and Answers; (3) Space Age Philosophy.

----- Gray Barker's book of saucers. Clarksburg, W. Va., Saucerian Books, 1965. 77 p.

Book catalogues UFO sightings in all parts of the world, 1962-1963. Saucer landings, communication between saucer crews and humans, seizure of terrestrials by saucer crews, mating of extraterrestrials with terrestrials, and "the men in black" are discussed.

Barton, Michel X. Flying saucer revelations. Los Angeles, Futura Press, 1957. 38 p.

Discusses role of interplanetary beings in man's origin and evolution. Considers stories of contact between extraterrestrials and earth men and the implications. Reports on flying saucer sighting at Giant Rock Airport, Yucca Valley, Calif., on Mar 12, 1955, during Interplanetary Spacecraft Convention.

Bender. Albert K. Flying saucers and the three men. Annotated and with introd. and epilogue by Gray Barker. Clarksburg, W. Va., Saucerian Books, 1962. 194 p.

Discussion of activities of and reports of UFO sightings made to International Flying Saucer Bureau, organized by Bender in April 1952 in Bridgeport, Conn., and of Bender's contact with extraterrestrial beings which he claims resulted in his dissolving IFSB in November 1953. Published also by Paperback Library, Inc. (53-686), New York.

Bethurum, Truman. Aboard a flying saucer. Los Angeles, De Vorss & Co., 1954. 192 p.

Story of alleged contact between author and flying saucer and crew from planet Clarion at Mormon Mesa, Nevada, during eleven visits between July and November 1952.

----- The voice of the planet Clarion. Prescott, Ariz., The Author, [195-] 88 p.

Collection of poetry and prose written by Bethurum while he was allegedly under the telepathic control of Aura Rhanes, the female captain of a spacecraft from the planet Clarion.

Bowen, Charles. Fantasy or truth? Flying saucer review, v. 13, July-Aug. 1967: 11-14.

Details of case where an individual was allegedly transported from Salzburg, Austria, to another planet and back in a flying saucer on May 15, 1951, are reexamined in the light of subsequent similar contact claim cases.

A Brazilian contact claim. Flying saucer review, v. 7, Sept.-Oct. 1961: 18-20.

Translation of report of contact with extraterrestrial beings and ride in flying saucer by Prof. João de Freitas Guimaraes on Aug. 27, 1957, near São Sebastião, Brazil. Originally appeared in Discos Voadores, Bulletin No. 4, July 1, 1959, issued by Dr. W. Buhler in Rio de Janeiro, Brazil.

Buckle, Eileen. Tne Scoriton mystery. London, Neville Spearman, 1967. 303 p.

Full details of investigation by British Unidentified Flying Object Research Association (BUFORA) of E.A. Bryant's claim that on April 24, 1965, near Scoriton, England, he encountered three individuals from a landed extra-terrestrial spacecraft, one of whom told him, "My name is Yamski" (George Adamski having died April 23, there being suggested reincarnation).

Chambers, Howard V. UFOs for the millions. Los Angeles, Sherbourne Press, Inc., 1967. 158 p.

Book discusses UFO sightings, the persons who made them, the persons who made evaluations of the sightings, and what people who think they've made actual contacts with aliens think these sightings mean.

Clark, Jerome. A contact claim. Flying saucer review, v. 11, Jan.-Feb. 1965: 30-32.

Noting the way in which the "beings" associated with the 1897 "airship" sightings seemed interested in reinforcing the belief that the craft was of mundane origin, the author concludes that the extraterrestrials either were engaged in some unknown activity in which they did not want their real identity made known, or that they chose to hide their existence realizing that the comparative unsophistication of nineteenth century Americans would not permit them to accept the interplanetary answer.

----- The meaning of contact. Flying saucer review, v. 11, Sept.-Oct. 1965: 28-29.

Speculating that the UFO beings might put a false cover over their activities so as to keep officialdom or anyone else from coming close to the truth, the author suggests that contact claims become a tool with a two-fold purpose: to discourage legitimate inquiry into the saucer field by making it look ridiculous, and to instill false ideas into the minds of those who do go to investigate the subject.

----- Two new contact claims. Flying saucer review, v. 11, May-June 1965: 20-23.

On January 26, 1965, a landed flying saucer and its 3 1/2 ft. occupants were allegedly seen near Brands Flats, Virginia. On January 30, 1965, TV repairman Sid Padrick allegedly encountered a landed flying saucer and was invited aboard by its crew members.

Cox, Adrian. Thoughts on extended dimensions. Flying saucer review, v. 9, July-Aug. 1963: 8-9.

Article assumes that some, at least, of the contact claims are genuine and inquires into the possible motives of those who are allegedly visiting us.

Creighton, Gordon W. The Italian scene: Bruno Ghibaudi's contact claim. Flying saucer review, v. 9, May-June 1963: 18-20.

Summary of two articles which appeared in the Turin, Italy, newspaper Le ore on Jan. 24 and 31, 1963, regarding Bruno Ghibaudi's claim that he had talked to the humanoid pilots of UFOs in Summer 1961.

----- The Italian scene--Part 4. Flying saucer review, v. 9, July-Aug. 1963: 10-12.

Translation of articles in January 6 and 20, 1963, issues of Settimana Incom Illustrata reporting contact claims: (1) on Aug. 25, 1960, a Swedish student was allegedly drawn up into a flying saucer near Halmstad and then taken to a "subterranean space-base"; (2) a man who allegedly photographed the occupants of a landed flying saucer had the film confiscated by tall men with bronzed complexions and dark hair; (3) on June 3, 1961, a disc-shaped unidentified submarine object was seen in the Mediterranean off the coast of Italy.

----- Three more Brazilian cases. Flying saucer review, v. 13, May-June 1967: 5-8.

Translation from July 1959 SBEDV (Sociedade Brasileira de Estudos sobre Discos Voadores) Bulletin of three alleged contact/landing incidents in Brazil, 1958-1959.

----- The Villa Santina Case. Flying saucer review, v. 13, Jan.-Feb. 1967: 3-7.

Account of alleged encounter with a landed flying saucer and its pilots by Professor L.R. Johannis on Aug. 14, 1947, near Villa Santina, Carnia, Italy. Translated from "Ho visto un disco volante" in May 1964 Clypeus.

Crenshaw, James. The great Venusian mystery. Fate, v. 19, June 1966: 32-39.

Episode involving two beings who claimed to have come from Venus and to have landed their spacecraft near Barstow, Calif., in June 1953.

Dick, William. U.S. Air Force project uses doctor to prove cop's report of flying saucer by hypnotism. National enquirer, v. 42, May 19, 1968: 1, 3, 4.

On Dec. 2, 1967, police officer Herbert Schirmer allegedly encountered humanoid crew of extraterrestrial spacecraft that hovered over the ground near Ashland, Nebraska. While under hynotic trance by Dr. Leo Sprinkle, associate professor of psychology at the University of Wyoming, Schirmer was "unswerving" in relating details of incident.

Duclout, Jorge A., & Napy Duclout. Unico documento confirmado sobre el origen, estructura y destino de los platos voladores; transcripcion de las grabaciones, sobre alambre, registradas durante experimentaciones psiquicas en que se concerto una cita con un plato volador, la cual fue complida en la fecha preestablecida; 2da. Edicion, ampliada con los testimonios del pasaje de un plato volador, el 6 de Septiember de 1954. Buenos Aires, America Tecnica & Editorial J.A. Duclout, 1956. 179 p.

Elizabeth Klarer's flying saucer. Flying saucers from other worlds, June 1957: 65-69, 75.

Mrs. Elizabeth Klarer gives her account of a flying saucer landing near her home in Natal, South Africa, on April 7, 1956, of her contact with occupant and ride in the spacecraft.

Foght, Paul. Inside the flying saucers: pancakes. Fate, v. 14, Aug. 1961: 32-36.

Joe Simonton of Eagle River, Wisconsin, claims a flying saucer landed in his back yard on April 18, 1961, and the crew members gave him three fried cakes.

Fouere, Rene. Surhumains ou sous-humains, anges ou demons, que sont les extra-terrestres? Phénomènes spatiaux, Mar. 1966: 5-11.

Speculation on the nature of the extraterrestrial beings apparently visiting earth based in part on reports of "contactees. "

Fry, Daniel W. The White sands incident. Los Angeles, New Age Publishing Co., 1954. 66 p.

Author describes how on July 4, 1950, he was taken in remote-controlled extraterrestrial spacecraft on a ride from White Sands Missile Range, N. Mex. , to New York City and back in approximately 30 minutes, and claims he conversed telepathically with extraterrestrial being in UFO's base ship 900 miles above earth's surface.

----- The White Sands incident. Louisville, Ky. , Best Books, Inc. , 1966. 120 p.

Account of 20-minute roundtrip ride to New York in unmanned, extraterrestrial spacecraft which allegedly landed near White Sands Proving Grounds, New Mexico, and report of subsequent conversations with an extraterrestrial on science, technology, and philosophy.

Fuller, Curtis. The men who ride in saucers. Fate, v. 7, May 1954: 44-47.

Alleged contacts of earthmen with crewmen of flying saucers are reported, including the stories of Truman Bethurum, George Adamski, Orfeo Angelucci, John Black, and John Van Allen.

Fuller, John G. The interrupted journey. New York, Dial Press, 1966. 302 p.

Account of UFO experience Sept. 19, 1961, of Barney and Betty Hill near Cannon Mountain, N. H. , during which they were taken aboard an extra-terrestrial spacecraft, given a physical examination, and released. Data used were based on tape recordings made by the principals while under hypnosis during subsequent psychiatric treatment.

Gibbons, Gavin. They rode in space ships. London, Neville Spearman, Ltd.,
1957. 217 p.

Account of reported rides in extraterrestrial spacecraft by Daniel Fry
(on July 4, 1950, from White Sands Missile Range, N. Mex., to New York
and back in 20 minutes) and Truman Bethurum (on July 27, 1952, from
Mormon Mesa, Nevada).

Gilman, Peter. Do the cherubim come from Mars? Flying saucer review, v. 13,
Sept.-Oct. 1967: 19-21, 29.

On Apr. 24, 1964, Gary Wilcox, who was working his farm in Newark Valley,
N. Y., allegedly saw a UFO land in a nearby field. The crew were two
humanoid 4-ft.-tall entities who were holding specimens of soil and sod,
said they were from Mars, and who explained that although they had been
obtaining their food from the atmosphere, they had to find a way to
rehabilitate their soil to raise food. Author suggests that "food taken from
the atmosphere" might be analogous to the celestial manna described in
the Bible in Exodus; the angels involved in this manifestation were the
cherubim and therefore may have come from Mars. The entities also
said there would be coming changes in the universe which would affect our
solar system and that Mars may be where earth is now. Author draws a
parallel between this information and Velikovsky's theory in Worlds in
Collision.

Girvin, Calvin C. The night has a thousand saucers. El Monte, Calif.,
Understanding Publishing Co., 1958. 168 p.

Author claims to have been inducted into the Army in 1944; tells of being
fatally wounded in World War II; of a "Venusian" incarnating into his body
and healing his wounds; and of adventures as an agent for friendly extraterrestrials. Alleges physical contact with Venusians and visits to
Venusian "mother ship" aboard a flying saucer.

Hudson, Jan. Those sexy saucer people. Canterbury, N. H., Greenleaf Classics,
1967. 176 p.

A cross-section of contactee stories, largely concerned with messages and
messengers allegedly of extraterrestrial origin. Emphasis is on the
influence such experiences had on the lives of the contactee claimants, the
divorces that resulted, and the sexual experience of some contactees
with the UFO occupants.

Hugill, Joanna. On the road from Sydney to Melbourne. Flying saucer review,
v. 14, Mar.-Apr. 1968: 3, 11.

Story of the alleged refusal by an Australian motorcyclist on Aug. 24, 1967,
to respond to the invitation of two silver-clad figures standing beside a
saucer-shaped craft to board the craft. Author prepared article from a
transcript of taped interview with witness by Peter Norris, chairman of the
Victorian Flying Saucer Research Society, and M. Thornhill.

Important discoveries. Flying saucer review, v. 12, Nov.-Dec. 1966: 17.

Comparison of cases of Barney and Betty Hill who, on the night of Sept. 19, 1961, were allegedly captured by beings from a flying saucer and taken aboard the spacecraft for physical examination and that of Antonio Villas Boas who was allegedly abducted by extraterrestrial beings for sexual experiment aboard their landed spacecraft on Oct. 15-16, 1957.

The Italian scene: Part 2. Flying saucer review, v. 9, Mar.-Apr. 1963: 3-6.

Report on inquiry by Italian periodical Domenica del Corriere into stories of UFO incidents and contact claims in Italy 1956-1962.

James, Trevor. The case for contact. Flying saucer review, v. 8, Jan.-Feb. 1962: 9-11.

Use of occult science as a new tool in investigating claims by individuals of contact with extraterrestrial beings is suggested by author. He says the occult scientist would approach these reports with some assurance that the contactee had had experiences involving his perceptions and could evaluate situations that were not necessarily the way they seemed to the contactee.

----- Scientists, contactees and equilibrium. Flying saucer review, v. 6, Jan.-Feb. 1960: 19-21.

Author suggests that review of stories of persons allegedly contacted by extraterrestrial beings reveals a struggle between Christ and anti-Christ forces. Allegations should be evaluated not so much in the light of whether they are possible or valid but in the light of who contacted these people: were they forces of good or forces of evil?

Keel, John. The little man of Gaffney. Flying saucer review, v. 14, Mar.-Apr. 1968: 17-19.

Details of encounter by Gaffney, South Carolina, police officers with a landed flying saucer and its humanoid occupant on Nov. 17, 1967.

----- Strange messages from flying saucers. Saga, v. 35, Jan. 1968: 22-25, 69-70, 72-74.

Similarities are noted in the details of messages given contactees throughout the world.

----- An unusual contact claim from Ohio. Flying saucer review, v. 14, Jan.-Feb. 1968: 25-26.

On July 18, 1967, Reverend Anthony de Polo of Boardman, Ohio, allegedly encountered and carried on telepathic communication with a humanoid being he believes to be of extraterrestrial origin.

Kobler, John. He runs flying saucer headquarters. Saturday evening post, v. 228, Mar. 10, 1956: 26-27, 69, 72.

Report on activities of James S. Rigberg of New York City--head of Flying Saucer News Club--who collects reports of UFO sightings and "contact" claims as telephoned or written to him.

Kraspedon, Dino. My contact with flying saucers. Translated from the Portuguese by J. B. Wood. London, Neville Spearman, 1959. 205 p.

Discusses in detailed technical terms the forces that UFOs use to navigate in earth's atmosphere and to travel through space on interplanetary voyages. Presented in question-and-answer form, information synthesizes series of five alleged meetings between author and captain of an extraterrestrial spacecraft.

Lemaitre, Jules. Angels or monsters? Flying saucer review, v. 5, Nov.-Dec. 1959: 3-5.

An inquiry into contact reports in Europe and the U.S.

Leslie, Desmond and George Adamski. Flying saucers have landed. London, Werner Laurie, 1953. 232 p.

Account of alleged contact by Adamski with a landed extraterrestrial spacecraft and meeting with a man from Venus on Nov. 20, 1952, near Desert Center, Calif. Photographs of spacecraft. Review by Leslie of material from old manuscripts referring to sightings of unidentified objects throughout antiquity.

Lindsay, Gordon. The riddle of the flying saucers. Dallas, Tex., The Voice of Healing Publishing Co., 1966. 31 p.

Author says reports do not ring true of flying saucers landing, nor of claims of their extraterrestrial origin, creatures of high evolutionary development, or of bringing knowledge to the human race to save it from disaster. He suggests that the whole thing has the earmarks of the diabolical.

Lorenzen, Coral and Jim Lorenzen. Flying saucer occupants. Introd. by Dr. Frank B. Salisbury. New York, Signet Books, The New American Library, 1967. 213 p.

Reports from men and women who have allegedly seen and communicated with extraterrestrial creatures. Authors, directors of the Aerial Phenomena Research Organization, claim that eyewitness reliability has been checked by psychiatric and other scientific methods. Also, an in-depth analysis of the role of the CIA in the study of UFO sightings is presented.

Luciano Galli's contact claim. Flying saucer review, v. 8, Sept.-Oct. 1962: 29-30.

Account of July 7, 1957 (or 1959), alleged encounter near Bologna, Italy, with a landed flying saucer from Venus and its crew and ride aboard spacecraft to "mother ship." Based on interview by Renate Albanese in June 1962 Domenica della Sera.

Martin, D. M. Seven hours aboard a space ship. Detroit, Mich., The Author, [1959?] 29 p.

Author claims that in June 1956 beings from Venus took him for a ride in one of their spacecraft during which they explained its operation, discussed conditions on their planet and spoke of the law-enforcing "central authority" of the solar system.

The Mel Noel story: the inside story on the U. S. Air Force secrecy on UFOs. Inglewood, Calif., The Author, 1966. 26 p.

Author, an ex-USAF lieutenant, gives details of a 1953-1954 USAF assignment that was allegedly specifically oriented towards the search for UFOs. He claims that on three different occasions, he, the two pilots, and the commanding colonel saw a group of 16 UFOs, 5 UFOs, and again 5 UFOs and had communication with their pilot during the third sighting. The commanding colonel allegedly later met these beings and boarded their spacecraft.

Menger, Howard. From outer space to you. Clarksburg, W. Va., Saucerian Books, 1959. 256 p.

Report of contacts with visitors from other planets and discussion of their philosophy.

----- The Howard Menger story. Flying saucer review, v. 4, July-Aug. 1958: 10-12, iii.

Author's account of alleged personal contacts with extraterrestrial spacecraft and their occupants.

Mr. Cooke goes to Zomdic. Flying saucer review, v. 4, July-Aug. 1958: 26-27.

Report of alleged contact with extraterrestrial beings and ride in spacecraft to planet Zomdic in another solar system.

Michael, Cecil. Roundtrip to Hell in a flying saucer. New York, Vantage Press, 1955. 61 p.

Account of author's alleged contact in 1952 with extraterrestrial beings who had the power to materialize and dematerialize at will and who took him to their planet, Hell, in his astral body aboard a flying saucer.

Mitchell, Helen and Betty Mitchell. We met the space people. Clarksburg, W. Va., Saucerian Publications, 1959. 17 p.

Addresses delivered by Helen and Betty Mitchell during Buck Nelson
Convention, June 28-29, 1958, concerning alleged contact with Martians and
Venusians and ride in Martian spacecraft. Extraterrestrials warn of impending
change in plane of earth's axis and concomitant cataclysms.

Miller, Max B. The men who ride in saucers. Fate, v. 13, Feb. 1960: 32-38.

Report on first national convention of the Amalgamated Flying Saucer Clubs
of America in Los Angeles, July 11-12, 1959.

Mundo, Laura. Pied piper from outer space. Los Angeles, The Planetary Space
Center Working Committee, 1964. 152 p.

Author describes alleged visit to Mars and philosophical, political, and
educational institutions there. Her "guide" on the visit discusses earth's
past history, role in God's plan, and ultimate destiny.

Nebel, Long John. The flying saucer story. New York, American Music Library,
1966. Matrix no. AML-201. 2s. 12 in. 33 1/3 rpm microgroove.

Interviews by the author of individuals involved in UFO controversy.

----- The way out world. Englewood Cliffs, N. J., Prentice-Hall, 1961. 225 p.

Tales and word portraits of men and women who claim to have sighted, contacted, flown in, traveled to other planets, systems, and galaxies in flying
saucers.

Nelson, Buck. I visited Mars, Venus, and the moon. Search, Dec. 1956: 6-20.

Extract from a lecture given before the Study Group on Interplanetary
Relationships, Detroit, Mich., July 26, 1955. Nelson describes alleged
interplanetary voyage with extraterrestrials who landed their spacecraft
on his farm.

----- My trip to Mars, the moon, and Venus. Mountain View, Mo., The Author,
1956. 44 p.

Contact with crews of flying saucers 1954-1955 and alleged voyages aboard
spacecraft while in his corporeal body are described by author.

Norkin, Israel. Saucer diary. New York, Pageant Press, 1957. 137 p.

Publication consists of correspondence between author and persons claiming
contact with extraterrestrial occupants of UFOs.

Oberth, Hermann. Katechismus der Uranidem. Wiesbaden-Schierstein, Ventla-
Verlag, 1966. 160 p.

Communication with an extraterrestrial being through a psychic medium has caused Oberth to adopt this view: there is a soul which outlives the body; this world serves as a training-ground for the soul; the soul will continue life (on a planet where conditions are in keeping with its degree of development) after death.

Owens, Ted. Flying saucer intelligences speak. New Brunswick, N. J., Interplanetary News Service, 1966. 7 p.

Author claims to be the only human representative of the Saucer Intelligences (UFO occupants) on earth; that he is able to receive intelligence from these people and transmit it to humans; and that he is able to prove out the intelligence that has been transmitted. He gives an account of his experiences.

Pascalis, Bernardino. Werkelijkheid of fantasie? Panorama, Feb. 21-27, 1967: 31-38.

Feature article on UFO reports in which there was alleged communication with the occupants or crew of the objects.

Rampa, T. Lobsang. My visit to Venus. Clarksburg, W. Va., Saucerian Books, 1966. 42 p.

Allegedly autobiographic, the book tells how the author and six "telepathic" lamas were taken aboard an extraterrestrial spacecraft to Venus to observe that planet's superior civilization. Voyage was sponsored by a brotherhood of "guardian" incarnate and discarnate entities from many different planets "who safeguard life in all forms."

Reeve, Bryant and Helen Reeve. Flying saucer pilgrimmage. Amherst, Wis., Amherst Press, 1957. 304 p.

Account of two-year private research by authors into UFO phenomenon which involved 23,000 miles of travel to interview individuals claiming contact with extraterrestrial beings. Religious, philosophic, and prophetic implications of UFO appearances are also discussed.

Rocha, Hugo. Outros mundos outras humanidades. Porto, Editora Educação Nacional, 1958. 371 p.

First part of book presents arguments from the literature and from scientific, philosophical, and religious writings supporting and opposing the theory of a plurality of inhabited worlds. Second part gives reports of individuals claiming contact with extraterrestrials, including Adamski, Bethurum, Fry, Allingham, Jorge and Napy Duclout, Kraspedon, and Ramatis and de Freitas Guimaraes.

Schmidt, Reinhold O. The Kearney incident. Flying saucers, Oct. 1959: 31-45.

Author allegedly sighted a landed flying saucer on Oct. 25, 1957 and was taken for a ride by its crew. Incident occured near Kearney, Nebraska.

Schmidt, Reinhold. The Reinhold Schmidt story. Los Angeles, Amalgamated
Flying Saucer Clubs of America, 1960. 18 p.

Author relates his claim that on Nov. 5, 1957, he encountered a landed flying
saucer and its crew near Kearney, Nebraska, and tells of his subsequent
experiences with "space people. "

Science: cups or saucers? Time, v. 70, Sept. 9, 1957: 67.

Commentary on claim of João de Freitas Guimaraes, a professor of Roman
law at the Santos, Brazil, Catholic University that he had taken an hour-long
ride through outer space in a flying saucer and communicated telepathically
with the occupants.

Silvano, Ceccarelli. Mario Zuccala's strange encounter. Flying saucer review,
v. 8, July-Aug. 1962: 5-7.

On April 10, 1962, Mario Zuccala allegedly encountered a landed flying saucer
near Florence, Italy, was taken aboard by its humanoid crew and later
released.

Simões, Auriphebo Berrance. Os discos voadores; fantasia e realidade. São Paulo,
Edart Livraria Editora Ltda., 1959. 390 p.

Survey of world literature on UFO phenomena with emphasis on contacteo
claims. Current theories on possibility of life on other planets are evaluated.

Space ships--and the people they visit. Flying saucers, Feb. 1959: 6-7, 15.

Survey of reports of persons claiming contact with extraterrestrial beings.

A speech by Wilbert B. Smith. Flying saucer review, v. 9, Sept. -Oct. 1963: 13-16.

Author, a Canadian electrical engineer and head of Project Magnet, summarizes
findings of two-year UFO investigation, including a series of communications
with intelligences claiming to be extraterrestrial and laboratory experiments
suggested by these entities that confirmed the validity of their alien science.
Transcript of tape recorded speech delivered at Ottawa, Canada, on Mar. 31,
1958.

Spraggett, Allen. Kidnapped by a UFO. Fate, v. 20, Jan. 1967: 34-41.

Account of UFO's abduction of Barney and Betty Hill on Sept. 19, 1961, near
Franconia Notch, N. H.

Stranges, Frank E. Stranger at the Pentagon. Van Nuys, Calif., International
Evangelism Crusades, 1967. 201 p.

Account, as allegedly told to author, of visit to earth by Valiant Thor of Venus
and his address to a special group at the United Nations and meeting with high
officials at the Pentagon.

Thomas, Franklin. We come in peace. Los Angeles, New Age Publishing Co.,
1955. 53 p.

Account of alleged flying saucer landing in Austria and of message of peace
conveyed by the Martian occupant.

Twitchell, Cleve. The UFO saga. Lakemont, Ga., CSA Press, 1966. 94 p.

Summary of experiences of individuals who claim to have seen UFOs, or
ridden in them, or communicated with their crews.

Van den Berg, Basil. My discovery will prove Adamski's claim. Flying saucer
review, v. 8, Nov.-Dec. 1962: 3-5.

Author claims to have deciphered the hieroglyphics on a photographic plate
allegedly given Adamski by Venusians and to have constructed an anti-gravity
device based on them.

Van Tassel, George. The council of seven lights. Los Angeles, De Vorss & Co.,
1958. 156 p.

The "middle viewpoint" of life, religion, planet earth, and other worlds is
given by author on basis of knowledge gleaned from the "organized intelligences of other places."

Veit, Karl. Planeten-menschen. Wiesbaden-Schierstein, Ventla-Verlag, 1961.
223 p.

Author surveys scientific opinion on the possibility of life on other worlds and
summarizes UFO sighting reports from 1947 to date. Details are given of
"contactee" reports and the alleged appearance and behavior of beings from
outer space.

Vogt, Cristian. El misterio de los platos voladores. Buenos Aires, Editorial
"La Mandragora" [1956] 190 p.

Contains general discussion of UFO phenomenon and summaries of explanatory hypotheses relating to it. Activities of governmental and private
research projects and contactee claims are also reported.

Zenabi, J. El misterio de los discos voladores. Santiago de Chile, The Author,
1953. 77 p.

Account of author's alleged contact with landed flying saucer and its Martian
crew and trip to Mars aboard spacecraft. He describes in detail physical
features of Mars, its science, culture, and political institutions. Experience
reportedly took place in September 1952.

Brooks, Angus. Remarkable sighting near Dorset coast. Flying saucer review,
v. 14, Jan.-Feb. 1968: 3-4.

Report of UFO observed Oct. 26, 1967, at Moinge Downs, between Weymouth
and Lulworth Cove, Dorset, England. In "hover" position, object consisted
of four "fuselages" at equidistant position around a central chamber. Further
construction details are given.

Fry, Daniel W. Steps to the stars. Lakemont, Ga., CSA Publishers, 1956.
83 p.

The basic physical concepts underlying the construction and operation of a
vehicle that could undertake interplanetary travel are discussed.

Is this the real flying saucer? Look, v. 19, June 14, 1955: 44-46.

Design study for a flying-saucer fighter prepared for Look by Republic
Aviation Corp. engineer Thomas Turner. Sketches indicate appearance of
a craft that would fulfill following requirements: (1) ability to take off and
land vertically; (2) high speed of over Mach 2.; (3) high rate of climb;
(4) excellent maneuverability; (5) heavy armament; (6) ability to operate at
60,000 ft.

Schroeder, W. Only 4 hours to reach the moon. Flying saucer review, v. 4,
Jan.-Feb. 1958: 12-14.

Author considers ideal design for spacecraft that could travel outside earth's
atmosphere and concludes that (1) it must be circular; (2) it must have the
rocket motor on top and the remainder of the structure underneath; and (3)
the lower parts must be wider than the upper ones and have a hole in the
middle for unobstructed flow from the rocket motor. He says UFOs fit this
description because the design consideration applies universally.

Stanley, Neil and Chester S. Geier. The flying saucer jigsaw puzzle. Fate,
v. 1, Fall 1948: 101-104.

Speculates that possible reason for different sizes and shapes of observed
flying discs is that they are specialized units that fit together like a jigsaw
puzzle to compose a complete unit. Advantages of fragmentation would be
(1) greater speed and functioning efficiency; (2) protection against loss;
and (3) greater ease and safety in landing.

Winder, R.H.B. Comment on the Angus Brooks sighting. Flying saucer review,
v. 14, Jan.-Feb. 1968: 4-5.

Speculating on the reason for the crosslike configuration during hover of the
UFO seen over England Oct. 26, 1967, by Angus Brooks, author suggests
observations or measurements demanding instruments located at the four
corners of a square or requiring two or four linear devices (possibly antennae),
intersecting at right angles.

Winder, R. H. B. Design for a flying saucer. Flying saucer review, v. 12, Nov. -Dec. 1966: 21-26.

Article considers in broad outline the engineering design of a spacecraft capable of reproducing performance and effects characteristically noted in reported UFO sightings.

----- Design for a flying saucer. Flying saucer review, v. 13, Jan. -Feb. 1967: 13-18.

Continues discussion of design considerations of spacecraft capable of performing in manner noted in reported UFO sightings.

----- Design for a flying saucer: Part II - construction and performance. Flying saucer review, v. 13, Jan. -Feb. 1967: 13-18.

Author discusses the practical application of a fusion-powered hydromagnetic spacecraft and problems of operation in the planetary atmosphere.

----- Design for a flying saucer: Part III -- characteristics and effects. Flying saucer review, v. 13, Mar. -Apr. 1967: 20-23.

Author describes ionization and hydromagnetic phenomena associated with the use of hydromagnetic propulsion. He relates this to reported UFO behavior.

----- Design for a flying saucer: Part IV -- characteristics and effects. Flying saucer review, v. 13, May-June 1967: 9-12.

In discussion of characteristics and effects of a disc-shaped craft with hydromagnetic propulsion, the author considers: (1) permissible and forbidden flight configurations; (2) kinds of electromagnetic radiation emitted by machine; (3) visual consequences of ionization in the air; and (4) physiological effects of strong magnetic fields.

DETECTORS

Aho, Arthur C. Magnetic UFO detector. Flying saucers, Feb. 1961: 25-26.

Do-it-yourself directions for making a portable flying saucer detector.

Lafonta, Paul. Detecteurs magnetiques. Phenomenes spatiaux, Mar. 1966: 12-16.

Blueprint for making a magnetic detector for UFOs.

Lloyd, Dan. UFO detector network in the United Kingdom. Flying saucer review, v. 14, Mar. -Apr. 1968: 27-28.

UFO detector network equipped with McCarthy detectors is described and regional list given of detector owners with a telephone.

Thompson, T. A. means of detecting UFOs. BUFORA journal and bulletin, v. 1, Spring 1966: 6-8.

Description of a prototype UFO detector.

ELECTROMAGNETIC EFFECTS

Attention aux soucoupes! Phénomènes spatiaux, Mar. 1966: 29-30.

Several cases are cited where beams of rays from UFOs caused damage to the eyes. It is speculated that this is caused by the electro-magnetic field surrounding the objects.

Binder, Otto O. How flying saucers can injure you. Mechanix illustrated, v. 64, Jan. 1968: 64-66, 136-137.

Discusses physiological reactions of the human body to electromagnetic effects (EM) caused by UFOs.

Cade, C. Maxwell. A long, cool look at alien intelligence: It's all in the mind. Flying saucer review, v. 14, Mar.-Apr. 1968: 7-9.

Author suggests the possibility that UFOs and poltergeists are among phenomena which could be "experienced" with completely convincing realism, due to effects of electromagnetic fields. He also suggests that this electro-magnetic radiation could be either terrestrial or extraterrestrial in origin; it could be either a stochastic natural process or the planned product of an alien intelligence.

Campione, Michael J. Reality of UFOs, their danger, their hope. Cinnaminson, N. J., The Author, 1965. 16 p.

General discussion of the UFO phenomenon, including recognizable characteristics, physiological effects on humans, statistics on sightings and landings, theories on their origin, and USAF policy.

Cleary-Baker, John. A UFO stops the clocks. BUFORA journal and bulletin, v. 1, Summer 1965: 19.

Electro-magnetic watches and clocks stopped for 45 minutes when a cylindrical, white UFO flew over the Azores on July 9, 1965.

-----. Report on Warminster. BUFORA journal and bulletin, v. 1, Autumn 1965: 6-8.

Accounts of the mysterious aerial sights and sounds reported frequently in Warminster, England. Author speculates that the dull, crunching noise arises out of an electromagnetic interaction between a low-flying UFO and the ground (especially when there are deposits of ferromagnetic material). He suggests that the "humming" sound might come from altitude-finding devices on the UFOs.

Creighton, Gordon. Astronauts forced down by UFOs? Flying saucer review, v. 11, May-June 1965: 15-18.

January 1965 issue of Die Andere Welt is quoted as saying: "In Moscow there are persistent rumors that the last manned satellite [Voskod I, launched Oct. 11, 1964, with three-man crew] was repeatedly overtaken by extremely fast flying discs which struck the craft violent shattering blows with their powerful magnetic fields. "

-----. Mysterious psychological effects of flying saucers. Flying saucers review, v. 13, July-Aug. 1967: 5-6.

Apparent effect on heart, bladder, and bowels of individuals allegedly in proximity to flying saucers, and/or their occupants is discussed. It is speculated that phenomenon may be due to electromagnetic rays.

Edwards, Frank Edwards report: UFO sightings and alibis. Fate, v. 11, Mar. 1958: 27-34.

Author says that according to USAF officials, persons who report seeing UFOs are suffering from hallucinations; however, since cars and tractors reportedly have their ignition systems killed by proximity to these objects, he suggests that surely new "alibis" are needed.

Finch, Bernard E. Physiological effect on witness at Hook. Flying saucer review, v. 13, Nov.-Dec. 1967: 7, 27.

Apparent side-effects of UFO force field on the body of the individual sighting it Oct. 26, 1967, near Hook, England, are discussed.

Fontes, Olavo T. Brazilian top secret report revealed. Flying saucers, Feb. 1960: 6-14, 24.

Three instances are related in which UFOs sighted in Brazil in 1957 seemed to have hostile intent and to possess a weapon used as a means of defense and attack that completely disrupts electrical systems.

Maney, Charles A. Scientific measurement of UFOs. Fate, v. 18, June 1965: 31-39.

Cites instances where the strengths of magnetic fields associated with UFOs have been measured by physical devices.

Michel, Aime. Flying saucers in Europe: saucers--or delusions? Fate, v. 11, Jan. 1958: 73-79.

Cases of UFO sightings in France during 1954 are reported in which electric circuit "paralysis" of motor vehicles was a concomitant feature.

New clues to UFO electrical interference. The UFO investigator, v. 3, Nov.-Dec. 1965: 3-4.

Reported UFO sightings prior to or during the Nov. 9, 1965, "blackout" are reviewed; reports of smaller-scale instances of electromagnetic interference are surveyed for comparison.

Norman, Paul. Electro-magnetic effects of UFOs. Flying saucer review, v. 11, Sept.-Oct. 1965: 26-28.

Summary of known cases where UFO sightings were accompanied by electro-magnetic phenomena: interference with radio and television sets; dimmed headlights and stilled motor car engines; and power and light failures. Account taken from paper read by author at the Ballarat (Australia) Astronomical Society's 1965 conference.

Romig, Mary F. and Donald L. Lamar. Anomalous sounds and electromagnetic effects associated with fireball entry. Santa Monica, The Rand Corp., 1963. 60 p. (Rand Corp. Memorandum RM-3724-ARPA.)

Memorandum describes nature of certain hissing sounds and electromagnetic effects associated with the passage of very bright meteors or fireballs and discusses their possible origin from the standpoint of atmospheric electricity and reentry physics. Study was motivated by possibility that a better under-standing of these phenomena will lead to new techniques for determining the size, nature, and path of any large body entering earth's atmosphere.

Strange effects from EM waves. The UFO investigator, v. 3, Nov.-Dec. 1965: 5.

Experiments and research by Prof. Clyde E. Ingalls, Cornell University, are summarized and seem to indicate that electromagnetic waves can be "heard." Reports of odd effects and EM (electromagnetic) interference concomitant with UFO sightings are briefly surveyed.

Sur les effets biologiques des champs magnetiques intenses. Phénomènes spatiaux, Dec. 1965: 8-10.

Many of the individuals who have allegedly been in proximity to flying saucers or their occupants report being stricken by paralysis. Problems with vision, electric shock, and a sensation of heat (burns are often suffered), accompany this paralysis. It is suggested that exposure to a sufficiently intense magnetic field could be the causal factor.

Vogt, Christian. Non dramatique incident. Phenomenes spatiaux, Feb. 1965: 5-6.

A tragic accident allegedly occurred on May 24, 1954, near Las Vegas, Nevada, when an experimental jet aircraft was destroyed   as   it attempted to shoot down a flying saucer.

Winder, R. H. B.   Vehicle stoppage at Hook.   Flying saucer review, v. 13, Nov. -Dec. 1967: 6-7.

Report of motor vehicle electrical system failure in conjunction with UFO sighting Oct. 26, 1967, near Hook, England.

LANDINGS

L'affaire de Valensole. Phenomenes spatiaux, Sept. 1965: 5-24.

On the morning of July 1, 1965, Maurice Masse of Valensole, France, allegedly saw a landed football-shaped machine in a lavender field on his property. The apparent "pilot" of the craft was about the height and weight of an eight year old boy. Article reports newspaper accounts of incident and gives details of official government investigation.

Allingham, Cedric. Flying saucer from Mars. New York, British Book Center, 1955. 153 p.

Report of UFO landing Feb. 18, 1954, near Lossiemouth, North Scotland, and author's contact with a Martian.

Bowen, Charles. Crash-landed UFO near Mendoza. Flying saucer review, v. 11, May-June 1965: 7-9.

A cigar-shaped capsule estimated to be about 8 meters long and 1 meter in diameter allegedly fell at San Miguel, Argentina, in January 1965, and was photographed by an aircraft from the Provincial Aeronautical Bureau. According to newspaper account in La Cronica, local inhabitants said the object was a flying saucer and that they had seen little individuals working around the craft in uniforms like divers' suits that gave off a strange phosphorescence.

-----. A significant report from France. Flying saucer review, v. 11, Sept. - Oct. 1965: 9-11.

Summary of newspaper accounts of alleged UFO landing July 1, 1965, on the farm of Maurice Masse near Valensole, France.

Bowen, Charles. Who hoaxes who? Flying saucer review, v. 11, July-Aug.
1965: 6-9.

Details are given of the alleged landing of a spacecraft at Brooksville, Fla.,
on Mar. 2, 1965, in which two papers containing hieroglyphics were reportedly
dropped by an occupant of the spacecraft. Although the incident was labeled a
"hoax" by USAF, the author suggests that "perhaps the attempt to deceive is
not as straightforward as it would at first appear."

Bowen, Charles and Gordon Creighton. The Storrington reports: landings in
Sussex? Flying saucer review, v. 14, Mar.-Apr. 1968: 4-6.

Report of alleged UFO sightings near Storrington, England: (1) on Oct. 29,
1967, an ice-cream-cone-shaped object was seen; (2) on Nov. 16, 1967, the
object viewed had a trumpet shape at what appeared to be the front, a dome
shaped center, and two tails on the right-hand side. A gliding humanoid
figure was seen in connection with the latter sighting.

Cahn, J. P. Flying saucers and the mysterious little men. True, v. 32, Sept.
1952: 17-19, 102-112.

Report of investigation into allegations in Frank Scully's book, Behind the
Flying Saucers (New York, Henry Holt, 1950), that a crashed flying saucer
and corpses of its three-foot-tall crew had been taken into custody by the
U.S. Air Force. Claims prove untrue and the book a hoax.

Clark, Jerome. Two new contact claims. Flying saucer review, v. 11, May-June
1965: 20-23.

On January 26, 1965, a landed flying saucer and its 3 1/2 ft. occupants were
allegedly seen near Brands Flats, Virginia. On January 30, 1965, TV repairman Sid Padrick allegedly encountered a landed flying saucer and was
invited aboard by its crew members.

-----. UFO landings in South America. Flying saucers, Oct. 1966: 24-25.

Author reports alleged landings of UFOs during September in Brazil and
Peru and describes the "ufonauts" observed.

Cleary-Baker, John. The Scoriton affair. BUFORA journal and bulletin, v. 1,
Autumn 1965: 10-11.

On June 7, 1965, E. Arthur Bryant sighted a UFO that appeared to descend
onto a nearby field. Next morning, throughout the area where he estimated
the object had come to earth, the foliage and grass were singed. A small,
turbine-like fitting with curved blades was found as well as a glass phial
containing "silver sand" and a piece of paper on which was written:
"Adelphos Adelpho."

Creighton, Gordon. The extraordinary happenings at Casa Blanca. Flying saucer review, v. 13, Sept.-Oct. 1967: 16-18.

On Aug. 22, 1955, a group of children playing in the garden of a home in Casa Blanca, California, allegedly first sighted silvery, spinning discs and later 3-ft.-tall transparent beings who emerged from landed craft. Author considers accounts of incident by Coral Lorenzen in Flying Saucer Review's The Humanoids and by Winona Cromwell in a 1955 issue of the Journal of the Borderland Sciences Research Association.

Do flying saucers ever land? Flying saucers, Oct. 1966: 30.

Lists reports of flying saucer landings worldwide and encounters with humanoid occupants 1964-1966.

Duchêne, J. L. La repartition des atterrissages de soucoupes volantes en France. Phénomènes spatiaux, May 1965: 21-25.

By plotting the points of alleged UFO landings over a period of years on a map of France, the author observes that they seem to be aligned circularly around a "neutral" center.

Dunn, William J., Jr. An analysis of the 1965 Brookville landing case. Saucer news, v. 13, June 1966: 6-8.

Reviews information on March 1965 sightings of airborne and landed UFOs and contact with presumed crew near Weeki Wachi Springs, Florida.

Elizabeth Klarer's flying saucer. Flying saucers from other worlds, June 1957: 65-69, 75.

Mrs. Elizabeth Klarer gives her account of a flying saucer landing near her home in Natal, South Africa, on April 7, 1956, of her contact with occupant and ride in the spacecraft.

Enquête à Valensole. Phénomènes spatiaux, Sept. 1965: 42-46.

Report of a magistrate on his inquiry into claim by Maurice Masse of Valensole, France, that a football-shaped flying machine had landed in his lavender field July 1, 1965, and he had seen the diminutive pilot of the craft.

Fawcett, George D. Flying saucers: explosive situation for 1968. Flying saucers, Apr. 1968: 22-25.

Study of 1967 reports of UFO incidents from 40 states and 20 foreign countries. Included are 75 landings, 56 photographs, 52 car chases, 30 pilot pursuits, 14 "occupant" reports, 11 radar trackings and 7 UFO-related power failures. Many of these incidents occured in North Carolina, Pennsylvania, New England, Florida, California, Ohio, England, Canada, Argentina, Australia, Peru, and Mexico.

Fouere, Rene and Francine Fouéré. Le plateau de Valensole serait-il un haut
lieu du tourisme insolite? Phénomènes spatiaux, Sept. 1966: 10-20.

There have been four of five UFO sightings at Valensole, France, within
a year of the time Maurice Masse allegedly saw a landed spacecraft and
its occupant in his lavender field (July 1, 1965), according to reports
cited by the authors.

Girvan, Waveney. The Wiltshire crater mystery: the meteor that never was.
Flying saucer review, v. 9, Sept. -Oct. 1963: 3-7.

Details of incident where "something" landed in farmer Ray Blanchard's
field in Charlton, Wilshire, England, on July 16, 1963, leaving a saucer-
shaped depression eight feet in diameter and about four feet in depth.
In the center of depression was a three-feet-deep hole variously described
as from five inches to one foot in diameter. Radiating from central hole
were four slot marks, four feet long and one foot wide.

Greenbank, Anthony. Creatures from outer space (stepping from flying saucer).
In The book of survival. New York and Evanston, Harper & Row, 1967. p. 34.

Advice on what to do in the event of encounter with crew disembarking from
landed flying saucer: (1) avoid rapid forceful movement; (2) use no shrill
sounds; (3) breathe quietly; (4) avoid giving a direct menacing gaze.

Holledge, James. Flying saucers over Australia. London, Melbourne, Sidney,
Howitz Publications, Inc., 1965. 130 p.

Book gives eye witness accounts of flying saucers sighted over Australia
as well as saucer landings in Australia.

The humanoids. Flying saucer review, Oct. -Nov. 1966. 32 p.

A survey of worldwide reports of landings of unconventional aerial objects
and their alleged occupants: The Villa Santina [Italy] Case; Few and Far
Between [Landing and occupant reports a rarity in the British Isles],
Charles Bowen; The Pattern Behind the UFO Landings [Report on the
analysis of 200 documented observations made in 1954], Jacques Vallee;
The Landing at Villares Del Saz [Spain], Antonio Ribera; The Humanoids
in Latin America, Gordon Creighton; The Landing at Socorro, N.M. [New
light on a classic case], W. T. Powers; UFO Occupants in United States
Reports, Coral Lorenzen; Questions on the Occupants, Donald B. Hanlon;
The Problem of Non-Contact, Aime Michel; Was it a Landing at Silverton
[South Africa] ?, Ed Pitlo and Edgar Sievers.

Keel, John A. From my Ohio Valley note book. Flying saucer review, v. 13,
May-June 1967: 3-5.

Report on unpublicized UFO "ground level activities" in Ohio and West
Virginia, October 1966-January 1967.

Keel, John. The little man of Gaffney. Flying saucer review, v. 14, Mar.-Apr. 1968: 17-19.

Details of encounter by Gaffney, South Carolina, police officers with a landed flying saucer and its humanoid occupant on Nov. 17, 1967.

Kunkel, Wallace. The little man who wasn't there. Fate, v. 7, May 1954: 48-52.

Special report: a crowd gathered in a canyon in the Sierra Nevada mountains near Oroville, Butte County, Calif., on July 20, 1953, and vainly awaited arrival of a flying saucer and its pilot. Miner John Black and John Van Allen had allegedly seen craft three times on the 20th of the month--in March, May, June--and believed it would return July 20th.

Leslie, Desmond and George Adamski. Flying saucers have landed. London, Werner Laurie, 1953. 232 p.

Account of alleged contact by Adamski with a landed extraterrestrial spacecraft and meeting with a man from Venus on Nov. 20, 1952, near Desert Center, Calif. Photographs of spacecraft. Review by Leslie of material from old manuscripts referring to sightings of unidentified objects from antiquity.

Lorenzen, Coral. Diving for lost UFO. Fate, v. 17, May 1964: 62-65.

Efforts are being made to salvage a flying saucer which seemed in mechanical difficulty when it allegedly sank in the Peropava River, Brazil, on October 31, 1963.

Lorenzen, Coral and Jim Lorenzen. UFOs over the Americas. New York, Signet Books, The New American Library, 1968. 254 p.

Authors report that 1967 brought an unprecedented number of UFO landings, low-level hovering maneuvers, and landings with occupants visible. They suggest that the almost constant UFO activity from 1965 to the present indicates that close approaches of the planet to Mars to earth is no longer a factor; there are no longer cyclical recurrences of UFO activity peaks. An interpretation of this might be that UFOs are interplanetary in origin and the occupants have established bases close enough to earth so that long journeys are no longer necessary, the authors say.

Michel, Aimé. Flying saucers in Europe: meeting with the Martian. Fate, v. 10, Sept. 1957: 43-46.

Account of alleged encounter by Antoine Mazaud on Sept, 10, 1954, near Limoges, France, with a creature apparently from a landed "flying saucer." Other inhabitants of Limoges reported sighting on the same evening a reddish disc that left a bluish trail.

----- Flying saucers in Europe: the little men. Fate, v. 10, Nov. 1957: 72-76.

On Sept. 10, 1954, Marius Dewilde allegedly saw two creatures that appeared to be crew of a "flying saucer" that had landed on railroad tracks in an area near Valenciennes, France. Details of subsequent investigation are given.

----- Flying saucers over Europe: French flying saucer. Fate, v. 10, Dec. 1957: 33-38.

A flying saucer allegedly landed in a field in Saint-Seine-l'Abbaye, France, (near Dijon), was seen by several people, and left an excavated hole in the ground. Occurrence was on Oct. 4, 1954.

----- The mystery at Marignane. Fate, v. 9, Dec. 1956: 22-30.

French customs officer Gabriel Gachignard reported that a weird, football-shaped object landed at Marignane airport (France) on Oct. 26-27, 1952. Reprinted from author's book, The Truth About Flying Saucers (New York, Criterion Books, 1956).

----- Valensole. Phénomènes spatiaux, Mar. 1966: 21-26.

Author's investigation of claim by Maurice Masse that on July 1, 1965, he saw a landed football-shaped flying machine and its pilot in his lavender field produces new facts. Among them: (1) during the week preceding the alleged incident, Masse and his father noticed that young lavender plants were damaged as though someone were taking cuttings from them; (2) when the UFO flew away, it accelerated rapidly and then vanished completely twenty yards away; (3) Masse's "paralysis" may have been due to post-hypnotic suggestion since "real" paralysis would have stopped the heart muscles; and (4) Masse may not be revealing all the details of his encounter with the UFO "pilot." Reprinted from Flying Saucer Review.

----- The Valensole affair. Flying saucer review, v. 11, Nov.-Dec. 1965: 7-9.

Comment by author on July 1, 1965, sighting at Valensole, France, of UFO and its humanoid crew based in his own investigation.

Michel, Aimé and Charles Bowen. A visit to Valensole. Flying saucer review, v. 14, Jan.-Feb. 1968: 6-12.

Aimé Michel and Charles Bowen interview Maurice Masse (in August 1967) at Valensole, France, about his alleged experience with the humanoid occupants of a flying saucer that landed on his property July 1, 1965. Mention is also made of UFO sighting on Sept. 17-18, 1965, from St. Michel Observatory, France, by three astronomers.

More about Marliens. Flying saucer review, v. 13, Sept.-Oct. 1967: 14-15.

Report quoting extensively from the Lausanne (Switzerland) newspaper, Feuille d' Avis, on marks discovered May 9, 1967, in a clover field in Marliens, France, that seem to indicate a flying saucer landing.

Nelson, Buck. I visited Mars, Venus, and the moon. Search, Dec. 1956: 6-20.

Extract from a lecture given before the Study Group on Interplanetary Relationships, Detroit, Mich. , July 26, 1955. Nelson describes alleged interplanetary voyage with extraterrestrials who landed their spacecraft on his farm.

1966 Tully. Australian flying saucer review, No. 9, Nov. 1966: 16-18.

On Jan. 19, 1966, banana grower George Pedley saw a "vapor-like saucer" take off from a "nest" in the reeds near Tully, Australia. Two more "nests" were discovered by cane farmer Tom Warren and school teacher Hank Penning during the month.

Perego, Alberto. The Monguzzi case [Basle, 1965] . 2 p.

English translation by Lou Zinsstag of pertinent section of Peego's Svelato il mistero dei dischi volanti (Rome, Edizioni del C. I. S. A. E. R. , 1957).

Que s'est-il passe à Marliens. Phénomènes spatiaux, June 1967: 24-30.

Newspaper accounts of May 6, 1967, incident in Marliens, France, in which . markings were found in a field for which there was no conventional explanation.

Retour sur Attignéville: l'incident de Xertigny. Phénomènes spatiaux, Dec. 1966: 13-17.

Details of further inquiry into incident at Attigneville, France, Mar. 26, 1966, in which a strange white wheel with red spokes at its periphery was seen traveling at a constant speed of about 30 kilometers an hour. A circular depression discovered by a farmer at Xertigny, France, on Sept. 4, 1966, that he originally thought was a meteor crater, is also discussed.

Retour sur Valensole: les conclusions de notre enquêteur. Phénomènes spatiaux, Dec. 1965: 11-16.

The unanimous opinion of persons interrogating Maurice Masse concerning his alleged July 1, 1965, encounter with landed U FO and its occupant is that his account of the incident is a truthful one.

Ribera, Antonio. The Madrid landing. Flying saucer review, v. 12, May-June 1966: 28-31.

Statements of witnesses to appearance and brief "touch down" of UFO at Aluche, near Casa de Campo, Spain, on Feb. 7, 1966.

Rifat, Alain. Was it a landing at Marliens? Flying saucer review, v. 13, Sept-Oct. 1967: 11-13.

Report on strange hole and associated marks found in a clover field in Marliens, France, May 9, 1967. Marks were similar to the Charlton crater of 1963, and to those found at Valensole in 1965.

Rymdbesök--eller vad? Sökaren, v. 5, no. 1, 1968: 8-10.

On August 23, 1967, in Sweden, a "creature" was sighted by two witnesses in conjunction with a UFO sighting. The following day, footprints were found at the site of the encounter.

Sanderson, Ivan T. "Something" landed in Pennsylvania. Fate, v. 19, Mar. 1966: 33-35.

Details are given of the crash of a fiery object--flying rather than falling at 1,062.5 mph and observed to make a 25° turn--near Pittsburgh, Pa., on Dec. 9, 1965.

Senelier, Jean. Observations sur le rapport d'analyse de la terre de Marliens; remarques sur de pretendus débris d' O. V. N. I. Phénomenes spatiaux, Dec. 1967: 12-15.

On May 6, 1967, markings were found in a field in Marliens, France, that were interpreted by some as indicating that an aircraft--terrestrial or extraterrestrial--had landed there. Laboratory analysis of soil samples revealed no traces of material not indigenous to earth: this was also true of analysis of burnt organic material found.

La "soucoupe" carrée de Bolazec ou le tracteur volant. Phénomènes spatiaux, Mar. 1966: 17-20.

Alleged landing of a square-shaped UFO near Bolazec, France, on Jan. 16, 1966, is reported. Newspaper accounts of incident are cited.

Thomas, Franklin. We come in peace. Los Angeles, New Age Publishing Co., 1955. 53 p.

Account of alleged flying saucer landing in Austria and of message of peace conveyed by the Martian occupant.

Thomas, Robert B. "Flying saucers" or "fairy rings"? Farmer's almanac, v. 175, 1967: 50-51.

Fairy ring phenomenon, supposedly caused by discharge of lightning upon the earth, is discussed. It is suggested that it could be caused by UFO landings.

The Tully "nests": How freakish can whirlwinds be? Flying saucers, Apr. 1968: 6-9.

Author examines question of whether areas in Tully, Australia, where the reeds "were without exception bent below water level, dead and swirled around in a clockwise manner, as if they had been subjected to some terrific rotary force" could be explained in terms of known atmospheric processes. Conclusion is negative. Reprinted from Australian Flying Saucer Review.

UFO: flying saucers. Poughkeepsie, N.Y., Western Publishing Co., 1968. 64 p.

Comic book. Accounts of UFOs in ancient history, UFO kidnappings, and "classic" sightings and landing cases, including those where occupants were allegedly seen.

Wilkins, H. Percy. Mysteries of space and time. London, Frederick Muller, Ltd., 1955. 208 p.

Mysteries on the land, in the sea, in the air, and in outer space are discussed. Chapter 2 is devoted to "Flying Things in Space" and investigates the reliability of various accounts and probability of impending "invasion" of earth. Author feels it is improbable that alien life could exist in our atmosphere without a period of acclimatation in some inaccessible and remote spot such as the interior of South America or amid the snows of the Himalayas.

Zulli, Alphonse. Glassboro UFO landing reviewed. Fate, v. 19, Sept. 1966: 32-39.

Mysterious holes, scorched earth, injured trees, and unidentified chemicals give evidence that a 30-foot "something" landed on Sept. 4, 1964, at Glassboro, N.J.

MEN IN BLACK

Barker, Gray. Gray Barker's book of saucers. Clarksburg, W. Va., Saucerian Books, 1965. 77 p.

Book catalogues UFO sightings in all parts of the world, 1962-1963. Saucer landings, communication between saucer crews and humans, seizure of terrestrials by saucer crews, mating of extraterrestrials with terrestrials, and "the men in black" are discussed.

----- They knew too much about flying saucers. New York, University Books, 1956. 256 p.

Instances are cited in which flying saucer investigators have allegedly been frightened into silence by various visitors, including "three men in black."

Bender, Albert K. Flying saucers and the three men. Annotated and with introd. and epilogue by Gray Barker. Clarksburg, W. Va., Saucerian Books, 1962. 194 p.

Discussion of activities of and reports of UFO sightings made to International
Flying Saucer Bureau, organized by Bender in April 1952 in Bridgeport,
Conn., and of Bender's contact with extraterrestrial beings which he claims
resulted in his dissolving IFSB in November 1953. Published also by
Paperback Library, Inc. (53-686), New York.

Easley, Robert S. and Rick R. Hilberg. MIB: a report on the mysterious men in
black who have terrorized UFO witnesses and investigators in all parts of
the nation. Cleveland, Ohio, UFO Magazines Publications, 1968. 24 p.

Article discusses increasing numbers of "hush up" cases where witnesses
to important UFO sightings are being systematically silenced by the "men in
black."

Keel, John A. The "silencers" at work. Flying saucer review, v. 13, Mar.-Apr.
1967: 10.

Col. George P. Freeman, Pentagon spokesman for Project Blue Book, is
alleged to have said in a press interview that "mysterious men dressed
in Air Force uniforms or bearing impressive credentials from government agencies have been 'silencing' UFO witnesses." Similar mystery
men have reportedly turned up and confronted UFO witnesses in the states
of Washington, Texas, Connecticut, and on Long Island, N. Y.

----- UFO "agents of terror." Saga, v. 33, Oct. 1967: 29-31, 72-74, 76-79, 81.

Report on activities of "men in black" who masquerade as government
investigators, but whose real job is to seize pictures of flying saucers,
suppress evidence of sightings and contacts, and frighten witnesses into
silence.

----- UFO report: the sinister men in black. Fate, v. 21, Apr. 1968: 32-39.

Cites many reports of appearance of "men in black." Suggests they might
come from some group or organization directly related to the UFO phenomenon and are successfully infiltrating our cities and villages. Their
mission seems to be to "silence" individuals who have had UFO experiences.

Steiger, Brad. What price silence? Flying saucers, June 1968: 31.

A private citizen investigates an alleged UFO landing and is given a piece of
metal that supposedly fell from the machine. The metal sample is taken
away from him during a visit by what seemed to be representatives of "the
men in black."

Adamski, George. Flying saucers farewell. London, New York, Abelard-
Schuman, 1961. 190 p.

Adamski discusses the reasons spacecraft from other planets are visiting
earth and man's place in the universe as reportedly revealed to him through
contact with beings from Venus, Mars, and Saturn. Published also with
title Behind the Flying Saucer Mystery by Paperback Library (53-439),
New York.

Ashtar. In days to come. Los Angeles, New Age Publishing Co., 1955. 91 p.

Prophesies the coming of legions of "space people" to assist in establishing
the new Golden Age. Message received through automatic writing.

Barker, Gray. Chasing the flying saucers. Flying saucers, Feb. 1961: 22-24, 58.

Discusses conclusion by some UFO researchers that UFOs are hostile and
suggests that the occasional injuries they have caused might be accidental.

The book of spaceships in their relationship with the earth. Los Angeles,
DeVorss & Co., 1967. 47 p.

Discussion of origin and intent of extraterrestrial spacecraft in earth's atmosphere by one who alleges to be a traveler in these spacecraft as well as an
aerial traveler without any kind of vehicle but his own body.

Clark, Jerome. Why UFOs are hostile. Flying saucer review, v. 13, Nov. -
Dec. 1967: 18-20.

Author postulates that because UFOs have killed and injured seemingly
innocent persons, we should not conclude that the saucers have sinister
motives; because UFOs usually do not bother us, we should not conclude
that they are indifferent to us; because UFO beings are sometimes kind
to us, we should not conclude that they like us. We should conclude,
though, that they are intimately concerned with us--to the extent that they
have gone to fantastic lengths to prevent us from knowing what they are
doing.

Clarke, Arthur C. When earthmen become the "UFO" of other planets. Flying
saucers, Aug. 1968: 8-17.

The story of the movie "2001: A Space Odyssey," translating the challenges
posed by extraterrestrial life into a motion picture.

Cove, Gordon. Who pilots the flying saucers. London, The Author, 1955. 80 p.

Flying saucers, according to the author, are celestial warnings of an impending Divine interruption of the course of world events: they are to warn men of the coming judgement and to encourage the believer.

Cox, Adrian. Thoughts on extended dimensions. Flying saucer review, v. 9, July-Aug. 1963: 8-9.

Article assumes that some, at least, of the contact claims are genuine and inquires into the possible motives of those who are allegedly visiting us.

Creighton, Gordon W. Amazing news from Russia. Flying saucer review, v. 8, Nov.-Dec. 1962: 27-28.

Translation of an article by Signor Alberto Fenoglio stating that the USSR's munitions plants, atomic installations, airfields, and missile bases are under constant UFO surveillance. Article appeared in Oltre il cielo: missili & razzi, Issue No. 105, June 1-15, 1962.

----- The most amazing case of all. Analysis of the Brazilian farmer's story. Flying saucer review, v. 11, Mar.-Apr. 1965: 5-8.

Author analyses details of Antonio Villas Boas story that he was taken aboard a landed flying saucer and seduced by a white-skinned, red-haired, slant-eyed woman. He speculates that the mission of some extraterrestrial visitors might be to breed a mixed race--a new race which would have inherited some of our characteristics, including our ability to live in a mixture of 80% nitrogen and 20% oxygen.

----- Postscript to the most amazing case of all. Flying saucer review, v. 11, July-Aug. 1965: 24-25.

Author suggests that far from being sensational, the account of the seduction of a Brazilian farmer aboard a landed flying saucer by an apparently extra-terrestrial woman "is nothing new in the long history of the planet earth." He cites instances of apparently similar incidents.

----- A small "experiment"? Flying saucer review, v. 13, Nov.-Dec. 1967: 16-17, 20.

Report of a series of five cases of sudden and inexplicable loss of conscious-ness at Barra de Tijuca, Brazil, accompanying UFO sightings. All presented identical features, and all occurred in a very restricted area and within an absolute limit of thirty minutes. Corroborated by reputable physicians and hospital staff. It is suggested that a UFO might have been carrying out some "test" on earthmen designed to ascertain such things as degree of "susceptibility" of the "targets," and the speed with which ambulances and doctors can respond in emergencies.

Duclout, Jorge A., and Napy Duclout. Unico documento confirmado sobre el
origen, estructura y destino de los platos voladores; transcripcion de
las grabaciones, sobre alambre, registradas durante experimentaciones
psiquicas en que se concerto una cita con un plato volador, la cual fue
complida en la fecha preestablecida; 2da. Edicion, ampliada con los
testimonios del pasaje de un plato volador, el 6 de Septiember de 1954.
Buenos Aires, America Tecnica & Editorial J. A. Duclout, 1956. 179 p.

Edwards, Frank. Frank Edwards' report: what do flying saucers want? Fate,
v. 10, Sept. 1957: 19-27.

A scientist (who asked to remain anonymous) theorizes that beings from
Mars are transporting minerals mined on the moon and water taken
from the earth back to their own planet in what we call "flying saucers."

----- Frank Edwards' report: why shoot the moon? Fate, v. 11, May 1958: 41-47.

Cites evidence of unusual UFO activity near both polar regions, with numerous
reports of UFOs moving north and south at considerable altitude, presumably in transit from one pole to the other. Suggests that "unknowns" may
have established a base on the moon.

----- The spies from outer space. Real, v. 5, Nov. 1954: 20-21, 58-60.

Evidence is given by the author to support his belief that a "blanket of
silence" imposed by the Government is preventing the public from getting
all the facts about unidentified flying objects. He also suggests that flying
saucers are extraterrestrial and engaged in reconnaissance activities.

Farish, Lucius. Cattle rustling by UFO. Fate, v. 19, Apr. 1966: 42-45.

"Rustling" of a heifer from the farm of Alexander Hamilton by UFO on
April 21, 1897, is described.

Fawcett, George D. Current UFO status. Flying saucers, June-1968: 18-19.

During 1967, 93 UFO landings, 81 UFO car chases, 62 UFO photographs,
36 UFO plane encounters, 30 UFO occupant reports, 11 radar trackings of
UFOs, and 9 power failures related to UFO appearances were reported
worldwide.

----- The flying saucers are hostile. Flying saucers, Feb. 1961: 12-21, 58.

Chronicles apparently hostile acts by UFOs 1944-1960. Lists statements
that UFOs are extraterrestrial spacecraft by Air Chief Marshall Lord
Dowding; Dr. Hermann Oberth; Lt. Col. John O'Mara; Wilbur B. Smith;
Albert M. Chop; and General L. M. Chassin.

Ferguson, William. A message from outer space. Oak Park, Ill., Golden Age
Press, 1955. 54 p.

A translation decoding the Book of Revelations allegedly given to author telepathically by "Khauga, the angel who gave it to St. John." Flying saucers are said to be the spacecraft of "perfected beings" who are "progressed to a four dimensional state of reality" and who are "preparing earth for the second coming of Jesus."

Flanders, C. M. Superman--does he really exist? Flying saucers, Oct. 1959: 16-19, 45.

Author postulates a "Federation" of super beings who are keeping earth man's efforts to invade space under surveillance.

The flying saucer menace. New York and London, Universal Publishing and Distributing Corp., 1967. 64 p.

Facts and photographs that would seem to indicate UFO hostility.

Fontes, Olavo T. Brazilian top secret report revealed. Flying saucers, Feb. 1960: 6-14, 24.

Three instances are related in which UFOs sighted in Brazil in 1957 seemed to have hostile intent and to possess a weapon used as a means of defense and attack that completely disrupts electrical systems.

----- Dying girl saved by humanoid surgeons. Flying saucer review, v. 13, Sept.-Oct. 1967: 5-6.

Entities from a flying saucer allegedly "operated" with an instrument resembling a flashlight on a girl dying of cancer (Oct. 25, 1958.). Incident occured in Petropolis, Brazil. A complete cure was reportedly effected.

----- Project Argus and the "anonymous" satellite. Flying saucers, Oct. 1959: 8-12.

Author suggests that the mission of nuclear missile launching Project Argus may have been to destroy an unidentified satellite that circled the earth from Aug. 16, 1959, until Argus' warheads were exploded in space Aug. 27, Aug. 30, and Sept. 6. Satellite may have been associated with UFOs, author speculates.

Gaddis, Vincent H. Survey of mysterious disappearances In his Invisible horizons. Philadelphia, Chilton Co., 1965 p. 161-225.

Describes disappearances of men and aircraft under circumstances that would suggest kidnapping by extraterrestrials.

Giles, Gordon A. The UFOs have taken over the earth. Monsieur, v. 9, Apr. 1967: 10-13, 54-55.

It is claimed that reported UFO activities seem to fall into a definite pattern consistent with the idea of an "earth patrol" carried on by other beings.

Gli UFO debattuti all' ONU. Centro unico nazionale per lo studio del fenomeni ritenuti di natura extraterrestre. Notiziario, No. 6, 1967:

Report on Dr. James E. McDonald's June 7, 1967, speech before the U. N. Outer Space Committee expressing belief that UFOs may be extraterrestrial spacecraft on reconnaisance missions to earth.

Grant, W. V. Men from the moon in America. Dallas, Texas, The Author, [195-] 31 p.

"Space men" who have allegedly contacted certain humans are supernatural beings from an evil (anti-Christ) source and are not from the moon, other planets, or a Russian satellite, the author postulates. Their goal of ruling the world is to be accomplished by deceiving and thereby influencing mankind.

----- Men in the flying saucers identified. Dallas, Tex. , The Author, [195-] 32 p.

Author postulates that flying saucers are real and that there are supernatural beings in them; however, he claims that these spirits are demoniac anti- Christ forces attempting to dupe man and take over our world.

Hapgood, Charles H. The Piri Reis map of 1513. Keene, N. H. , The Author, 1962. 48 p.

The accuracy of both latitude and longitude throughout the Piri Reis map of 1513 is inexplicable in terms of our present ideas of the extent of geographical knowledge and cartographic science in ancient times or in the Renaissance, the author contends. It has been speculated that data used were from aerial survey by an extraterrestrial spacecraft.

Hecker, Randall C. Did UFO sabotage Mariner IV? Fate, v. 20, May 1967: 32-37.

Appearance of UFO near Tidbinbilla [Australia] tracking station and con-comitant loss of Mariner IV [space probe] signals on July 14, 1965, is suggested as defensive measure by intelligences controlling UFO to prevent relay of information that life exists on Mars.

Heline, Corinne. America's invisible guidance. Los Angeles, New Age Press, 1949. 175 p.

An "invisible hierarchy" is postulated by the author composed of an "exalted brotherhood" that has elected to render world service by guarding and guiding world destiny "from the higher levels of the inner planes. "

Is the U. S. government expecting invaders from space? Flying saucers
from other worlds, Aug. 1957: 16-21.

Presents "factual" though circumstantial evidence to support theory that
USAF knows that some of the unidentified objects observed are from other
worlds and is taking measures to repulse an extraterrestrial invasion force.

Keel, John A. Secret UFO bases across the U. S. Saga, v. 36, Apr. 1968: 30-33,
86, 89-90, 92-94, 96.

Author suggests that "while everyone has been studying the skies, searching
for a clue to the origin of the UFOs, the objects and their occupants may
have been happily nesting almost in our very midst, quietly preparing for
their 'D-Day'!"

----- The UFO kidnappers. Saga, v. 33, Feb. 1967: 10-14, 50, 52-54, 56-60, 62.

Documents instances where UFOs have tracked and sometimes kidnapped
humans. Reports cases where airborne planes have been engulfed by UFOs.

----- UFO report: the sinister men in black. Fate, v. 21, Apr. 1968: 32-39.

Cites many reports of appearance of "men in black." Suggests they might
come from some group or organization directly related to the UFO phenomenon and are successfully infiltrating our cities and villages. Their
mission seems to be to "silence" individuals who have had UFO experiences.

Keyhoe, Donald E. The flying saucers are real. New York, Fawcett Publications,
1950. 175 p.

Author states his conclusions about the UFO phenomenon: (1) the earth has been
under periodic observation from another planet, or other planets, for at least
two centuries; (2) this observation suddenly increased in 1947, following the
series of A-bomb explosions begun in 1945; (3) the observation, now intermittent, is part of a long-range survey and will continue indefinitely.

Larson, Kenneth L. Charles Fort and the UFO. Flying saucers, July 1959:
20-23, 42.

Speculates on whether sightings of unidentified flying objects between
November 1896 and April 1897 reported by Charles Fort implied that
an aerial survey of the world took place.

Layne, Meade. The coming of the guardians. Vista, Calif., Borderland
Sciences Research Associates Foundation, Inc. (P.O. Box 548), 1964. 72 p.

UFO phenomenon is discussed, the nature and origin of the spacecraft, and
the reasons for their incursion into earth's atmosphere. Author postulates
they do not belong to the world of three-dimensional matter, but emerge
from denser etheric worlds.

Lindsay, Gordon. The riddle of the flying saucers. Dallas, Tex., The Voice of Healing Publishing Co., 1966. 31 p.

Author says that reports of flying saucers landing in the desert, claiming to come from other planets, claiming to be creatures of a high state evolutionary development, claiming to bring knowledge to the human race to save it from disaster -- do not ring true. He suggests that the whole thing has the earmarks of the diabolical.

Lorenzen, Coral. The Fitzgerald investigation: what it means. Flying saucers, May 1959: 47-50.

On Sept. 21, 1958, Mrs. William Fitzgerald of Sheffield Lake, Ohio, allegedly saw an apparently intelligently controlled metallic object about 22 feet in diameter and six feet thick; luminescent smoke seemed to issue from nozzles in apertures on the rim. Author compares this report to similar ones throughout the world that were accompanied by mention of electrical interference and power failure and concludes that the craft may be engaged in weapons testing.

----- Flying saucers: the startling evidence of the invasion from outer space. New York and Toronto, Signet Books, New American Library, 278 p.

Author presents evidence in support of theory that UFOs are reconnoitering earth's water reserves and military defenses, gathering flora and fauna, and tracking our space missiles. Original title: The Great Flying Saucer Hoax (New York, William-Frederick Press, 1962).

----- The great flying saucer hoax; the UFO facts and their interpretation. New York, William-Frederick Press, for the Aerial Phenomena Research Organization of Tucson, Ariz., 1962. 257 p.

Author, director of Aerial Phenomena Research Organization, presents documented information to support theory that UFOs are not only real, but are extraterrestrial and unfriendly and that visitations follow a pattern indicating military reconnaissance and biological and ecological survey. Published also with title Flying Saucers in paperback edition by New American Library, Inc. (Signet book T3058), New York.

Luna, Walter F. Los UFOs y su posible mision en la tierra. Montevideo, The Author, 1968. 15 p.

Assuming that UFOs are extraterrestrial spacecraft under intelligent control, the author speculates on their mission to the planet earth.

McDonald, James E. Are UFOs extraterrestrial surveillance craft? Tucson, Ariz., The Author, 1968. 4 p.

Stressing the need for establishment of a vigorous investigation program of the UFO phenomenon, the author noted that close-range sightings of machine like objects of unconventional nature and unconventional performance characteristics, seen at low altitudes, appeared to be occurring all over the globe, possibly with increasing frequency. Suggestions that such observations can be explained away in terms of meteorological optics or in terms of atmospheric plasmas cannot be supported with cogent scientific arguments, he said. Talk given Mar. 26, 1968, before the American Institute of Aeronautics and Astronautics, Los Angeles, Calif.

Marais, D. Are we being watched? Personality, v. 1410, Jan. 1, 1954: 26-28.

Misraki, Paul. Les extraterrestres, par Paul Thomas [pseud.] Paris, Plon, 1962. 224 p.

Develops hypothesis that from earliest antiquity to modern times, extra-terrestrial beings have kept earth under surveillance, have at times visited this planet, and have frequently modified the course of history by means of spectacular appearances. Cites biblical passages and ancient manuscripts.

The mystery satellite: a study in confusion. Flying saucer review, v. 6, May-June 1960: 25-26.

Possible extraterrestrial origin is discussed of satellite discovered circling earth in near-polar orbit in February 1960. Reconnaissance mission possible.

Oberth, Hermann. Flying saucers come from a distant world. American weekly, Oct. 24, 1954: 4-5.

Author states that flying saucers are possibly manned by intelligent observers who are members of a race that may have been investigating earth for centuries and that they possibly have been sent to conduct systematic, long-range investigations, first of men, animals and vegetation, and more recently of atomic centers, armaments, and centers of armament production.

Philip, Brother. Secret of the Andes. Clarksburg, W. Va., Saucerian Books, 1961. 151 p.

Discusses the connection of lost cities of South America and the UFO pheno-menon. Postulates that current presence of numerous extraterrestrial spacecraft in earth's atmosphere is to assist in evacuation of earth following an impending catastrophe.

Ribera, Antonio. More about UFOs and the sea. Flying saucer review, v. 11, Nov.-Dec. 1965: 17-18.

Author summarizes events which may indicate underwater reconnaissance by UFOs of submarine bases.

Sanctillean. Flying saucers: portents of these "last days." Santa Barbara, Calif., I. F. Rowny Press, 1950. 39 p.

Some of the "mystery ships" which so puzzle mankind today are said to be observation scouts from other planets and dimensions seeking to discover where next there may be a rocket experiment or an atomic bomb explosion.

Settimo, Gianni. Gli U. F. O. preparano un "Rapporto Kinsey" interplanetario? Clypeus, v. 5, Feb. 1968: 33-34.

Article suggests that some UFOs might be studying the sex habits of humans and cites cases that would seem to support the theory.

Sprinkle, R. Leo. Patterns of UFO reports. Laramie, Wyoming, The Author, 1967. 15 p.

References are cited which survey the literature on UFO reports, including explanatory hypotheses. Results of various investigators are summarized, with emphasis on evidence indicating that UFOs are spacecraft controlled by intelligent beings who are conducting an intensive survey of the earth. Suggestions are offered with regard to psychological procedures and techniques for investigating UFO reports, with emphasis on hypnotic techniques and the pendulum technique for comparing the reliability of conscious and subconscious information from UFO observers. Speech given at Sept. 1-5, 1968, meeting of American Psychological Association, Washington, D. C., under title "Psychological Problems of Gathering UFO Data."

Steiger, Brad. Flying saucers on the attack. Saga, v. 34, 1967: 32-35, 76, 78-81, 83-84.

UFO cases are cited which would seem to indicate hostile intent.

Steiger, Brad and Joan Whritenour. Flying saucers are hostile. New York, Award Books, 1967. 160 p.

Documented cases in which UFOs have allegedly been involved in murders, kidnappings, auto crashes, destruction of airplanes, and other acts of aggression.

The strange intruder. Newsweek, v. 56, July 4, 1960: 83.

Radio astronomer Ronald Bracewell comments on possibility that an unidentified satellite from an extraterrestrial civilization is orbiting the sun.

Tomas, Andrew. Their purpose of coming? Australian flying saucer review, no. 9, Nov. 1966: 5-7.

Summary of theories that attempt to explain the purpose of extraterrestrial spacecraft visitations in the past, in modern history, and currently.

Wellman, Wade. Sense and speculation. Flying saucer review, v. 11, Sept. - Oct. 1965: 30-31.

The belief is expressed that two or more races are participating in scrutiny of our planet and may long since have "taken it over," without our knowledge, since their doings might not attract our notice.

Willems, Louis. De lieve invasie. A.B.C., Oct. 8, 1966: 14-16.

Speculation on whether increasing reports of worldwide sightings of UFOs harbinger an invasion ჟy extraterrestrial ჟeings.

----- Wordt de aarde door andere planeten bespied? A.B.C., June 4, 1966: 6-11.

Summary of information that would seem to indicate that earth has been under surveillance by extraterrestrial pilots of the spacecraft oჟserved in earth's atmosphere since earliest recorded history.

Wilkins, Harold T. Flying saucers on the attack. New York, Citadel Press, 1954. 329 p.

Author traces reports of cosmic visitors to earth's skies as far back as 729 A.D. Conjectures that sinister or hostile forces of unknown interplanetary origin may act to keep space explorers from earth well within limits of substratosphere. London ed. has title: Flying Saucers from the Moon. Published also in paperback edition by Ace Books (A-11), New York.

----- Flying saucers uncensored. New York, Citadel Press, 1955. 255 p.

Author catalogues UFO sightings and incidents over U.K., Western Europe, U.S., and Australia from 1947 through 1955 and speculates that extraterrestrial visitants are possibly established in bases on moon and other planets; a cosmic general staff may receive reports on terrestrial affairs as well as biological and ecological samples from earth for purposes of study and experimentation. Published also in British edition(London, Arco, 1956), and in paperback edition by Pyramid Pubns., Inc. (T1651), New York.

Williamson, George Hunt. Other tongues--other flesh. Amherst, Wis., Amherst Press, 1953. 448 p.

Author affirms that extraterrestrial visitors have been coming to earth in spacecraft for several millenia and quotes references to them in the Bible, ancient mythology, and old documents. He relates technological and sociological progress on earth to influence of space intelligences and cites references from latest authenticated UFO sightings to support theory that visitors from space are now making themselves known to the world as a whole to lead mankind to a new, enlightened age.

----- Secret places of the lion. Amherst, Wis., Amherst Press, 1958. 230 p.

Author cites Biblical passages and material in ancient manuscripts to
support theory that many leaders of the past were men and women from
other worlds in time and space who had migrated to earth in what today are
called UFOs to assist mankind in its climb from beasthood to manhood.
He discloses discoveries suggesting that ancient civilizations in South America,
especially, had continuing contact with extraterrestrial visitors.

Williamson, George Hunt and John McCoy. UFOs confidential!; the meaning
ɔehind the most closely guarded secret of all time. Corpus Christi, Tex.,
Essene Press, 1958. 100 p.

NEWS MANAGEMENT

Bryant, Larry W. A hard look at UFO news management. Fate, v. 17, Feb. 1964:
41-44.

Author asserts that "paper curtain" around UFO news includes the local as
well as national level.

Edwards, Frank. Frank Edwards' report: is the UFO "curtain" lifting? Fate,
v. 11, June 1958: 47-54.

Cites instances of apparent suppression of UFO news by the Air Force and
analyzes current official actions that seem to indicate a change in policy.

Strentz, Herb. Seeing saucers. Columbia journalism review, Fall 1966: 23-25.

Press coverage of reported UFO sightings is treated.

OCCUPANTS

Barker, Gray. The case for non-human space visitors. Flying saucers, Feb. 1959:
18-23.

Cites landing/contact reports that would seem to indicate that some saucers
either contain or are piloted by non-humanoid entities. Mentions speculation
that alien animals might ɔe deposited on earth, then taken up again to undergo
laboratory examination to determine how the atmosphere, disease germs, and
other environmental factors on earth had affected them.

----- Gray Barker's book of saucers. Clarksburg, W. Va., Saucerian Books,
1965. 77 p.

Book catalogues UFO sightings in all parts of the world, 1962-1963. Saucer landings, communication between saucer crews and humans, seizure of terrestrials by saucer crews, mating of extraterrestrials with terrestrials, and the "men in black" are discussed.

Barker, Gray. The monster and the saucer. Fate, v. 6, Jan. 1953: 12-17.

Account of author's investigation of sighting on September 12, 1952, near Flatwoods, W. Va., of a "ten-foot, red-faced monster, which sprayed a foul, sickening gas." There were seven witnesses whose stories agreed.

Bowen, Charles. Crash-landed UFO near Mendoza. Flying saucer review, v. 11, May-June 1965: 7-9.

Details of case in which a mysterious artefact "fell" at San Miguel, Argentina (January 1965). According to newspaper account, local inhabitants declared the object was a flying saucer and that they saw "little" individuals walking around the craft in uniforms like divers' suits.

----- The spectre of Winterfold. Flying saucer review, v. 14, Jan.-Feb. 1968: 15-17.

Encounter of young couple on Nov. 13, 1967, near Cranleigh, England, with a 4 1/2 foot luminous entity that was accompanied by a nauseating odor. Description of entity was similar to that of the "Flatwoods monster."

Brandt, Ivan. The problem of the Frankensteins. Flying saucer review, v. 13, May-June 1967: 16-19.

Incidents are summarized which seem to support the author's speculation that some extraterrestrials have arrived at a stage of chemical and physiological knowledge which has enabled them to produce a very advanced type of biological robot which they send or bring with them to our planet to help with their research.

Cahn, J. P. Flying saucers and the mysterious little men. True, v. 32, Sept. 1952: 17-19, 102-112.

Report of investigation into allegations in Frank Scully's book, Behind the Flying Saucers (New York, Henry Holt, 1950), that a crashed flying saucer and corpses of its three-foot-tall crew had been taken into custody by the U. S. Air Force. Claims prove untrue and the book a hoax.

Caputo, Livio. Rapporto sui dischi volanti: qualcuno ha parlato con "loro." Epoca, v. LXIV, Sept. 11, 1966: 30-38.

Report of creatures seen in or near spacecraft of apparently extraterrestrial origin in countries throughout the world, 1950-1965.

Clark, Jerome. A contact claim. Flying saucer review, v. 11, Jan.-Feb. 1965: 30-32.

Noting the way in which the "beings" associated with the 1897 "airship" sightings seemed interested in reinforcing the belief that the craft was of mundane origin, the author concludes that the extraterrestrials either were engaged in some unknown activity in which they did not want their real identity made known, or that they chose to hide their existence realizing that the comparative unsophistication of nineteenth century Americans would not permit them to accept the interplanetary answer.

----- The meaning of contact. Flying saucer review, v. 11, Sept.-Oct. 1965: 28-29.

Speculating that the UFO beings might put a false cover over their activities so as to keep officialdom or anyone else from coming close to the truth, the author suggests that contact claims become a tool with a two-fold purpose: to discourage legitimate inquiry into the saucer field by making it look ridiculous, and to instill false ideas into the minds of those who do go to investigate the subject.

----- UFO landings in South America. Flying saucers, Oct. 1966: 24-25.

Author reports alleged landings of UFOs during September in Brazil and Peru and describes the "ufonauts" observed.

Creighton, Gordon. The extraordinary happenings at Casa Blanca. Flying saucer review, v. 13, Sept.-Oct. 1967: 16-18.

On Aug. 22, 1955, a group of children playing in the garden of a home in Casa Blanca, California, allegedly first sighted silvery, spinning discs and later 3-ft.-tall transparent beings who emerged from landed craft. Author considers accounts of incident by Coral Lorenzen in Flying Saucer Review's The Humanoids and by Winona Cromwell in a 1955 issue of the Journal of the Boderland Sciences Research Association.

Do flying saucers ever land? Flying saucers, Oct. 1966: 30.

Lists reports of flying saucer landings worldwide and encounters with humanoid occupants 1964-1966.

Edwards, Frank. Frank Edwards' report: space men - or monsters: Fate, v. 11, Sept. 1958: 76-83.

Analysis of conflicting reports of alleged flying saucer occupants and discussions of how much truth reports contained.

Eiseley, Loren C. Little men and flying saucers. Harper's, v. 206, Mar. 1953: 86-91.

Reasons are given for the author's non-belief in the two-foot-tall beings described as crewmen of extraterrestrial spacecraft allegedly sighted: a normal human being cannot function with a capacity, at the very minimum, of less than 900 cubic centimeters of capacity; a man with a hundred-cubic-centimeter brain will not be a builder of flying saucers--he will be less intelligent than an ape.

Entities associated with Type I sightings. Part two: the scientific interpretation. Flying saucer review, v. 10, May-June 1964: 3-5.

Statistical characteristics found in considering selected accounts of "landing" and the "entities" described in the reports are reviewed and discussed in terms of scientific interest.

Étranges creatures. Phenomènes spatiaux, Dec. 1966: 32-34.

Description of "occupants" allegedly seen in conjunction with landed flying saucers in France, Argentina, Venezuela and Peru.

Evans, Gordon H. Do the UFOs use a paralysis ray? Fate, v. 19, Dec. 1966: 101-105.

Evidence is presented suggesting that extraterrestrials visiting earth use a paralysis device to stun or immobilize defensively.

Fawcett, George D. Flying saucers: explosive situation for 1968. Flying saucers, Apr. 1968: 22-25.

Study of 1967 reports of UFO incidents from 40 states and 20 foreign countries. Included are 75 landings, 56 photographs, 52 car chases, 30 pilot pursuits, 14 "occupant" reports, 11 radar trackings, and 7 UFO-related power failures. Many of these incidents occured in North Carolina, Pennsylvania, New England, Florida, California, Ohio, England, Canada, Argetina, Australia, Peru, and Mexico.

Flying saucers: UFO report--No. 2. New York, Dell Publishing Co., 1967. 64 p.

Summary of the "sense and nonsense speculation and theories" relating to the UFO phenomenon. Includes information on landings, saucer occupants, the Michigan "flap," commonly reported UFO types, and UFO research organizations. Details are given of sighting at Wanaque Reservoir (N. J.) on Jan. 13, 1966, and mysterious glowing particles seen by John Glenn while in orbit around the earth Feb. 20, 1962.

Fontes, Olavo T. Dying girl saved by humanoid surgeons. Flying saucer review, v. 13, Sept.-Oct. 1967: 5-6.

Entities from a flying saucer allegedly "operated" with an instrument resembling a flashlight on a girl dying of cancer (Oct. 25, 1958.). Incident occured in Petropolis, Brazil. A complete cure was reportedly effected.

Fouéré, René. Seraient-ils des revenants du futur? Phenomenes spatiaux,
June 1966: 11-14.

Author speculates on an explanation for the fact that UFO occupants do not
attempt widespread contact with humans: they might be time travelers
returning to the past from the future.

----- Surhumains ou sous-humains, anges ou démons, que sont les extra-
terrestres? Phénomènes spatiaux, Mar. 1966: 5-11.

Speculation on the nature of the extraterrestrial beings apparently visiting
earth based in part on reports of "contactees."

----- Une lumiere qui traverse les murs. Phenomenes spatiaux, Mar. 1967:
23-24.

Accounts of incidents in Argentina during October 1963 and January 1965 when
UFOs caused individuals observing them to lose all mobility by directing at
the houses they occupied what appeared to be a beam of light.

Fuller, Curtis. Little men from all over. Fate, v. 8, Mar. 1955: 30-33.

Descriptions of flying saucer occupants sent to Fate from all over the world
are summarized. Reports were from Muenster, Germany; Quarouble,
France; Mofjell, Norway; Bucine, Tuscany, Italy; Sudbury, Ont., Canada;
and Coldwater, Kansas.

----- The men who ride in saucers. Fate, v. 7, May 1954: 44-47.

Alleged contacts of earthmen with crewmen of flying saucers are reported,
including the stories of Truman Bethurum, George Adamski, Orfeo Angelucci,
and John Black and John Van Allen.

Gilman, Peter. Do the cherubim come from Mars? Flying saucer review, v. 13,
Sept. -Oct. 1967: 19-21, 29.

On Apr. 24, 1964, Gary Wilcox, who was working his farm in Newark Valley,
N. Y., allegedly saw a UFO land in a nearby field. The crew were two
humanoid 4-ft. -tall entities who were holding specimens of soil and sod,
said they were from Mars, and who explained that although they had been
obtaining their food from the atmosphere, they had to find a way to
rehabilitate their soil to raise food. Author suggests that "food taken from
the atmosphere might be analogous to the celestial manna described in the
Bible in Exodus; the angels involved in this manifestation were the cherubim
and therefore may have come from Mars." The entities also said there would
be coming changes in the universe which would affect our solar system and
that Mars may be where earth is now. Author draws a parallel between
this information and Velikovsky's theory in Worlds in Collision.

Goupil, Jean. L'hypothèse du champ repulsif: essaie d'explications des incidents de Kelly. Phénomènes spatiaux, Mar. 1967: 18-23.

A hypothesis is advanced to explain behavior of the "creatures" seen at Kelly, Kentucky, on Aug. 21, 1955.

Grant, W. V. Men in the flying saucers identified. Dallas, Tex. , The Author, [195-] 32 p.

Author postulates that flying saucers are real and that there are supernatural beings in them; however, he claims that these spirits are demoniac anti-Christ forces attempting to dupe man and take over our world.

Greenbank, Anthony. Creatures from outer space (stepping from flying saucer). In The book of survival. New York and Evanston, Harper & Row, 1967. 34 p.

Advice on what to do in the event of encounter with crew disembarking from landed flying saucer: (1) avoid rapid forceful movement; (2) use no shrill sounds; (3) breathe quietly; (4) avoid giving a direct menacing gaze.

Helland, Albert E. They caught a spaceman. Fate, v. 11, Mar. 1958: 62.

Author quotes from ancient manuscript to cite instance when an apparently extraterrestrial being was captured and released during the 13th century.

Hugill, Joanna. On the road from Sydney to Melbourne. Flying saucer review, v. 14, Mar. -Apr. 1968: 3, 11.

Story of the alleged refusal by an Australian motocyclist on Aug. 24, 1967, to respond to the invitation of two silver-clad figures standing beside a saucer-shaped craft to come aboard. Author prepared article from transcript of taped interview with witness by Peter Norris, chairman of Victorian Flying Saucer Research Society, and M. Thornhill.

The humanoids. Flying saucer review, Oct. -Nov. 1966. 32 p.

A survey of worldwide reports of landings of unconventional aerial objects and their alleged occupants: The Villa Santina [Italy] Case; Few and Far Between [Landing and occupant reports a rarity in the British Isles], Charles Bowen; The Pattern Behind the UFO Landings [Report on the analysis of 200 documented observations made in 1954], Jacques Vallée; The Landing at Villares Del Saz [Spain], Antonio Ribera; The Humanoids in Latin America, Gordon Creighton; The Landing at Socorro, N. M. [New light on a classic case] , W. T. Powers; UFO Occupants in United States Reports, Coral Lorenzen; Questions on the Occupants, Donald B. Hanlon; The Problem of Non-Contact, Aimé Michel; Was it a Landing at Silverton [South Africa]?, Ed Pitlo and Edgar Sievers.

Ibson, Jack. Did a space visitor land in Bradford? Flying saucer news, Autumn 1955: 4-5.

A small humanoid being about 4-ft tall, dressed in skin tight black clothing, arms down by sides and feet together, was allegedly seen in Yorkshire, England, on August 15, 1955. It did not walk, but hopped with both feet together. A cigar-shaped UFO was seen in the sky earlier in the evening.

Jansen, Clare John. Little tin men in Minnesota. Fate, v. 19, Feb. 1966: 36-40.

Sighting of rocket-like UFO and its tin can-shaped occupants on Oct. 23, 1965, near Long Prairie, Minn., is reported.

Keel, John A. Never mind the saucer! Did you see the guys who were driving? True, v. 48, February 1967: 36-37, 78, 80-83.

Article cites cases reported worldwide of creatures observed in vicinity of grounded UFOs. Similarities and differences in alleged appearance, behavior, and dress are noted.

----- New landing and creature reports. Flying saucer review, v. 12, Nov.-Dec. 1966: 5-8.

Reports of strange objects and lights in the skies above Erie, Pa., and surrounding districts during July 1966 are discussed and a UFO landing and unearthly creature sightings during the same period detailed.

Knight, Oscar F. Wolverton trail event: a visitor from Venus. Strathmore, Calif., 1963. 11 p.

During a camping trip in Sequoia National Park, Calif. on July 1, 1955, author observed a "mother ship" from which a number of smaller UFOs were discharged. He later encountered a being whose strangeness of manner and speech led to speculation that he may have been an occupant of the strange craft.

Ley, Willy. The mighty invaders from outer space. Catholic digest, v. 22, Apr. 1958: 25-29.

"Portrait" of the man from planet X: (1) he breathes air; (2) he eats both plants and meat; (3) he is probably not much larger than the largest human being; (4) he weighs at least 40 pounds and probably more; (5) he has a skull of some kind; (6) he has two eyes and ears; (7) his eyes and ears are near the brain; and (8) he has hands and feet. Condensed from This Week, Nov. 10, 1957.

Lloyd, Dan. Crawling lights--a new development. Flying saucer review, v. 13, May-June 1967: 29-30.

Report on alleged sightings in Ohio during March 1966 of strange objects including two types of spaceship-like craft; doughnut-shaped pulsating lights that "crawled" along the walls of a house; and moving, stump-like creatures.

Lorenzen, Coral. Besieged by UFOs. Fate, v. 17, June 1964: 34-38.

On October 18, 1963, truck driver Eugenio Douglas was reportedly accosted by three "robots" near Monte Maix, Argentina. On October 21, the entire Moreno family in Cordoba province, Argentina, allegedly saw a landed UFO; five other discs kept the family under seige with beams of light that made the house "hot as an oven."

----- The reality of the little men. Flying saucers, Dec. 1958: 26-34.

Relates incidents where "little men" were reportedly seen in connection with landed UFOs in South America, 1950-1955.

Lorenzen, Coral and Jim Lorenzen. Flying saucer occupants. Introd. by Dr. Frank B. Salisbury. New York, Signet Books, The New American Library, 1967. 213 p.

Reports from men and women who have allegedly seen and communicated with extraterrestrial creatures. Authors, directors of the Aerial Phenomena Research Organization, claim that eyewitness reliability has been checked by psychiatric and other scientific methods. Also, an in-depth analysis of the role of the CIA in the study of UFO sightings is given.

Michel, Aimé. Flying saucers in Europe: meeting with the Martian. Fate, v. 10, Sept. 1957: 43-46.

Account of alleged encounter by Antoine Mazaud on Sept. 10, 1954, near Limoges, France, with a creature apparently from a landed "flying saucer." Other inhabitants of Limoges reported sighting on the same evening a reddish disc that left a bluish trail.

----- Flying saucers in Europe: the little men. Fate, v. 10, Nov. 1957: 72-76.

On Sept. 10, 1954, Marius Dewilde allegedly saw two creatures that appeared to be crew of a "flying saucer" that had landed on railroad tracks in an area near Valenciennes, France. Details of subsequent investigation are given.

Miller, Max B. Recent dramatic saucer reports. Fate, v. 13, Jan. 1960: 29-32.

Details are given of UFO sightings in New Zealand, Australia, and New Guinea during June-July 1959 where occupants were observed by responsible persons.

"M.O.C." et leurs occupants vus au sol en 1967. Lumieres dans la nuit, no. 93, Mar.-Apr. 1968: 14-16.

Landed UFOs and their occupants seen during 1967 in Chile, Spain, Argentina, and the U.S.

The New Zealand "flap" of 1909. Flying saucer review, v. 10, Nov. -Dec. 1964: 32-33.

Discussion of newspaper reports of cigar-shaped flying objects and their occupants observed over New Zealand in 1909.

Oberth, Hermann. Flying saucers come from a distant world. American weekly, Oct. 24, 1954: 4-5.

Author states that flying saucers are possibly manned by intelligent observers who are members of a race that may have been investigating earth for centuries and that they possibly have been sent out to conduct systematic, long-range investigations, first of men, animals and vegetation, and more recently of atomic centers, armaments, and centers of armament production.

Ormond, Ron. I found a little green man. Flying saucers from other worlds, Aug. 1957: 22-26.

Miner claims that flying saucers led him to cave where he discovered mummified remains of two creatures 15-16 inches tall.

Pereira, Flavio A. O livro vermelho dos discos voadores. São Paulo, Edicoes Florenca Ltda. , 1966: 486 p.

Handbook containing summary tables of information on all aspects of the UFO phenomenon worldwide: sightings, occupants, electromagnetic effects, radar detection, professions of witnesses, physiological effects, geographical distribution, and statements by prominent individuals.

Retour sur Valensole: les conclusions de notre enquêteur. Phénomènes spatiaux, Dec. 1965: 11-16.

The unanimous opinion of persons interrogating Maurice Masse concerning his July 1, 1965, encounter with landed UFO and its occupant is that his account of the incident is a truthful one.

Ribera, Antonio. What happened at Fatima? Flying saucer review, v. 10, Mar. -Apr. 1964: 12-14.

Resume of the miracle at Fatima, north of Lisbon, Portugal, which extended from May 13 to Oct. 7, 1917, in context of the UFO phenomenon. Author suggests that UFO occupants may present themselves in terms familiar to "contactees, " usually as divine manifestations.

Roberts, Keith. Reconsidering the mysterious "little men. " Saucer news, v. 12, Mar. 1965: 7-9.

Article reconsiders stories of crashed UFOs containing corpses of "little men. "

Robinson, Jack and Mary Robinson. The case for extraterrestrial little men. Saucer news, v. 13, Fall 1966: 7-9.

Presents scientifically feasible biological hypothesis for existence of humanoid extraterrestrial beings.

A saucer, two men, and "little creatures." Flying saucers, May 1959: 57-60.

Two young men, Hans Gustavson and Stig Rydberg, driving home from a dance near Halsingborg, Sweden, allegedly sighted a landed flying saucer and were attacked by four jelly-like lead-grey creatures a little more than four feet tall. Incident allegedly occurred Dec. 20, 1958. Reprinted from A.P.R.O. Bulletin.

Scully, Frank. Behind the flying saucers. New York, Henry Holt, 1950. 230 p.

Presents information to support position that UFOs are real and that official disclaimers of their existence by DOD are calculated to deceive the public. Claims that a crashed flying saucer and the corpses of its three-foot-tall crew were taken into custody by USAF.

Steep Rock flying saucer. Fate, v. 5, Feb.-Mar. 1952: 68-72.

Article consists of a letter originally published in the September and October 1950 issues of Steep Rock Echo, a house magazine of Steep Rock Iron Mines, Ltd., Steep Rock Lake, Ontario, Canada. Written by a senior employee of the mine, the letter reports a flying saucer sighted July 2, 1950, that landed on water and was apparently manned by robots.

Steiger, Brad. Strangers from the skies. New York, Award Books, 1966. 158 p.

Author cites cases (1897 to date) on a worldwide scale involving sightings of flying saucers and their crews by humans.

Steiger, Brad and Joan Whritenour. Abominable spacemen. Saga, v. 35, Feb. 1968: 34-35, 58-60, 62, 64.

Article postulates a connection between UFO sightings and landings and the recent reported appearance of gorilla-like humanoids throughout the U.S.

Thompson, William C. Houston bat man. Fate, v. 6, Oct. 1953: 26-27.

Figure of a man with wings like a bat, dressed in gray or black tight-fitting clothing was reportedly seen in Houston, Tex., on June 18, 1953. Figure was framed in a glow of light. Appearance of apparition paralleled in many ways object seen by seven residents of Flatwoods, W. Va., September 12, 1953.

UFO: flying saucers. Poughkeepsie, N.Y., Western Publishing Co., 1968.
64 p.

Comic book. Accounts of UFOs in ancient history, UFO kidnappings, and
"classic" sightings and landing cases, including those where occupants
were allegedly seen.

Vallée, Jacques. A descriptive study of the entities associated with the Type 1
sighting. Flying saucer review, v. 10, Jan.-Feb. 1964: 6-12.

Report on study of UFO sightings in which witnesses perceived forms in human
shape which they believed to be the pilots of the spacecraft. List of 80 UFO
sightings from 1909 through 1960 where pilots were observed with statistical
interpretation.

Wilkins, H. Percy. Mysteries of space and time. London, Frederick Muller,
Ltd., 1955. 208 p.

Mysteries on the land, in the sea, in the air, and in outer space are discussed. Chapter 2 is devoted to "Flying Things in Space" and investigates
the reliability of various accounts and probability of impending "invasion"
of earth. Author feels it is improbable that alien life could exist in our
atmosphere without a period of acclimatation in some inaccessible and remote
spot such as the interior of South America or amid the snows of the
Himalayas.

Winder. R.B.H. The little blue man on Studham common. Flying saucer review,
v. 13, July-Aug. 1967: 3-4.

Schoolboys playing on the common near Studham Village Primary School,
England, Jan. 28, 1967, allegedly saw a 3-ft.-tall man wearing a helmet and
emanating a greyish-blue glow. He wore a one-piece vestment extending down
to a broad black belt supporting a black box at the front about six inches square.
When pursued by the boys, he disappeared three times in a cloud of
yellowish mist.

ORIGIN AND NATURE

Allen, W. Gordon. Spacecraft from beyond three dimensions. New York,
Exposition Press, 1959. 202 p.

Develops thesis that the mind of man seems to be a many-levelled
(intellectual levels) receiver that tunes to the "universal thought source"
and that UFOs might therefore be thought-controlled "thought form
phenomena. "

Are "contact group" sightings metaphysical? Flying saucers, July-Aug. 1958:
12-15, 19.

Referring to the group of UFO investigators who place a mystical, religious, or metaphysical interpretation on the entire UFO phenomenon, author states these concepts cannot be rejected but must be considered. They could comprise a facet of the overall picture.

Avignon, Andre. Des animaux-machines? Phenomenes spatiaux, Nov. 1964: 13-14.

Compares physical details of UFO sighted at Vauriat, France, on Aug. 29, 1962, with objects sighted 1849-1872 and recorded by Charles Fort in Book of the Damned. Suggests a machine-like animal indigenous to space might be involved.

Barker, Gray. Hostile spacecraft. Flying saucers, Dec. 1958: 12-23, 78.

Review of Trevor James' book, They Live in the Sky (Los Angeles, New Age Publishing Co., 1958), and background information on James' involvement in UFO research. James suggests that UFOs may be invisible animals indigenous to our atmosphere.

Barton, Michael X. We want you. Los Angeles, Futura Press, 1960. 34 p.

Author suggests that not all UFOs come from outside or inside the planet earth but that some of them are Nazi-built (from the blueprints of Vikton Schauberger) at an armed fortress in Patagonia (Argentina) to which Adolph Hitler fled in July 1945. He speculates that the story of Hitler's suicide was fraudulent and that Hitler is still alive. The unfulfilled predictions of Karl Michalek between 1958 and 1960 are also analyzed.

Bessor, John P. Are the saucers space animals? Fate, v. 8, Dec. 1955: 6-12.

Flying disks, the author contends, are a form of space animal, or creature, of a highly attenuated (ectoplasmic?) substance, capable of materialization and dematerialization, whose propellant is a form of kinetic energy.

----- UFOs: animal or mineral? Fate, v. 20, Nov. 1967: 32-39.

Presents facts to substantiate theory that typical flying saucers are sky animals of an "ectoplasmic" substance and are capable of materialization and dematerialization.

The book of spaceships in their relationship with the earth. Los Angeles, DeVorss & Co., 1967. 47 p.

Discussion of origin and intent of extraterrestrial spacecraft in earth's atmosphere by one who alleges to be a traveler in these spacecraft as well as an aerial traveler without any kind of vehicle but his own body.

Bowen, Charles. Mystery animals. Flying saucer review, v. 10, Nov.-Dec. 1964: 15-17.

Marked increase in England during 1963-1964 in appearance of large mystery animals of the cat family is discussed. Reports indicate that depredations by the animals are sometimes accompanied by UFO sightings.

Bray, Derek, R. M. Flying saucers: a startling theory. Panorama, v. 1, Nov. 1962: 4-7.

Author points out that whenever angelic beings have made themselves visible to man, clothed in normal costume and speaking the language of the country, they have not been identified as such until they chose to make themselves known by an overt act of superhuman power or by identifying themselves by word of mouth; throughout the ages there must have been, and very probably still are, visitations by angels--probably in most cases appearing as normal human beings.

Bull, F. Malcolm. UFO handbook 2. London, British UFO Research Assn., [1964] 31 p.

Details are given of the various natural and man-made phenomena that could be misinterpreted as unidentified flying objects.

Campbell, John W., Jr. How do saucers fly? Pic, v. 23, Nov. 1952: 16-17, 73-74.

Reasons are given for the author's belief that flying saucers are intelligently manned extraterrestrial spacecraft. He speculates on where they come from and on why their pilots seem to prefer the western U. S.

Campione, Michael J. Reality of UFOs, their danger, their hope. Cinnaminson, N. J., The Author, 1965. 16 p.

General discussion of the UFO phenomenon, including recognizable characteristics, physiological effects on humans, statistics on sightings and landings, theories on their origin, and USAF policy.

Clarke, Arthur C. Flying saucers. Journal of the British Interplanetary Society, V. 12, May 1953: 97-100.

In author's opinion, UFOs are not material bodies because: (1) they have been observed to travel at accelerations which no material body could stand, and (2) despite the enormous speeds reported, no sonic booms are ever heard. He considers it possible that UFOs may "turn out to be of intelligent extra-terrestrial origin" but "if they are artificial, and come from other planets, it is fairly certain they are not spaceships... they will be something very much more sophisticated. "

----- What's up there? Holiday, v. 25, Mar. 1959: 32, 34-37, 39-40.

Author describes personal UFO sightings that proved to have conventional explanations. He suggests that many hard core unexplained UFOs may be "plasmoids" -- ball lightning.

Cohen, Daniel. Myths of the space age. New York, Dodd, Mead & Co., 1967: 278 p.

Author discusses "myths" -- including flying saucers -- that have persisted into modern times although mankind should by now know better. In his discussion of UFOs, he cites several "classic" sightings and gives the "scientific" explanation

Constance, Arthur. The inexplicable sky. London, W. Laurie, 1956. 308 p.

Discusses sky phenomena, including meteors, fireballs, mirages, and things that fall from the heavens. Cites cases of reported extraterrestrial visitations and advances theory with supporting arguments that non-terrestrial intelligences are coming to, or emerging from other dimensions into, earth's atmosphere. American ed. (New York, Citadel Press) published 1957.

Coughlin, William J. The UFO as a plasma. Space/aeronautics, v. 49, Mar. 1968: 91.

Review of Philip Klass' book, UFOs- Identified (Random House, 1968) in which it is postulated that UFOs do indeed exist and are freak atmospheric electrical phenomena known as "plasma." Theory purports to explain (1) why UFOs fly such erratic flight profiles; (2) why UFOs are able to stop so abruptly and change direction; (3) why UFOs can be seen by radar; (4) why UFOs can suddenly disappear; and (5) why UFOs cause electrical interference.

Day, Langston. Flying saucers: fact or fiction? Chambers' journal, Nov. 1950: 668-670.

Digard-Combet, Simonne. Les soucoupes: leur provenance, leur but. Paris, Aryana, 1954. 43 p.

Version of origin and mission of flying saucers.

Duclout, Jorge A., and Napy Duclout. Unico documento confirmado sobre el origen, estructura y destino de los platos voladores; transcripcion de las grabaciones, sobre alambre, registradas durante experimentaciones psiquicas en que se concerto una cita con un plato volador, la cual fue complida en la fecha preestablecida; 2da. Edicion, ampliada con los testimonios del pasaje de un plato volador, el 6 de Septiember de 1954. Buenos Aires, America Tecnica & Editorial J.A. Duclout, 1956. 179 p.

Fawcett, George D. The flying saucers are hostile. Flying saucers, Feb. 1961: 12-21, 58.

Chronicles apparently hostile acts by UFOs 1944-1960. Lists statements that UFOs are extraterrestrial spacecraft by Air Chief Marshall Lord Dowding; Dr. Hermann Oberth; Lt. Col. John O'Mara; Wilbur B. Smith; Albert M. Chop; and General L. M. Chassin.

Ferguson, William. A message from outer space. Oak Park, Ill., Golden Age Press, 1955. 54 p.

A translation decoding the Book of Revelations allegedly given to author telepathically by "Khauga, the angel who gave it to St. John. " Flying saucers are said to be the spacecraft of "perfected beings" who are "progressed to a four dimensional state of reality" and who are "preparing earth for the second coming of Jesus. "

Finds saucers exist solely in imagination. Science digest, v. 37, Jan. 1955: 24.

Flying saucer controversy; meteorological balloons, and weather conditions which may provide explanations of the phenomenon. Illustrated London news, v. 223, Dec. 5, 1953: 936-937.

The flying saucer mystery. Science news letter, v. 57, Mar. 25, 1950: 188.

The "most likely" explanations of reported flying saucers are reported as: (1) the planet Venus; (2) balloons; (3) meteors; (4) secretly tested aircraft; (5) mass hallucinations; (6) secret disc-like devices being tested by the armed forces.

Flying saucers. The engineer, v. 191, Mar. 30, 1951: 416-417.

Office of Naval Research's official announcement that flying saucers are Skyhook balloons prompted speculation as to why, if this is true, so much time and effort were lavished on "Project Saucer. "

Flying saucers. Public opinion quarterly, v. 14, Fall 1950: 597-598.

Results of poll in which question was asked: What do you think flying saucers are? Asked of 94% of a national sample who had heard or read of UFOs. 23% believed they were Army or Navy experiments or new weapons; 16% thought them to be an optical illusion or hoax; 5% said they were comets, shooting stars, or something from another planet.

Fouéré, René. Leurres et réalités. Phénomenes spatiaux, Mar. 1967: 13-17.

Phenomena often mistaken for UFOs are discussed.

----- Méteors à hublots. Phenomènes spatiaux, Feb. 1965: 7-9.

Meteors and atmospheric phenomena have often been mistaken for flying saucers. Plasmas resembling flying saucers have been synthesized in the laboratory. However, none of these phenomena have features that even remotely resemble the "portholes" described in many alleged sightings. Presence of portholes would then preclude a meteoric or other "natural" explanation for a UFO sighting.

Fouere, Rene. Seraient-ils des revenants du futur? Phenomenes spatiaux, June 1966: 11-14.

Author speculates on an explanation for the fact that UFO occupants do not attempt widespread contact with humans: they might be time travelers returning to the past from the future.

----- Surhumains ou sous-humains, anges ou demons, que sont les extra-terrestres? Phenomenes spatiaux, Mar. 1966: 5-11.

Speculation on the nature of the extraterrestrial beings apparently visiting earth based in part on reports of "contactees."

Fuller, Curtis. Let's get it straight about the saucers. Fate, v. 5, Dec. 1952: 20-31.

Details of UFO sightings over Washington, D.C., during July 1952 are reported and some theories that have been advanced to explain the UFO phenomenon discussed.

----- The saucers are flying. Fate, v. 8, Aug. 1955: 6-16.

Postulates five possible explanations of flying saucers: (1) they are space ships piloted by intelligent beings from somewhere else in the universe; (2) they are space animals which live in space; (3) they are natural phenomena such as aggregations of electrons, or some other kind of energy which we do not understand; (4) they originate on earth and are man-made: (5) they are hallucinations.

----- Saucers and ionization. Fate, v. 6, Feb. 1953: 8-10.

Theory is advanced that "flying saucer" phenomenon is due to ionized areas in the air which follow electrical and magnetic patterns originating from the high ionization powers of radioactive materials, thunderstorms, radiation from the sun, or even the slow disintegration of natural ores.

Fuller, John G. A communication concerning the UFOs. Saturday Review, v. 50, Feb. 4, 1967: 70-72.

In SR's science sections for August 6, September 3, and October 1, John Lear, SR's science editor, discussed various aspects of the UFO controversy. Among several books from which he took excerpts was John Fuller's "Incident at Exeter." Fuller takes exception to Lear's articles and defends his own position.

Gaddis, Vincent H. Mysterious lights and fires. New York, David McKay Co., 1967. 280 p.

In three sections, "Earth's Glowing Ghosts," "Electro-Dynamic Man," and "Premature Cremations," the book deals with the enigmatic aspects of fires and lights. UFOs are treated in the first section. Agreeing that some of these objects appear to be metallic craft piloted by humanoid beings, the author points out that many reported sightings could be what he calls "electro-animals"--a form of upper-atmospheric life perhaps feeding on pure energy. Firefalls, ball lightning, fireballs and similar phenomena are also treated in the first section.

Girvan, Ian Waveney. Flying saucers and common sense. London, Frederick Muller, Ltd., 1955. 160 p.

Discusses mental processes by which author came to accept validity of theory that UFOs emanate from somewhere outside earth's atmosphere and that they are piloted or remotely controlled by intelligent beings. Also writes of the impact of the subject of UFOs on the public mind.

Great balls of fire. Newsweek, v. 68, Sept. 5, 1966: 78.

Summary of Philip Klass' theory that many UFO sightings are really ball lightning.

Green, Gabriel and Warren Smith. Let's face the facts about flying saucers. New York, Popular Library, 1967. 127 p.

Reports from research members of the Amalgamated Flying Saucer Clubs of America (AFSCA) that would seem to indicate that UFOs are vehicles from other planets piloted by extraterrestrials.

Green, Vaughn M. Flying monsters. Fate, v. 8, Jan. 1955: 112-114.

As our earth evolved, great winged creatures evolved which could live in outer space, the author speculates. Living in outer space outside earth's atmosphere, such creatures could live for hundreds of years, stirred into activity only when meteoric particles disturbed them or when by chance they were drawn into earth's atmosphere. He suggests that perhaps many UFO sightings could be explained in this way.

Guieu, Jimmy. Flying saucers come from another world. Translated by Charles Ashleigh. London, Hutchison & Co., 1956. 248 p.

Halsey, Wallace C. Cosmic end-time secrets. Los Angeles, Futura Press, 1965. 102 p.   .

Contains collected writings, lectures, and charts of the author. UFOs, their origin and purpose, are discussed, as well as the story of creation; the Tower of Babel; our solar system's imbalance; functions of the Pyramids: the Infinite Light; squaring the body; pineal gland or "third eye" development; teleportation; the work of the Melchizedek Order; cosmic high noon; the transitor beam; the White Stone; and the Solar Tongue.

Hansen, L. Taylor. The mystery ship. Fate, v. 1, Winter 1949: 30-33.

Author speculates on possible origin of wingless spacecraft seen over
Montgomery, Ala. on July 23, 1949, and hints that it could have come from
Mars.

Hull, Joe. Men in motion; obituary of the flying saucers. The air line pilot,
v. 22, Sept. 1953: 13-14.

Dr. Donald H. Menzel's book, Flying Saucers, is hailed as having solved the
flying saucer riddle by proving that natural atmospheric phenomena account
for UFO sightings. The author therefore postulates that 1953 should mark "the
end" of flying saucers.

Hynek, J. Allen. Unusual aerial phenomena. Journal of the Optical Society of
America, v. 43, Apr. 1953: 311-314.

Author reports that several hundred serious reports of "unidentified aerial
objects" have been studied in detail in an attempt to get a pattern classification. It appears to him that reported phenomena which do not admit of a
ready and obvious explanation exhibit fairly well-defined patterns and that
these are worthy of further study. One pattern in particular, that of a
hovering nocturnal light, does not appear to him to be readily explainable on
an astronomical basis or by mirages, balloons, or conventional aircraft.

James, Trevor. Saucers and psychism. Flying saucer review, v. 5, Nov.-Dec.
1959: 24-27.

Any investigation, government or personal, which does not take into account
the psychic aspects of the UFO phenomena, cannot be considered either
truly scientific or exhaustive, the author postulates. He believes that UFOs
come from and return to an optically invisible realm; UFOs are predominently
of an intradimensional nature, and are not physical ships launched from another
world to journey across space to land on physical earth.

----- Space animals--a fact of life. Flying saucer review, v. 6, July-Aug.
1960: 3-7.

Article and supporting photographs suggest that UFO phenomena observed in
the skies of the world are of two kinds: (1) extraterrestrial spacecraft under
the intelligent control of human or humanoid pilots; and (2) amoeboid,
self-luminous creatures of circular shape--resembling molluscs of the
ocean--who exist in the heat state, are metallic, maneuver intelligently,
and are their own energy source.

----- They live in the sky. Los Angeles, New Age Publishing Co., 1958. 270 p.

Author postulates that reevaluation of the UFO phenomenon is needed:
"Blanket terms, such as the 'space people' need to be eliminated, and
careful attention paid not only to the invisible animals that fly in our air,
but to the various orders of beings who either visit us or who have their
natural habitat in invisible domains surrounding and interpenetrating our
own."

Jessup, Morris K. The case for the UFO, unidentified flying objects. Introd. by Frank Edwards. New York, Citadel Press, 1955. 239 p.

Author analyzes and correlates many paranormal phenomena of scientific record and theorizes that objects such as stones, ice, water, colored rain, organic matter, living organisms, and vegetable matter that have fallen to earth from the heavens come from intelligently operated extra-terrestrial spacecraft or are in some way formed, guided, or influenced by the operators of such spacecraft.

----- The expanding case for the UFO. New York, Citadel Press, 1957. 253 p.

In this sequel to The Case for the UFO, the author further develops the theory that paranormal phenomena, when collated and analyzed, support belief in the existence of intelligence functioning in space. He suggests that UFOs may be a sentient animal life form that originated on earth aeons ago but which now lives naturally in open space.

Kaempffert. Waldemar. Expert sees flying object--saucer or balloon. Science digest, v. 31, Feb. 1952: 74.

Account of Charles B. Moore's sighting of UFO while tracking a Skyhook balloon with a theodolite. Moore was project engineer for Project Skyhook; UFO sightings have often been explained as Skyhook balloons.

Keyhoe, Donald Edward. Flying saucers from outer space. New York, Holt, 1953. 276 p.

Reports USAF information on UFOs allegedly leading to Intelligence admission that these are extraterrestrial and under intelligent control.

Klass, Philip J. Many UFOs are identified as plasmas. Aviation week & space technology, v. 85, Oct. 3, 1966: 54-55, 57, 59, 61, 65, 67, 69, 71, 73.

Evidence is presented in support of theory that high-level UFOs could be created by electric discharge between clouds or between invisible layers of charged dust/ice particles. Occasional daylight sightings of what have been reported as well-structured or silhouetted objects are explainable as plasmas that give the illusion of metal structure, possible due to whirling charged dust or ice particles. Conclusions based on analysis of reports collected by National Investigations Committee on Aerial Phenomena.

----- Plasma theory may explain many UFOs. Aviation week & space technology, v. 85, Aug. 22, 1966: 48-50, 55-56, 60-61.

Theory is advanced that many low-altitude UFOs are a form of ball lightning (plasma), also called kugelblitz, that is generated by lightning or by corona discharge along high-voltage power lines under appropriate conditions. Idea was prompted by numerous UFO sightings on or near high-tension lines, especially at Exeter, N.H., during 1965, and the similarity of their characteristics to those reported for some kugelblitz sightings.

Klass, Philip. That was no saucer, that was an echo. Aviation week, v. 59, July 20, 1953: 26, 28, 30.

CAA study of unidentified radar plots is reported as showing that the spurious targets are caused by radar energy which ricochets off small atmospheric areas, strikes the ground, and returns an echo via the same path. These isolated refracting areas are normally found under temperature inversion conditions and travel with the wind, giving moving-target indications on radar scopes. Findings contained in CAA T.D. Report No. 180 entitled "A Preliminary Study of Unidentified Targets Observed on Air Traffic Control Radars" by Richard C. Borden and Tirey K. Vickers.

----- UFOs -- identified. New York, Random House, 1968. 290 p.

Theory is advanced that most UFOs seem to be "natural plasmas of ionized air, sometimes containing charged dust particles or tiny charged ice particles." These plasmas may be closely related to St. Elmo's fire and ball lightning. They appear to whirl and float, sometimes maneuvering as though they were controlled by an intelligent being; they can also give off light. Hypothesis is applied to explain reported UFO sightings near Exeter, New Hampshire, and to an alleged saucer landing in Socorro, New Mexico.

Klemin, Alexander. The flying saucer. Aero digest, v. 32, Mar. 1950: 129-130.

Author examines "flying saucer stories" from point of view of aerodynamic feasibility and practicality and concludes there is "nothing in them."

Kor, Peter. Perspective: flying saucers--physical or psychic? Saucer news, v. 13, Fall 1966: 10-12.

Inquiry into the language and concepts that have been used to determine the nature of the UFO phenomenon.

Layne, Meade. The coming of the guardians. Vista, Calif., Borderland Sciences Research Associates Foundation, Inc. (P.O. Box 548), 1964. 72 p.

UFO phenomenon is discussed, the nature and origin of the spacecraft, and the reasons for their incursion into earth's atmosphere. Author postulates they do not belong to the world of three-dimensional matter, but emerge from denser etheric worlds.

----- Flying discs--the ether ship mystery and its solution. San Diego, Borderland Sciences Research Associates, 1950. 38 p.

Theorizes that UFOs are supra-physical: the spacecraft do not come from another planet of our solar system or from any other heavenly body known to us; they come from the region of existence called the etheric plane.

Le Poer Trench, Brinsley. The flying saucer story. London, Neville Spearman, 1966. 208 p.

Author presents evidence to support his belief that UFOs are extraterrestrial and that they have visited earth for millenia.

----- The three W's. Saucer news, v. 11. Dec. 1964: 7-10.

Discusses three questions important in UFO research: (1) where do they come from? (2) who crews them? (3) why are they coming?

Liddel, Urner. Phantasmagoria or unusual observations in the atmosphere. Journal of the Optical Society of America, v. 43, Apr. 1953: 314-317.

Author says he can categorically state that there is no evidence which leads one to doubt the physical laws of motion and inertia or to believe in interplanetary travel at this time. All reliably reported UFO incidents can be fully explained when sufficient scientific data are provided. Most of the incidents are the result of reflection, refraction, meteors and meteor trails, and diffraction.

Lindsay, Gordon. The riddle of the flying saucers. Dallas, Tex., The Voice of Healing Publishing Co., 1966. 31 p.

Author says reports do not ring true of flying saucers landing in the desert, nor do claims of their origin on other planets, existence of creatures of higher evolutionary development, and their bringing knowledge to the human race to save it from disaster. He suggests that the whole story has the earmarks of the diabolical.

Loftin, Robert. Identified flying saucers. New York, David McKay Co., 1968. In press.

General summary of the various aspects of the UFO controversy. Author states that although evidence he has gathered over a fifteen year period would tend to support the extraterrestrial hypothesis, it is still an hypothesis.

Lorenzen, Coral and Jim Lorenzen. UFOs over the Americas. New York, Signet Books, The New American Library, 1968. 254 p.

Authors report that 1967 brought an unprecedented number of UFO landings, low-level hovering maneuvers, and landings with occupants visible. They suggest that the almost constant UFO activity from 1965 to the present indicates that close approaches of the planet to Mars to earth is no longer a factor; there are no longer cyclical recurrences of UFO activity peaks. An interpretation of this might be that UFOs are interplanetary in origin and the occupants have established bases close enough to earth so that long journeys are no longer necessary, the authors say.

McDonald, James E. Are UFOs extraterrestrial surveillance craft? Tucson, Ariz., The Author, 1968. 4 p.

Stressing the need for establishment of a vigorous investigation program of the UFO phenomenon, the author noted that close-range sightings of machine-like objects of unconventional nature and unconventional performance characteristics, seen at low atlitudes, appeared to be occurring all over the globe, possibly with increasing frequency. Suggestions that such observations can be explained away in terms of meteorological optics or in terms of atmospheric plasmas cannot be supported with cogent scientific arguments, he said. Talk given Mar. 26, 1968, before the American Institute of Aeronautics and Astronautics, Los Angeles, Calif.

----- Science, technology, and UFOs. Tucson, Ariz., the author, 1968, 14 p.

Noting that throughout the entire world only a small handful of scientists have taken the trouble to attempt direct checks on the puzzling and recurrent reports of UFO phenomena, author presents evidence, based on personal investigation, to support his hypothesis that UFOs are extraterrestrial probes or vehicles--products of some technology other than our own. He also reviews competitive hypotheses. Speech presented Jan. 26, 1968, at a General Seminar of the United Aircraft Research Laboratories, East Hartford, Conn.

----- Statement on unidentified flying objects. Tucson, Arizona, The Author, 1968. 39 p.

In his statement, the author reviews his experiences in interviewing UFO witnesses in the U.S. and abroad and discusses ways in which his professional experience in the field of atmospheric physics and metorology illuminates the past and present attempts to account for UFO phenomena. Presented at the Symposium on Unidentified Flying Objects, Committee on Science and Astronautics, House of Representatives, July 29, 1968.

----- UFOer -det strste videnskabelige problem i vor tid? Denmark, UFO-NYTs Forlag, 1967. 64 p.

Translation of "UFOs: the greatest scientific problem of our times," delivered at the convention of the American Society of Newspaper Editors, Washington, D.C., April 22, 1967.

----- UFOs--extraterrestrial probes? Astronautics & aeronautics, v. 5, Aug. 1967: 19-20.

Author states his belief that the extraterrestrial-origin hypothesis for the UFO phenomenon must be given serious scientific attention. He points out that most arguments against feasibility of interstellar travel are couched in terms of present-day scientific knowledge and technology.

Manas, John H. Flying saucers and space men: a scientific and metaphysical dissertation in interplanetary traveling. New York, Pythagorean Society, 1962. 124 p.

Maney, Charles A. Donald Menzel and the Newport News UFO: a critical report. Fate, v. 18, Apr. 1965: 64-75.

Evidence is offered that Dr. Menzel's orthodox explanations of flying saucers fail to explain observed phenomena.

Maney, Charles A. and Richard Hall. The challenge of unidentified flying objects. Washington, The Authors, 1961. 208 p.

Book is a series of separate articles by authors in which each presents his own version and interpretation of UFO phenomena.

March of the news: new light on "flying saucers." U.S. news & world report, v. 62, Mar. 20, 1967: 16.

When ammonium vapor is ignited with a high-voltage spark, the result is a mass of glowing gas that assumes the shape associated with UFOs--a disc-shaped subject with an inverted-saucer top and sometimes the appearance of tiny windows around the rim. It can be tracked by radar and produces a "charge field" that could affect radio performance nearby. Research was by Dr. Robert S. Powell, Melpar Inc., Falls Church, Va.

Mauer, Edgar F. Of spots before the eyes. Science, v. 116, Dec. 19, 1952: 693.

The author, a physician, suggests that flying saucers are muscae volitantes (motes before the eyes caused by shadows cast upon the retina by cells in the vitreous humor) "or perhaps some abnormal cortical discharges in the migrainous."

Meerloo, Joost A. Flying saucer syndrome and the need for miracles. Journal of the American Medical Association, v. 203, Mar. 18, 1968: 170.

Analysis of subjective interpretation and failures in objectivity that may explain flying saucer reports: (1) memory distortions; (2) personal search for magic; (3) optical illusions; (4) psychological perceptual distortion; (5) physical distortion of images; (6) anxiety; (7) flying saucer cult; (8) rumor and propaganda.

Menzel, Donald H. Flying saucers. Cambridge, Harvard University Press, 1953. 319 p.

Phenomena underlying the 20% of UFO sightings that USAF lists as unexplained are reported as meteorological optical effects: mirages, reflections in mist, refractions and reflections by ice crystals. Author asserts there is no evidence that UFOs are interplanetary spacecraft manned by extraterrestrial beings.

----- UFO: fact or fiction? Cambridge, Mass., The Author, 1967. 15 p.

With respect to UFOs, the author states his position as being that natural explanations exist for "unexplained" sightings. He attempts to show that arguments advanced in favor of the interplanetary nature of UFOs are fallacious.

Menzel, Donald H. and Lyle G. Boyd. The world of flying saucers. Garden City, N.Y., Doubleday, 1963. 302 p.

Authors describe the common types of UFO sighting and analyse some of the representative and most interesting cases in each category. It is concluded that specific UFOs can be accounted for in terms of normal physical phenomena.

Michel, Aimé. The truth about flying saucers. New York, Criterion Books, 1956. 255 p.

Author presents and comments on UFO sightings reported throughout the world from 1947. Sources include: Project Saucer records; communiques or records of the air forces in U.S.A., U.K., Canada, South Africa, France, and Sweden; USAF's Air Technical Intelligence Center; National Meteorological Office (France and the French Union); French and foreign technical periodicals; personal inquiries; and information in the files of NICAP. Summarizes current theories and explanations of UFO phenomena.

Miller, R. DeWitt. You do take it with you. New York, Citadel Press, 1955. 238 p.

Discussion of strange and unusual phenomena which seem to demonstrate existence of a world beyond the range of physical measurement. Author believes that flying saucers can be intelligently evaluated only in this context.

Moorehouse, Frederick G. The case of the flying saucers. Argosy, v. 329, July 1949: 22-24, 92.

Author states that: (1) there are flying saucers; (2) they represent the most advanced form of guided missile yet to appear; (3) they use a new source of propulsion which derives from a compact "soft fission' atomic powerplant that affords amazing performance in terms of range and speed; (4) they use a new scheme for guidance and control that gives a never-before-reached degree of precision. He documents his claims.

Moseley, James W. UFOs, the universe, and Mr. John M. Cage. Fate, v. 15, Sept. 1962: 78-84.

Cage suggests that UFOs are not machines but are "sentient life forms of a highly tenuous composition, charged with and feeding upon energy in the form of negative electricity."

Mulholland, John. Magicians scoff at flying saucers. Popular science, v. 161, Sept. 1952: 96-98.

Author, a professional magician, states his opinion that flying saucers may be optical illusions.

The mystery of other worlds revealed. Greenwich, Conn., Fawcett Publications, 1952. 144 p.

Chapter headings include: life on other worlds; communication with other worlds; the expanding universe; possibilities for an invasion base on the moon; a case for flying saucers; investigation of the Carolina saucer; are the flying saucers Russian-owned?

New light on flying saucers. U.S. news & world report, v. 62, Mar. 20, 1967: 16.

Report that Dr. Robert S. Powell at Melpar, Inc., had succeeded in making "flying saucers" in the laboratory by igniting ammonia vapor with a high voltage spark.

Oberth, Hermann. Dr. Hermann Oberth discusses UFOs. Fate, v. 15, May 1962: 36-43.

Author says that in the absence of a more plausible explanation, one might assume that UFOs are "flying machines" that (1) are not built by human beings; (2) fly by means of artificial gravity fields; and (3) produce high-tension electric charges to push the air out of their paths so that it does not start glowing, and strong magnetic fields to interact with ionized air at higher altitudes. Transitions of UFOs from half-transparent to invisible state might be related to creation of artificial gravity fields. Oberth "would bet 100 to one that some of the contact persons are normal and have seen and experienced something."

----- Flying saucers come from a distant world. American weekly, Oct. 24, 1954: 4-5.

Author states that flying saucers are possibly manned by intelligent observers who are members of a race that may have been investigating earth for centuries and that they possibly have been sent to conduct systematic, long-range investigations, first of men, animals and vegetation, and more recently of atomic centers, armaments, and centers of armament production.

Palmer, Ray. Saucers from earth: a challenge to secrecy. Flying saucers, Dec. 1959: 8-21.

Author suggests that the most logical origin for flying saucers is our own earth and that the hollow earth theory, which suggest the interior of the earth is populated by a highly evolved race with great technological skill, merits serious attention.

Perret, Jacques. Barbu, marc de cafe, hallebardes. Mercure de France, Mar. 1, 1953: 408-427.

Commentary on difficulty of ascertaining whether or not UFOs are hallucinations.

Psychoanalyzing the flying saucers. Air force, v. 33, Feb. 1950: 15-19.

Psychological study prepared by USAF's Aeromedical Laboratory. Writer concludes that there are sufficient psychological explanations for the reports of unidentified flying objects to provide plausible explanations for reports not otherwise explainable. Errors in identifying real stimuli result chiefly from inability to estimate speed, distance, and size.

Rougeron, Camille. Soucoupistes et antisoucoupistes. Illustration, V. 6, Apr. 29, 1950: 422.

Russian UFOs. Soviet science in the news, v. 5, July 1968: 1-2.

Soviet scientists claim the hypothesis that UFOs originate in other worlds merits serious examination and are calling for a worldwide investigation.

Sanctillean. Flying saucers: portents of these "last days." Santa Barbara, Calif., I. F. Rowny Press, 1950. 39 p.

Some of the "mystery ships" which so puzzle mankind today are said to be observation scouts from other planets and dimensions seeking to discover where next there may be a rocket experiment or an atomic bomb explosion.

Sanderson, Ivan T. Uninvited Visitors. New York, Cowles Education Corp., 1967. 244 p.

Author, a biologist, speculates on the nature of the UFO phenomenon. Chapter headings: What Could UFOs Be?; Things in the Sky; A Thing on the Ground; The Shape and Substance of UFOs and UAOs; What Do They Do?; Could UFOs or UAOs Be Alive?; Other Strange Things Come Down From the Sky; Our Uninvited Visitors; And More Uninvited Visitors!; Where Do They Come From? How?; When Did They Start Coming and Why?; A Concept of Cosmic Evolution.

Santesson, Hans S., ed. Flying saucers in fact and fiction. New York, Lancer Books, 1968. 224 p.

Anthology of science fiction stories in which the central themes revolve around "flying saucers" and imaginative solutions to the mystery. Two non-fiction essays, one pro-UFO by Ivan T. Sanderson, and one anti-UFO by Lester Del Rey, are included. Other outstanding science fiction writers such as Robert Bloch, Judith Merril, Theodore Sturgeon, John Stephens, Miriam Allen deFord, Bertram Chandler, Edward D. Hoch, Aidan van Alm, John Nicholson, and Richard Wilson are represented.

Saucers and smoking. Newsweek, v. 52, Aug. 11, 1958: 85.

Swiss psychologist Carl Jung is quoted as having written in the Bulletin of the Aerial Phenomena Research Organization (date not given) that the postwar sightings of flying saucers and other unidentified flying objects (UFOs) were not hallucinations.

Saucers explained. Science newsletter, v. 77, Apr. 30, 1960: 279.

Summary of report by Dr. Richard P. Youtz of Barnard College to Eastern Psychological Association meeting that most unexplained UFOs are probably a peculiarity of perception known to psychologists as "afterimage. "

Saucers under glass. Newsweek, v. 40, Aug. 18, 1952: 49.

Physicist Noel Scott reports that he has produced flying saucers in miniature in the laboratory. When ionized air is introduced into a partial vacuum, he can produce orange-red balls, discs, and mushrooms capable of registering on a radar screen. Scott is employed at the Research and Development Laboratories at Fort Belvoir, Va.

Schoenherr, Luis. UFOs and fourth dimension. Flying saucer review, v. 9, Mar.-Apr. 1963: 10-12.

Discussing the relationship between UFOs and the fourth dimension, the author suggests the following possibilities: (1) the fourth dimension is a means of connection between different three-dimensional space; (2) space travelers are indeed coming from outer space but they use the fourth dimension for their traveling; (3) the UFOs are not three-dimensional but actually four-dimensional objects.

----- UFOs and the fourth dimension. Flying saucer review, v. 10, Jan.-Feb. 1964: 16-20.

Outlines four hypotheses concerning the nature of the UFO phenomenon: (1) UFOs are a machine emanating from a region of the cosmos unobservable in our space-time continuum; (2) UFOs originate in our space-time continuum but voyage outside it using the fourth dimension; (3) UFOs are four-dimensional structures and that part of the UFO observable to us is the three-dimensional projection of the structure in that part of the cosmos observable to us; (4) UFOs may be time machines, assuming that the fourth dimension is time.

----- UFOs and the fourth dimension. Flying saucer review, v. 11, Nov.-Dec. 1965: 12-13, 18.

Author enlarges on hypothesis that UFOs could be a sort of spacecraft traveling to our space along the fourth dimension and suggests that they are not necessarily a means of transportation in the conventional sense of the word, but instead, they could be technical devices for the production of local spatial curvatures which extend into the space to be contacted. Once this has been accomplished, beings from the other space could transcend into ours.

Schopfer, Siegfried. Fliegende Untertassen: ja oder nein? Stuttgart, Walter Hadecke Verlag, 1955. 32 p.

Evidence relating to UFOs is examined and author concludes that although hallucinations, images, and fantasies relating to the phenomenon may be real, there is no such thing as a flying saucer.

Shalett, Sidney. What you can believe about flying saucers. Saturday evening post, v. 221, May 7, 1949: 36, 184-186.

Applies "logical" explanations to reported facts of UFO sightings and concludes they are results of tricks played by sun, stars, and senses.

Sharp, Peter F. An appraisal of the present UFO position. Flying saucer review, v. 7, 1961: 19-22.

Analysis of current hypotheses which attempt to explain UFO phenomena.

Slim chance for saucer sightings. Science digest, v. 43, Feb. 1958: 60.

USAF says there are less than two chances in 100 that UFO sightings cannot be identified as familiar objects, reports Chemical and Engineering News. The six categories into which USAF places UFOs are: balloons, aircraft, astronomical, other (i.e., reflections, searchlights, birds, clouds, hoaxes, ice crystals, fireballs), insufficient data, and unknowns.

Some "saucers" may be electrical. New scientist, v. 31, Sept. 1, 1966: 463.

Discussion of Philip J. Klass' theory that corona discharges, in the shape of balls of luminous gas, occur when there are salt deposits on very high voltage transmission lines and account for many UFOs.

Something in the air. Time, v. 60, Aug. 11, 1952: 58.

Radar impulses bouncing off a temperature inversion are suggested as the explanation for mysterious radar "blips" believed by some to be caused by flying saucers over the Capitol in Washington, D.C., July 20-21, 1952.

Space visitors: examples of mysterious and well-authenticated unidentified flying objects, by "Theorist." Practical mechanics, v. 24, Dec. 1956: 138-141.

Sprinkle, R. Leo. Patterns of UFO reports. Laramie, Wyoming, The Author, 1967. 15 p.

References are cited which survey the literature on UFO reports, including explanatory hypotheses. Results of various investigators are summarized, with emphasis on evidence indicating that UFOs are spacecraft controlled by intelligent beings who are conducting an intensive survey of the earth. Suggestions are offered with regard to psychological procedures and techniques for investigating UFO reports, with emphasis on hypnotic techniques and the pendulum technique for comparing the reliability of conscious and subconscious information from UFO observers. Speech given at Sept. 1-5, 1968, meeting of American Psychological Association, Washington, D.C., under title "Psychological Problems of Gathering UFO Data."

Stanford, Rex G. Brev fran Rex Stanford. Sokaren, v. 5, no. 3, 1968: 16.

Author's response to questions submitted to him by the editor, Sven Magnusson. He states his belief that flying saucers come from and are controlled by beings from outer space. The author's book, Look Up, was translated into Swedish with title Kontakt med Rymdmanniskor (Halsingborg, Parthenon, 1959). Also discussed is Project Starlight International, organized by his brother, Ray Stanford, Corpus Christi, Tex., to collect physical proof of the existence of UFOs.

Steiger, Brad and Joan Whritenour. The Allende letters. New York, Award Books, 1968. 155 p.

When the Office of Naval Research published a limited edition of a strangely annotated copy of Morris Jessup's book, The Case for the UFO, it included two letters received by Jessup from Carlos Allende, who was apparently one of the annotators. This book explores Allende's role in the UFO controversy.

Stranges, Frank E. Danger from the stars. Venice, Calif., International Evangelism Crusades, Inc., 1960. 14 p.

Author postulates that planet earth has been host to generations of interstellar visitors who can travel with or without what we call flying saucers and who fall into four classifications: ministering angels; guardian angels; angel reapers; and fallen angels. He discusses their characteristics and traits and then warns against "counterfeit" flying discs causing crashes, near collisions, near-havoc, and all manner of fear and superstition. He lists occurrences 1945-1960 that seem to indicate a pattern of violence and deliberate interference.

Stumbough, Virginia. The anatomy of mirages. Fate, v. 6, Apr. 1953: 85-93.

Stating that an important segment of scientific opinion believes that flying saucers can be explained as mirages, the author discusses phenomena that are proven mirages and the conditions necessary for the phenomenon to be manifested. She says that while many UFO sightings fit into a mirage theory, scores do not.

Study radar "ghosts." Science news letter, v. 62, Aug. 16, 1952: 99.

Article states that a DOD panel is trying to discover the phenomena that can be picked up by radar. It is hoped that findings will help dispel impression that unexpected "blips" appearing on radar screens are "flying saucers."

Sykes, Egerton. Flying saucers and negative matter. Atlantis, v. 5, Sept. 1962: 49-51.

It has been established, asserts the author, that if heavy matter can be volatized instantaneously, it may under certain circumstances recombine on the negative side of the scale. This secondary stage will be shortlived, but will have characteristics similar to those of fireballs.

Temperature inversions cause "flying saucers." Science news letter, v. 62, Dec. 20: 1952: 388.

Reports the CAA had confirmed that the "flying saucers" seen on radar scope at National Airport near Washington, D.C., during July 1952 were result of temperature inversions bending the radar waves.

Those flying saucers; an astronomer's explanation. Time, v. 59, June 9, 1952: 54-56.

Dr. Donald H. Menzel, Harvard professor of astrophysics, analyzes frequently-reported characteristics of flying saucers and uses scientific deduction to show that sightings were caused by terrestrial rather than extraterrestrial phenomena.

Tufty, Barbara. 8 planet-probe robots. Science newsletter, v. 84, Oct. 12, 1963: 227.

Ufology. Newsweek, v. 62, Aug. 5, 1963: 44.

Review of Donald H. Menzel and Lyle G. Boyd's book The World of Flying Saucers (New York, Doubleday, 1963).

Unger, George. Flying saucers: physical and spiritual aspects. Foreword by Dr. H. Poppelbaum. East Grinstead, Sussex, Eng., New Knowledge Books, 1958. 43 p.

An anthroposophist convinced of spiritual relationship between the cosmos and earth, author postulates that while UFOs are real phenomena, they are not spacecraft from other planets; the spreading of sensational news about their appearances may be considered a large-scale diverting manoeuvre by adverse spiritual forces to distract mankind from task of spiritual development.

Uriondo, Oscar A. Objetos aéreos no identificados: un enigma actual. Buenos
Aires, The Author, 1965. 155 p.

State-of-the-art report on theories and research relating to the UFO
phenomenon. Author concludes that at present it is impossible to either
prove or disprove the reality of flying saucers. He urges international
cooperation in a program to resolve the problem.

U.S. space plans offer clue to UFO problem. The UFO investigator, v. 2,
Jan.-Feb. 1963: 6-7.

Assuming that there are inhabited planets, some of which are technically far
ahead of us and may have achieved space travel long ago, article postulates
that fundamental space-travel requirements would be basically the same
for any world and examines U.S. space plans for clues to the nature and
operations of advanced space explorers, including any now observing earth.

Vaeth, J. Gordon. Skyhooks as flying saucers. In 200 miles up. New York,
Ronald Press Co., 1951. p. 111-116.

Details of appearance and properties of Skyhook balloons for high altitude
research are given to explain why Skyhook sightings have often been
interpreted as flying saucer or other unusual phenomena. The sighting of a
UFO--not a balloon--that occurred during a Skyhook operation near Arey,
N. Mex., on April 24, 1949, is discussed.

Vallée, Jacques and Aleksandr Kazantsev. Flying saucer review, v. 13, Nov.-Dec.
1967: 11-12.

General discussion of theories and hypotheses relating to the UFO phenomenon.
Reprinted from Tekhnika Molodezhi, v. 8, Aug. 1967.

Vallée, Jacques and Janine Vallée. Astronomers' verdict: flying saucers are
real. Fate, v. 20, Apr. 1967: 62-72.

An objective review of major hypotheses on origin of UFOs leads author to
conclude that (1) all sightings cannot be attributed to conventional causes;
(2) existence of alien intelligence must be considered; (3) extreme caution must
be used in developing latter hypothesis because of phenomenon's complexity.
Excerpted from Challenge to Science: UFO Enigma, published in Chicago
by H. Regnery Co., 1966.

Wassilko-Serecki, Zoe. Startling theory on flying saucers. American
astrology, v. 23, Sept. 1955: 2-5.

Taking into consideration all enumerated characteristics of UFOs, the
probability is suggested that they represent hitherto unknown type of animal
life indigenous to earth's ionosphere. Their bodies are postulated as being
hollow, composed of a minimum of dense matter, and charged with electricity.
It is also suggested that these creatures could be something like a "missing
link" between organic and inorganic life and that this is the reason they
give a machine-like impression.

129

Webster, Robert N. The saucers aren't balloons. Fate, v. 4, May-June 1951: 4-7.

Attacks theory by Office of Naval Research chief of the nuclear physics branch Dr. Urner Liddel that "Skyhook" balloons account for all saucer reports. Cites five UFO sighting reports that cannot be explained by Dr. Liddel's theory.

----- Saucers: material or immaterial? Fate, v. 6, Oct. 1953: 4-5.

Author discusses his theory that flying saucers are a kind of "ectoplasmic ghost animal. "

Wellman, Wade. Extra-solar UFOs. Flying saucer review, v. 8, Mar.-Apr. 1962: 8-10.

Suggestion is made that UFOs come from outside earth's solar system-- possibly from 61 Cygni or 70 Orphiuchi.

----- The psychology of scepticism. Flying saucer review, v. 9, Sept.-Oct. 1963: 32-34.

Review of Donald H. Menzel's book, The World of Flying Saucers (New York, Doubleday & Co., 1963).

What were the flying saucers? Popular science, v. 159, Aug. 1951: 74-75, 228.

Results of an unofficial Popular Science survey in which eye-witnesses to UFO phenomena were asked to choose the explanation that seemed most plausible to them: 52% believe they saw "man-made aircraft"; 16% believe they saw "something commonplace"; 4% believe they saw a "visitor from afar"; 28% are still uncertain, but more than half of them think they saw either man-made aircraft or visitors from afar.

Wilkins, Harold T. Flying saucers. The contemporary review, v. 78, July 1950: 49-53.

Well-corroborated UFO incidents are cited by author as proof that the phenomenon cannot be dismissed as misinterpretation of natural objects.

Wilson, Harvey. Found: flying saucer base in outer space. The national police gazette, v. 173, Aug. 1968: 14, 24.

It is speculated that pulsating signals from the region of the star Vega are indicative of a flying saucer base there.

Wilson, Richard. A nuclear physicist exposes flying saucers. Look, v. 15, Feb. 27, 1951: 60-62, 64.

Report on Office of Naval Research's Skyhook project which has resulted in many reports of flying saucer sightings.

Wood, Robert H. Saucers, secrecy & security. Aviation week, v. 54, Feb. 19, 1951: 50.

Editorial comment on Feb. 27, 1951, Look magazine story quoting Dr. Urner Liddel, chief of the nuclear physics branch of ONR as saying, "There is not a single reliable report of an [UFO] observation which is not attributable to the cosmic [Skyhook] balloons."

Wylie, C. C. Saucers elude astronomers. Science newsletter, v. 61, June 14, 1952: 375.

Author, professor of astronomy at the University of Iowa, states that not one "saucer" has been reported as the result of astronomical observation. He says the fact that each saucer has been reported from only one point suggests that most have been spots of reflected light.

Wylie, Philip. Of stress and saucers. Saturday review, v. 42, Aug. 8, 1959: 17.

Carl Jung, in Flying Saucers: A Modern Myth of Things Seen in the Sky (New York, Harcourt Brace, 1959), asserts that UFOs are compensatory images projected by the frightened. Wylie takes issue with some of the Swiss psychiatrist's conclusions.

----- UFOs: the sense and nonsense. Popular science, v. 190, Mar. 1967: 76-79.

In what he terms an "informal consensus" of scientific opinion, author considers (1) the possible nature of UFOs sighted but not explained, and (2) whether reported sightings are evidence that alien beings are reaching earth.

Young, John R. The negative universe. Fate, v. 11, Apr. 1958: 87-89.

Hypothesizes that intelligent beings may exist in a "negative universe" that interpenetrates and coexists with ours without our being conscious of it. Suggests that this might explain poltergeist manifestations and flying saucers.

ORTHOTENY

Cleary-Baker, John. Leys, orthotenies, and the UFOs. BUFORA journal and bulletin, v. 2, Summer 1967: 6-7.

The author states that the attempt to link UFOs with a discredited archeological fallacy (the leys of Great Britain) and the abandoned orthoteny theory is to hamper the real work of UFO investigators.

Duchêne, J. L. La repartition des atterrissages de soucoupes volantes en France.
Phénomènes spatiaux, May 1965: 21-25.

By plotting the points of alleged UFO landings over a period of years on a map
of France, the author observes that they seem to be aligned circularly around a
"neutral" center.

Fontes, Olavo T. Brazil under UFO survey. Flying saucer review, v. 7, Mar.-
Apr. 1960: 10-14.

Dr. Fontes documents the intensive UFO survey to which Brazil was subjected
on night of May 13, 1960. Sightings followed orthotenic pattern first discovered
by Aime Michel in France in 1954.

Goddard, J. New light on ancient tracks. Flying saucer review, v. 10, Mar.-
Apr. 1964: 15-16.

Theory is proposed that the "leys," old straight tracks stretching for miles over
the English countryside, were built by the intelligences behind the flying saucers
for navigational purposes or in order to find readily a form of magnetic current
that is helpful to them. It is suggested that leys and orthotenies are similar.

Haythornthwaite, P. K. Bavic as a permanent alignment. BUFORA journal and
bulletin, v. 1, Autumn 1965: 16-18.

Analytical calculations are made to test the significance of orthotenic
alignments.

----- Bavic plotted as a world circle line. Flying saucer review, v. 9, Nov.-
Dec. 1963: 17-18.

For those who wish to calculate their own orthotenic world lines, author gives
the formula relating lattitude and longitude on a great circle line:

$$\cos \emptyset = \sqrt{\frac{1-k^2}{1-K^2 \cos^2 (\theta + x)}}$$

where $\emptyset$ is latitude
θ is longitude

and k and x are two constants for the given great circle which may be found
by substituting into the formula the values of θ and $\emptyset$ for two known points
on the line.

Maney, Charles A. An evaluation of Aimé Michel's study of the straight line
mystery. Flying saucer review, v. 5, Nov.-Dec. 1959: 10-14.

Stating that Michel's book, Flying Saucers and the Straight-Line Mystery,
is "outstanding," Maney summarizes its contents. A public lecture given
at Akron, Ohio, on March 14, 1959, sponsored by the Research Committee
of Akron.

Menzel, Donald H. Do flying saucers move in straight lines? Flying saucer review, v. 10, Mar.-Apr. 1964: 3-7.

It is contended that orthoteny (occurrence of UFO sightings from places that lie on the same "straight line"), as discovered by Aimé Michel, is invalid because it is based on questionable statistics.

----- Global orthoteny. Flying saucer review, v. 10, July-Aug. 1964: 3-4.

Author attacks Aimé Michel's claim that local orthotenic alignment discovered during UFO sightings could be extended to constitute great world circle lines and also criticizes claims of further developments in orthotenic research by Jacques Vallee.

----- Orthoteny -- a lost cause. Parts I and II. Flying saucer review, v. 11, May-June 1965: 9-11; July-Aug. 1965: 26-28.

Critique of orthoteny. Author suggests Aimé Michel's straight lines are only accidental alignments of randomly dispersed points and that his statistics are incorrect. (Michel had theorized that UFO sighting points could be joined together by straight lines all radiating from the point where a "cigar-shaped" mother-ship had been seen.)

Michel, Aimé. Flying saucers and the straight-line mystery. Pref. by L. M. Chassin. New York, Criterion Books, 1958. 285 p.

Author discusses his discovery that UFO sightings of a single day during late Summer and early Fall 1954, even though they might occur as far apart as England, France, and northern Italy, fell clearly and precisely along straight lines forming highly characteristic patterns suggesting systematic aerial exploration. Translated from Mystérieux objets célestes and edited by the Research Division of Civilian Saucer Intelligence of New York. Appendix on latest U.S. sightings by Alexander D. Mebane.

----- Global orthoteny. Flying saucer review, v. 9, May-June 1963: 3-7.

Michel announces that "local" orthotenic alignments previously discovered in UFO sightings can be extended to constitute great world circle lines.

----- New thoughts on orthoteny. Flying saucer review, v. 12, Jan.-Feb. 1966: 19.

Michel speculates that his presumed discovery of an underlying order in manifestations of UFO phenomena on a planetary scale--orthoteny--was but a false trail.

----- Reflections of an honest liar. Flying saucer review, v. 11, May-June 1965: 11-14.

Author points out discrepancies in Dr. Menzel's analyses of orthotenic statistics.

Michel, Aimé. Where Dr. Menzel has gone wrong. Flying saucer review, v. 10, Mar.-Apr. 1964: 8-10.

Author answers Menzel's criticism of statistical method on which theory of orthoteny is based.

Ribera, Antonio. "Bavic" in the Iberian peninsula. Flying saucer review, v. 9, Sept.-Oct. 1963: 30-32.

Evidence is presented that confirms statements made about global orthoteny and the Bayonne-Vichy line which Aime Michel discovered and illustrated in his book, Flying Saucers and the Straight Line Mystery (New York, Criterion Books, 1958). "Bavic" consisted of six UFO sighting points over France: Bayonne, Lencouacq, Tulle, Ussel, Gelles, and Vichy, and the incidents all occurred on Sept. 24, 1954. Michel later discovered that his line could be further extended until it encircled the globe. Author's verification is of the Spanish stretch of "Bavic."

----- Spanish orthotenies in 1950. Flying saucer review, v. 7, Nov.-Dec. 1961: 9-11.

Wave of UFO sightings in 1950 off the Iberian peninsula that form straight-line orthotenies when plotted on a map are discussed.

----- UFO survey of Spain: more evidence. Flying saucer review, v. 9, Jan.-Feb. 1963: 14-17.

Author submits orthotenic map of Spain as proof that the Iberian peninsula was subjected to deliberate survey by UFOs during Spring 1950.

----- UFO waves follow a certain pattern. Flying saucer review, v. 5, May-June 1959: 12-14.

Report on discoveries by Eduardo Buelta, a Spanish engineer and UFO researcher, that (1) UFO sightings follow a pattern in both time and space and (2) the peak of sightings indicates a movemnet eastward as if earth were being submitted to close and methodical survey. Complements work by Aimé Michel on theory of orthoteny.

Seevior, Peter M. Foundations of orthoteny. Flying saucer review, v. 11, Mar.-Apr. 1965: 10-12.

Discussion of discrepancies in orthotenic results so far published and inquiry into possible ways of basing further study on a more solid foundation.

Toulet, Francois. Mathematic de l'orthotenie. Phenomenes spatiaux, June 1967: 7-11.

Mathematical formulae that may be applied to orthotenic studies.

Vallée, Jacques. The Menzel-Michel controversy. Flying saucer review, v. 10, July-Aug. 1964: 4-6.

In answer to Donald Menzel's attack on Aimé Michel's claim that local orthotenic alignments discovered during UFO sightings could be extended to form great world circles, author discusses method used for computation of great circles as well as new indications about the statistical significance of the lines, based on IBM computer data.

----- Recent developments in orthotenic research. Flying saucer review, v. 9, Nov.-Dec. 1963: 3-6.

General outline of methods perfected for analyzing orthotenic alignments.

----- Towards a generalisation of orthoteny and its application to the North African sightings. Flying saucer review, v. 8, Mar.-Apr. 1962: 3-7.

Apparent confirmation of orthoteny in UFO sightings in the Morocco-Algeria-Tunisia area is reported.

The Warminster phenomenon. Flying saucer review, v. 11, July-Aug. 1965: 3, 9.

In a letter published in the Warminster Journal (June 4, 1965), amateur geologist and naturalist David Holton wrote that recorded instances of phenomenon consisting of persistent "whirrings," humming sounds, and vibrations of several degrees of intensity were occurring at places which when linked, formed "straight lines" on the map and that three of these lines passed through Warminster (England) itself. He also told how a number of witnesses to whom he had spoken about the noise also had fleeting glimpses of a luminous object overhead.

PERCEPTION

Comella, Tom. UFO's: problems in perception. Fate, v. 12, Jan. 1959: 92-96.

Details are given of UFO sighting in Cleveland, Ohio, October 21, 1955. There were several witnesses.

Durham, Anthony and Keith Watkins. Visual perception of UFOs. Flying saucer review, v. 13, May-June 1967: 27-29.

Fine details of the structure of the eye that may be relevant to the accuracy of UFO reports are noted.

----- Visual perception of UFOs: Part II. Flying saucer review, v. 13, July-Aug. 1967: 24-26.

After considering problems in perception presented to the brain in UFO sightings, the authors note that if the data coming in were completely new, it is probable the brain would pick a simplifying hypothesis based on the observer's experience and attitudes. The observer would then see and remember this interpretation of the data, and one could not tell what the original experience was really like.

Finch, Bernard E. Can they see us? Flying saucer review, v. 14, Mar. -Apr. 1968: 31.

Reports of the movements of flying saucers, including near misses of trees, buildings, overhead cables, and hills suggest to author that whoever is in control appears to have very poor vision in our atmosphere. He feels that this could account for the strange and paradoxical reported movements of UFOs.

Fuhs, Allen E. Visual sensitivity of residents of other planets. ARS Journal, v. 30, June 1960: 577.

Visual sensitivity of hypothesized intelligent beings outside our solar system is discussed.

Hughes, F. P. Letters: a trained eye on UFOs. Science, v. 156, June 9, 1967: 1311-1312.

Drill designed to aid discriminating observation of aerial and/or atmospheric phenomena.

Illusions of nature. Science illustrated, v. 2, Oct. 1947: 42-44.

Examples of illusions of nature that can fool man into major misconceptions.

Luckiesh, Matthew. Seeing is deceiving. Science illustrated, v. 1, June 1946: 86-87.

Instances in which if one believes what he sees, he often is believing what isn't true.

Perret, Jacques. Barbu, marc de cafe, hallebardes. Mercure de France, Mar. 1, 1953: 408-427.

Commentary on difficulty of ascertaining whether or not UFOs are hallucinations.

Smith, E. R. UFOs and artificial satellites. Flying saucer review, v. 7, Sept. -Oct. 1961: 6-11.

Some conventional methods of observing things seen in the sky are discussed for benefit of UFO researchers. Possibility of confusing satellites with UFOs--and vice versa--is treated.

Wertheimer, Michael. A case of "autostasis" or reverse autokinesis. Perceptual and motor skills, v. 26, Feb. 1968: 417-418.

Three of 5 observers of a light in the night sky that was actually moving continuously along a linear course reported it as stationary as long as the light was on. The phenomenon, "autostasis," seems to be opposite to the wellknown phenomenon of autokinesis, or apparent motion of an actually stationary light in an undifferentiated field. This work was helped by the Air Force Office of Scientific Research which supported the University of Colorado's program to conduct a scientific study of unidentified flying objects.

PERSONALITIES

Barker, Gray. Chasing the flying saucers. Flying saucers, May 1959: 19-43.

General discussion of activities of UFO researchers and alleged contactees. Claims made by "Prince Neosom of the Planet Tythian" are mentioned.

----- Chasing the flying saucers. Flying saucers, Dec. 1959: 22-29.

Tells how Long John Nebel Show in New York was ordered cut off the air during discussion of flying saucers by Gray Barker, James Moseley, and Jonah ibn Aharon.

Buckner, H. T. The flying saucerians: a lingering cult. New society, v. 9, Sept. 1965: 14-16.

Cohen, Daniel. The return of flying saucers. The nation, v. 201, Sept. 13, 1965: 131-134.

Overall survey of UFO events in the U.S. from 1947 and of the personalities and organizations involved.

Draper, Hal. Afternoon with the space people. Harper's magazine, v. 221, Sept. 1960: 37-40.

An observer's view of visitors and speakers at the September 1959 Northern California Spacecraft Convention in San Francisco sponsored by the Amalgamated Flying Saucer Clubs of America. Summarizes AFSCA's apparent aims.

Edwards, Frank. Frank Edwards' report: authorities who believe in flying saucers. Fate, v. 14, Jan 1961: 29-35.

Among astronomers who have seen and/or photographed unidentified flying objects are Sr. José Bonilla, director of observatory at Zacatecas, Mexico; Dr. H. Percy Wilkins; Dr. James Bartlett, Jr.: Frank Halstead, curator of the University of Minnesota observatory; and Clyde Tombaugh.

Grescoe, Paul. This man knows UFOs. Canadian magazine, May 25, 1968: 9, 11.

On July 6, 1967, Warren Smith, Lorne Grovue, and Craig Dunn photographed an unidentified flying object while on a prospecting trip near Calgary, Canada. Article describes investigation of incident by Dr. J. Allen Hynek.

Kobler, John. He runs flying-saucer headquarters. Saturday evening post, v. 228, Mar. 10, 1956: 26-27, 69, 72.

Report on activities of James S. Rigberg of New York City--head of Flying Saucer News Club--who collects reports of UFO sightings and "contact" claims as telephoned or written to him.

Leslie, Desmond. George Adamski. Flying saucer review, v. 11, July-Aug. 1965: 18-19.

Obituary for George Adamski who died at age 75 on April 23rd, 1965, at a sanatorium in Takoma Park, Md., following a heart attack.

The new report on flying saucers. Greenwich, Conn., Fawcett Publications, Inc., 1967. 80 p.

Contains UFO sighting reports and photographs; interviews with Project Blue Book Chief Maj. Hector Quintanilla and broadcaster Long John Nebel; and statements by Wernher von Braun, Dr. J. Allen Hynek, John Fuller, and Maj. George W. Ogles.

Ogden, Richard C. - The case for the R. E. Straith letter. Flying saucers, Dec. 1959: 34-39, 47.

A letter released to the public by George Adamski and signed by R. E. Straith of the State Department said in part: "It will no doubt please you to know that the Department has on file a great deal of confirmatory evidence bearing out your own claims, which as both of us must realize, are controversial, and have been disputed generally." Letter was labeled a forgery since the State Department claimed that R. E. Straith was unknown to them. Author presents evidence that he believes proves the "Straith letter" to be authentic.

On the flying saucer trail. The American magazine, v. 157, Apr. 1954: 56.

Coral Lorenzen, founder and head of the Aerial Phenomena Research Organization, tells in interview how she evaluates flying saucer sightings reported by APRO members in attempt to find solution to UFO mystery.

Out-of-the-blue believers. The New Yorker, v. 35, Apr. 18, 1959: 36-37.

Commentary on a symposium relating to UFO phenomena sponsored by Civilian Saucer Intelligence of New York.

The people who see "flying saucers." The UFO investigator, v. 1, Jan. 1958: 23-24.

Listing of witnesses to UFO sightings; professions are given.

Roberts, August C., and Dominick Lucckesi. Saucers in the wee hours: the "Long John" party line. Flying saucers from other worlds, May 1958: 14-19.

Profile of individuals associated with ufology that have been heard on the Long John Nebel Show in New York City. Mentioned are Gray Barker, Mark Probert, George Van Tassel, Art Aho, John Otto, Daniel Fry, M. K. Jessup, Howard Menger, Ralph Slater, Joe Eddleman, James Moseley, Dr. Leon Davidson, Hannes Bok, Courtlan Hastings, and Lex Mebane.

Saucer flap. The New Yorker, v. 42, Apr. 9, 1966: 32-33.

Possible significance of Michigan "flap" of UFO sightings during March 1966 is discussed with three ufologists: Jose Cecin, head of the New York Subcommittee of the National Investigations Committee on Aerial Pehnomena; James W. Moseley, President of the Saucer and Unexplained Celestial Events Research Society; and Michael J. Campione, New Jersey representative of the Amalgamated Flying Saucer Clubs of America.

Van Sommers, Tess. These are our ufologists. Pix, v. 78, July 31, 1965: 14.

Veit, Karl. Mainzer Weltkongres der UFO-Forscher. UFO-nachrichten, Dec. 1967: 1, 3.

Proceedings of the 7th International UFO Congress, Mainz, Germany, Nov. 3-6, 1967.

Zinsstag, Lou. Conversations with Dr. Jung. Flying saucer review, v. 9, July-Aug. 1963: 14-16.

The author, a relative of Dr. Jung, discusses with him the UFO phenomenon and reports his comments.

----- On George Adamski. Basle, Switzerland, The Author, 1959. 5 p.

Impressions of George Adamski recorded during his trip to Europe in 1959.

PHOTOGRAPHS

Adamski, George. I photographed space ships. Fate, v. 4, July 1951: 64-74.

Adamski reports on his sightings of flying saucers through 6-inch and 15-inch telescopes from his home on Mt. Palomar 1944-1950. He describes his attempts to photograph the objects.

Archers' Court Research Group. Biometric analysis of the "flying saucer" photographs. Archers' Court, Hastings, Sussex, 1954. 27.

Baker, Robert M. L. Future experiments on anomalistic observation data. The
journal of the astronautical sciences, v. 15, Jan.-Feb. 1968: 44-45.

Requirement is given for additional experiments in the area of anomalistic
phenomena, based upon the paucity of "hard data"; relevant data collected by
astronomers, meteoriticists, and meteorologists, which would be either over-
looked or not detected; and the possible "filtering" and/or "editing" out of pertinent data by various space surveillance systems prior to its evaluation. Experiment involving two cameras slaved to a detection radar is outlined and it
is concluded that such a system should be constructed for use in meteoritic,
astronautical, and "UFO" study programs.

----- Observational evidence of anomalistic phenomena. The journal of the astronautical sciences, v. 15, Jan.-Feb. 1968: 31-36.

Summary is presented of data from a series of analyses and experiments initi-
ally carried out by author under auspices of Douglas Aircraft Co. and based
on movie film containing anomalistic data originally provided by U.S. Air Force.
It is concluded that on the basis of the photographic evidence, the images cannot
be explained by presently known natural phenomena.

Birch, A. Flying saucers photographed in England. Fate, v. 16, Jan. 1963: 26-27.

14 year-old schoolboy Alexander Birch sighted and photographed a flying saucer
in late February or early March 1962 in Mosborough, Sheffield, England. Photo has been declared genuine by experts.

Bowen, Charles. Crash-landed UFO near Mendoza. Flying saucer review, v. 11,
May-June 1965: 7-9.

Details of case in which a mysterious artifact "fell" at San Miguel, Argentina
(January 1965). According to newspaper account, local inhabitants declared
the object was a flying saucer and that they saw "little" individuals walking
around the craft in uniforms like divers' suits.

----- The Russell photograph. Flying saucer review, v. 13, Jan.-Feb. 1967: 29.

Spectacular photographs of a UFO were taken on Dec. 15, 1966, over a south
London suburb.

The camera sees flying saucers. True, v. 27, July 1950: 44-45. 82.

A selection of flying saucer photographs. Editors of True have verified that
each is a true photographic image appearing in the original negative.

Creighton, Gordon W. The mysterious Templeton photograph. Flying saucer review, v. 10, Nov.-Dec. 1964: 11-12.

Developed picture that James P. Templeton, a Carlisle, England, fireman took of his daughter in May 1964 shows a man in the background in white garb which resembles a padded space suit; on his head is a helmet, apparently transparent. Templeton emphatically stated that except for his little girl in front of him when he snapped the picture there was no one in sight.

Cremaschi, Inisero and Guiseppe Pederiali. Dischi volanti: benvenuti. Bologna, Carroccio, 1967. 157 p.

Summary of evidence in support of theory of extraterrestrial origin of UFOs. UFO photographs from many parts of the world are analyzed and discussed as are contactee reports.

Edwards, Frank. Frank Edwards' report: authorities who believe in flying saucers. Fate, v. 14, Jan. 1961: 29-35.

Among astronomers who have seen and/or photographed unidentified flying objects are Sr. José Bonilla, director of observatory at Zacatecas, Mexico; Dr. H. Percy Wilkins; Dr. James Bartlett, Jr.; Frank Halstead, curator of the University of Minnesota Observatory; and Clyde Tombaugh.

----- Frank Edwards' report: how to fake a flying saucer. Fate, v. 10, Dec. 1957: 46-54.

Author lays down "ground rules" for becoming a "saucer celebrity." He reveals how to fake UFO photos and what pitfalls to avoid in describing an imaginary visit to another world.

Fawcett, George D. A camera's eye analysis of 411 flying saucers from 281 photographs taken around the world. Fate, v. 15, Feb. 1962: 67-87.

Study analyzes visual characteristics of UFOs from photographs alone.

Ferriere, Joseph L. We photographed UFOs. Fate, v. 20, Mar. 1967: 52-55.

Two-man photographic team successfully records on film during daylight hours UFO activity over Woonsocket, R. I., July 24, 1966.

Flying saucers pictorial. Tucson, Ariz., Arizill Realty and Pub. Co., 1967.

Fogl, T. Saucer photographed at sea. Flying saucers, July 1959: 6-9.

While author was with the British ship SS Ramsey enroute from Vancouver to Port Elizabeth via Panama during 1957, he sighted and took two photographs of a UFO.

Fontes, Olavo T. The Brazilian navy sighting at the island of Trinidade. Flying saucers, Feb. 1961: 27-54.

Details of UFO sighting Jan. 16, 1958, by Brazilian ship Almirante Saldanha which was on IGY mission near Trinidade Island. Photographs taken were certified as genuine by the Brazilian government. Reprinted from A. P. R. O. Bulletin.

Fontes, Olavo T. Trinidade observationerne-der fremtvang officiel brasiliansk anerkendelse af UFO-ernes eksistens. Randers, Denmark, UFO-NYTs Forlag, 1967. 30 p.

UFO was sighted and photographed by Brazilian ship on IGY mission off Trinidade Island, Brazil, on Jan. 16, 1958. Reprinted from February 1961 APRO Bulletin.

Galindez, Oscar A. Unusual photographs from Argentina. Flying saucer review, v. 13, Jan.-Feb. 1967: 8-9.

On July 3, 1960, Capt. Hugh F. Niotti, graduate of the National School of Aeronautics at Cordoba, Argentina, photographed a cone-shaped UFO. Photo was published as an exclusive feature in No. 222 of La Revista Nacional de Aeronautica, official organ of the Argentine Air Force. On Dec. 1, 1965, Father Benito Reyna photographed UFOs silhouetted against the moon from the Adhara Observatory at San Miguel, Buenos Aires, Argentina.

Heath, David. The Kingsford Heights, Indiana, sighting. Flying saucers, Oct. 1966: 16-17.

On April 3, 1966, author saw and photographed two football-shaped UFOs.

Hinman, Grace. How to take a UFO photograph. Fate, v. 20, Nov. 1967: 78-80.

Robert J. Low, project coordinator for UFO investigation being conducted at the University of Colorado, provides instructions for taking useful UFO pictures.

Kowalezewski, Stanislaw. U.F.O. photographed over Poland. Flying saucers, Feb. 1960: 27-28.

Details of UFO sighted and photographed by author on Dec. 22, 1958, near Muszyna, Poland. Polish photographic experts believe photograph is genuine. Information first published in Zycie Warszawy on Feb. 23, 1959.

Lorenzen, Coral. Brazilian official report on the Trinidade UFO. Fate, v. 18, Mar. 1965: 38-48.

UFO is photographed near Trinidade Island on January 16, 1958, by Brazilian navy training ship on IGY mission.

Mayher, Ralph. I proved flying saucers are real. Pic, v. 25, June 1954: 12-15, 66-67.

Ex-Marine photographer tells how on July 29, 1952, he photographed a UFO traveling in a left-to-right direction at speed estimated by the University of Miami as 7,550 mph.

Palmer, Ray. 1914 UFO   photo puzzles experts. Flying saucers, Aug. 1966: 7-9.

Photo that has lain in an album since it was taken in Pennsylvania in 1914 seems to show a disc-shaped UFO.

Powers, W. T. Photographic surveillance for UFOs: Is it feasible? Flying saucer review, v. 14, Jan.-Feb. 1968: 14, 17.

Information is given on proposed equipment and estimated cost for one year's operation of an "all-sky camera network" that would photograph low-level, close-range UFOs.

Rankow, Ralph. The disc with the domed top. Fate, v. 19, Aug. 1966: 54-61.

Highway inspector discribed encounter with soundless aerial object that he was able to photograph.

----- The Heflin photographs. Flying saucer review, v. 14, Jan.-Feb. 1968: 21-24.

Author, professional photographer in New York and former photographic consultant to NICAP, describes conditions under which four photographs of a UFO were taken by Rex Heflin on Aug. 3, 1965, in Orange County, California.

----- The Martin B-57 and the changing UFO. Fate, v. 19, Nov. 1966: 36-45.

Evidence that an apparently genuine UFO photograph taken near Edwards AFB in 1954 as a publicity portrait for the Martin Company was doctored up and made to look like a fake.

Ribera, Antonio. Two more facts for the UFO file. Flying saucer review, v. 8, July-Aug. 1962: 14-15.

Striking similarity is noted between UFO photograph in Jan. 8, 1961, Komsomolskaya Pravda and UFO photograph taken in Barcelona on Aug. 27, 1959.

Roberts, August C. The Nicholson photos. Flying saucers, July-Aug. 1968: 84-85.

Ralph E. Nicholson of Patterson, N. J., snapped three photos of UFOs in November 1957 from the roof of his home while trying to photograph one of the Sputniks.

Roberts, August C. The Skywatch Tower case. Flying saucers from other worlds, Aug. 1957: 8-15.

Details of UFO sighting on July 28, 1952, from Civilian Defense Skywatch Tower, New York City, and photographing of object.

Ross, John C. UFOs and the record flight of the X-15. Fate, v. 15, Aug. 1962: 38-44.

UFOs were allegedly filmed by rear-facing cameras on NASA test pilot Joseph A. Walker's X-15 aircraft during May 1961 flight when world altitude record was set.

Schönherr, Luis. Spindles in the sky. Flying saucer review, v. 11, Jan.-Feb. 1965: 9-11.

General discussion of optical phenomena that may cause apparent UFO photographs.

Speaking of pictures: a rash of flying disks breaks out over the U.S. Life, July 21, 1947: 14-16.

Reports UFO sightings in 43 states and the District of Columbia between June 25 and July 10, 1947. Explanatory theories summarized.

Steiner, Ralph. How to expose flying saucers. Popular science, v. 162, Jan. 1953: 227-229.

Instructions for photographing flying saucers through a diffraction grating that will reveal the chemical composition of object's light source.

Strauch, Arthur A. I photographed a UFO. Fate, v. 19, June 1966: 67-72.

Report on UFO seen and photographed on Oct. 21, 1965, near Gibbon, Minn.

UFOs? No! Lens flare? YES! Flying saucer review, v. 11, Jan.-Feb. 1965: 7-9.

Discussion of common shapes of lens flares and how they can be mistaken for photographs of UFOs.

Veestraeten, Door J. Ze zien ze weer vliegen. Panorama, Apr. 19-25, 1966: 56, 57.

UFO photograph taken by Jacqueline Wingfied on Dec. 26, 1965, near Waterford, Ireland, is discussed.

Wilson, Harlan. Photographers analyze UFO picture. Fate, v. 13, Oct. 1960: 70-73.

On March 2, 1960, a photograph was taken of a bright, glowing object 50 feet above the ground in Leibnitz, Austria. It was described as milky white, rotated, and emitted intense heat. Vienna meterological station said it could not have been a balloon or other meteorological instrument, nor ball lightning, nor a meteor.

X-15 pilot shows his film. Flying saucer review, v. 8, July-Aug. 1962: 3-4, 13.

X-15 pilot Joseph A. Walker, in lecture to Second National Conference on Peaceful Uses of Space Research in Seattle, Wash., May 11, 1962, showed slides of 5 or 6 cylindrical or discoid objects taken by a camera mounted on the rear of his supersonic plane. The objects, he said, appeared as the plane reached the arc of its flight and began heading back for earth.

PROPULSION

Angelucci, Orfeo. The secret of the saucers. Amherst, Wis., Amherst Press, 1955. 167 p.

Account of author's alleged ride in extraterrestrial spacecraft and contact with extraterrestrial beings associated with the objects. Propulsion of spacecraft explained as converted magnetic energy "inherent in all the universe."

Beach, David. Some UFO thoughts from Britain. Flying saucers, June 1968: 27-28.

Author speculates on the motive force causing reported UFO behavior.

Burridge, Gaston. Townsend Brown and his anti-gravity discs. Fate, v. 11, Nov. 1958: 40-48.

Describes propulsion principle based on Biefeld-Brown effect said to be successfully used to fly saucer-like disc. Anti-gravitic potentials discussed.

Chase, Frank Martin. Document 96; a rationale for flying saucers. Clarksburg, W. Va., Saucerian Publications, 1968. 128 p.

"At least 70% of the contents of this book is completely new materials; this relates to the possible advent of ZAMN power for propulsion of flying discs" - Gray Barker, publisher, p. [vi.]

Comella, Thomas M. Why the real saucer is interplanetary. Fate, v. 8, Dec. 1955: 17-23.

Postulating that the maneuvers and speeds of the "saucers" reported by reliable witnesses are proof that they operate "by some totally revolutionary process which outdates rocket and jet propulsion," the author reviews "evidence" in support of the extraterrestrial-origin hypothesis.

Cramp, Leonard G. A challenge to the technical press. Flying saucer review, v. 9, Jan.-Feb. 1963: 6-10, iii.

Author re-states the G-field theory proposed in his book, Space, Gravity, and the Flying Saucer (London, T. Werner Laurie, 1954). He contends that recent reported behavior of UFOs during sightings conforms to that predicted by his theory.

----- Piece for a jigsaw. Cowes (I.O.W.), Eng., Somerton Publishing Co., 1966. 388 p.

Briefly appraises current developments in and state-of-the-art of aero-astronautics. Reviews, analyzes and correlates technically corroborative evidence of contra-gravitational theory of UFO propulsion in authenticated UFO sightings and events. Offers evidence verifying existence of visiting extraterrestrial spacecraft.

----- Space, gravity, and the flying saucer. Introd. by Desmond Leslie. London, T. Werner Laurie, Ltd., 1954. 182 p.

Postulating that UFOs are intelligently controlled extraterrestrial spacecraft, author introduces theory and supporting arguments that they are propelled by a controlled gravitational field.

Edwards, Frank. Frank Edwards' report. Fate, v. 10, Aug. 1957: 51-57.

Cites claimed discovery in 1926 by Dr. Charles F. Bush that lintz basalt defies laws of gravity by not accelerating in free fall. Claims that in April 1957 five major aeronautical companies were engaged in anti-gravity research projects. Alleges that the U.S. Air Force has a multi-million dollar plant equipped for investigation of anti-gravity and counter-gravitational forces. Suggests that research activity relates to determining propulsion mode of UFOs.

Evans, Gordon H. UFO: theories of flight. Science and mechanics, v. 38, Aug. 1967: 48-51, 72-74.

Evaluation of current theories that attempt to explain UFO propulsion.

Finch, B. E. The saucer--a flying plasma. Flying saucer review, v. 7, July-Aug. 1961: 13-16.

Arguments are presented to support "plasma jet" theory of UFO propulsion.

Flying saucers and science. American mercury, v. 85, July 1957: 121-125.

Stating that DOD will shortly confirm that flying saucers are "space ships," article speculates that the power units in UFOs must involve one of the following: nuclear fission, mass conversion of energy, cosmic rays, or the electromagnetic forces existent everywhere.

Goupil, Jean. L'hypothèse du champ magnétique canalisé: tentative d'explication de quelques phenomènes étranges. Phénomènes spatiaux, June 1967: 2-4.

Observed UFO behavior and phenomena associated with sightings are explained by theory of a controlled magnetic field that serves as a means of propulsion.

----- Une consequence curieuse de l'hypothèse du champ repulsif: la forme des "O. V. N. I. " Phénomènes spatiaux, June 1967: 9-11.

It is shown that the shapes reported for flying saucers are the ideal configurations for spacecraft using a repelling force field as a means of propulsion.

Gradecak, Vjekoslav. Electricity for space exploration. Flying saucer review, v. 8, May-June 1962: 16-19.

Author discusses role electric propulsion will play in making extensive space trips possible and summarizes feasibility studies carried out at Ryan Aeronautical Co., San Diego, Calif.

Harder, James A. The UFO propulsion problem. Berkeley, Calif., The Author, 1968. 10 p.

Author states that "concerning the propulsion of UFOS, a tentative hypothesis would be that it is connected with an application of gravitational fields that we do not understand." Statement made at the Symposium on Unidentified Flying Objects, Committee on Science and Astronautics, House of Representatives, July 29, 1968.

Holden, A. R. Flying saucer propulsion. Flying saucer review, v. 4, Jan.-Feb. 1958: 18-21.

Author theorizes that negative charge of earth tends to induce electrical charges on smaller bodies in proximity to it, thus creating an attractive or gravitational force. UFOs may be constructed to not only neutralize these induced charges, but also to set up opposing charges that would alter the force of attraction; the spacecraft could be made to rise or descend as required depending on the amount of charge it released to its poles.

Jones, Bob. Magnetic space propulsion. Flying saucers, Aug. 1966: 25.

Author gives reasons why it is easy to draw up physically sound means of using magnetic force for propulsion but impractical to put them into operation.

Keyhoe, Donald E. How the saucers fly. Fate, v. 7, Nov. 1954: 27-43.

Excerpt from author's book, Flying Saucers from Outer Space. Cites conclusions of Canadian geomagnetic engineer Wilbur B. Smith that it is possible to produce a magnetic "sink" within the earth's field; that is, a region into which magnetic flux will flow at a controlled rate, giving up some of its potential energy in the process. Smith noted that most of the descriptions of flying saucers are in accordance with the design which would be necessary to exploit the properties of a "magnetic sink."

Keyhoe, Donald E. I know the secret of the flying saucers. True, v. 47, Jan. 1966: 34-36, 94-95.

Author suggests that control over gravity is the only explanation for the astounding maneuvers that "flying saucers" are said to make.

----- Tefatens hemlighet: antigravitation. Sökaren, v. 4, no. 6, 1967: 7-10.

Observed behavior of UFOs leads author to speculate that they are propelled by an anti-gravity device.

Korcsmaros, Jesse. Flying discs, clouds, and falling ice. Flying saucers, Dec. 1959: 30-33.

Author suggests that flying saucers employ water as a coolant which in turn is changed into water vapor by the propulsion system; this vapor is seen as a cloud and accounts for the cloudlike aspect of UFOs sighted near sources of fresh water. If the flying saucer was at an extreme altitude and exuding large amounts of water vapor, this vapor could freeze and account for ice falls reported from a clear sky.

----- Radar--clue to UFO propulsion? Fate, v. 10, Aug. 1957, 64-69.

A theory of UFO propulsion involving vortices generated in the ether is suggested by the fact that radar often detects UFOs when the eye does not.

Krafft, Carl F. The atom and the UFO. Fate, v. 10, Oct. 1957: 51-53.

Author suggests that since the current nuclear theory does not seem to explain how UFOs operate, a new theory may be needed.

----- Atomic structure in relation to spaceship propulsion. Flying saucer review, v. 5, Sept.-Oct. 1959: 21-22.

Possibility of synthesizing a material that would make use of electro-magnetic repulsion between electrically charged ions for (ionic) propulsion of interplanetary spacecraft is discussed.

Kraspedon, Dino. My contact with flying saucers. Translated from the Portuguese by J. B. Wood. London, Neville Spearman, 1959. 205 p.

Discusses in detailed technical terms the forces that UFOs use to navigate in earth's atmosphere and to travel through space on interplanetary voyages. Presented in question-and-answer form, information synthesizes series of five alleged meetings between author and captain of an extraterrestrial spacecraft.

Lauritzen, Hans. Disclosure of the motive power systems of the flying saucers. Het interplanetaire nieuwsbulletin, v. 1, Sept. 1966: 10-12.

Speculation that the reactions of diamagnetic and paramagnetic materials under the action of magnets might afford motive power to flying saucers.

Lauritzen, Hans. Flying saucers -- superconducting whirls of plasma. Flying saucers, Mar. 1967: 10-11.

Author hypothesizes that UFOs are super-conducting ring-shaped whirls of plasma trapped by earth's magnetic lines of force. Phenomena accompanying UFO sightings are explained in this context.

----- Magnetic motors: power systems of the flying saucers? Flying saucers, Mar. 1967: 13-21.

Author states that in its space program the Soviet Union is using the mechanical accelerator as the propulsion system. Experiments seem to indicate that its range comprises all fields of velocity through the speed of light and perhaps many times faster than light. Proposals for experiments with this mode of propulsion are detailed.

----- The motive power of the flying saucers. Saucer news, v. 13, Winter 1966-1967: 7-9.

Describes theoretical and experimental work carried out to determine the motive power of flying saucers.

Lafonta, Paul. Delendus est clypeus. Phenomenes spatiaux, Nov. 1964: 8-12.

Lists phenomena associated with UFO sightings and draws conclusions about mode of propulsion based on interpretations of these phenomena.

Look! It's flying discs again. Popular mechanics, v. 96, Aug. 1951: 120-121.

Description of electrical principle that permits saucer-type metal plate used for display purposes to rotate in mid-air without apparent support.

Moorehouse, Frederick G. The case of the flying saucers. Argosy, v. 329, July 1949: 22-24, 92.

Author states that: (1) there are flying saucers; (2) they represent the most advanced form of guided missile yet to appear; (3) they use a new source of propulsion which derives from a compact "soft fission" atomic powerplant that affords amazing performance in terms of range and speed; (4) they use a new scheme for guidance and control that gives a never-before-reached degree of precision. He documents his claims.

Norman, Paul. Gravity powered objects? Flying saucer review, v. 11, Mar.-Apr. 1965: 18-20.

Professor Fred Hoyle is quoted as saying that quasars "must be gravity power-ed" and that "if these stars are gravity-powered they will be found to be pulsat-ing." It is suggested that the observed pulsations of UFOs might well suggest they are gravity-powered.

Oberth, Hermann. Dr. Hermann Oberth discusses UFOs. Fate, v. 15, May 1962: 36-43.

Author says that in the absence of a more plausible explanation, one might as-sume that UFOs are "flying machines" that (1) are not built by human beings; (2) fly by means of artificial gravity fields; and (3) produce high-tension elec-tric charges to push the air out of their paths so that it does not start glowing, and strong magnetic fields to interact with ionized air at higher altitudes. Transitions of UFOs from half-transparent to invisible state might be related to creation of artificial gravity fields. Oberth "would bet 100 to one that some of the contact persons are normal and have seen and experienced something."

Ogden, Richard C. The creation of the solar system. Flying saucer review, v. 4, July-Aug. 1958: 14-18.

Author reveals that there are more than nine planets in our solar system and gives locations of three newly-discovered planets; that our solar system con-tains more than one asteroid belt; and gives information on how man can defy gravity and apply this knowledge toward building a spacecraft that can maneu-ver outside earth's atmosphere.

Plantier, Jean. La propulsion des soucoupes volantes par action directe sur l'atome. Tours, Maison Mame, 1955. 123 p.

Presents theory and supporting arguments that UFOs are propelled through use of a controlled force field. Explains observed anomalies in behavior of UFOs by this theory.

Ross, John C. Canada hunts for saucers. Fate, v. 7, May 1954: 12-15.

Canada's Project Magnet with equipment that could be used to investigate the possibility of flying saucers powered by magnetic propulsion is described.

Slater, Robert M. Solving the secret of UFO propulsion. Flying saucers, June 1968: 15-17.

Author proposes a hypothetical propulsion system for UFOs based on phenome-na observed in relation to the objects. He theorizes that the machines are powered by a small fusion reactor which operates by combining deuterium with helium.

Strong, James Godwin. Flight to the stars. New York, Hart Publishing Co., 1965. 178 p.

Speculative discussion of future galactic flight by man, including possible means of propulsion and galactic worlds that may be congenial for habitation.

Van As, I. A. Anti-gravity: the science of electrogravitics. Flying saucer review, v. 8, Jan.-Feb. 1962: 22-24.

Principle is proposed for an anti-gravity diamagnetic spacecraft of aluminum and bismuth that would travel along the lines of force of the planets.

Watson, W. H. Ufology and the ion rocket. Flying saucer review, v. 4, Sept.-Oct. 1958: 22-23.

Author develops hypothesis that UFOs are ion rocket propelled and presents supporting evidence.

Winder, R. H. B. Design for a flying saucer: construction and performance. Flying saucer review, Feb. 1967: 13-18.

Author discusses the practical application of a fusion-powered hydromagnetic spacecraft and problems of operation in the planetary atmosphere.

----- Design for a flying saucer: Part III -- characteristics and effects. Flying saucer review, v. 13, Mar.-Apr. 1967: 20-23.

Author describes ionization and hydromagnetic phenomena associated with the use of hydromagnetic propulsion. He relates this to reported UFO behavior.

----- Design for a flying saucer: Part IV -- characteristics and effects. Flying saucer review, v. 13, May-June 1967: 9-12.

In discussion of characteristics and effects of a disc-shaped craft with hydro-magnetic propulsion, the author considers: (1) permissible and forbidden flight configurations; (2) kinds of electromagnetic radiation emitted by machine; (3) visual consequences of ionization in the air; and (4) physiological effects of strong magnetic fields.

PSYCHIC ASPECTS

Allen, W. Gordon. Spacecraft from beyond three dimensions. New York, Exposition Press, 1959. 202 p.

Develops thesis that the mind of man seems to be a many-levelled (intellectual levels) receiver that tunes to the "universal thought source" and that UFOs might therefore be thought-controlled "thought form phenomena."

Asimov, Isaac. UFOs--what I think. Science digest, v. 59, June 1966: 44-47.

Commenting on the compulsion of "believers" to identify unidentified flying objects, the author says that "its not what you see that is suspect, but how you interpret what you see." He suggests that persons who want to believe that the spacecraft crews are benevolent guardians of our welfare are "insecure person[s] clinging desperately to a fantasy of security."

Barker, Gray. Chasing the flying saucers. Flying saucers, July-Aug. 1958: 20-35.

General report of activities of UFO researchers. Mentions messages from extraterrestrial beings allegedly received by John Otto of Chicago, beginning November 28, 1954.

Barton, Michael X. Release your cosmic power. Los Angeles, Futura Press, 1961. 3 p.

A "way of life" based on the "cosmic secret of balance" is described. Information allegedly transmitted to author telepathically by extraterrestrial beings.

----- Secrets of higher contact. Los Angeles, Futura Press, 1959. 30 p.

Technique by which human beings may "reach up into the high consciousness of the Interplanetary Beings and contact them" is revealed. Information transmitted telepathically to author by "Space Brothers."

----- The spacemasters speak. Los Angeles, Futura Press, 1960. 34 p.

Messages from beings on Mars, Venus, and Antares allegedly transmitted telepathically to author for delivery during the Harmony Grove (Escondido, Calif.) Spacecraft Convention, July 2-4, 1960.

Carter, Joan F. Fourteen footsteps from outer space. Dallas, Tex. Royal Publishing Co., 1966. 168 p.

Describing herself as clairvoyant and gifted with ESP, the author discusses sightings, visions, and experiences involving UFOs as well as alleged personal encounters with extraterrestrials.

Cleary-Baker, John. The "psychological" saucer. BUFORA journal and bulletin, v. 1, Winter 1965: 17-18.

Discussion of the UFO as a contemporary visionary manifestation.

Donnelly, Joseph W. Diary of a psychic. Hollywood, Fla., The Author, 1966. 60 p.

Anecdotes and personal experiences of author in the development of extrasensory perception allegedly written under guidance of "spirit mentors." Includes discussion of psychic-occult-UFO matters.

Girvin, Calvin C. The night has a thousand saucers. El Monte, Calif., Understanding Publishing Co., 1958. 168 p.

Author claims to have been inducted into the Army in 1944; tells of being fatally wounded in World War II; of a "Venusian" incarnating into his body and healing his wounds; and of adventures as an agent for friendly extraterrestrials. Alleges physical contact with Venusians and visits to Venusian "mother ship" aboard a flying saucer.

Hampton, Wade T. How to hypnotize by telepathy. Fate, v. 9, Nov. 1956: 88-94.

Tests indicate that a subject may be entranced by mental command.

----- Mystery of hypnotic "ecstacy." Fate, v. 10, Jan. 1957: 94-99.

Discussion of the "visions" of ecstatics and the bearing that the phenomenon might have on the existence of a "spirit world" and on communication with beings on another plane of existence.

Howard, Dana. The keys to the citadel of space. Los Angeles, Llewellyn Publications, Ltd., 1960. 203 p.

Much of the knowledge leading to scientific and technological advance today is being channeled to man by thought transfer from "brothers" on advanced planets, postulates the author. She suggests that by cultivating extrasensory perception, the human mind could readily tap other grades of consciousness to obtain knowledge that will enable the civilization on earth to attain a higher (vibrational) plane of existence.

----- Over the threshold. Los Angeles, Llewellyn Publications, 1957. 140 p.

Subjective report of paranormal contact between author and a being from Venus who, in mission to "guide men in the ways of perfection, " discourses on such subjects as: The Intuitions; Disease and Destruction; Reincarnation; Religion; The Subworlds; The Alchemy of Finance; The Secret of Youth; and The Meaning of Consciousness.

Inglefield, Gilbert S. Fatima: the three alternatives. Flying saucer review, v. 10, May-June 1964: 5-6.

Events at Fatima, Portugal, on Oct. 13, 1917, must have one of three explanations, claims the author: (1) the dancing sun was a phenomenon that science can explain; (2) it was a pure miracle; or, (3) it was due to UFO intervention either on its own or with the liaison of Christian agency.

James, Trevor. The case for contact. Flying saucer review, v. 8, Jan.-Feb. 1962: 9-11.

Use of occult science as a new tool in investigating claims by individuals of contact with extraterrestrial beings is suggested by author. He says the occult scientist would approach these reports with some assurance that the contactee had had experiences involving his perceptions and could evaluate situations that were not necessarily the way they seemed to the contactee.

James, Trevor. Saucers and psychism. Flying saucer review, v. 5, Nov.-Dec. 1959: 24-27.

Author postulates that any investigation, government or personal, which does not take into account the psychic aspects of UFO phenomena, cannot be considered either truly scientific or exhaustive. He defines psychic as "beyond known physical processes" and suggests that cases of psychic contacts indicate UFO experiences of an intradimensional nature.

----- Scientists, contactees and equilibrium. Flying saucer review, v. 6, Jan.-Feb. 1960: 19-21.

Author suggests that review of stories of persons allegedly contacted by extraterrestrial beings reveals a struggle between Christ and anti-Christ forces. Allegations should be evaluated not so much in the light of whether they are possible or valid but in the light of who contacted these people: were they forces of good or forces of evil?

Jung, Carl Gustav. Flying saucers; a modern myth of things seen in the skies. Translated from the German by R. F. C. Hull. New York, Harcourt, Brace, 1959. 186 p.

Text treats UFOs primarily as a psychological phenomenon with particular emphasis on their occurrence in dreams and in modern poetry. Explains basic emotional pattern and actions of individuals claiming contact with occupants of UFOs. Translation of Ein moderner Mythus (Zürich, Rascher-Verlag, 1958). Issued also in British edition (London, Routledge & Paul, 1959).

Kor, Peter. Perspective: flying saucers--physical or psychic? Saucer news, v. 13, Fall 1966: 10-12.

Inquiry into the language and concepts that have been used to determine the nature of the UFO phenomenon.

Lee, Gloria. The going and the glory. Aukland, New Zealand, Heralds of the New Age, 1966. 73 p.

Book was allegedly dictated telepathically to Verity by Gloria Lee after her demise on Dec. 2, 1962. Discusses the condition of the soul after death. Postulates that "space people" are etheric beings and that earth people in their present stage of development would not be able to see them "in their own environs." "Space people" materialize only when they "convert to earth's frequency."

Martin, Mitch. Space travelers in 1870? Fate, v. 11, Sept. 1958: 44-50.

Account of reports on psychometric exploration of outer space--especially Mars--by the Denton family of Wellesley, Mass., between 1860 and 1873. William Denton was convinced that the men on Mars had "traced us out as a people" in 1873.

Meerloo, Joost A. Flying saucer syndrome and the need for miracles. Journal of the American Medical Association, v. 203, Mar. 18, 1968: 170.

Analysis of subjective interpretation and failures in objectivity that may explain flying saucer reports: (1) memory distortions; (2) personal search for magic; (3) optical illusions; (4) psychological perceptual distortion; (5) physical distortion of images; (6) anxiety; (7) flying saucer cult; (8) rumor and propaganda.

Michael, Cecil. Roundtrip to Fell in a flying saucer. New York, Vantage Press, 1955. 61 p.

Account of author's alleged contact in 1952 with extraterrestrial beings who had the power to materialize and dematerialize at will and who took him to their planet, Hell, in his astral body aboard a flying saucer.

Miller, Will and Evelyn Miller. We of the new dimension. Los Angeles, The Authors, [195-] . 115 p.

Intelligences from other worlds and dimensions allegedly dictate the book telepathically to the authors. The role of the individual in the universe and how he can advance into a well-balanced, fuller life is discussed.

Oberth, Hermann. Katechismus der Uranidem. Wiesbaden-Schierstein, VentlaVerlag, 1966. 160 p.

Communication with an extraterrestrial being through a psychic medium has caused Oberth to adopt this view: there is a soul which outlives the body; this world serves as a training-ground for the soul; the soul will continue life (on a planet where conditions are in keeping with its degree of development) after death.

Pelley, William D. Star guests... design for mortality. Noblesville, Ind., Soulcraft Press, 1950. 318 p.

Description of experiments in clairaudient writing and psychical contact with beings "of the more harmonious planes... above the planes of earth. "

Perturbations psychiques. Phénomènes spatiaux, Dec. 1966: 21-23.

Psychic effect on witnesses of encounters with flying saucers is discussed.

Ribera, Antonio. What happened at Fatima? Flying saucer review, v. 10, Mar.Apr. 1964: 12-14.

Resumé of the miracle at Fatima, north of Lisbon, Portugal, which extended from May 13 to Oct. 7, 1917, in context of the UFO phenomenon. Author suggests that UFO occupants may present themselves in terms familiar to "contactees, " usually as divine manifestations.

Unger, George. Flying saucer: physical and spiritual aspects. Foreword by Dr. H. Poppelbaum. East Grinstead, Sussex, Eng., New Knowledge Books, 1958. 43 p.

An anthroposophist convinced of spiritual relationship between the cosmos and earth, author postulates that while UFOs are real phenomena, they are not spacecraft from other planets; the spreading of sensational news about their appearances may be considered a large-scale diverting maneuver by adverse spiritual forces to distract mankind from task of spiritual development.

Walsh, William T. Our Lady of Fatima. New York, Macmillan, 1947. 227 p.

Three shepherd children from Serra da Aire, Portugal, reported six times in 1917 that they had seen a circular globe of light descend from the heavens and had spoken with a lady--later thought to be the Virgin Mary--who had stepped from inside it.

RADAR

Browning, Keith A. and David Atlas. Velocity characteristics of some clear-air dot angels. Journal of the atmospheric sciences, v. 23, Sept. 1966: 592-604.

Nature of the targets responsible for certain clear-air dot angel echoes, and their suitability as wind tracers, are deduced from pulse Doppler radar observations of their velocity characteristics.

Edwards, Frank. Frank Edwards' report: Have UFOs learned to outwit radar? Fate, v. 12, Dec. 1959: 50-55.

Sightings of UFOs flying either very high or very low may indicate radar detection evasion maneuvers.

Glover, Kenneth M., Kenneth R. Hardy, Thomas G. Konrad, W. N. Sullivan, and A. S. Michaels. Radar observations of insects in free flight. Science, v. 154, Nov. 25, 1966: 967-972.

It is concluded that the mysterious discrete "dot angel" echoes observed from invisible targets in the apparently clear atmosphere are, in large measure, due to insects.

Klass, Philip. That was no saucer, that was an echo. Aviation week, v. 59, July 20, 1953: 26, 28, 30.

CAA study of unidentified radar plots is reported as showing that the spurious targets are caused by radar energy which ricochets off small atmospheric areas, strikes the ground, and returns an echo via the same path. These isolated refracting areas are normally found under temperature inversion conditions and travel with the wind, giving moving-target indications on radar scopes.

Findings contained in CAA T.D. Report No. 180 entitled "A Preliminary Study of Unidentified Targets Observed on Air Traffic Control Radars" by Richard C. Borden and Tirey K. Vickers.

Mallan, Lloyd. These saucers nearly fooled the Air Force. This week, May 7, 1967: 4-5.

Report on investigation of radar sightings near Guam of what appeared to be UFOs. Objects were identified as U.S. aircraft flying below horizon.

Saucers over Paris. Flying saucers from other worlds, June 1957: 76-77.

UFO was tracked by radar from Orly Airport, near Paris, France, on February 19, 1956. Speed was calculated at 2,250 miles an hour.

Something in the air. Time, v. 60, Aug. 11, 1952: 58.

Radar impulses bouncing off a temperature inversion are suggested as the explanation for mysterious radar "blips" believed by some to be caused by flying saucers over the Capitol in Washington, D. C., July 20-21, 1952.

Study radar "ghosts." Science news letter, v. 62, Aug. 16, 1952: 99.

Article states that a DOD panel is trying to discover the phenomena that can be picked up by radar. It is hoped that findings will help dispel impression that unexpected "blips" appearing on radar screens are "flying saucers."

Temperature inversions cause "flying saucers." Science news letter, v. 62, Dec. 20, 1952: 388.

Report the CAA had confirmed that the "flying saucers" seen on radar scopes at National Airport near Washington, D. C., during July 1952 were results of temperature inversions bending the radar waves.

RADIATION EFFECTS

Foght, Paul. Guilty: the mystery ray that kills. Fate, v. 14, Mar. 1961: 31-33.

A young man is found dead in his car, his skin and flesh destroyed while his clothing and hair were intact. The car was hot enough to melt a religious statue on the dashboard although nothing was burned. It is suggested that a nuclear energy ray would have had this effect.

Haythornthwaite, P. K. Radioactivity and the UFO. BUFORA journal and bulletin, v. 1, Summer 1965: 13-14.

Possible radiation effects of UFOs are considered.

Hervey, Michael. The strange growing in Martinique. Fate, v. 9, Sept. 1956: 27-41.

Radioactive deposits of an unknown nature on the island of Martinique seem to affect the growth of animals, insects, plants, and man to a remarkable degree. It is suggested that an extraterrestrial spacecraft crashed on Monte Pelée in 1948 and that the radiation is emanating from the wreck which has buried itself deeply in the ground.

Slaboda, Emil. He collected on a flying saucer. Fate, v. 10, June 1957: 66-69.

Night watchman Harry J. Sturdevant was granted medical compensation for disability caused by injuries he said he suffered when a UFO zoomed past him while he was on duty. Alleged incident took place near Trenton, N. J., on Oct. 2, 1956.

Smith, Alson J. Psychic warnings of Pelée eruption. Fate, v. 13, May 1960: 27-34.

Many omens of disaster preceded the eruption of Mt. Pelée, Martinique, on May 8, 1902. A single fiery blast incinerated the 40,000 occupants of the city of St. Pierre in less than one minute. It has been speculated that explosion of an extraterrestrial spacecraft within the mountain's crater was responsible for the destruction.

Young, Mort. The flying saucer invasion that panicked the Pentagon. Saga, v. 34, July 1967: 22-25, 70, 72, 74-76.

It is claimed that after the flurry of UFO sightings in Michigan in March 1966, investigators found traces of radioactivity, peculiar impressions in the ground, and that all plant and animal life in the immediate sighting area had been killed. Excerpted from UFO--Top Secret (New York, Simon & Schuster, 1967).

RESEARCH

Bowman, Norman J. The need for critical analysis of flying disc reports. Journal of spaceflight, v. 5, Nov. 1953: 11.

UFO data that has been gathered by Government and civilian research groups should be analyzed statistically to indicate what is probably unreliable, determine averages, etc., the author suggests. He feels that this is the only way the UFO problem can be approached to yield conclusions of significance.

Caputo, Livio. Anche gli astronauti hanno visto i dischi volanti. Epoca, v. LXIV, Aug. 28, 1966: 16-23.

Report on UFO sightings, chiefly in the U. S., from 1897 to 1966 and on investigation of phenomenon by Project Blue Book. Research programs of NICAP and APRO are mentioned.

Chartrand, Robert L. and William F. Brown. Facts about unidentified flying objects. Washington, D. C., Library of Congress, Legislative Reference Service, 1966. 29 p.

Includes the following: description of various types of UFOs; trends in UFO activity; historical sightings of aerial phenomena; identification of flying objects (versus UFOs); U. S. Government monitoring of UFO activity; special studies of UFOs; special briefings on UFO activity; public reaction to UFOs; Air Force Regulation 200-2.

Cohen, Daniel. UFOs--what a new investigation may reveal. Science digest, v. 60, Dec. 1966: 54-56, 58, 60-63.

Reviews USAF's Project Blue Book investigation of UFO reports and summarizes aims of independent 15-month study by University of Colorado.

Davidson, Leon. Flying saucers: an analysis of the Air Force Project Blue Book Special Report No. 14. [3rd ed., rev. and enl.] Ramsey, N. J., Ramsey-Wallace Corp., 1966. 84 p.

Author states that throughout its investigation of UFO phenomena, USAF has withheld information, photographs, and other evidence it has amassed. He suggests that full text of Project Blue Book Special Report No. 14 (analysis of reports of unidentified aerial objects)--an offset copy dated May 5, 1955 is in the appendix--probably was not made readily available to the public because in 20% to 30% of cases in main study, origin of objects sighted was declared unknown. He also points out that the report did not discuss whether or not there was evidence to prove or disprove the theory that UFOs might be extraterrestrial objects or devices. First and second editions published by author (White Plains 1956, 1957).

Edwards, Frank. Frank Edwards, report: ten years of UFOs. Fate, v. 10, Oct. 1957: 65-69.

Summarizes government research into the attitudes concerning UFO phenomenon 1947-1957.

Everett, Eldon K. Saucers over Puget Sound. Flying saucers, July-Aug. 1958: 52-60.

Author relates experiences in flying saucer investigations from 1948 to 1954, including the Maury Island (Wash.) incident.

Fawcett, George D. UFO repetitions. Flying saucers, Aug. 1966: 28.

Lists aspects of UFO sightings that are repeatedly reported.

Fontes, Olavo T. A suggested scientific investigation of the UFO phenomenon. Flying saucer review, v. 13, Nov.-Dec. 1967: 22-24.

In setting up a scientific investigation into the UFO phenomenon, it is suggested that the following steps be taken: (1) cancellation of unnecessary security restrictions; (2) a systematic rather than haphazard search for UFO appearances; (3) use of the most effective detection methods available; (4) determination of the best locations to set up detection instruments; (5) use of a convergent procedure to alert given areas of a possible UFO sighting; (6) distribution of available equipment and trained observers in reasonable proportions in different areas; (7) consideration of effect the search procedure might have on the searched object.

Fouere, Rene. Sommes-nous a un tournant? Phenomènes spatiaux, Dec. 1966: 6-12.

Author postulates that UFO research seems to have reached a crucial turning point and cites as indications of this the fact that (1) USAF has begun to make its Project Blue Book files more accessible to researchers, and (2) establishment of the Condon Project at the University of Colorado to study UFO phenomena.

Gibbons, Russel W. Ohio Northern investigates the saucers. Fate, v. 6, Oct. 1953: 18-20.

Basic objectives of Ohio Northern's Project A, begun in July 1952, are summarized: (1) to objectively collect data from all possible sources dealing with "flying saucers," and to analyze this data in various departments of the university; (2) to make public the results of research of a private institution unhampered by bureaucratic restrictions; (3) to stimulate and promote objective study of all types of illusory phenomena by individual observers, and to issue reports of the project investigations; and (4) to aid in creating more accurate observers for the civilian air defense program.

Gli UFO dal' Inghilterra all'URSS. Centro unico nazionale per lo studio del fenomeni ritenuti di natura extraterrestre. Notiziario, No. 6, 1967: 13-20.

Newspaper accounts of "official" Soviet interest in flying saucers are summarized. Government commission to study UFO phenomenon is discussed.

Greenfield, Irving A. The UFO report. New York, Lancer Books, 1967. 141 p.

Summary of the author's personal investigations into the numerous UFO sighting reports on Long Island, N. Y., in the spring of 1966, including many first-hand accounts and a review of the history of the phenomenon. Supports the extraterrestrial thesis and the "Air Force conspiracy" allegations.

Hatvany, Edgar A. Dr. Hynek & the UFOs. BUFORA journal and bulletin, v. 1, Autumn 1966: 5-8.

Commentary on letter from Dr. J. Allen Hynek dated Aug. 1, 1966, and submitted to but not published by Science, in which he urges scientific attention to the UFO phenomenon.

Hickman, Warren and Eric Turner. Report from Ohio Northern. Fate, v. 6, Oct. 1953: 21-25.

Highlights from analysis of the 54 UFO sightings reported to Ohio Northern University's Project A are: (1) the objects fly with a peculiar step-like pattern of flight, moving in a horizontal path, then rising vertically, then moving horizontally again, in a series of steps; (2) trained observers who have been close to the "saucers" state they are material objects; (3) they are disc-like in shape and their domes give off an amber light. At night the color seems reddish. The rest of the disc is silver-colored except for a hazy blue light around the edges; (4) observers only yards from the objects sighted have ruled out explanations of light reflection, cloud formation, ionization, and similar theories.

Hynek, J. Allen. The scientific problem posed by unidentified flying objects. Evanston, Ill., The Author, 1968. 15 p.

Author makes the following recommendations: (1) that a mechanism be set up whereby the problem posed by the reports from all over the world, but especially in the U.S., from people of high credibility, can be adequately studied, using all methods available to modern science; and (2) that the U.S. seek the cooperation of the United Nations in establishing a means for the impartial and free interchange among nations of information about unidentified flying objects. Statement made at the Symposium on Unidentified Flying Objects, Committee on Science and Astronautics, House of Representatives, July 29, 1968.

----- The UFO gap. Playboy, v. 14, Dec. 1967: 144-146, 267, 269-271.

Author says that from what "hard" information he has, the U.S.S.R. may have been studying the UFO phenomenon with dispassionate thoroughness for years; the U. S. is only now beginning to consider treating the problem seriously. He outlines what he believes to be a thorough and efficient way to obtain scientific knowledge of UFOs.

I nostri aderenti ci hanno chiesto il parere sull' AIAS. Centro unico nazionale per lo studio del fenomeni ritenuti di natura extraterrestre. Notiziario, no. 4, 1967: 1-4.

Report on founding in Rome of l'Associazione Italiana Avvistatori Spaziali which proposes to scientifically study the UFC phenomenon and to serve as an international clearinghouse for UFO information.

Keel, John. UFOs--the statistical problem. Flying saucers, Aug. 1968: 18-19.

Author states that random UFO sighting reports do not provide data of sufficient depth or "keys to the many hidden factors" of the phenomenon. He suggests that UFO researchers revise their approach to the subject and "search for new and possibly illogical (by our standards) clues buried in the more controversial cases."

Kor, Peter. Perspective: flying saucers--physical or psychic? Saucer news, v. 13, Fall 1966: 10-12.

Inquiry into the language and concepts that have been used to determine the nature of the UFO phenomenon.

Kor, Peter. UFOs from the critic's corner: the myth of the flying saucer mystery. Flying saucers, Dec. 1959: 48-53.

Author, a non-believer in UFOs, gives reasons for his non-belief and critically analyzes current UFO "research."

McDonald, James E. A need for an international study of UFOs. Flying saucer review, v. 14, Mar.-Apr. 1968: 11.

Author writes an endorsement to Soviet scientist Zigel's plea for "a joint effort of all the scientists of the world" to determine the nature of UFOs. From a Dec. 10, 1967, New York Times story by Henry Kamm.

Mallan, Lloyd. What we are doing about UFOs. Science & mechanics, v. 38, Jan. 1967: 38-43, 62-67, 76.

Survey of activities of official and private organizations engaged in UFO research.

Maney, Charles A. Scientific aspects of UFO research. Flying saucer review, v. 4, Sept.-Oct. 1958: 10-12, 30.

Maney discusses role of scientific method in UFO research in speech at opening of Planetary Center, Detroit, Mich., June 14, 1958.

Margolis, Howard. The UFO phenomenon. Bulletin of the atomic scientists, v. 23, June 1967: 40-42.

Problems and difficulties inherent in the University of Colorado study of unidentified flying objects are discussed by the author. He concludes that it is unlikely that the final report will resolve the issue and speculates that it may "add more fuel to the controversy."

Michel, Aime. A note on William of Occam. Flying saucer review, v. 14, Mar.-Apr. 1968: 10-11.

Author points out that William of Occam's dictum that "for the purpose of explanation, things not known to exist should not...be postulated as existing" is a dangerous intellectual narcotic. He asserts that all discoveries without exception have been made by rebels who rejected the "simplest hypothesis," and likens these pioneers to UFO researchers who refuse to adhere to the "misinterpretation" theory about UFOs.

Miller, Max B. Report on the UFO. Fate, v. 9, Dec. 1956: 31-34.

Review of Edward J. Ruppelt's book about the U.S. Air Force's UFO investigations, The Report on Unidentified Flying Objects (New York, Doubleday, 1956).

Miller, Stewart. On scientific dogma. Flying saucer review, v. 13, Mar.-Apr. 1967: 26-27.

Speculation about UFOs must be expressed within a coherent and consistent framework, the author postulates; otherwise UFO researchers must not level accusations of narrow-mindedness at those who point out mistakes.

Munday, John C. On the UFOs. Bulletin of the atomic scientists, v. 23, Dec. 1967: 40-41.

Author urges independent, exhaustive studies into the UFO phenomenon.

Oberth, Hermann. Warum Ufoforschung? In Mitteilungen der Gesellschaft für Interplanetarik. Wien, Europäischer-Verlag, 1961. p. 1-7.

After summarizing hypotheses that might explain the UFO phenomenon, the author predicts that scientific institutions will enter seriously into UFO research once the field has been more clearly defined so that it can be assigned to the appropriate specialists and when enough evidence has been collected so that the facts can no longer be denied or ridiculed.

Plenty going on in the skies. U.S. news & world report, v. 36, Jan. 1, 1954: 27-28.

Excerpts from text of USAF report on its investigation of unidentified flying objects during 1952.

Priestly, Lee. Inside APRO...a saucer fan club. Fate, v. 12, Jan. 1959: 59-65.

Account of the activities of the Aerial Phenomena Research Organization (APRO) of Tucson, Arizona.

The Project A report. Ada, Ohio, Ohio Northern University, 1953. 9 p.

Scientific analysis of unidentified flying objects reported in the year 1952. Conducted by the faculty and staff of Ohio Northern University, Ada, Ohio.

Psychoanalyzing the flying saucers. Air force, v. 33, Feb. 1950: 15-19.

Psychological study prepared by USAF's Aeromedical Laboratory. Writer concludes that there are sufficient psychological explanations for the reports of unidentified flying objects to provide plausible explanations for reports not otherwise explainable. Errors in identifying real stimuli result chiefly from inability to estimate speed, distance, and size.

Rehn, K. Gösta. The question of proof -- a new slant. Bromma, Sweden, The Author, 1967. 5 p.

It is the author's contention that in the study of the UFO phenomenon, philosophy of science has jurisdiction and must rule on the problem, claiming precedence over other disciplines.

Rogers, Warren. Flying saucers. Look, v. 31, Mar. 21, 1967: 76-80.

Background information on the USAF-sponsored study of the UFO phenomenon by the University of Colorado--what it hopes to accomplish and how.

Ruppelt, Edward F. Inside story of the saucers. Science digest, v. 39, Apr. 1956: 35-41.

Condensed from a chapter of the book, The Report on Unidentified Flying Objects, published in New York by Doubleday, 1956. Author describes his activities as head of USAF's Project Blue Book, 1951-1953. He states that while balloons, airplanes, stars, and many other common objects have been reported as UFOs, there are hundreds of other UFO reports which carry the verdict, "Conclusion Unknown."

----- What our Air Force found out about flying saucers. True, May 1954: 19-20, 22, 24, 26, 30, 124-134.

Ruppelt, in charge of USAF's Project Blue Book from 1951 to 1953, reports what he learned about flying saucers during this period. He states his opinion that the saucers are either interplanetary or do not exist.

Science and space: UFO-watcher watcher. Newsweek, v. 69, Mar. 20, 1967: 111.

Interview with physicist Dr. Edward U. Condon about procedures and techniques planned in UFO investigation he heads at the University of Colorado. Project is supported by Air Force Office of Scientific Research.

Serious flaws in AF Special Report 14 revealed by NICAP analysis. The UFO investigator, v. 1, Jan. 1958: 16-18.

Analysis of the main points of USAF Project Blue Book report.

Sharp, Peter F. The truth: some suggestions for the investigator. Flying saucer review, v. 9, Nov.-Dec. 1963: 7-9.

Advice to UFO researchers: (1) the investigator should always bear in mind the scarcity factor, i.e., his normal reaction is to become increasingly sceptical as the unusualness of the case increases; (2) theories must only be built on wide experience and documentation.

Shuldiner, Herbert. The great UFO probe. Popular science, v. 191, Oct. 1967: 120-123.

Report on the objectives of a $313,000 USAF-sponsored study of the UFO phenomenon at the University of Colorado, headed by Dr. Edward U. Condon. Findings would be released in Fall 1968.

Simons, Howard. American newsletter. New scientist, v. 32, Oct. 27, 1966: 174.

Announcement that the Air Force had enlisted Dr. Edward U. Condon of the University of Colorado to head a 15-month study of unidentified flying objects (UFOs) under a $313,000 grant.

Sprinkle, R. Leo. Patterns of UFO reports. Laramie, Wyoming, The Author, 1967. 15 p.

References are cited which survey the literature on UFO reports, including explanatory hypotheses. Results of various investigators are summarized, with emphasis on evidence indicating that UFOs are spacecraft controlled by intelligent beings who are conducting an intensive survey of the earth. Suggestions are offered with regard to psychological procedures and techniques for investigating UFO reports, with emphasis on hypnotic techniques and the pendulum technique for comparing the reliability of conscious and subconscious information from UFO observers. Speech given at Sept. 1-5, 1968, meeting of American Psychological Association, Washington, D. C., under title "Psychological Problems of Gathering UFO Data."

----- Some uses of hypnosis in UFO research. Laramie, Wyoming, The Author, 1968. 18 p.

A brief review of UFO literature is presented. Examples are described in the use of hypnotic techniques in investigation of persons who have observed UFO phenomena. Advantages and disadvantages of hypnosis are discussed in regard to obtaining more detailed information from UFO observers. Speculations are offered regarding possible relationships of paranormal or ESP processes and observations of UFO phenomena. Cases are described which indicate possible relationships of hypnotic and psychic experiences of UFO observers. Suggestions are presented for further investigation of UFO phenomena through use of hypnotic and parapsychological procedures. Speech delivered May 9, 1968, at Rocky Mountain Psychological Association Meeting.

Szachnowski, Antoni. The necessity of a global international federation of UFO groups. BUFORA journal and bulletin, v. 1, Spring 1965: 5-9.

Lecture at the Southern Region UFO Research Groups Conference, Oxford, England, May 8, 1965.

Tacker, Lawrence J. Flying saucers and the U.S. Air Force. Princeton, N. J., Van Nostrand, 1960. 164 p.

Author, a former USAF public information officer on UFOs, discusses UFO sightings reported to Aerospace Technical Intelligence Center (Project Blue Book), Wright Patterson Air Force Base, from Summer 1947 through Summer 1960 in attempt to demonstrate that, in general, they were misinterpretations of known objects. He also gives history of USAF's research effort into UFO phenomena, including Project Saucer and Project Grudge.

UFOs again. Ordnance, v. 51, Mar.-Apr. 1967: 450

Announcement that USAF had awarded a $313,000 contract to the University of Colorado for scientific evaluation of UFO phenomenon. Project would be headed by Dr. Edward U. Condon.

165

U.S. Air Force. Air Materiel Command. Unidentified aerial objects; Project Sign. Dayton, Ohio, Wright-Patterson Air Force Base, 1949. 35 p. (Its Technical Report No. F-TR-2274-IA)

Descriptive and analytical study of 243 domestic and 30 foreign reported UFO sightings between 1947 and 1948. Individual cases are described in brief form as an appendix. Methods and reasoning applied in evaluating data are presented. Project Sign was initiated by the Technical Intelligence Division, Air Materiel Command, on January 22, 1948.

----- Unidentified flying objects; Project Grudge. Dayton, Ohio, Wright-Patterson Air Force Base, 1949. 366 p. (Its Technical Report No. 102-AC 49/15100)

Report discusses in full the history of Project Grudge, the problems encountered, and the procedures followed in the investigation and evaluation of reports of unidentified flying objects through January 1949.

U.S. Air Force. Air Technical Intelligence Center. Special report no. 14. (Analysis of reports of unidentified aerial objects). Dayton, Ohio, Wright-Patterson Air Force Base, 1955. 308 p. (Project no. 10073)

Results of 1953 study of UFOs by committee chaired by H. P. Robertson, theoretical physicist at California Institute of Technology. Examination of distributions of important characteristics of sightings and study of sightings evaluated as "unknown" led to conclusion that a combination of factors, principally the reported maneuvers of the objects and unavailability of supplemental data such as aircraft flight plans or balloon-launching records, resulted in failure to identify as "knowns" most of the reports of objects classified as "unknowns."

The U.S. Air Force news release. Flying saucer review, v. 8, July-Aug. 1962: 11-13.

Statement on UFO report evaluation for 1961 issued by USAF in February 1962.

U.S. Congress. House. Committee on Armed Services. Unidentified flying objects. [Washington, U.S. Govt. Print. Off., 1966] 84 p. (89th Cong., 2d sess. House. Report no. 55)

Information concerning U.S. Air Force activities in the area of reported sightings of unidentified flying objects.

Vallee, Jacques. How to classify and codify saucer sightings. Flying saucer review, v. 9, Sept.-Oct. 1963: 9-12.

Article sets forth briefly principles which can be used in the classification and coding of flying saucer sightings.

----- How to select significant UFO reports. Flying saucer review, v. 11, Sept.-Oct. 1965: 15-18.

Author believes that the scientific way to process UFO data is to divide the problem into two parts: (1) consider all the reports from all available sources, trying to explain them in terms of conventional objects; (2) when all identified cases have been eliminated, the residue must contain reference to the UFO phenomenon if it exists as an unconventional, objective agent in the generation of reports.

Vallée, Jacques. A survey of French UFO research groups. Flying saucer review, v. 13, Sept.-Oct. 1967: 22-24.

Evaluation of the five major French publications devoted to UFO research: Ouranos (Commission Internationale d' Enquêtes Scientifiques Ouranos); GEPA Bulletin (Groupement d' Etude de Phénomenès Aériens); Lumières dans la Nuit; Le Courier Interplanétaire; and the CEREIC Bulletin (Centre d' Etude et de Recherche d' Eléments Inconnus de Civilization).

----- A ten point research proposal. Flying saucer review, v. 12, Sept.-Oct. 1966: 12-14.

Author suggests that UFO research is an ordinary field of science and lists ten problems which can be resolved by applying conventional scientific techniques (i.e., problems which do not require the development of new methods and do not pre-suppose new discoveries in other fields of knowledge).

----- UFO research in the U.S.A. Flying saucer review, v. 11, Nov.-Dec. 1965: 32-36.

Author lists civilian groups active in UFO research and attempts to assess their reliability.

----- UFO research in the U.S.A. Flying saucer review, v. 12, Jan.-Feb. 1966: 6-11.

Author reports on his impressions of trends--motivations and theories--in American ufology.

Vallée, Jacques and Janine Vallée. Les phénomènes insolites de l'espace; le dossier des mystérieux objets célestes. Paris, La Table Rond, 1966. 321 p.

Part I (Chapters 3-5) is devoted to a discussion of whether the location of sightings follows a precise law; Part II (Chapters 7-10) discusses variations in the frequency of sighting reports and their possible correlation with known phenomena; Part III (Chapters 11-13) is an attempt to establish as accurate a classification categories as possible for different types of sighting reports and descriptions of the physical characteristics of the objects sighted.

Veit, Karl L. Erforschung ausserirdischer Weltraumschiffe -- ein wissenschaftliches Anliegen des 20. Jahrhunderts. Wiesbaden-Schierstein, Ventla-Verlag, 1963. 95 p.

Discussion of ideas on the current state of European astronomy is followed by a report on UFO's by Ruppelt, by statements of scientists on life in the universe, a report on UFO research activities in the USA, reports of UFO landings and a list of astronomers who have seen UFOs. On the question of how UFOs and space research will influence the belief in God and our relationship to the religions, statements by scientists indicate that the two areas are mutually exclusive, but that increased space research tends to lead to increased spiritual awareness. A brief summary of the current state of UFO research in Europe is followed by a discussion of opposing views, a list of persons who have actually seen UFOs, a call for increased research, and a list of UFO publications.

Vezina, Allan K. Canada 1967 -- a big year for UFO research. Flying saucers, June 1968: 8-10.

Summarizes 1967 UFO incidents in Canada. Mentions power cut-offs and burning of an individual in association with sightings. Disc-shaped UFO allegedly crash-landed into Shag Harbour, Nova Scotia; although there were many witnesses, neither the UFO nor its wreckage was found.

Webster, Robert N. and John C. Ross. Air Force report on UFOs. Fate, v. 12, Feb. 1959: 54-66.

Critique of USAF's Special Report No. 14, originally issued on May 5, 1955, summarizing its investigations of unidentified flying objects through 1952.

Zigel, Felix. The UFO problem -- a challenge to science. Flying saucers, June 1968: 25-26.

The joint effort of all scientists in the world should be applied to discovering the nature of the UFO phenomenon, the author says. Details given of sightings in the U.S.S.R. 1965-1967.

SEDUCTIONS

Creighton, Gordon W. Even more amazing. Flying saucer review, v. 12, July-Aug. 1966: 23-27; Sept.-Oct. 1966: 22-25; Nov.-Dec. 1966: 14-16. v. 13, Jan.- Feb. 1967: 25-27; v. 14, Jan.-Feb. 1968: 18-20.

English version of original declaration made by Antonio Villas Boas that on the night of October 15-16, 1957, he was abducted by helmeted, uniformed creatures from his farm near Francisco de Sales, Brazil, onto a landed spacecraft of apparently extraterrestrial origin; there, he was seduced by a naked, fair-skinned, red-haired woman with slanting eyes in what may have been a biological experiment. A translation of the medical report confirms the possibility of the alleged experience.

----- The most amazing case of all: Part 1 -- a Brazilian farmer's story. Flying saucer review, v. 11, Jan.-Feb. 1965: 13-17.

On Oct. 15, 1957, Antonio Villas Boas, a Brazilian farmer, was allegedly taken aboard a flying saucer and seduced by a white-skinned, red-haired woman with "slanted" eyes. Based on account in the April/July 1962 bulletin of the Sociedad Brasileira de Estudos Sobre Discos Voadores.

Creighton, Gordon. The most amazing case of all. Part II - Analysis of the Brazilian farmer's story. Flying saucer review, v. 11, Mar.-Apr. 1965: 5-8.

Author analyses details of Antonio Vilas Boas story that he was taken aboard a landed flying saucer and seduced by a white-skinned, red-haired, slant-eyed woman. He speculates that the mission of some extraterrestrial visitors might be to breed a mixed race -- a new race which would have inherited some of our characteristics, including our ability to live in a mixture of 80% nitrogen and 20% oxygen.

----- Postscript to the most amazing case of all. Flying saucer review, v. 11, July-Aug. 1965: 24-25.

Author suggests that far from being sensational, the account of the seduction of a Brazilian farmer aboard a landed flying saucer by an apparently extraterrestrial woman "is nothing new in the long history of the planet earth." He cites instances of apparently similar incidents.

Fontes, Olavo T. Even more amazing... Part V. Flying saucer review, v. 13, May-June 1967: 22-25.

Comments by the author on deposition by Antonio Villas Boas who claimed he was taken aboard a flying saucer and seduced by a red-haired woman.

Hudson, Jan. Those sexy saucer people. Canterbury, N. H., Greenlead Classics, 1967. 176 p.

A cross-section of contactee stories, largely concerned with messages and messengers allegedly of extraterrestrial origin. Emphasis is on the influence such experiences had on the lives of the contactee claimants, the divorces that resulted, and the bizarre sexual experiences of some contactees with UFO occupants.

Sheldon, Jean. I was seduced by a flying saucer. The National tattler, v. 6, Apr. 2, 1967: 1, 8-9.

Report of a Michigan girl who was allegedly forced to have sexual relations with a crew member of a UFO.

SIGHTINGS

1800s

Bowen, Charles. Cross country cog wheels. Flying saucer review, v. 12, Sept.-Oct. 1966: 16-17

Details of maneuvers of cogwheel-like mechanisms--possibly sonde devices from another world designed to record relief of earth's surface--sighted on Mar. 26, 1966, near Attigneville, France; on May 31, 1955, at Puy-Saint-Galmier, France; and on Feb. 8, 1855, in Devonshire, England.

Caputo, Livio. Anche gli astronauti hanno visto i dischi volanti. Epoca, v. LXIV, Aug. 28, 1966: 16-23.

Report on UFO sightings, chiefly in the U.S., from 1897 to 1966 and on investigation of phenomenon by Project Blue Book. Research programs of NICAP and APRO are mentioned.

Clark, Jerome. A contact claim. Flying saucer review, v. 11, Jan.-Feb. 1965: 30-32.

Noting the way in which the "beings" associated with the 1897 "airship" sightings seemed interested in reinforcing the belief that the craft was of mundane origin, the author concludes that the extraterrestrials either were engaged in some unknown activity in which they did not want their real identity made known, or that they chose to hide their existence realizing that the comparative unsophistication of nineteenth century Americans would not permit them to accept the interplanetary answer.

----- More on 1897. Flying saucer review, v. 13, July-Aug. 1967: 22-23.

Story in the April 23, 1897, Harrisburg (Ark.) Modern News is quoted, relating the visit of an "airship" and conversation of the "aeronaut" with an ex-Senator.

----- The strange case of the 1897 airship. Flying saucer review, v. 12, July-Aug. 1966: 10-17.

Account of large numbers of piloted aircraft, carrying brilliant searchlights and human-like passengers, capable of flying against the wind, landing and taking off when approached, which first appeared in northern California in November 1896 and reappeared all over the western and midwestern United States in March 1897.

Farish, Lucius. An 1880 UFO. Flying saucer review, v. 11, May-June 1965: 34-35.

A balloon described as having the shape of a fish and "apparently guided by a large fanlike apparatus" was seen, with occupants, over Gallisto Junction, N.M., on March 26, 1880. Account appeared in the Daily New Mexican, Santa Fe, 1880, and in June 1964 True West magazine.

----- Unidentified "airships" of the Gay Nineties. Fate, v. 19, Nov. 1966: 94-104.

Newspaper items are cited as evidence of aerial activity over a large portion of the U.S. during 1896-1897. Passengers of aircraft also reportedly observed.

Goble, H. C. Did Jones chart an unknown world? Fate, v. 10, Apr. 1957: 68-70.

Analysis of the 700-page observations of Zodiacal Light made Apr. 4, 1853 to Feb. 3, 1855, by Rev. Jones, Chaplain of Commodore Perry's expedition to Japan, seems to indicate that some components of the "light" were artificially-propelled luminous objects with behavior identical to that of UFOs.

Hanlon, Donald B. Texas odyssey of 1897. Flying saucer review, v. 12, Sept. - Oct. 1966: 8-11.

Wave of UFO sightings over Texas during 1897 as reported in the press is discussed.

Hanlon, Donald B. and Jacques Vallee. Airships over Texas. Flying saucer review, v. 13, Jan. -Feb. 1967: 20-25.

Article documents the analysis of the 1896-1897 wave of UFO sightings over the U. S. by presenting thirty hitherto unpublished reports.

Larson, Kenneth L. Charles Fort and the UFO. Flying saucers, July 1959: 20-23, 42.

Speculates on whether sightings of unidentified flying objects between November 1896 and April 1897 reported by Charles Fort implied that an aerial survey of the world took place.

Lore, Gordon and Harold H. Deneault. Mysteries of the skies: UFOs in perspective. Englewood Cliffs, N. J., Prentice-Hall, 1968. 237 p.

Historical aspects of the UFO phenomenon are presented. The 1897 "airship" reports are treated in detail.

Miller, Robert W. and Rick R. Hilberg. The saucer enigma. Cleveland, Ohio, UFO Magazine Publications, 1968. 23 p.

In "A Brief History of the Saucers, " UFO sightings, 1619-1897, are listed; a general summary of the UFO controversy follows.

Ribera, Antonio. El gran enigma de los platillos volantes, desde la prehistoria hasta la epoca actual. Santiago de Chile, Buenos Aires, Mexico, Barcelona, Editorial Pomaire, 1966. 431 p.

Author summarizes worldwide reports of unexplained aerial phenomena (1800s-1960s) with emphasis on U. S. accounts and on the 1954 wave of UFO sightings in France. Current theories on the possibility of life in other worlds are discussed. Hypotheses attempting to explain the UFO phenomenon are surveyed.

Watson, W. H. 19th century paraglider? Flying saucer review, v. 13, Nov. -Dec. 1967: 21.

Descriptions of the "airships" reportedly seen over the U.S. between 1880 and 1897 and descriptions of similar aeronautical devices currently being tested in U.S. and U.K. suggested idea to author that UFOnauts are generally a few decades ahead of us with their devices.

1900s

Chaloupek, Henri. Une observation en Moravie en 1913. Phenomenes spatiaux, Mar. 1967: 28.

Report of alleged UFO sighting near Brno, Czeckoslovakia, in late summer 1913.

Creighton, Gordon. Saucers and South Africa. Flying saucer review, v. 8, July-Aug. 1962. 18-21.

Account of UFO sightings during 1914 over South Africa. Resume from first chapter of Edgar Sievers' Flying Saucer Über Sudafrika (Pretoria, Sagittarius Verlag, 1955).

Edwards, Frank. UFOs, natural satellites, or meteors? Fate, v. 16, Dec. 1963: 49-54.

Flaring lights seen in the skies of Saskatchewan on February 9, 1913, were said by scientists to be meteors although they traveled parallel to earth in formation.

Gearhart, Livingston. Bombed by meteors. Fate, v. 18, Mar. 1965: 80-82.

On November 5, 1906, SS St. Andrew was caught in an apparent meteor shower; fall included a saucer-shaped meteor 10-15 feet in diameter.

The New Zealand "flap" of 1909. Flying saucer review, v. 10, Nov.-Dec. 1964: 32-33.

Discussion of newspaper reports of cigar-shaped flying objects and their occupants observed over New Zealand in 1909.

Observations etrangères. Phenomenes spatiaux, Feb. 1965: 32-33.

Report of UFO sightings in Transvaal (1906) and in U.S.A. (1964-1965).

Arnold, Kenneth A. I did see the flying disks. Fate, Spring 1948: 4-10.

Details of Arnold's June 24, 1947, sighting of nine disc-shaped objects flying in formation near Mt. Rainier.

----- The flying saucer as I saw it. Boise, Idaho, The Author, 1950. 16 p.

Author's account of UFO sighting June 24, 1947, near Mt. Rainier, Washington.

----- Mystery of the flying disks. Fate, Spring 1948: 19-48.

Apparent censorship by newspapers of reports of UFO sightings after July 10, 1947, is discussed. UFO sightings by reliable witnesses are cited to support author's belief in the reality of flying saucers.

Arnold, Kenneth A. and Ray Palmer. The coming of the saucers. Boise, Idaho, The Authors, 1952. 192 p.

Detailed account of Arnold's sighting on June 24, 1947, of chain of nine saucer-like objects flying in formation near Mt. Rainier and of June 21, 1947, reported sighting of six disc-shaped UFOs off Maury Island, Wash., by Harold A. Dahl. Photographs.

Berry, Bruce D. Flying saucer over the Golden Gate. Fate, v. 11, Feb. 1958: 52-54.

A tear-shaped UFO is allegedly seen on Sept. 11, 1948, near San Francisco's Golden Gate park.

Bloecher, Ted. Report on the UFO wave of 1947. Introd. by Dr. James E. McDonald. Washington, D. C., The Author, 1967. 1 v. (various pagings)

Primarily a reference work, this report provides a chronological listing of more than 850 UFO sightings made during June-July, 1947. Sightings were made in 48 states, the District of Columbia, and Canada. Newspapers provided basic source of information. Cases selected as representing special aspects of the UFO phenomenon are reported in detail.

Busson, Bernard and Gerard Leroy. Visitors from the skies. In The last secrets of the earth. New York, G. P. Putnam's Sons, 1956. p. 13-34.

Summary of "modern" reports of UFO sightings from 1947, with emphasis on the 1954 "wave" of flying saucers over France.

Calvillo Madrigal, Salvador. Plativología, ensayo nesciente. Mexico, 1954. 21 p.

Listing of worldwide sightings of UFOs from 1947 with emphasis on those viewed throughout Mexico in 1952.

Chaloupek, Henri. Observations en Tchécoslovaquie et en Bulgarie. Phénomènes spatiaux, Mar. 1968: 20-24.

Following UFO sightings are noted: (1) July 1, 1966, at Snopousov, Czechoslovakia; (2) summer 1944 at Blovice, Czechoslovakia; and (3) Nov. 21, 1967, at Sofia, Bulgaria.

Dagenis, Arleigh J. Do you believe in flying saucers? Michigan technic, Jan. 1960: 16-17, 50-51.

Author summarizes details of June 1947 sighting by Kenneth Arnold of flying disc-shaped objects; the January 1948 crash of Capt. Mantell while chasing a UFO; and the June 1952 appearance of mysterious objects over the White House and Capitol. He reviews the various explanatory theories.

Edwards, Frank. Are our satellites hunting the saucers? Fate, v. 16, May 1963: 29-35.

Within the 24-month period following 1947-1948 appearance of UFOs in the region of the South Pole, Argentina, Chile, Australia, France, Great Britain, the United States, Sweden, and the Soviet Union sent expeditions to the Antarctic. Tangible developments were (1) motion and still pictures of disc-shaped objects that circled ships under Chilean commander Orrego; and (2) realization that objects presumably entered earth's atmosphere at polar regions for a reason. On March 2, 1958, telemetry from Explorer satellites confirmed existence of zone of intense radiation - Van Allen belt - encircling earth about 600 miles out from equator. There is no such belt above either of the polar regions.

----- To see or not to see. In his My first 10,000,000 sponsors. New York, Ballantine Books, 1956. p. 110-125.

Reports are given of UFO sightings 1947-1954 by apparently reliable witnesses, especially airlines pilots, and subsequent apparent "muzzling" of witnesses and suppression of news stories ostensibly by a Government agency.

Everett, Eldon K. Saucers over Puget Sound. Flying saucers, July-Aug. 1958: 52-60.

Author relates experiences in flying saucer investigations from 1948 to 1954, including the Maury Island (Wash.) incident.

Flying saucers definitely proved. Fate, v. 1, Winter 1949: 47-51.

Story of a half-hour encounter Oct. 1, 1948, over Fargo, N. Dak., between an Air National Guard plane and flying disc. Four witnesses confirm story.

Gregg, Doris D. I am being watched by a UFO. Fate, v. 14, Nov. 1961: 27-33.

After sighting several UFOs in 1948 near Longview, Texas, author alleges she has been under continual surveillance by the objects up to the present.

Heard, Gerald. The riddle of the flying saucers. Is another world watching? London, Carroll & Nicholson, 1950. 157 p.

Lists in chronological order the UFO phenomena reported throughout the world between Midsummer 1947 and early Autumn 1950. Revised edition with new material published in New York in 1953 by Bantam Books.

Janssen, John H. My encounter with the flying discs. Fate, v. 2, Sept. 1949: 12-16.

An aircraft at 6,000 ft. altitude reportedly encounters a flying saucer on July 23, 1947, over Morristown, N. J.; the engine stops but the aircraft remains in normal level-flight attitude although motionless.

Jones, S. H. The Swedish ghost rockets. Flying saucer news, Summer 1955: 10-12.

Analysis, in the light of recent knowledge and events, of the many UFOs seen over Scandinavia in the summer of 1946.

Lang, Daniel. Something in the sky. In From Hiroshima to the moon. New York, Simon and Schuster, 1959. p. 320-346.

Overview of UFO sighting reports 1947-1954; summary of explanatory hypotheses; and discussion of the "official" USAF position.

Michel, Aimé. The truth about flying saucers. New York, Criterion Books, 1956. 255 p.

Author presents and comments on UFO sightings reported throughout the world from 1947. Sources include: Project Saucer records; communiques or records of the air forces in U. S. A., U. K., Canada, South Africa, France, and Sweden; USAF's Air Technical Intelligence Center; National Meteorological Office (France and the French Union); French and foreign technical periodicals; personal inquiries; and information in the files of NICAP. Summarizes current theories and explanations of UFO phenomena. Translation of Lueurs sur les soucoupes volantes.

National Investigations Committee on Aerial Phenomena. [NICAP Headquarters UFO Newspaper Clipping File, 1947-1966]. Washington, D. C., 1967. 37 v. (looseleaf) 35 mm.

Material constituted the newspaper clippings file of Civilian Saucer Intelligence (CSI), New York, now defunct. Microfilm made by the Science and Technology Division, Library of Congress, 1967.

Olsen, Thomas M. The reference for outstanding UFO sighting reports. Rider-wood, Md. UFO Information Retrieval Center, Inc., 1967. 1 v. (various pagings) (UFORIC - 6661)

Collection of 160 outstanding UFO reports as originally published. A numerical value of reliability is formulated for each case, the reports are presented in chronological order and cross-indexed by date, geographical location and source.

Palmer, Ray. New report on the flying saucers. Fate, v. 4, Jan. 1951: 63-81.

Excerpts from article entitled "The Flying Saucers--Fact or Fiction" printed in July 1950 Flying. Reports alleged UFO sightings on March 31, 1950, by Chicago and Southern Air Lines pilots Capt. Jack Adams and G. W. Anderson, Jr., near Little Rock, Ark.; in July 1948 by Eastern Air Lines pilots Capt. Clarence S. Chiles and John B. Whitted southwest of Montgomery, Ala.; on April 27, 1950, by Trans-World Air Lines pilots Capt. Robert Adickes and Robert Manning near South Bend, Ind.; and on May 29, 1950, by American Airlines pilot Capt. William T. Sperry near Washington, D. C.

Perego, Alberto. L'aviazione di altri pianeti opera tra noi. Rome, Edizioni del Centro Italiano, 1963. 563 p.

Report on worldwide UFO sightings between 1943-1963 with emphasis on those over Italy.

Ribera, Antonio. Objetos desconocidos en el cielo. Barcelona, Libraria Editorial Argos, 1961. 289 p.

Reports major UFO sightings throughout the world from 1947, reviews some of the literature on the subject, and summarizes theories currently proposed to explain the UFO phenomenon.

Signs, portents, and flying saucers. Newsweek, v. 30, July 14, 1947: 19-20.

Reports "flap" of UFO sightings coast-to-coast over U. S. during weekend of July 4, 1947.

Speaking of pictures: a rash of flying discs breaks out over the U.S. Life, July 21, 1947: 14-16.

Reports UFO sightings in 43 states and the District of Columbia between June 25 and July 10, 1947. Explanatory theories summarized.

U. S. Air Force. Air Materiel Command. Unidentified aerial objects; Project Sign. Dayton, Ohio, Wright-Patterson Air Force Base, 1949. 35 p. (Its Technical Report No. F-TR-2274-IA)

Descriptive and analytical study of 243 domestic and 30 foreign reported UFO sightings between 1947 and 1948. Individual cases are described in brief form as an appendix. Methods and reasoning applied in evaluating data are presented. Project Sign was initiated by the Technical Intelligence Division, Air Materiel Command, on January 22, 1948.

U.S. Air Force. Air Materiel Command. Unidentified flying objects; Project Grudge. Dayton, Ohio, Wright-Patterson Air Force Base, 1949. 366 p. (Its Technical Report No. 102-Ac 49/15100)

Report discusses in full the history of Project Grudge, the problems encountered, and the procedures followed in the investigation and evaluation of reports of unidentified flying objects through January 1949.

U.S. Air Force. Air Technical Intelligence Center. Special report no. 14. (Analysis of reports of unidentified aerial objects). Dayton, Ohio, Wright-Patterson Air Force Base, 1955. 308 p. (Project no. 10073)

Results of 1953 study of UFOs by committee chaired by H. P. Robertson, theoretical physicist at California Institute of Technology. Examination of distributions of important characteristics of sightings and study of sightings evaluated as "unknown" led to conclusion that a combination of factors, principally the reported maneuvers of the objects and unavailability of supplemental data such as aircraft flight plans or balloon-launching records, resulted in failure to identify as "knowns" most of the reports of objects classified as "unknowns."

Vallee, Jacques. Ghost rockets: a moment of history. Flying saucer review, v. 10, July-Aug. 1964: 30-32.

Article cites reports in French press of strange lights, apparently under intelligent control, seen in northern Europe during 1946.

What the Air Force believes about flying saucers. Fate, v. 2, Nov. 1949: 69-83.

Digest of official report of studies made by Project Saucer of the Air Materiel Command, Wright-Patterson Air Force Base, Ohio. Incidents involving Kenneth Arnold (June 24, 1947), Capt. Thomas F. Mantell (Jan. 7, 1948), Eastern Air Lines pilots Capt. C. S. Chiles and John B. Whitted (July 1948), and North Dakota National Guard Lt. George F. Gorman (Oct. 1, 1948) are discussed.

Wilkins, Harold T. Flying saucers uncensored. New York, Citadel Press, 1955. 255 p.

Author catalogues UFO sightings and incidents over U.K., Western Europe, U.S., and Australia from 1947 through 1955 and speculates that extraterrestrial visitants are possibly established in bases on moon and other planets; a cosmic general staff may receive reports on terrestrial affairs as well as biological and ecological samples from earth for purposes of study and experimentation.

Zinsstag, Lou and T. Allemann. UFO-sichtungen über der Schweiz, 1949-1958.
Basel, Zurich, UFO-Verlag, 1958. 48 p.

Compilation of reports of unidentified flying objects seen over Switzerland 1949-
1958.

An airline captain speaks out. The UFO investigator, v. 2, Oct. -Nov. 1962: 5-6.

Main details are given of July 14, 1952, UFO sighting by Pan American Airways pilot Capt. William B. Nash. Statement by Nash is published in reply to Dr. Donald Menzel's rejection of his report.

Anderson, Carl. Two nights to remember. Los Angeles, New Age Publishing Co., 1956. 55 p.

Flying saucers are allegedly viewed at close range by author and his family on Apr. 4, 1954, on the Mojave Desert, California, and in August 1955 at Yosemite National Park.

Barker, Gray. Chasing the flying saucers. Flying saucers, Dec. 1958: 43-56.

Summary of UFO sightings and activities of UFO researchers during summer 1958.

----- Chasing the flying saucers. Flying saucers, Feb. 1959: 24-34.

Report on high incidence of UFO sightings in 1958.

----- Chasing the flying saucers. Flying saucers, July 1959: 24-37.

Feb. 24, 1959, UFO sighting by American Airlines pilot Capt. Peter Killian is discussed in detail.

----- Chasing the flying saucers. Flying saucers, Feb. 1960: 15-24.

Describes interview with family of Weston, West Va., in which they described hearing an intense whining noise on July 9, 1959, that caused temporary paralysis. Source of the sound seemed to be a brightly glowing object back of their house.

----- The monster and the saucer. Fate, v. 6, Jan. 1953: 12-17.

Account of author's investigation of sighting on September 12, 1952, near Flatwoods, W. Va., of a "ten-foot, red-faced monster, which sprayed a foul, sickening gas." There were seven witnesses whose stories agreed.

Benard, Paul C. Who believes in flying saucers? Bluebook, v. 101, July 1955: 20, 110-113.

Results of author's inquiry into 123 UFO sightings reported during 1952-1955 near Blythe and Desert Center, Calif.

Bender, Albert K. Flying saucers and the three men. Annotated and with introd. and epilogue by Gray Barker. Clarksburg, W. Va., Saucerian Books, 1962. 194 p.

Discussion of activities of and reports of UFO sightings made to International Flying Saucer Bureau, organized by Bender in April 1952 in Bridgeport, Conn., and of Bender's alleged contact with extraterrestrial beings which he claims resulted in his dissolving IFSB in November 1953.

Bessor, John P. Some strange meteors. Fate, v. 7, July 1954: 78-79.

Among strange aerial objects described is a six-foot-diameter purple globe that landed in a Philadelphia, Pa., field in October 1950. When touched by a policeman, it dematerialized.

Bowen, Charles. Cross country cog wheels. Flying saucer review, v. 12, Sept-Oct. 1966: 16-17.

Details of maneuvers of cogwheel-like mechanisms--possibly sonde devices from another world designed to record relief of earth's surface--sighted on Mar. 26, 1966, near Attignéville, France; on May 31, 1955, at Puy-Saint-Galmier, France; and on Feb. 8, 1855, in Devonshire, England.

----- A South American trio. Flying saucer review, v. 11, Jan.-Feb. 1965: 19-21.

Three UFO sighting cases from South America: (1) In April, 1957, a resident of Cordoba, Argentina, allegedly encountered a landed flying saucer and was invited by one of the crew members to enter for an inspection tour; (2) On Jan. 10, 1958; an unidentified floating object was viewed off the coast of São Paulo, Brazil, by several witnesses before sinking out of sight; (3) During a fire near São Bernado do Campo, Brazil, in 1963, a flying saucer landed amid the flames, and several tall, good-looking "people" emerged from it and picked up pieces of burnt material, stones, and other debris.

A Brazilian contact claim. Flying saucer review, v. 7, Sept.-Oct. 1961: 18-20.

Translation of report of contact with extraterrestrial beings and ride in flying saucer by Prof. João de Freitas Guimaraes on Aug. 27, 1957, near São Sebastião, Brazil. Originally appeared in Discos Voadores, Bulletin No. 4, July 1, 1959, issued by Dr. W. Buhler in Rio de Janeiro, Brazil.

Brief saucer review. Fate, v. 11, Mar. 1958: 14-17.

Resume of UFO sightings during November 1957 reported from around the world.

Busson, Bernard and Gerard Leroy. Visitors from the skies. In The last secrets of the earth. New York, G. P. Putnam's Sons, 1956. p. 13-34.

Summary of "modern" reports of UFO sightings from 1947, with emphasis on the 1954 "wave" of flying saucers over France.

Caldbeck, David. Flying saucers over South Africa. Australian saucer record, v. 3, First quarter 1957: 3-8.

Summary of newspaper accounts of UFO sightings in South Africa, 1951-1956.

Calvillo Madrigal, Salvador. Plativologia, ensayo nesciente. México, 1954. 21 p.

Listing of worldwide sightings of UFOs from 1947 with emphasis on those viewed throughout Mexico in 1952.

Carnell, John. BOAC's flying jellyfish. Fate, v. 7, Nov. 1954: 16-23.

Report of seven black objects that followed a BOAC stratocruiser for 80 miles over the coast of Labrador on July 1, 1954, and then vanished when a jet fighter approached. It was said that there was a big central object which appeared to continuously change shape and six smaller objects that "dodged" around the "parent."

Carrouges, Michel. Les apparitions de martiens. Paris, Fayard, 1963. 275 p.

Study of UFO sightings reported during September-October 1954 as a sociological phenomenon.

Comella, Tom. UFO's: problems in perception. Fate, v. 12, Jan. 1959: 92-96.

Details are given of UFO sighting in Cleveland, Ohio, October 21, 1955. There were several witnesses.

Constance, Arthur. What blazed over Britain? Flying saucer news, Autumn 1955: 8-15.

Summary of numerous newspaper reports of UFO seen by hundreds of people in cities and towns throughout Great Britain on March 24, 1955.

Couten, Francois. Curieux et secret contact interplanetaire survenue en Argentine le 2 janvier 1953. Phénomènes spatiaux, Nov. 1964: 5-7.

Report of UFO landing in Argentina on Jan. 2, 1953.

Creighton, Gordon. A cigar-shaped UFO over Antarctica. Flying saucer review, v. 14, Mar.-Apr. 1968: 20-22.

A group of Chilean scientists observed two UFOs for two days off Robertson Island, Antarctica, during January 1956. Scientists were participating in 2nd International Geophysical Year 1956-58 expedition. Report supplied by UFO Chile of Santiago.

Creighton, Gordon. The extraordinary happenings at Casa Blanca. Flying saucer review, v. 13, Sept.-Oct. 1967: 16-18.

On Aug. 22, 1955, a group of children playing in the garden of a home in Casa Blanca, California, allegedly first sighted silvery, spinning discs and later 3-ft.-tall transparent beings who emerged from landed craft. Author considers accounts of incident by Coral Lorenzen in Flying Saucer Review's The Humanoids and by Winona Cromwell in a 1955 issue of the Journal of the Borderland Sciences Research Association.

----- UFOs in the South Atlantic. Flying saucer review, v. 14, Jan.-Feb. 1968: 13.

During the summer of 1952, "disc-shaped machines" were seen hovering a meter or so above the south Atlantic off the coast of Itenhaém, Brazil. From Os Discos Voadores-Fantasia e Realidad by Auriphebo Simoes (São Paulo, Livraria Edart, 1957. p. 375-376).

Cruttwell, Norman E. G. Flying saucers over Papua in 1959; points out general characteristics of series; and discusses their possible nature, origin, and purpose. UFO activity at Boianai, Papua, June 26-27, 1959, where humanoids were observed in hovering spacecraft by Anglican Mission director Father William B. Gill is given particular attention.

----- What happened in Papua in 1959? Flying saucer review, v. 6, Nov.-Dec. 1960: 3-7.

Details and analysis of sighting on June 26-27, 1959, at Boianai Mission, Papua, of UFO apparently manned by humanoids.

Dagenis, Arleigh J. Do you believe in flying saucers? Michigan technic, Jan. 1960: 16-17, 50-51.

Author summarizes details of June 1947 sighting by Kenneth Arnold of flying disc-shaped objects; the January 1948 crash of Capt. Mantell while chasing a UFO; and the June 1952 appearances of mysterious objects over the White House and Capitol. He reviews the various explanatory theories.

Dixon, William A. Saucers or illusions? Air facts, v. 14, Sept. 1, 1951: 37-43.

Report by TWA pilot Capt. Art Shutts of UFO sighting on Dec. 27, 1950 (Flight 361) near Bradford, Illinois. Crew members Capt. Robert Kaddock and hostess Mary Lind also saw object.

Dowling, J. Flying saucer over Durban. Outspan, v. 1449, Dec. 3, 1954: 14-17.

Edwards, Frank. Flying saucers over Brazil. Fate, v. 13, Sept. 1960: 42-49.

Reports UFO sightings in Brazil 1953-1958.

Edwards, Frank. Frank Edwards' report: flying saucers stopped the ball game!
Fate, v. 10, Nov. 1957: 35-41.

About 75 players and parents attending a Little League baseball game in
Paris, Ill., July 18, 1957, watched two shiny, disc-shaped objects pursue
a jet plane across the sky.

----- To see or not to see flying saucers. Fate, v. 10, May 1957: 17-32.

Instances of near-collisions between aircraft and UFOs (1954-1955) are noted.
Other sightings by credible observers are reported. Author suggests that
rather than insist that the objects do not exist, the Air Force should keep the
public informed of findings in investigations underway. Excerpted from
author's book, My First 10,000,000 Sponsors (N.Y., Ballantine, 1956).

----- UFO buzzes train. Fate, v. 12, Feb. 1959: 25-30.

On October 3, 1958, crew of freight train No. 91 were allegedly paced by
four UFOs for 1 hour 10 minutes on run between Monon, Indiana, and Indianapolis.

Flying saucer review. World roundup of UFO sightings and events. Introd. by
Brinsley le Poer Trench. New York, Citadel Press, 1958. 224 p.

Chronological listing of UFO sightings between late 1955 and December 1957 as
reported to Flying Saucer Review.

Flying saucer roundup: saucer report no. 1. Fate, v. 11, Feb. 1958: 29-37.

Summary of UFO sighting reports March-October 1957.

Fontes, Olavo T. The Brazilian navy sighting at the island of Trinidade. Flying
saucers, Feb. 1961: 27-54.

Details of UFO sighting Jan. 16, 1958, by Brazilian ship Almirante Saldanha
which was on IGY mission near Trinidade Island. Photographs taken were
certified as genuine by the Brazilian government. Reprinted from A.P.R.O.
Bulletin.

Fort-Lamy, 27 mars 1955. Phénomènes spatiaux, Mar. 1967: 25-27.

Report of UFO sighting allegedly witnessed by 70 people at Fort-Lamy airport,
France, on March 27, 1955.

Fuller, Curtis. Fate's report on flying saucers. Fate, v. 7, May 1954: 16-22.

Significant developments during 1953 in the investigation of unidentified aerial
objects are reported.

Fuller, Curtis. Let's get straight about the saucers. Fate, v. 5, Dec. 1952: 20-31.

Details of UFO sightings over Washington, D. C., during July 1952 are
reported and some theories that have been advanced to explain the UFO
phenomenon discussed.

----- Report from New Zealand. Fate, v. 10, June 1957: 15-16.

UFO sightings near Auckland, N. Z., on Sept. 4, 1956.

----- Saucers trail airliner. Fate, v. 12, Aug. 1959: 25-31.

On February 25, 1959, 39 persons on an American Airlines DC-6 airliner
piloted by Capt. Peter Killian observed three UFOs for 45 minutes while
the plane was enroute between Bradford and Erie, Pennsylvania.

Garreau, Charles. Alerte dans le ciel! Documents officiels sur les objets volants
non identifiés. Paris, Éditions du Grand Damier, 1956. 257 p. (Collection
"Cosmos")

Lists sightings of UFOs in Europe and the U. S. A. from June 1947 to Autumn
1954 and builds case to support theory they are of extraterrestrial origin.

Gibbons, Gavin. The coming of the space ships. London, Neville Spearman, Ltd.,
1956. 183 p.

Account of UFO sightings by author over North Wales from Dec. 1953 to March
1955 and of sightings reported to British Flying Saucer Bureau between May
1952 and Jan. 1956.

González Ganteaume, Horacio. Platillos voladores sobre Venezuela. Caracas,
1961. 250 p.

Account of authenticated UFO sightings over Venezuela from 1959 based on
published and unpublished official reports. General review of worldwide
manifestations of UFO phenomenon.

Hall, Richard H., ed. The UFO evidence. Washington, National Investigations
Committee on Aerial Phenomena, 1964. 184 p.

Documented report containing 746 UFO sighting cases selected from NICAP
files and covering NICAP's investigations from early 1957 to the end of
1963. Sightings are listed and analyzed by observer categories; historical
development of phenomenon and Congressional attitudes and activity are
treated. Evidence is presented to support hypothesis that UFOs are under
intelligent control and that some of them might therefore be of extraterrestrial origin.

Hamilton, Jared. Saucers over Italy. Fate, v. 8, Mar. 1955: 14-19.

Reports of unidentified flying objects seen over Italy September-November 1954.

Heard, Gerald. The riddle of the flying saucers. Is another world watching?
London, Carroll & Nicholson, 1950. 157 p.

Lists in chronological order the UFO phenomena reported throughout the
world between Midsummer 1947 and early Autumn 1950. Revised edition
with new material published in New York in 1953 by Bantam Books with
title Is Another World Watching? The Riddle of the Flying Saucers.

I saw a flying saucer. Flying saucers from other worlds, June 1957: 44-50.

Reports of alleged UFO sightings throughout the world May-August 1956.

I saw a flying saucer. Flying saucers from other worlds, Aug. 1957: 74-80.

Personal accounts of alleged UFO sightings 1953-1957.

Keyhoe, Donald E. Flight 117 and the flying saucer. True, v. 27, Aug. 1950:
24-25, 75.

Report of a red disk that paced a Trans World Air Lines DC-3 over Indiana
on April 27, 1950. Pilots were Robert F. Manning and Robert Adickes.

----- The flying saucer conspiracy. New York, Holt, 1955. 315 p.

Covers important developments 1953-55 in UFO sightings and events. Reports
paraphrased from official USAF records and cleared through USAF Press
Office, DOD.

Knight, Oscar F. Wolverton trail event: a visitor from Venus. Strathmore, Calif.,
1963. 11 p.

During a camping trip in Sequoia National Park, Calif., on July 1, 1955, author
observed a "mother ship" from which a number of smaller UFOs were discharged. He later encountered a being whose strangeness of manner and
speech led to speculation that he may have been an occupant of the strange craft.

Korean saucers. Newsweek, v. 39, Mar. 3, 1952: 44.

Three-foot-diameter flying saucer reportedly moved parallel to a B-29 flying
over North Korea at 200 mph about midnight Jan. 29-30, 1952. For five minutes it was in view of two crewmen and then disappeared.

Lang, Daniel. Something in the sky. In From Hiroshima to the moon. New York,
Simon and Schuster, 1959. p. 320-346.

Overview of UFO sighting reports 1947-1954; summary of explanatory hypotheses; and discussion of the "official" USAF position.

Letter from Paris. The New Yorker, v. 30, Oct. 23, 1954: 159-160.

Report of and commentary on flying saucers seen over France during September 1954.

Luciano Galli's contact claim. Flying saucer review, v. 8, Sept. -Oct. 1962: 29-30.

Account of July 7, 1957 (or 1959) encounter near Bologna, Italy, with a landed flying saucer from Venus and its crew and ride aboard spacecraft to "mother ship." Based on interview by Renate Albanese in June 1962 Domenica della Sera.

Luna, Walter Fernandez. La ufologia en el Uruguay. Montevideo, The Author, 1968. 14 p.

Details are given of authenticated UFO sighting in Uruguay July 7, 1958.

Maney, Charles A. The Campinas sighting. Flying saucer review, v. 8, May-June 1962: 3-6.

Summary of information relating to UFO sighting Dec. 13, 1954, at Campinas, Brazil, during which a liquid substance was seen to drop from the spacecraft.

Mann, Mary and Amey Hoag. We saw a flying saucer. Fate, v. 10, Apr. 1957, 54-56.

On Sept. 4, 1956, near Melbourne, Fla., a star-like object was sighted that changed in size and shape.

Michael. Canadian flying saucers. Ontario, Canada, The Brotherhood of Faithists, 1957. 26 p.

Record of UFO sightings in Canada 1955-1956 related at the 1956 meeting of the Brotherhood of Faithists, Casa Loma, Toronto, Canada.

Michel, Aimé. Bocaranga saucers. Fate, v. 9, Dec. 1956: 15-19.

On Nov. 22, 1952, eight men spent half an hour observing four flying saucers, their evolutions, variations of color and luminosity, and the whole range of their antics. Account is taken from records of the local Service Météorologique of the Oubangui Chari in French Equatorial Africa. Reprinted from author's book, The Truth About Flying Saucers (New York, Criterion Books, 1956).

----- Flying saucers in Europe: Italian flying saucer. Fate, v. 10, Oct. 1957: 19-24.

A UFO is sighted over Rome by many witnesses on Sept. 17, 1954. In France, a whole series of UFO observations was made on the same day.

Michel, Aimé. Flying saucers in Europe: saucers--or delusions? Fate, v. 11, Jan. 1958: 73-79.

Cases of UFO sightings in France during 1954 are reported in which electric - circuit "paralysis" of motor vehicles was a concomitant feature.

----- Flying saucers in Europe: the crisis of autumn, 1954. Fate, v. 10, Aug. 1957: 28-35.

Report on UFO sightings and landings in France during the fall of 1954.

----- The truth about flying saucers. New York, Criterion Books, 1956. 255 p.

Author presents and comments on UFO sightings reported throughout the world from 1947. Sources include: Project Saucer records; communiques or records of the air forces in U.S.A., U. K., Canada, South Africa, France, and Sweden; USAF's Air Technical Intelligence Center; National Meteorological Office (France and the French Union): French and foreign technical periodicals; personal inquiries; and information in the files of NICAP. Summarizes current theories and explanations of UFO phenomena. Translation of Lueurs sur les soucoupes volantes. Published also in paperback edition by Pyramid Pubns. (T1647), New York.

Miller, Max B. Recent dramatic saucer reports. Fate, v. 13, Jan. 1960: 29-32.

Details are given of UFO sightings in New Zealand, Australia, and New Guinea during June-July 1959 where occupants were observed by responsible persons.

----- UFOs invade Australian skies. Fate, v. 11, Feb. 1958: 48-51.

Report of UFO sightings over Australia during July 1957.

Mollohan, Hank. The Holly River sighting, as told to Gray Barker. Flying saucers from other worlds, May 1958: 36-41.

Report of a UFO sighting November 8, 1957, near Holly, West Virginia.

More saucers. Time, v. 59, Mar. 3, 1952: 92, 94.

USAF spokesman revealed that on Jan. 29, 1952, the tail gunner and fire-control man of a B-29 over Wonsan, North Korea, saw a disc-shaped object that seemed to fly with a revolving motion. It was orange in color with small, bluish flames around its rim. For five minutes it flew along with the bomber at 200 mph; then it disappeared.

Morgan, Dean. The Red Bud, Illinois photo. Flying saucers, Oct. 1959: 5-7.

Details are given of UFO sighted on April 23, 1950, near Red Bud, Illinois, and of the photograph taken.

National Investigations Committee on Aerial Phenomena. [NICAP Headquarters UFO Newspaper Clipping File, 1947-1966]. Washington, D. C., 1967. 37 v. (looseleaf). 35 mm.

Material constituted the newspaper clippings file of Civilian Saucer Intelligence (CSI), New York, now defunct. Microfilm made by the Science and Technology Division, Library of Congress, 1967.

The night of September 29. Fate, v. 12, Feb. 1959: 31-38.

Details of numerous UFO sightings reported throughout North America on September 29, 1958.

Norman, Samuel. Recent UFOs over Japan. Fate, v. 9, June 1956: 22-24.

Sightings of strange aerial objects over Japan during January 1956 are described.

Observations francaises plus anciennes. Phénomènes spatiaux, Nov. 1954: 26-36.

UFO sightings 1955-1963.

Observations francaises plus anciennes. Phénomènes spatiaux, Feb. 1965: 29-32.

UFO sightings in France 1951-1962.

Observations hors presse. Phénomènes spatiaux, Dec. 1966: 27-30.

Three previously unpublished UFO sighting reports: (1) On Aug. 18, 1952, a disc-shaped object was observed over the Indian Ocean by the crew of the "Oregon," (2) on Aug. 20, 1953, an object "like a ball of fire" was seen near Pres de Cronat, France; (3) On Dec. 2, 1957, a circular object was seen between Royère and Bourganeuf, France.

Olsen, Thomas M. The reference for outstanding UFO sighting reports. Riderwood, Md. UFO Information Retrieval Center, Inc., 1967. 1 v. (various pagings) (UFORIC - 6661)

Collection of 160 outstanding UFO reports as originally published. A numerical value of reliability is formulated for each case; the reports are presented in chronological order and cross-indexed by date, geographical location and source.

Palmer, Ray. New report on the flying saucers. Fate, v. 4, Jan. 1951: 63-81.

Excerpts from article entitled "The Flying Saucers--Fact or Fiction" printed in July 1950 Flying. Reports alleged UFO sightings on March 31, 1950, by Chicago and Southern Air Lines pilots Capt. Jack Adams and G. W. Anderson, Jr., near Little Rock, Ark.; in July 1948 by Eastern Air Lines pilots Capt. Clarence S. Chiles and John B. Whitted southwest of Montgomery, Ala.; on April 27, 1950, by Trans-World Air Lines pilots Capt. Robert Adickes and Robert Manning near South Bend, Ind.; and on May 29, 1950, by American Airlines pilot Capt. William T. Sperry near Washington, D. C.

Perego, Alberto. L'aviazione di altri pianeti opera tra noi. Rome, Edizioni del Centro Italiano studi aviazione elettromagnetica, 1963. 563 p.

Report on worldwide UFO sightings between 1943-1963 with emphasis on those over Italy.

----- The Monguzzi case. [Basle, 1965] . 2 p.

English translation by Lou Zinsstag of pertinent section of Perego's Svelato il mistero dei dischi volanti (Rome, Edizioni del C. I. S. A. E. R. , 1957).

Plenty going on in the skies. U. S. news & world report, v. 36, Jan. 1, 1954: 27-28.

Excerpts from text of USAF report on its investigation of unidentified flying objects during 1952.

The Project A report. Ada, Ohio, Ohio Nothern University, 1953. 9 p.

Scientific analysis of unidentified flying objects reported in the year 1952. Conducted by the faculty and staff of Ohio Northern University, Ada, Ohio.

Reports from everywhere. Fate, v. 7, May 1954: 23-31.

Reports on worldwide sightings of UFOs June-December 1953.

Ribera, Antonio. El gran enigma de los platillos volantes, desde la prehistoria hasta la època actual. Santiago de Chile, Buenos Aires, Mexico, Barcelona, Editorial Pomaire, 1966. 431 p.

Author summarizes worldwide reports of unexplained aerial phenomena (1800s-1960s)with emphasis of U. S. accounts and on the 1954 wave of UFO sightings in France. Current theories on the possibility of life in other worlds are discussed. Hypotheses attempting to explain the UFO phenomenon are surveyed.

----- Objetos desconocidos en el cielo. Barcelona, Libraria Editorial Argos, 1961. 289 p. (Documenta)

Reports major UFO sightings throughout the world from 1947, reviews some of the literature on the subject, and summarizes theories currently proposed to explain the UFO phenomenon.

Roberts, August C. The Skywatch Tower case. Flying saucers from other worlds, Aug. 1957: 8-15.

Details of UFO sighting on July 28, 1952, from Civilian Defense Skywatch Tower, New York City, and photographing of object.

Ross, John C. The big, fat UFO: saucer report no. 2. Fate, v. 11, Feb. 1958: 38-43.

A huge, glowing, cigar-shaped object was reportedly seen near Levelland, Tex., Elmwood Park, Ill., White Sands Proving Grounds, N. Mex., and Fiji Islands on Nov. 2-4, 1957. A silvery material that had apparently fallen from the sky appeared on the ground in conjunction with the sighting.

----- Fate's report on the flying saucer. Fate, v. 6, Oct. 1953: 6-13.

UFO sightings 1952-1953 throughout the U. S. are reported.

----- The lights that failed. Fate, v. 7, May 1954: 37-39.

Account of silent, blinking red lights that appeared daily near Camp Barrett, Va., during December 1953, and of the "scientific" explanation.

----- UFOs over New Guinea. Fate, v. 13, Mar. 1960: 44-52.

Article excerpted from 15-page report by the Reverend Father William Gill of the Boiani Anglican Mission of the Territory of Papua and New Guinea. Saucer-shaped objects were viewed from the mission on June 21 and 26-28, 1959. On June 26, four apparently humanoid figures allegedly waved to 38 humans from a saucer-shaped UFO that hovered overhead for 4 hours 19 minutes.

Roussel, Robert. La roue d' Attignéville. Phénomènes spatiaux, June 1966: 25-31.

On May 31, 1955, a luminous disc-shaped object 3-3 1/2 feet in diameter, encircled with spinelike projections of different lengths, was seen rolling across the grass in Puy-Saint-Galmier, France. A similar object was seen on March 26, 1966, at Tranqueville-Graux, France.

Ruppelt, Edward J. Report on unidentified flying objects. Fate, v. 10, Apr. 1957: 27-43.

An Air Force F-86 jet pilot, paced by a flying saucer during summer 1952, opened fire on it. Account excerpted from author's book, The Report on Unidentified Flying Objects (Garden City, N. Y., Doubleday, 1956).

Saucers and the Iron Curtain: a report from Czechoslovakia. Flying saucer review, v. 6, July-Aug. 1960: 31-32.

Report from Czechoslovakian publication Kridla Vlasti (No. 26, Dec. 22, 1959) on UFO sighting over Czech airfield Nov. 16, 1959, by ground crew and pilots.

Saucers in the news. Flying saucers from other worlds, May 1958: 76-77.

Reports of UFO sightings December 1957 - January 1958.

Saucers in the news. Flying saucers, July-Aug. 1958: 61-63.

Newspaper reports of flying saucer sightings November 1957-January 1958.

Saucers over Paris. Flying saucers from other worlds, June 1957: 76-77.

UFO was tracked by radar from Orly Airport, near Paris, France, on February 19, 1956. Speed was calculated at 2,250 miles an hour.

Saunders, Alex. Flying saucer scrap book. Search, Apr. 1959: 22-39, 53.

Newspaper clippings from scrapbook on UFOs are cited to provide details of little-known sightings during 1952-1955.

Seaman, E. A. A 1953 sighting. Science, v. 154, Dec. 2, 1966: 1118.

Seeing things. Newsweek, v. 50, Nov. 18, 1957: 41, 44.

130 reports of unidentified flying objects were received by U. S. Air Defense Command Headquarters at Colorado Springs, November 4-11, 1957. Some of the more interesting cases are cited.

Serpas, Paul F. The saucer that got away. Fate, v. 8, Mar. 1955: 34-37.

Flying saucer sighting on July 18, 1954, in New Orleans is described by the author.

Skillie from the sky. Newsweek, v. 50, Nov. 25, 1957: 38.

During week of Nov. 11, 1957, Cherokee Indians reported seeing a UFO resembling a fireball that settled on Great Smoky Mountains National Park near Cherokee, N. C.

Sklarewitz, Norman. Tokyo space ship. Fate, v. 11, Mar. 1958: 46-48.

Civilian engineer with U. S. Army in Japan describes UFO sighting on Lake Imba-numa on the Bozo Peninsula about 50 miles from Tokyo, Nov. 11, 1957.

Slaboda, Emil. He collected on a flying saucer. Fate, v. 10, June 1957: 66-69.

Night watchman Harry J. Sturdevant was granted medical compensation for disability caused by injuries he said he suffered when a UFO zoomed past him while he was on duty. Alleged incident took place near Trenton, N. J., on Oct. 2, 1956.

Sondy, Dominic. Space ship over Detroit. Fate, v. 10, June 1957: 86-89.

Author describes sighting of gigantic cigar-shaped object over Detroit on May 8, 1955.

Towner, Cliff R. Silver chaff from the sky. Fate, v. 10, Mar. 1957: 94-98.

Apparent fall from the sky on Aug. 27, 1956, of metallic shreds concomitant with reports of strange lights in the sky. Chickens consuming the material died.

Towner, Larry E. The night of August 9th. Fate, v. 7, May 1954: 32-36.

Report of chief Ground Observer Corps observer on UFO sighting the night of August 9-10, 1953, over Moscow, Idaho.

The truth about the "Orion Belt" sightings. Flying saucers, July 1959: 14-19.

On Feb. 24, 1959, an American Airlines DC-6 piloted by Capt. Peter Killian sighted three UFOs. Crew and passengers observed them for 45 minutes. Other aircraft were radioed and also reported seeing the same three objects, which were in the section of the sky where the constellation Orion was visible.

Two classic sightings. Flying saucer review, v. 9, May-June 1963: 11-12.

Summarizes information pertaining to UFO sightings near Nairobi, Kenya, in February 1951 and off the Straits of Madagascar in June 1947.

Vallée, Jacques and Janine Vallée. Challenge to science; the UFO enigma. Chicago, H. Regnery Co., 1966. 268 p.

Scientific study of UFO sightings reported throughout world from 1951. Book emphasizes global nature of phenomenon, showing how European sightings illuminate observations in U. S. and other parts of the world. Sightings in France are treated in detail and the methods developed for studying them are suggested as applicable to the phenomenon as a whole.

Veit, Karl. Planeten-menschen. Wiesbaden-Schierstein, Ventla-Verlag, 1961. 223 p.

Author surveys scientific opinion on the possibility of life on other worlds and summarizes UFO sighting reports from 1947 to date. Details are given of "contactee" reports and the alleged appearance and behavior of beings from outer space.

Vinther, Lawrence W. Another saucer mystery. Flying, v. 48, June 1951: 23, 56.

Author, a veteran Mid-Continent Airlines captain, gives details of UFO sighting Jan. 20, 1951, near Sioux City, Iowa.

Vogt, Christian. Non dramatique incident. Phénomènes spatiaux, Feb. 1965: 5-6.

A tragic accident allegedly occurred on May 24, 1954, near Las Vegas, Nevada, when an experimental jet aircraft was destroyed as it attempted to shoot down a flying saucer.

Volkman, Frank. Mystery lights over the orient. Fate, v. 8, Dec. 1955: 13-16.

Report of a weird, brilliant light with a revolving, disc-shaped nucleus seen over northern Japan on March 29, 1952, over Singapore on April 29, 1952, and over west Korea on Oct. 19, 1952.

Walling, Theodore L. Saucer sighting. Fate, v. 9, Dec. 1956: 35-37.

An enormous glowing object allegedly floated noiselessly past the author's house near Berkeley, Calif., on Sept. 20, 1955.

Washington's blips. Life, v. 33, Aug. 4, 1952: 39-40.

Report on July 20 and 26, 1952, incidents involving mysterious objects in the sky over Washington, D. C., recorded simultaneously by ground observers, by pilots in airplanes, and on radar screens. They were also chased by jet aircraft.

Webster, Robert N. Let's get up to date on the flying saucer. Fate, v. 5, Jan. 1952: 4-8.

Reports of strange aerial phenomena viewed between August 25 and October 9, 1951.

Wilkins, Harold T. Flying saucers uncensored. New York, Citadel Press, 1955. 255 p.

Author catalogues UFO sightings and incidents over U. K., Western Europe, U. S., and Australia from 1947 through 1955 and speculates that extraterrestrial visitants are possibly established in bases on moon and other planets; a cosmic general staff may receive reports on terrestrial affairs as well as biological and ecological samples from earth for purposes of study and experimentation. Published also in British edition (London, Arco, 1956), and in paperback edition by Pyramid Pubns., Inc. (T1651), New York.

Wilson, Harlan. The saucer that made tracks. Fate, v. 11, Feb. 1958: 44-47.

15-year-old Canadian Jack Stevens claims he watched a UFO for 45 minutes on July 30, 1957, as it hovered over a cornfield near Galt, Ontario, Canada. Subsequent investigation revealed a 35-foot-diameter circle burned into the field and 18-inch-long "footprints."

----- There are meteors after all. Fate, v. 7, May 1954: 40-43.

Report of aerial objects sighted during the last months of 1953 that seem to be meteors.

Woodley, Morris. The gyrating UFO of Cobalt. Fate, v. 8, Aug. 1955: 34-35.

Description of UFO sighted on Dec. 27, 1954, at Agaunica Cobalt Mine, Lake Timiskaming, Ontario, Canada.

Zinsstag, Lou and T. Allemann. UFO-sichtungen über der Schweiz, 1949-1958. Basel, Zurich, UFO-Verlag, 1958. 48 p.

Compilation of reports of unidentified flying objects seen over Switzerland 1949-1958.

1960s

An account of the Michigan incident through the experts and witnesses. Flying saucers, June 1967: 9-11.

The sighting of UFO on March 21-22, 1966, by girls and assistant dean of women at Hillsdale College, Michigan, is described in detail. Hillsdale County Civil Defense Director viewed the UFO; a twelve-minute time exposure was made by the deputy sheriff.

After Tully. Australian flying saucer review, No. 9, Nov. 1966: 18-21.

Account of UFO sighting reports in the vicinty of Tully, Australia, February-March 1966. Unexplained "footprints" that could not be identified were discovered and believed to be connected with the sightings.

Anderson, Dave. The saucer that terrorized a town. Saga, Aug. 1966: 12-15, 71-72.

UFO sighting over Wanaque, N. J., on Jan. 11, 1966, is described in detail. Corroborating remarks on incident by prominent city officials are reported.

Ann Arbor, Hillsdale et autres lieux. Phénomènes spatiaux, June 1966: 17-25.

Detailed account of UFO sighting incidents in the Ann Arbor-Dexter, Michigan, area, March 20-21, 1966.

Atterrissages de "M.O.C." en 1967. Lumières dans la nuit, no. 93, Mar.-Apr. 1968: 17-18.

UFO landings during 1967 in Spain, England, Chile, Argentina, and the U. S.

Australian scene 1965. Australian flying saucer review, no. 9, Nov. 1966: 8-11.

UFO sightings in Australia during 1965; locality, date, and witnesses are indicated. Compiled by the UFO Investigation Center, Sydney, Australia, with special contribution by Colin Norris, vice-president of the Australian Flying Saucer Research Society, Adelaide, Australia.

Babcock, Edward J. and Timothy G. Beckley. UFO plagues N. J. reservoir. Fate, v. 19, Oct. 1966: 34-44.

Account of mysterious aerial activity from UFOs over Wanaque Reservoir, N. J. on Jan. 11, 1966.

Barker, Gray. Chasing the flying saucers. Flying saucers from other worlds, Aug. 1957: 29-40.

General summary of reported UFO sightings during March 1966 and activities of UFO researchers.

----- Gray Barker's book of saucers. Clarksburg, W. Va., Saucerian Books, 1965. 77 p.

Book catalogues UFO sightings in all parts of the world, 1962-1963. Saucer landings, communication between saucer crews and humans, seizure of terrestrials by saucer crews, mating of extraterrestrials with terrestrials, and "the men in black" are discussed.

Bergendahl, P. E. UFO förföljde bilist. Sökaren, v. 4, no. 8, 1967: 8.

On March 21, 1967, a disc-shaped flying object followed a 22-year-old girl as she bicycled between Gullbringa and Tjuvkil, Sweden. Object was observed for 10-15 minutes and alternately rose and descended; it was seen at an altitude of 150 meters and at a distance of 400 meters. A powerful, intensely green light was emitted. Account accompanied by a report from civil engineer Sven Schalin, who interviewed the witness.

Bowen, Charles. Britain's busiest UFO days. Flying saucer review, v. 13, Nov. - Dec. 1967: 3-4.

Survey of significant UFO sighting reports in Great Britain October-November 1966.

----- Cross country cog wheels. Flying saucer review, v. 12, Sept. -Oct. 1966: 16-17.

Details of maneuvers of cogwheel-like mechanisms--possibly sonde devices from another world designed to record relief of earth's surface--sighted on Mar. 26, 1966, near Attignéville, France; on May 31, 1955, at Puy-Saint-Galmier, France; and on Feb. 8, 1855, in Devonshire, England.

Bowen, Charles. Michigan furore. Flying saucer review, v. 12, May-June 1966: 4-6.

Summary of newspaper reports of UFO sightings in the vicinity of Ann Arbor, Mich., on and after Mar. 20, 1966.

----- The mystery of the Morro do Vintem: How did the men with the lead masks die? Flying saucer review, v. 13, Mar.-Apr. 1967: 11-14.

Following a violent explosion at Altafona, Brazil, on June 13, 1966, a flaming object fell into the sea; there were many witnesses. On Aug. 17, 1966, two young electronics enthusiasts who had witnessed the phenomenon were found dead with strange masks of lead beside them on the Morro do Vintem hill at Niteroi. A prominent citizen then reported seeing an unusual object flying over the Morro do Vintem on the evening of August 17.

Bowen, Charles and Gordon Creighton. The Storrington reports: landings in Sussex? Flying saucer review, v. 14, Mar.-Apr. 1968: 4-6.

Report of alleged UFO sightings near Storrington, England: (1) on Oct. 29, 1967, an ice-cream-cone-shaped object was seen; (2) on Nov. 16, 1967, the object viewed had a trumpet shape at what appeared to be the front, a dome shaped center, and two tails on the right-hand side. A gliding humanoid figure was seen in connection with the latter sighting.

Brooks, Angus. Remarkable sighting near Dorset coast. Flying saucer review, v. 14, Jan.-Feb. 1968: 3-4.

Report of UFO observed Oct. 26, 1967, at Moinge Downs, between Weymouth and Lulworth Cove, Dorset, England. In "hover" position, object consisted of four "fuselages" at equidistant position around a central chamber. Further construction details are given.

Bryant, Larry W. The UFO cover-up at Langley Air Force Base. Flying saucers, June 1968: 11-14.

Author gives details of UFO sighting at Langley Air Force Base on Jan. 28, 1965, by responsible witnesses and of Air Force failure to investigate the incident and subsequent misrepresentation of the facts.

Buckle, Eileen. The Scoriton mystery. London, Neville Spearman, 1967.

Full details of investigation by British Unidentified Flying Object Research Association (BUFORA) of E. A. Bryant's claim that on April 24, 1965, near Scoriton England, he encountered three individuals from a landed extra-terrestrial spacecraft, one of whom told him, "My name is Yamski." (George Adamski had died on April 23.)

BUFORA research officer's annual report - 27th Nov. 1965. BUFORA journal and bulletin, v. 1, Spring 1966: 9-12.

Survey and summary of 1,200 reports of UFO sightings in the United Kingdom; summary of 200 worldwide UFO landing reports.

Cappa, Fidel A. Saucers over the Argentine. Flying saucer review, v. 8, May-June 1962: 29-30.

Report of multiple sightings of UFOs over Argentina Oct. 14-15, 1961.

Caputo, Livio. Rapporto sui dischi volanti-2: stanno per invaderci? Epoca, v. LXIV, Sept. 4, 1966: 32-37.

Report of UFO sightings, chiefly in the U. S. , during 1965-1966. Summary of various theories explaining UFO phenomenon.

Carpenter, Mark. The great UFO flap at Ann Arbor. Fate, v. 19, July 1966: 50-58.

Recapitulation of eyewitness accounts of UFOs seen over Dexter, Mich. , on Mar. 20, 1966.

Chaloupek, Henri. Observations en Tchécoslovaquie et en Bulgarie. Phénomènes spatiaux, Mar. 1968: 20-24.

Following UFO sightings are noted: (1) July 1, 1966, at Snopousov, Czechoslovakia; (2) summer 1944 at Blovice, Czechoslovakia; and (3) Nov. 21, 1967, at Sofia, Bulgaria.

Cheerio there, earthlings! America, v. 113, Aug. 21, 1965: 177.

Commentary on increase in reported UFO sightings during August 1965.

Clark, Jerome. The greatest flap yet? Flying saucer review, v.12, Jan. -Feb. 1966: 27-30.

Report on numerous sightings of UFOs all over the U.S. beginning the evening of Aug. 1, 1965.

----- The greatest flap yet? Flying saucer review, v. 12, Mar. -Apr. 1966: 8-11.

Details of UFO sightings in the U. S. during August 1965.

----- The greatest flap yet? Flying saucer review, v. 12, May-June 1966: 13-15.

Survey of UFO events in North America during September-October 1965.

----- The greatest flap yet? Flying saucer review, v. 12, Nov. -Dec. 1966: 9-13.

Wave of UFO sightings over U. S. during November-December 1965 is described.

----- The strange case of the 1897 airship. Flying saucer review, v. 12, July-Aug. 1966: 10-17.

Account of large numbers of piloted aircraft, carrying brilliant searchlights and human-like passengers, capable of flying against the wind, landing and taking off when approached, which first appeared in northern California in November 1896 and reappeared all over the western and midwestern United States in March 1897.

Cleary-Baker, John. The Scoriton affair. BUFORA journal and bulletin, v. 1, Autumn 1965: 10-11.

On June 7, 1965, E. Arthur Bryant sighted a UFO that appeared to descend onto a nearby field. Next morning, throughout the area where he estimated the object had come to earth, the foliage and grass were singed. A small, turbine-like fitting with curved blades was found as well as a glass phial containing "silver sand" and a piece of paper on which was written: "Adelphos Adelpho. "

Cramp, Leonard G. Report on UFO sighting and ground effect at Whippingham, Isle of Wright. BUFORA journal and bulletin, v. 2, Winter 1967/8: 5-9.

A UFO is sighted on July 10, 1967, and in a nearby field, there is damage similar to that that a whirlwind would have caused: the barley was flattened to the ground in a "whirligig" pattern hundreds of feet long.

Creighton, Gordon W. Argentina 1962. Flying saucer review, v. 10, July-Aug. 1964: 10-13.

Summarizes newspaper reports of remarkable UFO activity over Argentina in 1962.

----- Argentina 1963-1964. Flying saucer review, v. 11, Nov.-Dec. 1965: 14-17.

General resume of most important reported cases of UFO sightings in Argentina 1963-1964.

----- Argentina 1963-64. Flying saucer review, v. 12, Jan.-Feb. 1966: 23-26.

Sensational or unusual reports of UFO phenomena in Argentina 1963-64, including landing reports, contact claims, near approaches, multiple flyovers, and detailed descriptions of shapes and unusual effects.

----- Argentina 1963-64. Flying saucer review, v. 12, Mar.-Apr. 1966: 24-26.

Sightings of UFOs over Argentina during 1964 compiled from reports in the Argentine press.

----- Argentina 1963-64. Flying saucer review, v. 12, May-June 1966: 25-28.

Account of major UFO events in Argentina from June 1964 through the end of the year as reported in Argentine newspapers.

Darden, Mona. One UFO for the road. Fate, v. 20, June 1967: 66-70.

Details of incident [Nov. 28, 1966] in which author's car was allegedly paced by UFO on Interstate I-75 near Valdosta, Ga.

Did UFO bring death? Flying saucers, Oct. 1966: 11-14.

Harry F. Koch, Publicity and Research Director of Universal Research Society of America, sighted a UFO on Apr. 3, 1966, was apparently burned by radiation, reported the sighting and, weeks later, died of a supposed heart attack which had none of the usual systoms of heart disease.

Dufour, Jean C. Pigeon shoot at the Col d' Aspin. Flying saucer review, v. 14, Mar.-Apr. 1968: 29.

Two UFOs were observed by two responsible persons during a hunt in October 1965 at the Col d' Aspin, France.

Dunn, William J., Jr. An analysis of the 1965 Brookville landing case. Saucer news, v. 13, June 1966: 6-8.

Reviews information on March 1965 sightings of airborne and landed UFOs and contact with presumed crew near Weeki Wachi Springs, Florida.

Duplantier, Gene. Alien crafts curious about our cars and occupants. Flying saucers, June 1968: 22-24.

Details on incidents in Canada during 1967 where cars were chased by UFOs. Reprinted from Saucers, Space, and Science, no. 50, 1967-68.

----- Ontario's spring flood of UFOs. Flying saucers, Aug. 1966: 22-24.

Report of UFO sightings in Ontario, Canada, February-April 1966.

...ed ora parliamo di allucinazioni collettive. Centro unico nazionale per lo studio del fenomeni ritenuti di natura extraterrestre. Notiziario, no. 4, 1967: 5-25.

Numerous newspaper accounts of UFOs seen throughout Italy on the night of July 17, 1967, by responsible individuals are reproduced to support author's contention that it is most unlikely sightings were either mass hallucination or natural phenomenon.

Edwards, Frank. Flying saucers--here and now! New York, Lyle Stuart, 1967. 261 p.

Chronicle of worldwide UFO events with special emphasis on the period 1966-1967.

Edwards, Frank, My first UFO. Fate, v. 15, Feb. 1962: 27-31.

A glowing ball-shaped object over Indianapolis on October 12, 1961,--witnessed by many other persons--was Edwards' first UFO sighting.

----- Mystery blast over Nevada. Fate, v. 15, Aug. 1962: 68-74.

An aerial object that exploded over Nevada on April 18, 1962, seemed to be a meteor but, unlike metors, was tracked on radar and had been pursued by jets.

Enquêtes et observations diverses. Phénomènes spatiaux, Dec. 1965: 39-43.

Reports and investigations of UFO sightings in France and Argentina, November-December 1965.

Fawcett, George D. 1966--the year of saucers. Flying saucers, Aug. 1967: 6-11.

Postulating that the subject of flying saucers "has finally taken on respectability," author lists significant "breakthroughs" and analyzes major occurrences during 1966.

Flygande tefat över Lappland. Sökaren, v. 4, no. 3, 1967: 3.

Reports sighting of two disc-shaped, 30-meter-diameter objects by the Söderstrom family near Vilhelmina, Lapland, on March 4-5, 1967. Objects, seen at an altitude of 25-40 meters and at a distance of about 100 meters, were stationary for about 15 minutes and then accelerated rapidly and disappeared into the distance, giving off a reddish glow.

Fontes, Olavo T. Brazil under UFO survey. Flying saucer review, v. 7, Mar.-Apr. 1960: 10-14.

Dr. Fontes documents the intensive UFO survey to which he believes Brazil was subjected on night of May 13, 1960. Sightings followed orthotenic pattern first discovered by Aimé Michel in France in 1954.

Fouéré, René. Observations d' un astronome argentin. Phénomènes spatiaux, June 1966: 3-11.

On Nov. 14, 1964, the Reverend Father Benito Reyna of the Society of Jesus, saw and photographed a "flotilla" of flying saucers from the Adhara Observatory, San Miguel, Buenos Aires, Argentina. Incident is reported in detail and newspaper accounts quoted.

----- Rencontre avec Eugene Coquil; nouvelles soucoupes quadrangulaires; un mode de sustenation mystérieux. Phénomènes spatiaux, June 1967: 13-17.

Events surrounding the alleged sighting on Jan. 16, 1966, of a rectangular UFO at Bolazec, France, are reviewed and worldwide reports of rectangular UFOs discussed. Means by which objects are able to remain completely stationary in the air are speculated on.

Fouéré, René and Francine Fouéré. Le plateau de Valensole serait-il un haut lieu du tourisme insolite? Phénomènes spatiaux, Sept. 1966: 10-20.

There have been four of five UFO sightings at Valensole, France, within a year of the time Maurice Masse allegedly saw a landed spacecraft and its occupant in his lavender field (July 1, 1965), according to reports cited by the authors.

Fuller, Curtis. The boys who "caught" a flying saucer. Fate, v. 15, Jan. 1962: 36-42.

UFO sighted by many citizens and police officers over Waterford, Township, Michigan, on July 9, 1961.

----- The November 23 UFO. Fate, v. 14, Mar. 1961: 46-51.

Just before dawn on November 23, 1960, an unidentified flying object was allegedly seen from Missouri to Ohio by thousands of persons. "Official" explanations are listed.

Galindez, Oscar A. Argentine astronomer observes UFO buzzing Echo II. Flying saucer review, v. 12, Sept. -Oct. 1966: 31.

Jesuit priest claims that on Nov. 14, 1964, he observed a UFO in close proximity to Echo II (communications satellite) through the powerful telescope of the Adhara Observatory, Buenos Aires, Argentina.

Green Gabriel and Warren Smith. UFO raids inside Russia. Saga, v. 34, Aug. 1967: 34-36, 76, 78-81, 83-84.

Reports that on June 21, 1961, a metallic disc, judged to measure 300 feet in diameter, hovered over a ground-to-air missile base outside of Rybinek, U.S.S.R., about 92 miles north of Moscow, at an altitude of about 20,000 feet. Missiles launched toward the object exploded harmlessly in mid-air when they reached a distance of a mile and a quarter from it.

Greenfield, Irving A. The UFO report. New York, Lancer Books, 1967. 141 p.

Summary of the author's personal investigations into the numerous UFO sighting reports on Long Island, N. Y., in the spring of 1966, including many first-hand accounts and a review of the history of the phenomenon. Supports the extraterrestrial thesis and the "Air Force conspiracy" allegations.

Hall, Richard H., ed. The UFO evidence. Washington, National Investigations Committee on Aerial Phenomena, 1964. 184 p.

Documented report containing 746 UFO sighting cases selected from NICAP files and covering NICAP's investigations from early 1957 to the end of 1963. Sightings are listed and analyzed by observer categories; historical development of phenomenon and Congressional attitudes and activity are treated. Evidence is presented to support hypothesis that UFOs are under intelligent control and that some of them might therefore be of extraterrestrial origin.

Hanlon, Donald B. Virginia 1965 flap. Flying saucer review, v. 12, Mar.-Apr. 1966: 14-16.

Twenty-five accounts of UFO sightings in the state of Virginia between November 1964 and January 1965.

Happening at Hoogdal: an unidentified beeping object. Look, v. 31, Nov. 14, 1967: 42-43.

During the week of May 8, a metallic "beep-beep" began after dark in Hoogdal, Wash., and continued until dawn. "Fireball" activity was reported in the area during the same period.

Heavenly bogies. Time, v. 88, Sept. 2, 1966: 81-82.

Reviews of Frank Edwards' Flying Saucers--Serious Business and John G. Fuller's Incident at Exeter.

Hewes, Hayden C. The day the flying saucers came to Oklahoma. Flying saucers, June 1967: 7-8.

Numerous sightings of UFOs were reported throughout Oklahoma on Aug. 1, 1964. Objects were also tracked by radar from Tinker AFB.

Hunt, Richard. Canadian fireballs. Flying saucer review, v. 12, Mar.-Apr. 1966: 33-34.

Summary of newspaper clippings relating to brilliant balls of fire that lit the skies and landscape across British Columbia and parts of the northwestern U. S. on Mar. 31, 1965.

Immense triangular object over Majorca. Flying saucer review, v. 13, Jan.-Feb. 1967: 19, 33.

Sunday Express (London) for Oct. 9, 1966, reported that aviation expert Air Commodore Whitney Straight (Deputy Chairman of Rolls-Royce and former Managing Director of B.O.A.C.) and Lady Straight had observed a "very, very extraordinary unidentified flying object" over Majorca on September 1. Sighting confirmed by Michael Huggins who, with his wife, observed object over a four-hour period.

Jansen, Clare John. Little tin men in Minnesota. Fate, v. 19, Feb. 1966: 36-40.

Sighting of rocket-like UFO and its tin can-shaped occupants on Oct. 23, 1965, near Long Prairie, Minn., is reported.

Johnson, R. Dean. The priest and the saucer. Fate, v. 17, Jan. 1964: 26-31.

Author, priest-in-charge of all Souls Episcopal Church, Waukegan, Mich., reports observing a low-flying drum-shaped UFO on May 19, 1963, for 15-20 minutes.

Jonsson, Ake. Reports from Sweden. Flying saucer review, v. 14, Mar.-Apr. 1968: 12-16.

Article is based on a study of some 600 newspaper items covering the period March-May 1967 and reports 15 cases of UFO sightings in Sweden selected by author as the more interesting incidents.

Keel, John A. More from my Ohio Valley notebook. Flying saucer review, v. 13, July-Aug. 1967: 20-21.

During a visit to Sisterville, Ohio, for information about the 1897 UFO sighting there, author learns there have been numerous UFO sightings 1966-1967 and is told of an abortive attempt by a UFO to kidnap a blood-mobile in March 1967.

----- New landing and creature reports. Flying saucer review, v. 12, Nov.-Dec. 1966: 5-8.

Reports of strange objects and lights in the skies above Erie, Pa., and surrounding districts during July 1966 are discussed and a UFO landing and unearthly creature sightings during the same period detailed.

----- North America 1966: development of a great wave. Flying saucer review, v. 13, Mar.-Apr. 1967: 3-9.

Analysis of trends in U. S. UFO sighting reports during 1966.

----- Project 'B' 1966. New York, The Author, 1967. 5 p.

Analysis of UFO sighting reports during 1966.

Kelly, Peter J. Another Southampton flap. Flying saucer review, v. 11, Mar.-Apr. 1965: 3-4, 20.

Summary of events during UFO "flap" in Southhampton, England, October-November 1964.

Le Vauriat II. Phénomenes spatiaux, Dec. 1966: 26-27.

Account of a cigar-shaped machine allegedly sighted over Vauriat, France Oct. 4, 1962.

Liss, Jeffrey G. The light that chased a car. Fate, v. 16, Nov. 1963: 26-35.

Report of 18 year-old Ronnie Austin that a strange "light" pursued his car for almost an hour on August 5, 1963, near Fairfield, Illinois.

Lloyd, Dan. Crawling lights--a new development. Flying saucer review, v. 13, May-June 1967: 29-30.

Report on alleged sightings in Ohio during March 1966 of strange objects including two types of spaceship-like craft; doughnut-shaped pulsating lights that "crawled" along the walls of a house; and moving, stump-like creatures.

----- Things are hotting up in the Antarctic. Flying saucer review, v. 11, Sept. - Oct. 1965: 4-5.

Summary of newspaper accounts of UFO activity in Antarctic during July 1965.

Lorenzen, Coral. Besieged by UFOs. Fate, v. 17, June 1964: 34-38.

On October 18, 1963, truck driver Eugenio Douglas was reportedly accosted by three "robots" near Monte Maix, Argentina. On October 21, the entire Moreno family in Cordoba province, Argentina, allegedly saw a lánded UFO; five other discs kept the family under siege with beams of light that made the house "hot as an oven. "

----- Rocket-shooting saucers over Tucson. Fate, v. 15, Oct. 1962: 36-43.

On night of June 25-26, 1962, teen-age boys in Tucson, Arizona, allegedly observed rocket-like objects emerge from and return to a hovering UFO.

----- UFOs blanket South America. Fate, v. 19, Jan. 1966: 51-56.

Account of five-week wave of UFO sightings over South America during July-August 1965.

The Lowestoft sighting: object observed for an hour. Flying saucer, review, v. 9, Mar. -Apr. 1963: 17-18.

Article summarizes newspaper reports of UFO sightings over East Anglia, England, during December 1962. Accounts were in Eastern Daily Press (Dec. 5, 10, 20, 27, and 28).

Magee, Judith. UFO activity along the north-east coast of Australia. Flying saucer review, v. 11, Sept. -Oct. 1965: 12-13.

Summary of newspaper accounts of close-range sightings of UFOs along the New South Wales/Queensland coast of Australia, May-June 1965.

Maney, Charles A. The Antarctica sighting. Australian flying saucer review, No. 9, Nov. 1966: 24-25.

Details of July 3, 1965, UFO sighting off Deception Island, Antarctica, observed by scientists and naval personnel of Argentina, Chile, and Great Britain on mission there.

Mesnard, Joel. Quatre enquêtes. Phénomènes spatiaux, Dec. 1967: 18-24.

A family of four allegedly sighted a disc-shaped UFO at close range for several minutes over their chalet near Strasbourg, France, on May 6, 1967.

"M.O.C." observés à basse altitude en 1967. Lumières dans la nuit, no. 93, Mar.-Apr. 1968: 19-22.

Low-altitude UFO sightings during 1967 in the U.S., France, England, and Canada.

The mystery satellite: a study in confusion. Flying saucer review, v. 6, May-June 1960: 25-26.

Possible extraterrestrial origin is discussed of satellite discovered circling earth in near-polar orbit in February 1960.

National Investigations Committee on Aerial Phenomena. [NICAP Headquarters UFO Newspaper Clipping File, 1947-1966]. Washington, D.C., 1967. 37 v. (looseleaf) 35 mm.

Material constituted the newspaper clippings file of Civilian Saucer Intelligence (CSI), New York, now defunct. Microfilm made by the Science and Technology Division, Library of Congress, 1967.

New clues to UFO electrical interference. The UFO investigator, v. 3, Nov.-Dec. 1965: 3-4.

Reported UFO sightings prior to or during the Nov. 9, 1965, "blackout" are reviewed; reports of smaller-scale instances of electromagnetic interference are surveyed for comparison.

1966 Tully. Australian flying saucer review, No. 9, Nov. 1966: 16-18.

On Jan. 19, 1966, banana grower George Pedley saw a "vapor-like saucer" take off from a "nest" in the reeds near Tully, Australia. Two more "nests" were discovered by cane farmer Tom Warren and school teacher Hank Penning during the month.

La nuit du 17 au 18 juillet 1967. Phénomènes spatiaux, Mar. 1968: 11-18.

Statements of witnesses, including astronomers, of UFO sightings July 17-18, 1967, in France, Switzerland, and Italy. Newspaper references are cited.

Observations étrangères. Phénomènes spatiaux, Nov. 1954: 30-31.

UFO sightings worldwide March-October 1964.

Observations étrangères. Phénomenes spatiaux, Feb. 1965: 32-33.

Report of UFO sightings in Transvaal (1906) and in the U.S.A. (1964-1965).

Observations étrangères. Phénomènes spatiaux, May 1965: 37-47.

Worldwide reports of UFO sightings, 1964-1965.

Observations francaises récentes. Phénomènes spatiaux, Feb. 1965: 27-28.

UFO sightings in France November-December 1964.

Observations francaises récentes. Phénomènes spatiaux, May 1965: 35-37.

Reports of UFO sightings in France August 1964-May 1965.

Observations francaises récentes. Phénomènes spatiaux, Nov. 1964: 16-25.

UFO sightings in France July-October 1964.

Observations récentes. Phénomènes spatiaux, Dec. 1966: 30-32.

UFO sighting reports in France, Oct. -Nov. 1966.

Olsen, Thomas M. The reference for outstanding UFO sighting reports. Rider-
wood, Md. UFO Information Retrieval Center, Inc. , 1967. 1 v. (various
pagings) (UFORIC - 6661)

Collection of 160 outstanding UFO reports as originally published. A numerical
value of reliability is formulated for each case; the reports are presented
in chronological order and cross-indexed by date, geographical location and
source.

Opposition flap 1965. Flying saucer review, v. 11, May-June 1965: 3-6.

Report on increased intensity of UFO sightings during 1965, particularly in
the area of the eastern seaboard states of the U. S. , concomitant with
opposition of the planet Mars.

Palmer, Ray. Navy claps saucer sighters in psychiatric ward. Flying saucers,
Oct. 1966: 7-9.

Eight crew members of the USS WASP who reported sighting UFOs on May 24, 1966, were allegedly confined to the psychiatric ward in a U. S. Navy hospital and "treated" as schizophrenics.

Perego, Alberto. L'aviazione di altri pianeti opera tra noi. Rome, Edizioni del Centro italiano studi aviazione elettromagnetica, 1963. 563 p.

Report on worldwide UFO sightings between 1943-1963 with emphasis on those over Italy.

Physical evidence landing reports. The UFO investigator, v. 2, July-Aug. 1964: 4-6.

Details of alleged close-range UFO sighting by policeman Lonnie Zamora on Apr. 24, 1964, near Socorro, N. M.

Pi in the sky. Newsweek, v. 67, Apr. 4, 1966: 22, 27.

Details of UFO sightings in the area around Ann Arbor, Mich., during late March 1966. One night a University of Michigan scientist blinked the "pi" equation in code, explaining that this could be understood by extra-traterrestrial creatures.

Police chase low flying UFO. The UFO investigator, v. 3, Mar.-Apr. 1966: 1.

Account of April 17, 1966, UFO sighting incident near Ravenna, Ohio; object was seen by sheriffs Dale Spaur and W. L. Neff.

Poursuites dans le ciel. Phénomènes spatiaux, Mar. 1967: 29-30.

Newspaper accounts of incidents in which aircraft were paced by UFOs over Peru and Mexico during February 1967.

Priest astronomer's report: observations of an Argentine astronomer. Flying saucers, Apr. 1968: 15-17.

Reverend Father Benito Reyna of the Society of Jesus, teacher of mathematics and director of the Adhara Observatory near Buenos Aires, Argentina, photographed three UFOs on Nov. 14, 1964. Objects were following a route perpendicular to the orbit of Echo II and on the plane of its orbit.

Que s'est-il passe à Marliens? Phénomènes spatiaux, June 1967: 24-30.

Newspaper accounts of May 6, 1967, incident in Marliens, France, in which markings were found in a field for which there was no conventional explanation.

Que s'est-il passe à Plestan? Phénomènes spatiaux, Dec. 1965: 28-32.

Antics of a football-shaped flaming object on Nov. 12, 1965, in Plestan, France, are described. Possiblity that phenomenon was ball lightning is discounted.

Rathbun, Mabel. Flying saucer over San Salvador. Fate, v. 19, Feb. 1966: 41-43.

Aug. 18, 1965, sighting of UFO over San Salvador is detailed.

Retour sur Attigneville: l'incident de Xertigny. Phénomènes spatiaux, Dec. 1966: 13-17.

Details of further inquiry into incident at Attignéville, France, Mar. 26, 1966, in which a strange white wheel with red spokes at its periphery was seen traveling at a constant speed of about 30 kilometers an hour. A circular depression discovered by a farmer at Xertigny, France, on Sept. 4, 1966, that he originally thought was a meteor crater, is also discussed.

Ribera, Antonio. Cortège de soucoupes volantes sur Andorre-la Vieille. Phénomènes spatiaux, Dec. 1967: 29-30.

For over half an hour on Sept. 18, 1967, hundreds of people watched the acrobatics of a fleet of "flying saucers" over Andorre-la-Vieille, Andorra. Report based on newspaper account.

----- L'étrange affaire de Nuria. Phénomènes spatiaux, Mar. 1968: 27-30.

UFO sighting at Nuria, Spain, Sept. 25-26, and Nov. 18-19, 1967, accompanied by parapsychological effect on witnesses, including a priest, is described.

----- El gran enigma de los platillos volantes, desde la prehistoria hasta la epoca actual. Santiago de Chile, Buenos Aires, Mexico, Barcelona, Editorial Pomaire, 1966. 431 p.

Author summarizes worldwide reports of unexplained aerial phenomena (1800s-1960s) with emphasis on U. S. accounts and on the 1954 wave of UFO sightings in France. Current theories on the possibility of life in other worlds are discussed. Hypotheses attempting to explain the UFO phenomenon are surveyed.

----- Midsummer sightings over Andorra. Flying saucer review, v. 13, Nov. -Dec. 1967: 25.

Report of UFO sightings around Andorra-la-Veille, Andorra, during June 17-22, 1967.

Ross, John C. State cops race 'flying saucer.' Fate, v. 13, Dec. 1960: 44-47.

On night of August 13-14, 1960, Patrolmen Stanley Scott and Charles A. Carson sighted a football-shaped UFO near Corning, California, and pursued it for over two hours.

Roussel, Robert. La roue d'Attignéville. Phénomènes spatiaux, June 1966: 25-31.

On May 31, 1955, a luminous disc-shaped object 3-3 1/2 feet in diameter, encircled with spinelike projections of different lengths, was seen rolling across the grass in Puy-Saint-Galmier, France. A similar object was seen on March 26, 1966, at Tranqueville-Graux, France.

Russians say that flying saucers exist. National enquirer, v. 42, Mar. 31, 1961: 1-3.

1960-1965 UFO sightings in the U.S.S.R. are described. Dr. Felix Zigel, assistant professor of astronomy at Moscow Aviation Institute, is quoted as stating that observations indicate that UFOs behave intelligently and that "in a group formation flight, they maintain a pattern. " He also said they are often spotted over airfields, atomic stations, and other very new engineering installations.

Sacksteder, Fred V. Horned UFO sighted at La Porte. Flying saucers, Oct. 1966: 15.

Horned UFO sighted on Mar. 19, 1966, near La Porte, Indiana, is described as about the size of a railroad tank car, brilliant white, and surrounded by misty white rings; a round reddish light shone from near the center of the object.

Sanderson, Ivan T. "Something" landed in Pennsylvania. Fate, v. 19, Mar. 1966: 33-35.

Details are given of the crash of a fiery object--flying rather than falling at 1,062.5 mph and observed to make a 25° turn--near Pittsburgh, Pa., on Dec. 9, 1965.

Saucer flap. The New Yorker, v. 42, Apr. 9, 1966: 32-33.

Possible significance of Michigan "flap" of UFO sightings during March 1966 is discussed with three ufologists: Jose Cecin, head of the New York Subcommittee of the National Investigations Committee on Aerial Phenomena; James W. Moseley, president of the Saucer and Unexplained Celestial Events Research Society; and Michael J. Campione, New Jersey representative of the Amalgamated Flying Saucer Clubs of America.

Schang, Casimiro A. récents incidents. Phénomènes spatiaux, Sept. 1966: 25-28.

Newspaper accounts of UFO sightings in Argentina, November 1965-May 1966.

Sheffield's sensational week. Flying saucer review, v. 8, Nov.-Dec. 1962: 6-9.

Report on wave of UFOs sighted and filmed over Sheffield, England, Aug. 19-30, 1962.

Sherwood, John C. Flying saucers are watching you. Clarksburg, W. Va.,
Saucerian Books, 1967. 78 p.

Author cites newspaper releases in report on incidents which took place
during Michigan "flap" of UFO sightings in Spring 1966.

Shuttlewood, Arthur. The Warminster mystery. London, Neville Spearman, 1967.
207 p.

Account of strange aerial noises and pressure waves over Warminster,
England, often accompanying UFO sightings. Phenomenon allegedly began
Christmas 1964.

----- Warminster UFOs puzzling behavior. BUFORA journal and bulletin, v. 1,
Autumn 1966: 14-17.

Discussion of intense UFO activity over Warminster, England, January 1965-
June 1966.

The significant report from France. Flying saucer review, v. 11, Nov.-Dec.
1965: 5-6.

Report on investigation in behalf of the Groupement d'Etude des Phénomènes
Aériens et Objets Spatiaux Insolites (G. E. P. A.) of July 1, 1965, sighting at
Valensole, France, of UFO and its humanoid pilot.

Smith, Stephen L. The bent beams case. BUFORA journal and bulletin, v. 1,
Autumn 1966: 4-5.

Motorist nearly crashed off the road when his car headlight beams suddenly
appeared to bend to the right. Incident occurred Apr. 8, 1966, in Victoria
State, Australia. As he stopped his car, a UFO was seen to rise out of a
nearby field.

----- The bent beams case. Flying saucer review, v. 12, Sept.-Oct. 1966: iii.

Report that car headlight beams bent as automobile approached UFO on road
between Bendigo and St. Arnaud, Victoria, Australia, in April 1966.

La "soucoupe" carrée de Bolazec ou le tracteur volant. Phénomènes spatiaux,
Mar. 1966: 17-20.

Alleged landing of a square-shaped UFO near Bolazec, France, on Jan. 16,
1966, is reported. Newspaper accounts of incident are cited.

Soucoupes carrées avant Bolazec. Phénomènes spatiaux, June 1966: 14-16.

Reports of sightings of rectangular UFOs prior to Jan. 16, 1966, at Bolazec,
France. The Bolazec sighting had been thought to be the first in this
category.

Sur les solitudes glacées de l'antarctique. Phénomènes spatiaux, Sept. 1965: 25-31.

A "flotilla" of unidentified flying objects was seen on June 19, 1965, by Argentine, British, and Chilean scientists at bases in the Antarctic. Newspaper reports of incident are cited and official communiques quoted.

Trouble, Michel and René Fouéré. La grande panne USA-Canada et son explication technique. Phenomènes spatiaux, Mar. 1967: 8-13.

Discussion of Nov. 9, 1965, "blackout" that extended from Ontario, Canada, to New York, and concomitant UFO sightings.

UFO activity in Brazil during 1965. BUFORA journal and bulletin, v. 2, Summer 1967: 14-15.

Covers period September-December 1965.

"UFOs" -- they're back in new sizes, shapes, colors. U.S. news & world report, v. 61, Aug. 22, 1966: 58-60.

Of 1966 UFO sightings, USAF officials say: (1) more variety in sizes and shapes is reported; (2) there are lights of all kinds concomitant with sightings; (3) UFOs seem to be noisier than in the past; (4) appearance of objects allegedly seen during daylight hours is invariably that of some light-colored metal; (5) movement of reported UFOs continues to be erratic; (6) no "little green men" have appeared; (7) sightings have been concentrated more in the northeastern U.S. than in the past; and (8) objects exhibit apparent tendency to follow power lines.

Vallee, Jacques and Janine Vallee. Challenge to science; the UFO enigma. Chicago, H. Regnery Co., 1966. 268 p.

Scientific study of UFO sightings reported throughout world from 1951. Book emphasizes global nature of phenomenon, showing how European sightings illuminate observations in U.S. and other parts of the world. Sightings in France are treated in detail and the methods developed for studying them are suggested as applicable to the phenomenon as a whole.

The Vauriat sighting. Flying saucer review, v. 9, July-Aug. 1963: 3-5.

On Aug. 29, 1962, in the village of Vauriat, France, a number of people witnessed, in broad daylight, a veritable ballet dance by unknown aerial craft. Account taken from La Montagne, Aug. 30, 1962.

Veit, Karl. Planeten-Menschen. Wiesbaden-Schierstein, Ventla-Verlag, 1961. 223 p.

Author surveys scientific opinion on the possibility of life on other worlds and summarizes UFO sighting reports from 1947 to date. Details are given of "contactee" reports and the alleged appearance and behavior of beings from outer space.

Vezina, Allan K. Canada 1967 -- a big year for UFO research. Flying saucers,
June 1968: 8-10.

Summarizes 1967 UFO incidents in Canada. Mentions power cut-offs and
burning of an individual in association with sightings. Disc-shaped UFO
allegedly crash-landed into Shag Harbour, Nova Scotia; although there were
many witnesses, neither the UFO nor its wreckage was found.

A well-witnessed 'invasion' -- by something. Life, v. 60, Apr. 1, 1966: 24-31.

Illustrated report on numerous UFO sightings during March 1965 from
Australia to Michigan.

What the British press reports on flying saucers. Flying saucers, Aug. 1966:
29-33.

Newspaper accounts of UFO sightings August-October 1965. Reprinted from
Orbit, journal of the Tynside, England, U. F. O. Society.

Winder, R. H. B. Comment on the Angus Brooks sighting. Flying saucer review,
v. 14, Jan. - Feb. 1968: 4-5.

Speculating on the reason for the crosslike configuration during hover of the
UFO seen over England Oct. 26, 1967, by Angus Brooks, author suggests
observations or measurements demanding instruments located at the four
corners of a square or requiring two or four linear devices (possibly antennae,
intersecting at right angles.

Zigel, Felix. The UFO problem --a challenge to science. Flying saucers,
June 1968: 25-26.

The joint effort of all scientists in the world should be applied to discovering
the nature of the UFO phenomenon, the author says. Details given of sightings
in the U.S. S. R. 1965-1967.

STATEMENTS

Asimov, Issac. UFOs--what I think. Science digest, v. 59, June 1966: 44-47.

Commenting on the compulsion of "believers" to identify unidentified flying
objects, the author says that "its not what you see that is suspect, but how
you interpret what you see." He suggests that persons who want to believe
that the spacecraft crews are benevolent guardians of our welfare are
"insecure person /s/ clinging desperately to a fantasy of security."

Confusion in the sky. Fate, v. 8, Mar. 1955: 24-29.

   Article asserts that contradictory statements of the "experts" are responsible
   for confusion in the public's mind about the UFO phenomenon.

Dowding, Hugh C. I believe in flying saucers. Fate, v. 7, Nov. 1954: 24-26.

   Author, Britain's Air Chief Marshall Lord Dowding, states he is convinced
   that "flying saucers" exist and that they are not manufactured by any nation
   on earth. He says he "can therefore see no alternative to accepting the
   theory that they come from some extraterrestrial source." Reprinted from
   the London Sunday Dispatch.

Un document majeure: la déclaration du Dr. McDonald. Phénomènes spatiaux,
   Dec. 1967: 4-8.

   Text of letter sent by Dr. James McDonald to U.N. Secretary-General
   U. Thant urging international cooperation in studying the UFO phenomenon.

Edwards, Frank. Arthur C. Clarke looks at the universe. Fate, v. 12, May 1959:
   68-75.

   Astronomer and science fiction writer Arthur C. Clarke expresses his belief
   that intelligent beings unquestionably exist in other parts of the universe and
   might visit our solar system.

----- An astronomer reports on UFOs. Fate, v. 12, Mar. 1959: 34-41.

   Astronomer Frank Halstead, former curator of Darling Observatory, University of Minnesota, states his belief that UFOs are extraterrestrial spacecraft
   and describes circumstances under which he personally made a sighting.

----- Frank Edwards' report. Fate, v. 10, July 1957: 27-31.

   Dr. Maurice Ewing, director of Columbia Univ.'s Lamont Geological
   Observatory, is quoted as saying that there is a gigantic rift extending in an
   unbroken line about 45,000 miles around the earth and beneath its surface;
   presence of the rift possibly means the earth is in the process of change.
   NACA Director Dr. Hugh Dryden is quoted as telling the House Appropriations
   Committee on Feb. 19, 1957, that there is no such thing as a flying saucer.

----- Frank Edwards' report: Air Force warns flying saucers no joke. Fate,
   v. 13, July 1960: 44-52.

   Vice Admiral Robert Hillenkoetter, USN, retired, gave the press copies of
   an official USAF release issued December 24, 1959, by Major General
   Richard E. O'Keefe, Acting Inspector General, which stated in part:
   "unidentified flying objects...must be rapidly and accurately identified as
   serious USAF business."

Edwards, Frank. Frank Edwards' report: scientists and satellites. Fate, v. 11, Feb. 1958: 69-76.

Author says that the scientific community which, in 1957, "derided, denounced and dismissed" the possibility of a Soviet-launched earth satellite, is probably just as misguided currently in negative attitude regarding the reality of flying saucers.

Fuller, Curtis. Lyndon B. Johnson calls for UFO alert. Fate, v. 13, Nov. 1960: 27-29.

In letter to Major Donald E. Keyhoe dated July 6, 1960, Senator Lyndon B. Johnson said in part: "...the Preparedness Investigating Subcommittee... is keeping a close watch over new developments in this field with standing instructions to report to me any recent significant sightings of unidentified flying objects along with an analysis of the conduct and conclusions of the Air Force investigation of each such sighting."

Gibbs-Smith, Charles H. Flying saucers. The queen, v. 202, Nov. 17, 1954: 64.

A discussion of the UFO phenomenon by the well-known aeronautical historian. He states that one can rule out UFOs as being foreign aircraft and secret weapons and speculates that techniques may have been achieved in some other civilization in the universe that surmount matter and time as we know them--techniques no more startling for such a civilization than flying and radio appear to our civilization on earth.

Gibt es UFOs? Gesprach mit Hermann Oberth zur UFO - frage. Physikalische blatter, v. 17, Heft 2, 1961: 100-103.

In interview Oberth stated: (1) about 11% of all UFO sightings still cannot be explained as known scientific and technological phenomena; (2) he himself has never seen a UFO and his belief in whether or not they exist is irrelevant; (3) reported UFO phenomena should be investigated scientifically; (4) on the basis of his training in medicine and psychology, he believes some reports that individuals have had contact with extraterrestrial beings should be taken as real unexplained experiences; (5) he doubts the appearance of extraterrestrial beings in human form with human attributes; (6) UFOs may be flying machines, built by extraterrestrials, that are propelled by manipulation of gravity fields; and (7) there should be intensified study of the problem.

Hatvany, Edgar A. Dr. Hynek & the UFOs. BUFORA journal and bulletin, v. 1, Autumn 1966: 5-8.

Commentary on letter from Dr. J. Allen Hynek dated Aug. 1, 1966, and submitted to but not published by Science, in which he urged scientific attention to the UFO phenomenon.

Hiestand, Edgar W. Senators want saucer truth. Flying saucers, Feb. 1960: 25-26.

In extension of remarks, Congressman Edgar W. Hiestand (D. -Calif.) caused an article by Hollywood Valley Times commentator George Todt to be placed in the Congressional Record (July 15, 1959, Appendix, p. A6685). Article refers to NICAP's efforts to obtain open Congressional hearings on the UFO phenomenon. Statements of members of Congress in support of such hearings are quoted from June 1959 U. F. O. Investigator.

Hynek, J. Allen. Are flying saucers real? The Saturday evening post, v. 239, Dec. 17, 1966: 17-21.

Hynek, chairman of the department of astronomy at Northwestern Univ. and consultant to USAF's Project Blue Book, states that of the 15,000 cases of UFO sightings that have come to his attention, "several hundred are puzzling, and some of the puzzling incidents, perhaps one in 25, are bewildering. " He cites illustrative examples and urges a serious inquiry into the nature of the phenomenon.

Jones, Harold S. The flying saucer myth. The spectator, v. 185, Dec. 15, 1950: 686-687.

Author, the British Astronomer Royal, says that flying saucers are "improbable" and the extraterrestrial hypothesis "the strongest possible demonstration that the whole thing is a myth."

Keyhoe, Donald E. Flying saucers--fact or fancy? The air line pilot, v. 22, Oct. 1953: 9-10.

Major Keyhoe furnishes official statements from USAF's Air Technical Intelligence Center refuting Dr. Donald Menzel's explanations that UFO sightings are attributable to natural atmospheric phenomena. He also cites "an official Air Force document" which states that an increasing number of officials linked with the investigation are convinced "that the saucers are interplanetary. "

Lear, John. A reply. Saturday review, Feb. 4, 1967: 73.

SR's science editor restates his position in the UFO controversy and answers John Fuller's criticisms of him for publishing excerpts from Incident at Exeter (New York, G. P. Putnam's Sons, 1966) without permission and out of context.

McDonald, James E. Statement on unidentified flying objects. Tucson, Arizona, The Author, 1968. 39 p.

In his statement, the author reviews his experiences in interviewing UFO witnesses in the U. S. and abroad and discusses ways in which his professional experience in the field of atmospheric physics and meteorology illuminates the past and present attempts to account for UFO phenomena. Presented at the Symposium on Unidentified Flying Objects, Committee on Science and Astronautics, House of Representatives, July 29, 1968.

McDonald, James E. UFOs--an international scientific problem. Tucson, Ariz.,
The Author, 1968. 40 p.

Summarizing his position, the author states: (1) the UFO problem seems to be
a matter of great scientific interest; (2) machine-like objects--possibly
extraterrestrial in origin--have been repeatedly seen, often by observers of
very high credibility; (3) UFO observations are being made on a global scale
indicating an international scientific problem; (4) there has never been a
thorough scientific investigation of UFOs ; (5) there is no convincing evidence
of U. S. cover-up conspiracy operating to conceal true nature of UFO
problem; (6) Condon Committee's lack of scientific vigor in conducting USAF-
sponsored UFO study is disappointing; (7) UFO study programs by scientific
groups are needed throughout the world to systematically appraise conceivable hypotheses to account for UFO phenomena. Speech given Mar. 12,
1968, at the Canadian Aeronautics and Space Institute Astronautics Symposium,
Montreal, Canada.

----- UFOs--extraterrestrial probes? Astronautics & aeronautics, v. 5, Aug. 1967:
19-20.

Author states his belief that the extraterrestrial-origin hypothesis for the UFO
phenomenon must be given serious scientific attention. He points out that most
arguments against feasibility of interstellar travel are couched in terms of
present-day scientific knowledge and technology.

Markowitz, William. The physics and metaphysics of unidentified flying objects.
Science, v. 157, Sept. 15, 1967: 1274-1279.

Reported UFOs cannot be under extraterrestrial control if the laws of physics
are valid, the author asserts. He adds that the data published do not justify
the holding of investigations of the phenomenon.

The new saucer epidemic. New republic, v. 127, Aug. 18, 1952: 7

Commentary on increased reports of UFO sightings. Opinions of scientists
(including Donald H. Menzel and Noel Scott) who believe it unlikely that
flying saucers come from another planet are given.

Posin, Dan Q. An eye on space. Popular mechanics, v. 113, Feb. 1960: 103.

Commentary on reports of "hair-raising sights in the sky. " Unnamed
scientist is quoted as saying that while it is not probable that extraterrestrial
spacecraft have visited earth, "they can come and they might come --
any day. "

Professor Hermann Oberth defends the flying saucer. Flying saucer review, v. 8,
Sept. -Oct. 1962: 15-16.

In an interview in Barcelona by Antonio Ribera during the Second Congress of
Aeronautical and Space Medicine, Dr. Oberth said that in his opinion, the
higher forms of life in our planetary system are to be found only on earth.
If we are to seek the place of origin of the flying saucers, we must look to

other stellar systems, perhaps to the planets of Tau-Ceti and Epsilon Eridani, two of the suns nearest to us and belonging to the same spectrographic type as our own.

Ribera, Antonio. Professor Hermann Oberth revisits Barcelona. Flying saucer review, v. 11, Sept.-Oct. 1965: 32.

In a radio interview during the First Astronautical Week in Barcelona, May 3-9, 1965, Professor Hermann Oberth made the following statement on the UFO phenomenon: "We must consider real a fact of which we possess eight thousand certain sightings. I cannot say if they are or are not inter-planetary vehicles, but nobody can doubt any more their existence."

Russians say that flying saucers exist. National enquirer, v. 42, Mar. 31, 1961: 1-3.

1960-1965 UFO sightings in the U.S.S.R. are described. Dr. Felix Zigel, assistant professor of astronomy at Moscow Aviation Institute, is quoted as stating that observations indicate that UFOs behave intelligently and that "in a group formation flight, they maintain a pattern." He also said they are often spotted over airfields, atomic stations, and other very new engineering installations.

Saucers and smoking. Newsweek, v. 52, Aug. 11, 1958: 85.

Swiss psychologist Carl Jung is quoted as having written in the Bulletin of the Aerial Phenomena Research Organization (date not given) that the postwar sightings of flying saucers and other unidentified flying objects (UFOs) were not hallucinations.

Sherman, Carl. Why is the UN censoring the truth about UFOs? Saga, v. 35, Dec. 1967: 32-35, 58-60, 62.

Author states that in May 1967, U.N. Secretary-General U Thant claimed that the UFO mystery was one of the gravest problems facing humanity today--but later denied making the statement. He summarizes a statement by Dr. James McDonald to the U.N. Outer Space Affairs Group on June 7, 1967, urging immediate global action on the UFO problem.

Sightings by scientists. Flying saucers from other worlds, June 1957: 82-85.

Astronomers who have seen unidentified flying objects state their conclusions. They include Dr. Clyde Tombaugh; Dr. Seymour L. Hess; Dr. G. Duncan Fletcher; Dr. Frank Halstead, and Dr. H. Percy Wilkins.

UFOs for real? Newsweek, v. 168, Oct. 10, 1966: 70.

Astrophysicist J. Allen Hynek, consultant to USAF's Project Blue Book is quoted as saying about UFOs: "There is a phenomenon here. I've studied this for eighteen years and it's not all nonsense." He calls upon reputable scientists to investigate UFOs seriously.

"UFOs"--they're back in new sizes, shapes, colors. U.S. news & world report, v. 61, Aug. 22, 1966: 59-60.

Of 1966 UFO sightings, USAF officials say: (1) more variety in sizes and shapes is reported; (2) there are lights of all kinds concomitant with sightings; (3) UFOs seem to be noisier than in the past; (4) appearance of objects allegedly seen during daylight hours is invariably that of some light-colored metal; (5) movement of reported UFOs continues to be erratic; (6) no "little green men" have appeared; (7) sightings have been concentrated more in the northeastern U.S. than in the past; and (8) objects exhibit apparent tendency to follow power lines.

Waithman, Robert. These flying saucers. The spectator, v. 184, Apr. 14, 1950: 489-490.

Commentary on the flying saucer controversy.

UNIVERSITY OF COLORADO STUDY

Condon to head UFO study. Science, v. 154, Oct. 14, 1966: 244.

Fuller, Curtis. Air Force grants $313,000 to study UFOs. Fate, Feb. 1967: 32-39.

Details of University of Colorado contract for 15-month study of UFOs.

Fuller, John G. Flying saucer fiasco. Look, v. 32, May 14, 1968: 58, 60-64.

Incidents in the University of Colorado's UFO study leading to dismissal of Drs. Norman Levine and David Saunders and the resignation of the project's administrative assistant are discussed.

Lear, John. Research in America: University of Colorado study of UFOs. Saturday Review, v. 49, Dec. 3, 1966: 87-89.

Dr. Edward U. Condon, head of the USAF-financed independent study of the UFO phenomenon by the University of Colorado, describes his projected general plan of operation in long-distance telephone conversation with SR's science editor.

Libel suit may develop from UFO hassle. Scientific research, v. 3, May 13, 1968: 11-12.

Article reports that David R. Saunders and Norman E. Levine may sue Edward U. Condon for allegedly calling them "incompetent" when he fired them from the Air Force-sponsored University of Colorado UFO investigation. Events leading to the firings are detailed.

Margolis, Howard. The UFO phenomenon. Bulletin of the atomic scientists, v. 23, June 1967: 40-42.

Problems and difficulties inherent in the University of Colorado study of unidentified flying objects are discussed by the author. He concludes that it is unlikely that the final report will resolve the issue and speculates that it may "add more fuel to the controversy."

Press conference by Donald Keyhoe, Director of NICAP, on Tuesday, 30 April 1966: Washington, 1968. 22 p.

A transcription of the NICAP press conference on the University of Colorado study.

Rogers, Warren. Flying saucers. Look, v. 31, Mar. 21, 1967: 76-80.

Background information on the USAF-sponsored study of the UFO phenomenon by the University of Colorado--what it hopes to accomplish and how.

Shuldiner, Herbert. The great UFO probe. Popular science, v. 191, Oct. 1967: 120-123.

Report on the objectives of a $313,000 USAF-sponsored study of the UFO phenomenon at the University of Colorado, headed by Dr. Edward U. Condon. Findings would be released in Fall 1968.

Simons, Howard. American newsletter. New scientist, v. 32, Oct. 27, 1966: 174.

Announcement that the Air Force had enlisted Dr. Edward U. Condon of the University of Colorado to head a 15-month study of unidentified flying objects (UFOs) under a $313,000 grant.

Situation report: What is the unidentified flying object situation these days? American engineer, Mar. 1967: 55.

Two new developments relating to the UFO phenomenon are cited. (1) Dr. J. Allen Hynek's open letter to Science urging serious scientific investigation of the problem; and (2) the USAF-sponsored, 15-month study at the University of Colorado, headed by Dr. Edward U. Condon.

Stanton, L. Jerome. The final word on flying saucers? This week, Mar. 5, 1967: 6-7.

Report that on October 7, 1966, a contract was awarded to the University of Colorado to conduct a scientific investigation of UFO sightings and report findings to the U.S. Air Force, with recommendations for future operations of USAF's Project Blue Book UFO inquiry.

UFO study credibility cloud? Industrial research, v. 10, June 1968: 26-28.

Commenting on the controversy developing around the University of Colorado project investigating unidentified flying objects, Rep. J. Edward Rousch (D.-Ind.) is quoted as noting that it "raises great doubts as to the scientific profundity and objectivity of the project." Details of the controversy are reported.

UFOs again. Ordnance, v. 51, Mar.-Apr. 1967: 450.

Announcement that USAF had awarded a $313,000 contract to the University of Colorado for scientific evaluation of UFO phenomenon. Project would be headed by Dr. Edward U. Condon.

UFO-watcher watcher. Newsweek, v. 69, Mar. 20, 1967: 111.

Discussion of approach planned by Dr. Edward U. Condon in implementing a study of the UFO phenomenon at the University of Colorado under a $313,000 USAF grant.

MISCELLANEOUS

Authentic music from another planet. Slate Records 211 [1957?] 2 s 12 in. 33 1/3 rpm microgroove.

Narration and performance of the Song from Saturn by Howard Menger. Includes the songs Marla and Theme from the Song from Saturn.

Colorado horse death ruled no UFO case. The UFO investigator, v. 4, Oct. 1967: 4.

NICAP findings in the case of "Snippy the horse," found dead Sept. 9, 1967, under allegedly mysterious circumstances. Report quotes Dr. Robert Adams, an expert on horse diseases from Colorado State University's College of Veterinary Medicine and Biomedical Sciences, as stating that he detected nothing unusual or bizarre in connection with the death, and that "Snippy" probably died as a result of a severe hind leg infection.

Darby, Christian. World's first UFO murder case. Argosy, v. 365, Dec. 1967: 23-25, 60-63.

It is speculated that the deaths of two men found atop a hill in Niteroi, Brazil, on August 20, 1966, may have been caused by a flying saucer. Crude eyeless lead masks lay a few inches from their faces; there were no signs of a struggle; no hint of foul play.

De Tastelero, Mira. Flying saucers in the movies. Flying saucers from other worlds, June 1957: 40-43.

Listing of known flying saucer films through 1957.

Evans, Gordon H. What you don't know about space. Flying saucers, Nov. 1963: 16-32.

Public pronouncements justifying the space programs of both the U.S. and the U.S.S.R. are inadequate, states the author. He speculates that the real reasons very likely involve the UFO phenomenon.

Gray, Grattan. The town that believes in flying saucers. Maclean's, v. 80, Mar. 1967: 4.

Describes projected $14,000 landing pad for flying saucers to be erected for Centennial celebration of St. Paul, Alberta, Canada.

Herrmann, Joachim. Das falsche Weltbild. Stuttgart, Kosmos Verlag, Franckh' sche Verlagshandlung, 1962. 162 p.

Fact and fiction relating to UFO phenomenon are discussed.

Jones, S. H. The Swedish ghost rockets. Flying saucer news, Summer 1955: 10-12.

Analysis, in the light of recent knowledge and events, of the many UFOs seen over Scandinavia in the summer of 1946.

Lorenzen, Coral. The great UFO controversy: the Appaloosa from Alamosa. Fate, v. 21, Mar. 1968: 34, 36-44.

Proponents of UFO murder theory claim Snippy the horse fought valiantly but vainly when attacked by something from the sky in September 1967.

Merker, Donald. The great UFO controversy: the Appaloosa from Alamosa. Fate, v. 21, Mar. 1968: 35, 45-52.

Opponents of the UFO murder theory insist nothing was in the sky but stars when the horse, Snippy, died in September 1967 and blame mass media for trumped up enigma.

The mysterious chunk of hardware at Ottawa. Topside, Spring 1968: 1-4.

On June 12, 1960, a sonic boom was heard in Quebec City, Canada. At about the same time, a fiery object fell out of the sky, splitting into two pieces, both of which fell into the St. Lawrence River about 20 mi. upriver from Quebec City and were later recovered. X-ray diffraction analysis indicated the unidentified objects consisted of a metallic face-centered cubic compound, with a unit-cell dimension agreeing with those of austenitic steel and meteoric iron. The semi-quantitative spectrographic analysis showed there was insufficient nickel present for the material to be of meteoric origin; the subject was considered to be of terrestrial origin. Subsequent laboratory experiments on the metal by Wilbur B. Smith and co-workers resulted in a number of unusual reactions not consistent with the normal behavior of terrestrial metal.

Petersen, Clarence. Big money in swamp gas. Book world, Washington Post, Sept. 10, 1967: 33.

Author observes that Paperbound Books in Print lists 30 titles currently available on UFOs and related subjects. Discussed as examples are Edward J. Ruppelt's Report on Unidentified Flying Objects; Frank Edwards' Flying Saucers--Serious Business; Coral E. Lorenzen's Flying Saucers: The Startling Evidence of Invasion from Outer Space; John G. Fuller's Incident at Exeter and Interrupted Journey; and Harold T. Wilkins' Flying Saucers on the Attack and Flying Saucers Uncensored.

Smith, Stephen L. The bent beams case. BUFORA journal and bulletin, v. 1, Autumn 1966: 4-5.

Motorist nearly crashed off the road when his car headlight beams suddenly appeared to bend to the right. Incident occurred Apr. 8, 1966, in Victoria State, Australia. As he stopped his car, a UFO was seen to rise out of a nearby field.

----- The bent beams case. Flying saucer review, v. 12, Sept-Oct. 1966: iii.

Report that car headlight beams bent as automobile approached UFO on road between Bendigo and St. Arnaud, Victoria, Australia, in April 1966.

Sprinkle, R. Leo. Personal and scientific attitudes: a survey of persons interested in UFO reports. Laramie, Wyoming, The Author, 1968. 11 p.

A questionnaire survey on attitudes towards UFOs was conducted among three groups: 26 Ph. D. faculty and graduate students in a university Psychology Department; 59 graduate students enrolled in a NDEA Guidance Institute; and 259 members of the National Investigations Committee on Aerial Phenomena (NICAP). It was hypothesized that there would be no differences between the scores of the three groups on the Personal Attitude Survey (Form D, Dogmatism Scale, Rokeach, 1960) and the Scientific Attitudes Survey (Sprinkle, 1962). Results showed significant differences (P> 0.001) between the three groups with respect to their mean scores on both inventories, with the NICAP group scoring higher on both "dogmatic" and "scientific" inventories, followed by the guidance group and the psychology group, respectively. Investigation was supported by Grants-in-Air Committee, Scoiety for the Psychological Study of Social Issues (a division of the American Psychological Association).

UFO terminology. Cleveland, Ohio, Flying Saucer Digest, [1968]. 6 p.

Vocabulary used by UFO researchers.

Wright, Eric. UFO lands near pond and the water freezes in 50° weather. National enquirer, July 14, 1968: 32.

Minutes after a UFO was seen landing on Vashon Island near Seattle, Washington, a pond near the landing site froze although the temperature was 50°F. Incident occurred Feb. 18, 1968.

BIBLIOGRAPHY

Chartrand, Robert L. and William F. Brown. Facts about unidentified flying
  objects. Washington, D.C., Library of Congress, Legislative Reference
  Service, 1966. 29 p.

  Includes the following: descriptions of various types of UFOs; trends in UFO
  activity; historical sightings of aerial phenomena; identification of flying objects;
  U.S. Government monitoring of UFO activity; special studies of UFOs; special
  briefings on UFO activity; public reaction to UFOs; USAF Regulation 200-2.

Jain, Sushil K. and Christine Horswell. Twenty years of flying saucers: a select
  list of interesting books and periodical articles published during 1947-1966.
  Tenderden (Kent), England, Sushil Jain. Publications, 1967. 18 p.

U.S. Library of Congress, Legislative Reference Service. Unidentified flying
  objects, selected references (1966-1968). Louise G. Becker, research
  assistant, Science Policy Research Division, Washington, D.C., July 22, 1968.
  4 p.

  Bibliography prepared with special emphasis on books or articles of general
  interest, stressing public concern.

Page, H.M. Flying saucers...a bibliography. Foxboro, Mass., The Author, 1968.
  17 p.

  Lists UFO books and the sources from which they may be obtained as well as
  periodical articles, 1966-April 1968, a list of publishers and a list of private
  UFO research organizations.

Sable, Martin H. UFO guide, 1947-1967. Beverly Hills, Calif., Rainbow Press
  Co., 1967. 100 p.

  Contains international lists of books and magazine articles on UFOs, flying
  saucers, and life on other planets; worldwide directories of flying saucer
  organizations, professional groups and research centers concerned with space
  research and astronautics; a partial list of sightings; and an international
  directory of flying saucer magazines.

Origin of Life

Avenel, Antony. View from Orbit II. London, Werner Laurie, 1957. 167 p.

Part I deals with question of whether life is designed or is a chance occurrence. Part II is concerned with ways and means by which life could be guided by an outside agency. Part III considers the future of the human race.

Beischer, Dietrich E. Potentialities and ramifications of life under extreme environmental conditions. Journal of aviation medicine, v. 29, July 1958: 500-503.

Berget, Alphonse. The appearance of life on worlds and the hypothesis of Arrhenius. In The Smithsonian Institution. Annual report of the board of regents for the year ending June 30, 1912. Washington, U. S. Govt. Print. Off., 1913. p. 543-551.

Conception of Svante Arrhenius that life can be carried from one planet to another: Germs swept away by ascending air currents which carry them to the limits of the atmosphere are repelled by the electrically charged dust that has penetrated there, coming from suns that have driven it away by the repelling pressure of their radiation. After they have arrived in space they attach themselves to some straying grains of dust of greater dimensions than theirs that are consequently capable of obeying the attraction of a neighboring planet rather than the repelling force of radiation; they then penetrate into the atmosphere of this new planet and bring life to it, if life has not yet developed there.

Briggs, Michael H. Terrestrial and extraterrestrial life. Spaceflight, v. 2, Oct. 1959: 120-121.

Hypothesis for origin of life on earth is given based on three assumptions: (1) intelligent life existed somewhere in the universe prior to the beginning of life on earth; (2) interplanetary flight is possible by these intelligences;

224

and (3) lifeless earth was visited by extraterrestrials who either deliberately or accidentally left microbes behind when they departed. Variations of and objections to hypothesis are given.

Calvin, Melvin. Chemical evolution. In Cameron, A. G. W., ed. Interstellar communication. New York, W. A. Benjamin, 1963. p. 33-77.

From questions on the nature and characteristics of life, the author proceeds to hypotheses on chemical evolution and the establishment of an environment conducive to the origin of self-replicating macromolecules. Speculation on life on other planets, life elsewhere in the solar system, and life in the galactic systems is followed by a discussion of man's place in the universe. Of the two hundred million inhabitable planets in the visible universe, two areas selected for attempt at interstellar communication (Project Ozma) are Tau Ceti and Epsilon Eridani. Reasons are given for their selection.

Calvin, Melvin. Origin of life on earth and elsewhere. Annals of internal medicine, v. 54, May 1961: 954-976.

Traces chemical evolution to the point where a primitive organism is formed. Applies this reasoning to question of whether we are likely to find that similar events have occurred elsewhere than on earth.

Firsoff, V. Axel. Life, mind and galaxies. Edinburgh and London, Oliver & Boyd, 1967. 111 p.

Evidence is presented to show that life is not a freak occurrence in the universe of stars and nebulae, but an integral part of its general pattern, and will arise naturally from the inorganic substratum wherever and whenever conditions become suitable for it, and, that these may be suitable for life of a different chemical order even though unfit for our type of carbohydrate biology. It is postulated that no definite boundary can be fixed between the organic and the inorganic world, which shade into each other by imperceptible degrees.

Gatland, Kenneth W. and Derek D. Dempster. The inhabited universe. London, Alan Wingate, 1957. 182 p.

The theme throughout the book is that evolution is constantly bringing new forms of life into existence and that creation is a continuous process. Man is depicted as the product, not merely of a limited biological development, but of an inherent facet of cosmic evolution.

Huang, Su-Shu. Occurrence of life in the universe. American scientist, v. 47, September 1959: 397-402.

Prerequisites for the occurrence of life, especially in an advanced form, are discussed in the light of current knowledge of the stars and their evolution.

Munitz, Milton K. Theories of the universe from Babylonian myth to modern science. Glencoe, Ill., The Free Press, 1957. 437 p.

Survey of current trends in scientific cosmology against the background of earlier efforts and achievements. Beginning with one of the earliest ventures in the form of myth, materials are included exhibiting the principal stages of progress in cosmological inquiry from antiquity up to the present time.

Needham, A. E. Origination of life. Quarterly review of biology, v. 34, Sept. 1959: 189-209.

Formal solution of main problems concerning the origination of life is attempted, adopting as the fundamental axiom the assumption that it was a spontaneous natural sequence of "most probable" events.

Oparin, A. I. The origin of life in space. Space science review, v. 3, July 1964: 5-26.

Origin of life can be attributed to evolution of carbon compounds. On earth three stages can be traced: (1) formation of simple organic compounds such as hydrocarbon and cyanides and their oxygen, nitrogen, sulfur, phosphorus and other derivatives of low molecular weights; (2) polymerization and condensation of these compounds; and (3) formation of multimolecular compounds. First step is universal. Second step is possible on celestial bodies near earth. Final stage of formation of complex living organisms in space seems possible but is still debatable.

Sagan, C. On the origin and planetary distribution of life. Radiation research, v. 15, Aug. 1961: 174-192.

Author discusses current opinion and speculation concerning the origin and early history of life on earth, with particular emphasis on the role that radiation may have played, and with application to the problem of extraterrestrial life.

Sagan, Carl. The quest for life beyond the earth. In Smithsonian Institution. Annual report of the board of regents for the year ending June 30, 1964. Washington, D. C., U.S. Govt. Print. Off., 1965. p. 297-306.

Questions on the possibility of extraterrestrial life and the origin of life are discussed and alternative interpretations of available data given.

Strughold, Hubertus. Planetary ecology (astrobiology). In Lectures in aerospace medicine. Article 5. Brooks AFB, Tex., School of Aviation Medicine, 1960. p. 1-27.

Chemistry of the planetary atmospheres in their present state is discussed, including their origin and historical development.

Tocquet, Robert. Life on the planets. New York, Grove Press, Inc.,
1962. 192 p.

Discusses problem of origin of life and conditions in which it can develop on earth and elsewhere. Speculates on what man will find when
he is able to make interstellar trips.

Wald, George. The origin of life. In Moment, G. B., ed. Frontiers
of modern biology. Boston, Houghton Mifflin, 1962. p. 185-192.

Theories and accounts of the origin of life from Genesis to the present
are briefly delineated. Van Helmont, Redi, Spallanzani, Needham,
Pasteur, Mohler, Darwin, Haldane, Oparin, Miller, and Urey are cited
as contributors to development of the present state of knowledge. Author
concludes that life has originated and evolved elsewhere, that life has a
physical status in the universe, and that as men, we are "matter that
has begun to contemplate itself. "

Younghusband, Francis. The living universe. London, John Murray,
1933. 252 p.

Author postulates that the universe is a living universe and that the
primordial germ of life appeared as the result of the interaction of the
earth with life in the universe as a whole. He suggests that there may be
the same myriad forms of life in different planets as there are on earth.
All life is "derived from the same original source, and informed by the
same Spirit. "

Mankind

EVOLUTION

Avenel, Antony. View from Orbit II. London, Werner Laurie, 1957. 167 p.

Part I deals with question of whether life is designed or is a chance occurrence. Part II is concerned with ways and means by which life could be guided by an outside agency. Part III considers the future of the human race.

Blum, Harold F. Perspectives in evolution. American scientist, v. 43, Oct. 1955: 595-610.

Assuming life to exist on other planets of the billion solar systems now thought to comprise the known universe, the author says the next easy step is to assume that our own evolution here on earth has been paralleled elsewhere.

Buck, Richard M. Cosmic consciousness. New York, E. P. Dutton and Co., 1901. 384 p.

Evidence is presented that there have been, in the last three thousand years of human history, at least fourteen undeniable cases of complete and permanent "illumination," and that in addition to these, there have been many instances of partial, temporary, or doubtful "illumination," several of which have occurred during the past century. Noting the increasing frequency of the experience, the author deduces that very gradually -- and, sporadically -- the human race is in the process of developing a new kind of consciousness, far in advance of ordinary human self-consciousness.

Darwin, Charles G. The next million years. Garden City, N.Y., Doubleday & Co., 1953. 210 p.

228

Attempt to determine whether laws can be laid down from which the evolution of humanity can be foreseen. Discussion of the chief qualities of the human animal and changes that may be expected in the species homo sapiens in the next million years. Implications extend to possible older extraterrestrial civilizations.

Flammarion, Camille. Mysterious psychic forces. Boston, Small Maynard and Co., 1907. 466 p.

Study of psychical phenomena. Author concludes that man has in himself a fluidic and psychic force whose nature is still unknown, but which is capable of acting at a distance upon matter and of moving the same. This force, the expression of our will, is both psychical and physical.

Fry, Daniel W. The curve of development. Lakemont, Ga., CSA Printers and Publishers, 1965. 75 p.

Outlines development of the human soul "through stages of increasing ability and manifestation." Speculates that there may be other planets where life, intelligence and spiritual development have progressed beyond the average level achieved on earth; the earth human may at some stage of his development take up residence on such an advanced planet where the environment is more conducive to rapid progress.

Gatland, Kenneth W. and Derek D. Dempster. The inhabited universe. London, Alan Wingate, 1957. 182 p.

The theme throughout the book is that evolution is constantly bringing new forms of life into existence and that creation is a continuous process. Man is depicted as the product, not merely of a limited biological development, but of an inherent facet of cosmic evolution.

Geley, Gustave. From the unconscious to the conscious. New York and London, Harper & Bros., 1921. 327 p.

Interpretation of the evolution of the individual and the universe. Continuous development of the conscious is postulated as an evolutionary fact; this conscious, grown to its full stature, will be able to transcend all its limitations, to attain what is now inaccessible, to understand what is now incomprehensible.

Krafft, Carl F. Ether and matter. Richmond, Va., Dietz Printing Co., 1945. 117 p.

Defending the dynamic ether and vortex atom theory, the author believes that all phenomena of the physical universe are only different manifestations of the various modes of motion of the all-pervading ether. He refers to the pan-psychic doctrine that the consciousness has its origin in the ether. The ether would then be the common substrate of both mind and matter and would have psychical as well as physical attributes, both of which would be governed by similar or analogous laws and principles.

Muller, Hermann J. Out of the night: a biologist's view of the future. New York, Vanguard Press, 1935. 127 p.

Discussion of the possible courses that man's evolution might take.

Slater, Alan E. The probability of intelligent life evolving on a planet. In VIIIth International Astronautical Congress, Barcelona, 1957. Proceedings. Vienna, Springer-Verlag, 1958. p. 395-402.

Report traces briefly the evolution of the human species from primitive life forms and shows that the differentiation that eventually led to man was far from inevitable. Concludes that it seems improbable that other forms of intelligent life will be found by voyagers through space.

Smith, S. L. The problems of exobiology. Part II: life in the solar system. BUFORA journal and bulletin, v. 1, Spring 1966: 13-18.

Article discusses whether the processes that led to the evolution of man could have occurred beyond the solar system.

----- The problems of exobiology. Part III: life beyond the solar system. BUFORA journal and bulletin, v. 1, Summer 1966: 10-14.

Considers whether a process similar to that which led to the evolution of man could have occurred beyond the solar system; and if not, are there any other possible chemical processes that could lead to an alien form of life?

ORIGIN

Barton, Michel X. Flying saucer revelations. Los Angeles, Futura Press, 1957. 38 p.

Discusses role of interplanetary beings in man's origin and evolution. Considers stories of contact between extraterrestrials and earth men and the implications. Reports on flying saucer sighting at Giant Rock Airport, Yucca Valley, Calif., on Mar. 12, 1955, during Interplanetary Spacecraft Convention.

Becquerel, P. La vie terrestre provient-elle d'un autre monde? Astronomie, v. 38, 1924: 393-417.

Bible. Old Testament Apocryphal Books. Enoch. Transl. by R. H. Charles, London, Society for Promoting Christian Knowledge, 1917. 154 p.

Book of Enoch, especially verses VI-XI, is often cited as an historical account of extraterrestrial influences in man's origin.

Churchward, James. Cosmic forces as they were taught in Mu. New York, The Author, 1934. 246 p.

Translations of fragments of the "Sacred Inspired Writings -- Scientific Section" written over 70,000 years ago on the lost continent of Mu, on which a superior civilization is believed to have flourished.

----- The lost continent of Mu. New York, Ives Washburn, 1931. 335 p.

Information about Mu based on translations of two sets of ancient tablets: (1) the Naacal tablets discovered in India, and (2) stone tablets discovered by William Niven in Mexico. Some of the subjects embodied are an account of the creation in minute detail; life and its origin; the origin and workings of the "four Great Cosmic Forces"; and the creation of woman. Author asserts that both sets of tablets establish that at one time earth had an ancient civilization which was superior to our own and far in advance of us in important essentials.

----- The sacred symbols of Mu. New York, Ives Washburn, 1939. 296 p.

Evidence is presented that all religions have common origin in Lemuria's sacred writings: Moses condensed "The 42 Questions" on the Osirian religion into our Ten Commandments; the Lord's Prayer and our Proverbs are in the sacred writings of Mu.

Dewey, Mark. A man from space speaks. Houston, Texas, The Author, 1966. 38 p.

A philosophy of life allegedly dictated to author by Amano, a teacher on the planet Mars, during direct contact over a five-year period. Postulates that Martians are the ancestors of terrestrials.

Goble, H. C. Atlantis sank later than you think. Fate, v. 10, Aug. 1957: 19-24.

Records indicating that some remnants of the Atlantean continent may have existed near the Arctic Circle as late as the 16th century are cited by the author. He also suggests that the Greek navigator Pythias, the only man to sail to the North Country between 400 B. C. and 500 A. D., witnessed the final death throes of the sinking Atlantis. [Atlantis is thought by some to have been colonized by extraterrestrials.]

King, George. The nine freedoms. Los Angeles, The Aetherius Society, 1963. 200 p.

Gives a concise account of man's coming to earth, why he is here, and why he is at the bottom of the evolutionary ladder in this solar system. Outlines the exact path through evolution that man must take in order to become "God-man. " Reveals the way in which man will eventually attain the "glorious state of interplanetary existence. " Information allegedly delivered to author telepathically in nine consecutive transmissions by "a prominent Master of unquestionable Cosmic Status. "

Mugler, Charles Deux themes de la cosmologie grecaue: devenir cyclique et
pluralité des mondes. Paris, Librarie C. Klincksieck, 1953. 92 p.

Survey of Greek literature for indications of a belief in the extraterrestrial
origin of man and the existence of intelligent life throughout the universe.

Murray, Jacqueline. Flying saucers and Atlantis. Flying saucer review,
v. 5, May-June 1959: 18-19, 25.

Author postulates that certain beings who had been incarnate on the
planet Venus elected to reincarnate on earth to assist with its evolution
and thus started the civilization of Atlantis. When Atlantis was destroyed
by cataclysms, these Venusians may have been evacuated by flying saucers.

Oliver, Frederick S. A dweller on two planets, or The dividing of the way, by
Phylos the Tibetan. Los Angeles, Baumgardt Publishing Co. , 1905.
423 p.

High attainments of the Atlanteans before engulfment of their continent are
discussed. Rediscovery of Atlantean secrets is predicted and it is promised
that mankind will surpass Atlantis' greatness. Phylos the Tibetan allegedly
dicated manuscript telepathically to author.

Sendy, Jean. Les dieux nous sont nes. Paris, Bernard Grasset, 1966. 343 p.

Citing the Bible as a prime authority, the author postulates that the "gods"
were extraterrestrial beings who came to earth to create mankind and
promote civilization and who continue to exercise manipulative influence.
Flying saucers, the miracle of Fatima, evocations, premonition, precognition, and other psychic and hallucinatory experiences are discussed in
this context.

Watson, S. H. The secrets of time and space. In Palmer, Ray, ed. The
hidden world, No. A-9. Amherst, Wis. , Palmer Publications, 1963.
p. 1536-1723.

Allegories and myths relating to origin of mankind and of earth's solar
system are discussed in terms of author's personal beliefs.

Solar System

GENERAL REFERENCES

Arrhenius, Svante. The destinies of the stars. Transl. by J. E. Fries. New York and London, G. P. Putnam's Sons, 1918. 256 p.

Collection of articles on pre-history of the evolution of the planets. Included are (1) Origin of Star-Worship; (2) The Mystery of the Milky Way; (3) The Climatic Importance of Water Vapor; (4) Atmosphere and Physics of the Stellar Bodies; (5) Chemistry of the Atmosphere; (6) The Planet Mars; and (7) Mercury, the Moon, and Venus. Translation of Sjärnornas öden.

Berger, Rainer. The solar system and extraterrestrial life. In Advances in the astronautical sciences. v. 13. North Hollywood, Calif., Western Periodicals Co., 1963.

Discusses current experimental results, opinion, and speculation in research on problem of extraterrestrial life. Theories on chemical and prebiological evolution in space are examined in connection with theories on origin of life.

Berrill, Norman John. Worlds without end: a reflection on planets, life, and time. New York, Macmillan, 1964. 240 p.

Speculative investigation of possibilities of life on other planets: nearest and best-known planets are compared with earth; hypothetical planets similar to earth but with one or another feature altered in some manner are examined in order to predict how familiar living things might be affected; life on earth is evaluated to determine which characteristics may be regarded as universal under certain circumstances and which are special; and imaginative efforts of speculative writers to conceive and describe creatures different from those known to us on earth are presented.

Bún, Thomas P. and Flavio A. Pereira. "Biospheric index," a contribution to the problem of determination of the existence of extra-solar planetary biospheres. In VIIIth International Astronautical Congress, Barcelona, 1957. Proceedings. Vienna, Springer-Verlag, 1958. p. 63.

Authors report that planets within the solar system may be classified into three groups based on probable existence of life by comparative examination of regions of the solar ecosphere. Biospheric index for classification of given planet within indicated scale of groups may be established by comparison of spectroscopic absorption lines.

Cade, C. Maxwell. Are we alone in space? Discovery, v. 24, Apr. 20, 1963: 27-29.

Cramp, Leonard G. The cosmos--expanding or orbital? Flying saucer review, v. 7, May-June 1961: 8-12.

Author proposes an original and topical theory on how the universe began.

Da Silva, Renato I. No espaco não estamos sos. São Paulo, Edart, 1966. 213 p.

Theories relating to possibility of life on the moon and other planets are summarized. Parapsychological phenomena of mental telepathy, precognition, ESP, premonition, and astral projection are discussed as they might relate to contact with extraterrestrial entities or intelligences.

Dauvillier, Alexandre. L'origine des planetes; essai de cosmogonie. Paris, Presses Universitaires de France, 1956. 224 p. (Nouvelle collection scientifique)

Summarizes hypotheses successively proposed to explain the origin of our solar system. Attempts to show that there are countless unseen planetary systems in the galaxy, and that they only result from a specific kind of stellar interaction.

-----. Sur la nature de Pluton et de Triton. Acádemie des Sciences. Comptes rendus hebdomédaires des séances, v. 233, Oct. 22, 1951: 901-903.

De Grazia, Alfred, ed. The Velikovsky affair: the warfare of science and scientism. New Hyde Park, N. Y., University Books, 1966. 260 p.

In 1950, Worlds in Collision by Dr. Immanuel Velikovsky documented the evidence and sequence of castastrophes on earth and in the solar system. His historical and cosmological concepts constituted an assault on established theories of astronomy, geology, and historical biology and thereby gave rise to a controversy in scientific and intellectual circles about scientific theories and the sociology of science. This volume contains papers relating to the Velikovsky controversy by Ralph E. Juergens, Livio C. Stecchini, Alfred de Grazia, and Immanuel Velikovsky.

Drake, W. Raymond. Is our sun inhabited? Flying saucer review, v. 5,
Nov. -Dec. 1959: 15-17.

Author summarizes theories on the nature of the sun and speculates that the
heat and light reaching earth from it might be provided by methods other than
nuclear explosion on the sun itself. Habitability would then be within the
realm of possibility.

-----. Mercury, Jupiter, and others: can life exist? Flying saucer review,
v. 6, Sept. -Oct. 1960: 18-22.

Survey of facts and speculations on possibility of life on Mercury, Jupiter
and lesser known bodies in earth's solar system.

Ecosphere may shape life on distant planets. Science newsletter, v. 80, Oct. 21,
1961: 272.

Harrison, Philip. The case for the missing planet. Flying saucers, Aug. 1967.
16-18.

Discussion of the theory that there was once a planet in our solar system between
the orbits of Mars and Jupiter. The asteroid belt beyond the planet Mars
might represent fragments of this exploded planet, author speculates.

Heard, J. F. The physical nature of the planets and their probable course of
evolution. Canadian aeronautical journal, v. 5, May, 1959: 184-186.

Hoyle, Fred. Man in the universe. New York and London, Columbia University
Press, 1966. 81 p.

In astronomy, the author says, we are faced by contradictions. Not all the
apparent data of the moment can be correct; we do not know which fragments
are right and which are wrong. Because we cannot experiment with the
universe, we live in a kind of shifting uncertainty, shifting because as the
years pass the balance of certainty of a given piece of data changes.

Huang, Su-Shu. The sizes of habitable planets. Publications of the Astronomical
Society of the Pacific, v. 72, Dec. 1960: 489-493.

Conditions necessary for a habitable planet are reviewed. It is tentatively
concluded that a habitable planet most likely will have a radius lying between
1,000 and 20,000 km. It is also suggested that the rate of biological
evolution on a planet may increase with its surface area if other conditions
are equal.

-----. Some astronomical aspects of life in the universe. Sky and telescope,
v. 21, June 1961: 312-316.

Stellar life histories are briefly discussed as well as prerequisites for a
life-supporting planet. It is suggested that most single stars of the main
sequence between F5 and K5 could probably support life of an advanced form
on the planets revolving around them. Temperature and atmosphere of
Mars and Venus are discussed in detail and speculations made as to the
existence of life there.

Life on other planets -- what are the possibilities? Flying saucers, Oct. 1966:
8-11.

Summary of current scientific data on the possibility of intelligent life on
other planets in our solar system. Reprinted from the BUFORA (England)
Journal and Bulletin.

Limits of organic life in our solar system. American review of reviews, v. 43,
Feb. 1911: 242-243.

Moore, Patrick. The worlds around us. New York, Abelard-Schuman, 1956.
157 p.

Outlines conditions under which carbon-based life can survive and applies
them to sun, moon, planets, satellites, and asteroids in the solar system.
Hypothesizing that this is the only kind of life possible in the universe,
author concludes that men on earth are alone in the solar system. Asserts
that reports about visits to earth by extraterrestrial spacecraft are only
good stories.

Munitz, Milton K. Theories of the universe from Babylonian myth to modern
science. Glencoe, Ill., The Free Press, 1957. 437 p.

Survey of current trends in scientific cosmology against the background of
earlier efforts and achievements. Beginning with one of the earliest ventures
in the form of myth, materials are included exhibiting the principal stages
of progress in cosmological inquiry from antiquity up to the present time.

Ogden, Richard C. The creation of the solar system. Flying saucer review,
v. 4, July-Aug. 1958: 14-18.

Author reveals that there are more than nine planets in our solar system and
gives locations of three newly-discovered planets; that our solar system
contains more than one asteroid belt; and gives information on how man can
defy gravity and apply this knowledge toward building a spacecraft that can
maneuver outside earth's atmosphere.

Ovenden, Michael. Life in the universe. Garden City, N. Y., Doubleday, 1962.
160 p.

Recent discoveries in biology, chemistry, and physics that may provide clues
to possibilities of life in Solar System and beyond are discussed. Terrain
and atmospheres of Mars, Venus, Jupiter, and Saturn are considered as
well as probability of similar conditions existing on planets of other stars.

Posin, Daniel Q. Life beyond our planet. New York, McGraw-Hill, 1962. 128 p.

Non-technical discussion of planets of Solar System, consideration of whether life of any kind exists on them, and discussion of ways of communicating with these or planets of other solar systems.

Rush, Joseph H. Life in the universe. In The dawn of life. Garden City, N. Y., Hanover House, 1957. p. 188-217.

Appraisal of the possibility of life on the solar planets and beyond the solar system.

Sagan, Carl and W. W. Kellogg. The terrestrial planets. In Goldberg, Leo, Armin J. Deutsch, and David Layser, eds. Annual review of astronomy and astrophysics. v. 1. Palo Alto, Calif., Annual Reviews, Inc., 1963. p. 235-266.

Assessment of what we know and what we do not know about the nearer planets.

Sewall, Frank. Life on other planets as described by Swedenborg. Philadelphia, Swedenborg Scientific Association, 1911. 20 p.

Discussion of Swedenborg's description of planets in the solar system and their inhabitants which he claimed to have visited by astral projection.

Shapley, Harlow. The probable environment on other planets. In Pirie, N.W., ed. The biology of space travel. London, the Institute of Biology, 1961. p. 107-116.

Discussion topics includes: ozone barriers, the lunar surface and atmosphere, cosmochemistry--the local sampling, the Venus greenhouse and Martian deserts, the origin of life as one step in cosmic evolution, and life on the Lilliputian stars.

Space visitors: From which planets do they originate? Is there life on them? Newnes practical mechanics, v. 24, Jan. 1957: 203-204, 207.

Known information on the planetary atmospheres and physical conditions of the planets is summarized for the purpose of establishing whether or not life could be sustained on them. It is concluded that even the worst apparent location as an abode of life cannot be dismissed as entirely impossible.

Strughold, Hubertus. Planetary ecology (astrobiology). In Lectures in aerospace medicine. Article 5. Brooks AFB, Tex., School of Aviation Medicine, 1960. p. 1-27.

Chemistry of the planetary atmospheres in their present state is discussed, including their origin and historical development.

Strughold, Hubertus. The possibilities of an inhabitable extraterrestrial environment reachable from the earth. The journal of aviation medicine, v. 28, Oct. 1957: 507-512.

Ecological factors indispensible for the existence of terrestrial forms of life are presented. Each planet in our solar system is examined in the light of these factors, and a habitability index obtained. The possibility of life already existing on Mars is discussed.

MARS

Abbot, C. G. The habitability of Venus, Mars, and other worlds. In Annual report of the Board of Regents of the Smithsonian Institution for the year ending June 30, 1920. Washington, D. C., U. S. Govt. Print. Off., 1922. p. 165-171.

Considers the probability of the existence of intelligent life on heavenly bodies other than the earth and discusses means of communicating with the nearer planets.

Aitken, R. G. Why popular interest in Mars? Leaflets of the Astronomical Society of the Pacific, v. 2, July 1925: 3-6.

Antoncadi, E. M. The planet Mars. Sky, magazine of cosmic news, v. 31, July 1939: 6-7, 22.

Asimov, Isaac. The wellsprings of life. New York, Abelard-Schuman, 1960, 233 p.

In so vast a universe, it is possible there are billions of "earth type" planets. Mars is the only observable planet which may provide a habitat suitable for life.

Bennett, Dorothy A. Men from Mars. The sky, v. 3, Dec. 1938: 8-9.

Present knowledge of conditions on Mars is reviewed to support author's certitude that a Martian invasion is out of the question.

Bongers, Leonard H. Is there life on Mars? Space/aeronautics, v. 40, Aug. 1963: 86-88.

238

Possibility of life on Mars is discussed in terms of the Martian atmosphere and in terms of the hypothesis that the Martian surface markings are caused by vegetation.

Cade, C. Maxwell. Are we alone in space? Discovery, v. 24, Apr. 20, 1963: 27-29.

Various theories of origin of life on earth are reviewed with reference to possible development of similar life forms on other planets of other solar systems. Extraterrestrial origin of life on earth (panspermia hypothesis) is discussed critically from moment of a spore's escape from another planet to the arrival on earth's surface. Life on Mars, Venus, and other planets is briefly discussed. Conclusion of speculation is that intelligent life does exist in other parts of the universe.

Calvin, Melvin. Communication: from molecules to Mars. In A. I. B. S. Bull., v. 12, Oct. 1962: 29-44.

Current knowledge of chemical evolution on earth and the generation of molecular communities which give rise to terrestrial organisms is reviewed. It is hypothesized that given a corresponding set of molecules, temperature, and environment anywhere else in the universe, a similar sequence of evolution might have occurred as on earth. Mars is considered the most likely possibility for organic life.

Cross, C. A. Conditions on Mars. In Gatland, Kenneth W., ed. Spaceflight today. London, Iliffe Books, Ltd., 1963. p. 192-203.

Purpose of chapter is to show how knowledge of Mars can be deduced from what is actually observed astronomically. Author suggests that well-established deductions, which can confidently be accepted, can then be distinguished from conflicting hypotheses which await the accumulation of evidence before they can be accepted or rejected.

Cyr, Donald L. Mars revisited. Philadelphia, Dorrance & Co., 1959. 131 p.

A concept is advanced to aid in understanding the phenomenon of the variable surface markings of Mars.

Duckwell, W. E. Life in Mars. Popular astronomy, v. 49, Nov. 1941: 479-485.

Edwards, Frank. Frank Edwards' report: Soviet scientists claim life on Mars. Fate, v. 14, Apr. 1961: 40-46.

Views by Soviet scientists on the plurality of inhabited worlds are given. Among those who feel that Mars is inhabited by intelligent beings are V. Komarov, lecturer at Moscow planetarium; Dr. Martynov, director of the Shternberg Astronomical Institute; and Prof. N. Zhirov.

Edwards, Frank. Frank Edwards' report: what do flying saucers want?
Fate, v. 10, Sept. 1957: 19-27.

A scientist (who asked to remain anonymous) theorizes that beings from
Mars are transporting minerals mined on the moon and water taken from
the earth back to their own planet in what we call "flying saucers. "

Ellerby, Christopher. Saucers from Mars? Flying saucer review, v. 8,
Sept. -Oct. 1962: 16-18.

Mars, with weaker gravity than the earth's, may have permitted plant
and animal life to grow almost three times the normal size of that on
earth at a time when Martian surface conditions were more favorable.
Martian evolution may very well have developed almost three times as
fast as evolution on earth, thus permitting advanced forms of life to arise
on Mars and to protect themselves from the harsh conditions that now pre-
vail.

L'étrange histoire des satellites de Mars. Phénomènes spatiaux, Feb.
1965: 9-15.

Comments on speculation that the two satellites of Mars, Phobos and
Deimos, are artificial and were made by intelligent beings.

Evans, Gordon H. Image orthicon photographs of Martian canals. Flying
saucer review, v. 12, July-Aug. 1966: 7-9.

Discusses an image intensification technique for photographing
the Martian canal system.

Evans, Gordon H. Three unsolved Martian mysteries. Fate, v. 17,
June 1964: 27-33.

Author postulates that the case for an advanced Martian civilization is
almost better than the case for simple vegetable life forms. He discusses the canals, the motion of Phobos, and speculates that the violet
layer of the Martian atmosphere might be an artifically-produced shield
against ultraviolet light. He suggests that the discrepancy between optical and dynamical oblateness of Mars could be explained by a dome or
roof built over the planet by its inhabitants.

Evergreens will greet visitors in Mars. Science digest, v. 18, Nov.
1945: 88.

Gaston, Henry A. Mars revealed; or, seven days in the spirit world. San
Francisco, The Author, 1880. 208 p.

Account of trip to Mars by astral projection with descriptions of its
scenery, people, customs, educational institutions, religion, and laws.

Goddard, Jimmy. What Mariner IV saw. Flying saucers, Aug. 1966: 12-17.

Studies of pictures of the Martian surface sent back by Mariner IV seem to reveal symmetrical formations. Reprinted from Orbit, journal of the Tynside, England, U. F. O. Society.

Gossner, Simone D. Life may exist on Mars, but mistranslation made the canals. Natural history, v. 72, Apr. 1963: 56-57.

Gilman, Peter. Do the cherubim come from Mars? Flying saucer review, v. 13, Sept. -Oct. 1967: 19-21, 29.

On Apr. 24, 1964, Gary Wilcox, who was working his farm in Newark Valley, N. Y., allegedly saw a UFO land in a nearby field. The crew were two humanoid 4-ft. -tall entities who were holding specimens of soil and sod, said they were from Mars, and who explained that although they had been obtaining their food from the atmosphere, they had to find a way to rehabilitate their soil to raise food. Author suggests that "food taken from the atmosphere" might be analogous to the celestial manna described in the Bible in Exodus; the angels involved in this manifestation were the cherubim and therefore may have come from Mars. The entities also said there would be coming changes in the universe which would affect our solar system and that Mars may be where earth is now. Author draws a parallel between this information and Velikovsky's theory in Worlds in Collision.

Gould, Rupert R. Enigmas. New Hyde Park, N. Y., University Books, 1965: 248 p.

Information about mysteries which have not been resolved up to the present day. Evidence that there were once giants on the earth and that relates to the probability of intelligent life on Mars is discussed.

Horowitz, Norman. Is there life on other planets? Engineering and science, v. 24, Mar. 1961: 11-15.

Possible existence on Mars and Venus of terrestrial form of living matter based on proteins and nucleic acids is discussed.

Jackson, F. and P. Moore. Possibilities of life on Mars. In Mamikunian, Gregg and M. H. Briggs. Current aspects of exobiology. Pasadena, Calif., Jet Propulsion Laboratory, 1965. p. 243-259.

Conclusion that Mars may bear indigenous organisms of some kind is based on following observational arguments: (1) the various colors, including green, exhibited by the dark areas; (2) the seasonal changes in the visual albedo and polarization of the dark areas; (3) the ability of the dark areas to regenerate after an extensive "dust storm"; the presence of $2700-3000 cm^{-1}$ absorption bands, attributed to organic molecules.

Laine, Juliette. Gullivers' two moons on Mars. Fate, v. 10, Aug. 1957: 43-44.

Mars' two satellites were first viewed astronomically in 1877 by Asaph
Hall but had been accurately described in 1726--151 years earlier-- by
Jonathan Swift in Gullivers' Travels.

Levin, Gilbert V., Allen H. Heim, John R. Clendenning, and Mary-Francis
Thompson. Gulliver--a quest for life on Mars. Science, v. 138, Oct. 12,
1962: 114-121.

The "Gulliver" device utilizing a radioisotope technique to detect exotic
forms of life on Mars is discussed. The instrument would be incorporated
in a NASA-launched space probe. Data collection and analysis tecnniques
are described.

Ley, Willy. The history of the concepts about Mars. In Morgenthaler,
George W., ed. Exploration of Mars. North Hollywood, Calif., Western
Periodicals Co., 1963. p. 435-445 (Advances in the astronautical sciences,
v. 15)

Evolution of man's ideas and concepts about the planet Mars is traced from
the time of tne ancient Greeks to the present. The fanciful planetary trip
concepts of early fiction and 17 century chronicle are surveyed   Astronomical
writings describing the controversies over the "canals" and the existence
of life forms on Mars also are examined.

Liss, Jeffrey. The problem of life on Mars. Fate, v. 16, Aug. 1963: 39-47.

Hypothesis of plant physiologist Dr. Frank B. Salisbury that organisms
similar to higher terrestrial plants live in abundance on Mars, is reviewed.

Lowell, Percival. Proofs of life on Mars. Century, v. 2, 76, June 1908:
292-303.

Marshall, James S., ed. The planet Mars and its innabitants, by Eros Urides
(a Martian). Chico, Calif., James E. Marshall, 1956. 37 p.

All aspects of life on Mars are discussed. Information written down by
J. L. Kennon as given by a deep trance medium allegedly controlled by a
Martian, Eros Urides. First published in 1920.

Michel, Aimé. Do flying saucers originate from Mars? Flying saucer review,
v. 6, Mar. -Apr. 1960: 13-15.

Evidence supporting theory that intelligent life exists on Mars and that some
UFOs may originate there is reviewed.

Mundo, Laura. Pied piper from outer space. Los Angeles, The Planetary
Space Center Working Committee, 1964. 152 p.

Author describes alleged visit to Mars and philosophical, political, and educational institutions there. Her "guide" on the visit discusses earth's past history, role in God's plan, and ultimate destiny.

Nelson, Albert F. Tnere is life on Mars. New York, Citadel Press, 1955. 140 p.

Author considers the possibilities of life occurring on Mars and other planets throughout the universe under conditions with wnich we are familiar and based on the assumption that similar conditions are essential wherever life is to gain a hold.

Norman, Ernest L. The truth about Mars. Los Angeles, New Age Publishing Co., 1956. 61 p.

Account of trip to the planet Mars by astral projection and description of population, physical features, and socio-cultural-economic institutions.

Norman, Marke A. Many shall be called. El Monte, Calif., Understanding Publishing Co., 1959. 103 p.

Messages allegedly received by author through thought impression from what he believes to be an interplanetary space patrol craft from another dimension are related. Catastrophies on earth are prophesied and preparation advised.

Oparin, Aleksandr I. and V. Fesenkov. Life in the universe. New York, Twayne Publishers, Inc., 1961. 245 p.

On basis of most recent information in natural science, author discusses probability of universal existence of life-bearing planets, with special attention to Mars and Venus. Translation of Zhizn'vo veselennoi (Moscow, 1956).

Opposition flap 1965. Flying saucer review, v. 11, May-June 1965: 3-6. Report that UFO sighting apparently increased during opposition of Mars

Palmer, Ray. Mars' moons artificial. Flying saucers, Oct. 1959: 13-15.

Scientific fact is given to support theory that the two moons of Mars, Phobos and Deimos, are artificial satellites made by intelligent beings.

Pittendrigh, Colin S., Wolf Vishniac, and J. P. T. Pearman, eds. Biology and the exploration of Mars. Washington, D. C., National Academy of Sciences--National Research Council, 1966, 516 p. (NAS-NRC Publication 1296)

Report of a study held under auspices of the NAS-NRC Space Science Board. Contains a general summary chapter and 29 technical papers by various participants.

Pittenger, Norman W. Christianity and the man on Mars. Christian century, v. 73, June 20, 1956: 747-748.

Quiroga, R. A. La conquista de los grandes planetas. Revista Nacional de Aeronautica Espacial, v. 21, Jan. 1961: 8-9.

Discussion of the atmospheric and other characteristics of Mars and Venus which are of importance with respect to their habitability. The "population explosion" on earth is noted and the possibility of colonizing other planets is considered briefly, as is the possible existence there of living beings resembling man.

Rea, D. G. Evidence for life on Mars. Nature, v. 200, Oct. 12, 1963: 114-116.

Author states that while observations of seasonal changes on Mars seem to favor the probability of organic life, he prefers an inorganic explanation involving appropriate combinations of volcanic ash, lava, and winds.

Rember, Winthrop A. Eighteen visits to Mars. New York, Vantage Press, 1956. 439 p.

Narrative of journeys to, and exploration of the planet Mars, Oct. 6, 1892-Sept. 16, 1894. Through a phase of mediumship called "semi-automatism, " discarnate spirits dictate observations and experiences. Based on Sara Weiss' Journey to the Planet Mars; or Our Mission to Ento, Rochester, N. Y. , Austin Publishing Co. , 1905.

Russian report: Is there life on Mars? Fate, v. 13, Apr. 1960: 27-33.

Theories and data are presented supporting the view that conditions favorable to carbon-based life might exist on Mars. G. A. Tikhov, corresponding member of the U. S. S. R. Academy of Science, photographed Mars through colored heliofilters, observed the changing colors through the seasons, and concluded that they parallel the changing colors of the evergreen taiga in Siberia. He also concluded that if vegetation exists on Mars it does not show presence of chlorophyll but photographs white as do earth's Arctic plants. Translated from A Guest from the Cosmos by Aleksandr Kazantsev, Moscow, House of Geographical Literature, 1958.

Sagan, Carl. Biological exploration of Mars. In Morgenthaler, George W. , ed. Exploration of Mars. North Hollywood, Calif. , Western Periodicals Co. , 1963. p. 571-581 (Advances in the astronautical sciences. v. 15)

Present evidence strongly suggests, but does not conclusively prove, that life exists on Mars, the author states. He notes that intercomparison of Martian and terrestrial organisms, both on the biochemical and on the morphological levels, can provide a general perspective which is currently lacking in biology because all the life forms known to date have probably evolved from a single instance of the origin of life.

Sagan, Carl and W. W. Kellogg. The atmospheres of Mars and Venus. Washington, D. C., National Academy of Sciences - National Research Council, 1961. 151 p. (National Research Council. Publication 944)

Discusses in detail the state of our knowledge and some of the controversies concerning planetary atmospheres and explores experimental approaches most likely to lead to the resolution of these controversies. An expanded summary of a report by the Ad Hoc Panel on Planetary Atmospheres of the Space Science Board, National Academy of Sciences.

Salisbury, Frank. The inhabitants of Mars. Engineering and science, v. 18, Apr. 1955: 23-32.

Evidence for the existence of life on Mars is given. The influence of the Martian environment on the form this life may take is discussed, and problems demanding further investigation presented.

Schiaparelli, G. V. Mars den gådefulde planet. [Oversat af E. Slej.] Randers, Denmark, UFO-NYTs Forlag, 1965. 73 p.

Surface features of Mars, especially its "canals," are discussed as possible indications of intelligent life on that planet. Translation of article entitled "Über die beobachteten Erscheinungen auf der Oberfläche des Planeten Mars" in Himmel und Erde, v. 1, 1889.

Serviss, Garrett P. Curiosities of the sky. New York, Harper & Bros., 1909. 268 p.

A broad, general view of the chief mysteries and problems of astronomy is given; possibility of life and intelligence on the moon and on Mars is discussed.

Shapley, Harlow. The probable environment on other planets. In Pirie, N. W., ed. The biology of space travel. London, The Institute of Biology, 1961. p. 107-116.

Discussion topics include: ozone barriers, the lunar surface and atmosphere, cosmochemistry--the local sampling, the Venus greenhouse and Martian deserts, the origin of life as one step in cosmic evolution, and life on the Lilliputian stars.

Shneour, Elie A. and Eric A. Ottesen, comp. Extraterrestrial life: An anthology and bibliography. Washington, National Academy of Sciences--National Research Council, 1966. 478 p. (National Research Council. Publication 1296A)

Supplement to "Biology and the Exploration of Mars, " report of study under auspices of Space Science Board and published as NAS-NRC Publication 1296. Contains selected papers, including Mariner IV and sounding rocket observations of Mars made in 1965, and bibliography of 2,000 selected references to world literature published through mid-1964 with addendum of papers published from that date through late 1965.

Siegal, S. M., L. A. Halpern, C. Giumarro, G. Renwick, and G. Davis.
Martian biology: the experimentalist's approach. Nature, v. 197, Jan.
26, 1963: 329-331.

Reports tests showing that complex terrestrial organisms survive and
grow under conditions constituting extreme departure from normal terrestrial environment. Concludes that environments encountered during
future explorations of solar system which are not too extreme relative to
earth--those expected on Mars, for example--may support readily recognizable life forms.

Siguret, B. La vie sur mars. Phênomènes spatiaux, Dec. 1965: 3-7.

Review of theories relating to possibility of life on Mars. Data from
Mariner IV is considered.

Sinton, William M. Evidence of the existence of life on Mars. In Morgenthaler,
George W., ed. Explanation of Mars. North Hollywood, Calif., Western
Periodicals Co., 1963. p. 543-551. (Advances in the astronautical sciences.
v. 15)

Observational evidence that bears on the supposed existence of vegetation
in the dark regions of the planet Mars is discussed. The temperature
measurements of Mars are presented because, although they do not give
any direct support to the existence of vegetation, they do have a bearing on
the nature of the vegetation if such is present. From the temperature observation it is concluded that plants are likely to be shaped like cactuses.

Smoluchowski, R. Is there vegetation on Mars? Science, v. 148, May 14,
1965: 946-947.

Stevens, Stuart. Sighting peaks and planetary oppositions. Flying saucers,
Aug. 1966: 20-21.

Author suggests the UFO sighting peaks between the Martian oppositions
might mean there is also an opposition wave for other planets in our solar
system. Reprinted from Orbit, journal of the Tyneside, England, U.F.O.
Society.

The struggle for existence on the planet Mars. Current opinion, v. 54,
Jan. 1913: 40-42.

Strughold, Hubertus. The ecological profile of Mars: bioastronautical prospect. Advances in the astronautical sciences, v. 15, 1963: 543-551.

Strughold, Hubertus. Life on Mars in view of physiological principles.
In Epitome of space medicine. Article 3. Brooks AFB, Tex., School
of Aviation Medicine, 1958. p. 1-8.

Problem of extraterrestrial life is discussed in the light of current physiological experience. Particular attention is given the environmental factors of temperature and oxygen because of their close interrelation in biological processes. Speculation is advanced on the possibility of life on Mars and Venus.

Strughold, Hubertus. Physiological considerations on the possibility of life under extraterrestrial conditions. In Marbarger, John P., ed. Space medicine. Urbana, Ill., University of Illinois Press, 1951. p. 31-48.

Environmental conditions are discussed under which life as we know it can exist. It is concluded that from the standpoint of temperature, Mars and possibly Venus are the only planets, apart from earth, which at present possess the prerequisites. From the standpoint of vital oxygen pressure, man and animals except those of the very lowest species can be excluded from life on Mars with certainty.

Strughold, Hubertus. The possibilities of an inhabitable extraterrestrial environment reachable from the earth. The journal of aviation medicine, v. 28, Oct. 1957: 507-512.

Ecological factors indispensible for tne existence of terrestrial forms of life are presented. Each planet in our solar system is examined in tne light of these factors, and a habitability index obtained. The possibility of life already existing on Mars is discussed.

Strughold, Hubertus. Synopsis of Martian life theories. In Ordway, Frederick I. III, ed. Advances in space science and technology. v. 9. New York and London, Academic Press, 1967. p. 105-122.

Considering all the physicochemical and biological factors and their interrelations, and particularly the adaptability of life to adverse conditions and the effect of living matter upon the soil, it is concluded that the occurrence of life on Mars is more in the realm of probability than of possibility. The dark areas on the Martian surface might indeed represent an ecological system, or ecosystem, but of a level far below that found on earth. In terms of carbon biology and geocentric analogy, the conclusion is justified that the dark surface area can be of a biospheric nature.

Sytinskaĭa, N. N. Est' li zhizn' na drugikh planetakh [Is there life on other planets?] Moscow, Gosudarstvennoe izdatel 'stvo kul'turnoprosvetitel'noĭ literatury, 1952. 64 p.

A lecture dealing primarily with life on Mars and other planets. The author concludes that it is quite probable that vegetation exists on other planets, citing tne Russian astronomer, G. S. Tikhov, wno nas indicated that the color of polar caps on Mars is greenish, not white, an evidence of vegetation, and that the melting ice and snow produce the water necessary to sustain life.

Thomas, Dorotny. Life on Mars according to the great mystics. Los Angeles, New Age Publishing Co., 1958. 9 p.

Account of life on Mars as given by the mystics Jacob Lorber, C. W.
Leadbeater, Andrew J. Davis, and Flower Newhouse.

Tikhov, G. A. Reaching for the stars. Moscow, Foreign Languages Publishing House, 1962. 152 p.

Basic principles of astrobotany are discussed and development of this
science into astrobiology. Author explains how optical properties of
terrestrial plants growing in rigorous climates enabled scientists to
draw comparisons between them and those of Martian areas believed to
be patches of vegetation. Translation of V prostorakh vselennoĭ.

United States report: Is there life on Mars? Fate, v. 13, May 1960: 27-34.

Discoveries and conclusions of U. S. scientists regarding life on Mars
are presented. Research cited is by Harlow Shapley, Thomas Gold,
Melvin Calvin, Otto Struve, and Herman J. Muller.

Vallée, Jacques and Janine Vallée. Mars and the flying saucers. Flying
saucer review, v. 8, Sept.-Oct. 1962: 5-11.

Study of the periodicity of the flying saucer phenomenon in its correlation with the oppositions of Mars.

Von Braun, Werner. Mars: are its canals full of water; is there really
life there? Popular science, v. 183, Aug. 1963: 18.

Weiss, Sara. Journeys to the planet Mars; or Our mission to Ento (Mars).
Rochester, N. Y., Bradford Press, 1903: 548 p.

Narrative of journeys to and exploration of "planet astronomically known
as Mars" transcribed automatically while author was alleged by controlled
by discarnate spirits.

Wellman, Wade. Phobos and Deimos: an inquiry. Flying saucer review,
v. 9, May-June 1963: 26-27.

Information is considered suggesting that Phobos and Deimos, Mars'
moons, could be artificial space stations launched into orbit by the
race of beings responsible for the UFO phenomenon.

What's stirring on Mars? Franco-U. S. findings. Newsweek, v. 68, Oct. 31,
1966: 66.

Why are we keen about Mars? Literary digest, v. 86, Aug. 22, 1925: 19.

Wilks, Willard and Rex Pay. Quest for Martian life re-emphasized.
Technology week, v. 18, June 6, 1966: 26-28.

Zeñabi, J. El misterio de los discos voladores. Santago de Chile, The
Author, 1953. 77 p.

Account of author's alleged contact with landed flying saucer and its Martian
crew and trip to Mars aboard spacecraft. He describes in detail physical
features of Mars, its science, culture, and political institutions. Experience
reportedly took place in September 1952.

MOON

Abelson, Philip H. Extraterrestrial life. In U. S. National Academy of
Sciences. Proceedings. v. 47, Apr. 15, 1961: 575-581.

The paper reviews some of the cogent limitations on life as we know it
and examines some of the fundamental reasons these limitations exist.
A discussion of features of planetary and lunar environments which
strongly contraindicate the presence of life follows.

Anders, Edward. The moon as a collector of biological material.
Science, v. 133, Apr. 14, 1961: 1115-1116.

After considering the idea that the moon might serve as a repository
for microorganisms from outside the solar system, the author concludes that although terrestrial microorganisms might be found on the
moon, extra-solar-system biota would be undetectable.

Cyr, Guy J. Are there humanoids in space? Flying saucers, Aug. 1967:
12-14.

Author hypothesizes that the moon's so-called "crust" is actually the
filamentous, closely knitted, microphyllous foliage of various flourishing
florae held up to the sun for energy and meteoritic fertilizer. This "crust"
also serves as a global, protective roof for the superintelligent sentient
beings who live under it and who are among the various kinds of extraterrestrials exploring our world.

Da Silva, Renato I. No espaço não estamos sós. São Paulo Edart, 1966.
213 p.

Theories relating to possibility of life on the moon and other planets
are summarized. Parapsychological phenomena of mental telepathy,
precognition, ESP, premonition, and astral projection are discussed as
they might relate to contact with extraterrestrial entities or intelligences.

Edwards, Frank, Frank Edwards' report: from the hills of the moon. Fate,
v. 11, Apr. 1958: 59-65.

The question is raised as to whether the "hills" or "domes" currently observed in increasing numbers on the moon are natural or artificial objects.

Firsoff, Valdemar A. Life? In his Strange world of the moon. New York, Basic Books, 1959. p. 170-180.

Presents currently-known information on atmosphere, surface, and sub-surface of the moon. Chapter 16 postulates existence of underground water and gas on the moon as well as living beings equipped with a husk-like covering that would enable them to survive in a near vacuum.

Fouéré, René. Adamski's last chance. Flying saucer review, v. 10, Sept.-Oct. 1964: 27-29.

Article suggests that the description in Adamski's book, Inside the Spaceships, of snow, mountains, lakes, and rivers on the hidden side of the moon could be possible if intelligent beings there had created a gigantic dome of energy in which an atmosphere chemically created by them would remain captive and within which these weather phenomena could be made to occur. He says that the Adamski claim is indefensible and absurd otherwise.

Gilvarry, J. J. The possibilities of a primordial lunar life. In Mamikunian, Gregg and M. H. Briggs, eds. Current aspects of exobiology. Pasadena, Calif., Jet Propulsion Laboratory, 1965. p. 179-241.

Features of the lunar surface are discussed which would seem to indicate former presence of a hydrosphere and atmosphere with essentially complete internal consistency. Since these were the conditions that must have held at the inception of terrestrial life, it can be assumed that there was a pristine lunar life.

Gordon, Samuel. There's something in the moon. Fate, v. 12, July 1959: 47-53.

Reports observations by astronomers that seem to suggest the moon is being explored by an unknown race.

Hatcher, Judi Anne. Towers on the moon? Fate, v. 20, Dec. 1967: 32-37.

Author discusses the "six mysterious and statuesque shadows" that appeared in Lunar Orbiter II photographs of an area west of the moon's Sea of Tranquility released by NASA on Nov. 23, 1966, and comments on contradictory explanations issued by NASA.

Keyhoe, Donald, Enigma on the moon. Fate, v. 9, Aug. 1956: 36-43.

Strange lights, objects, and activities on the moon that were noted in early astronomical records are cited. Reprinted from The Flying Saucer Conspiracy (New York, Henry Holt, 1955).

King, George. Life on the planets. Hollywood, Calif., The Aetherius Society, 1958: 29 p.

Series of lectures dealing with life in general on the planets Mars, Venus, Jupiter, and Saturn. There is also a lecture dealing with the system of government--Interplanetary Parliament--adopted by residents of these planets. Information allegedly transmitted telepathically to author.

Layne, Stan. I doubted flying saucers. Boston, Meador Press, 1958. 177 p.

Imaginative account of visit to the moon in a sphere using magnetic lines of force for propulsion and description of civilization, philosophy, technology, customs, and artifacts there.

Moore, Patrick. Life on the moon? Irish astronomical journal, v. 3, March 1955: 133-137.

A summary is presented of current information on the lunar environment and of observations and theories concerning the possibility of indigenous life on the moon.

Nicolson, Marjorie Hope. Voyages to the moon. New York, Macmillan, 1948. 297 p.

The author traces through the literature from the 15th century the scientific and philosophical backgrounds of the idea of cosmic voyages.

Palmer, Ray. Mars' moons artificial. Flying saucers, Oct. 1959: 13-15.

Scientific fact is given to support theory that the two moons of Mars, Phobos and Deimos, are artificial satellites made by intelligent beings.

Reynolds, O. E. and F. H. Quimby. The search for organic material on the moon. In Malina, Frank J., ed. Life sciences research and lunar medicine. Proceedings. London, Pergamon Press, 1967. p. 51-53.

Paper develops a review of inquiries and methods applicable to the organic geochemical analysis of subsurface lunar material. Abstract only.

Serviss, Garrett P. Curiosities of the sky. New York, Harper & Bros., 1909. 268 p.

A broad general view of the chief mysteries and problems of astronomy is given; possibility of life and intelligence on the moon and on Mars is discussed.

There's intelligent life on the moon. Flying saucers, May 1959: 67-74.

Features of the moon that have been observed astronomically and that seem to indicate it is not a "dead" world are discussed.

Wells, Herbert George. The first men on the moon. London, G. Newnes, Ltd., 1901. 342 p.

Fictitious account of discovery of substance opaque to gravity and its use in constructing spacecraft which lands first men on the moon. Voyage, landing, and exploration of moon described in detail; human society criticized through depiction of a non-human culture.

VENUS

Abbot, C. G. The habitability of Venus, Mars, and other worlds. In Annual report of the Board of Regents of the Smithsonian Institution for the year ending June 30, 1920. Washington, D. C., U. S. Govt. Print. Off., 1922. p. 165-171.

Considers the probability of the existence of intelligent life on heavenly bodies other than the earth and discusses means of communicating with the nearer planets.

Aitken, R. G. Venus: the earth's twin planet. Leaflets of the Astronomical Society of the Pacific, v. 48, Jan. 1933: 195-198.

Any life on Venus is declared impossible. Science news letter, v. 40, July 12, 1941: 26.

Studies by Dr. Rupert Wildt of the Princeton University Observatory indicate that the clouds veiling the surface of Venus are solidified formaldehyde, a poisonous and extremely irritating gas often used as a disinfectant because of its germ-killing powers. It seems probable there would be enough free formaldehyde on the surface of Venus to make it most unpleasant, while the complete lack of oxygen would preclude the possibility of carbon-based life.

Cade, C. Maxwell. Are we alone in space? Discovery, v. 24, Apr. 20, 1963: 27-29.

Various theories of origin of life on earth are reviewed with reference to possible development of similar life forms on other planets of other solar systems. Extraterrestrial origin of life on earth (panspermia hypothesis) is discussed critically from moment of a spore's escape from another planet to the arrival on earth's surface. Life on Mars, Venus, and other planets is briefly discussed. Conclusion of speculation is that intelligent life does exist in other parts of the universe.

Edwards, Frank. Frank Edwards' report: keep your eye on Venus. Fate, v. 12, 1959: 57-63.

Author speculates that although Mars has seemed most likely to be the planet from which UFOs might originate, Venus is also a possibility.

Horowitz, Norman. Is there life on other planets? Engineering and science, v. 24, March 1961: 11-15.

Possible existence on Mars and Venus of terrestrial form of living matter based on proteins and nucleic acids is discussed.

Huang, Su-shu. Some astronomical aspects of life in the universe. Sky and telescope, v. 21, June 1961: 312-316.

Stellar life histories are briefly discussed as well as prerequisites for a life-supporting planet. It is suggested that most single stars of the main sequence between F5 and K5 could probably support life of an advanced form on the planets revolving around them. Temperature and atmosphere of Mars and Venus are discussed in detail and speculations made as to existence of life there.

Maney, Charles A. Is Venus inhabited? Flying saucer review, v. 11, Sept. - Oct. 1965: 6-8.

It is stated that U. S. scientists, as well as astrophysicists from the U.S.S.R., have found atomic oxygen and nitrogen in the dark light of Venus, providing evidence that the atmosphere of Venus is quite like that of earth. The author speculates that Venus may therefore be inhabited by human beings not too unlike the people on earth.

No chance of life on Venus; scientific data from Mariner II. Business week, Dec. 29, 1962: 22.

Oparin, Aleksandr I. and V. Fesenkov. Life in the universe. New York, Twayne Publishers, Inc., 1966. 245 p.

On basis of most recent information in natural science, author discusses probability of universal existence of life-bearing planets, with special attention to Mars and Venus. Translation of Zhizn' vo veselennoi (Moscow, 1956).

Serviss, Garrett P. Curiosities of the sky. New York, Harper & Bros., 1909. 268 p.

A broad general view of the chief mysteries and problems of astronomy is given; possibility of life and intelligence on the moon and on Mars is discussed.

Shapley, Harlow. The probable environment on other planets. In Pirie, N. W., ed. The biology of space travel. London, The Institute of Biology, 1961. p. 107-116.

Discussion topics include: ozone barriers, the lunar surface and atmosphere, cosmochemistry--the local sampling, the Venus greenhouse and Martian deserts, the origin of life as one step in cosmic evolution, and life on the Lilliputian stars.

Strughold, Hubertus. Life on Mars in view of physiological principles. In
Epitome of space medicine. Article 3. Brooks AFB, Tex., School of
Aviation Medicine, 1958. p. 1-8.

Problem of extraterrestrial life is discussed in the light of current
physiological experience. Particular attention is given the environmental
factors of temperature and oxygen because of their close interrelation in
biological processes. Speculation is advanced on the possibility of life
on Mars and Venus.

Strughold, Hubertus. Physiological considerations on the possibility of life
under extraterrestrial conditions. In Marbarger, John P., ed. Space
medicine. Urbana, Ill., University of Illinois Press, 1951. p. 31-48.

Environmental conditions are discussed under which life as we know it
can exist. It is concluded that from the standpoint of temperature, Mars and
possibly Venus are the only planets, apart from the earth, which at present
possess the prerequisites. From the standpoint of vital oxygen pressure,
man and animals except those of the very lowest species can be excluded
from life on Mars with certainty.

Thomas, Dorothy. Life on Venus according to the great mystics. Los
Angeles, New Age Publishing Co., 1958: 10 p.

Summary of descriptions of life on Venus by Andrew J. Davis, William D.
Pelley, Lee Crandall, Jacob Lorber, Dana Howard, Flower Newhouse, and
Emanuel Swedenborg.

Extraterrestrial Life

GENERAL REFERENCES

Abelson, Philip H. Extra-terrestrial life. In U. S. National Academy of Sciences. Proceedings. v. 47, Apr. 15, 1961: 575-581.

The paper reviews some of the cogent limitations of life as we know it and examines some of the fundamental reasons these limitations exist. A discussion of features of planetary and lunar environments which strongly contraindicate the presence of life follows.

Aharon, Y. N. ibn. The recent literature of extraterrestrialism. Saucer news, v. 12, Mar. 1965: 11-12.

Evaluates works on extraterrestrialism by Desmond Leslie and Dr. M. K. Jessup.

Allen, Thomas. The quest: a report on extraterrestrial life. Philadelphia, Chilton Co., 1965. 323 p.

State-of-the-art review of theories and speculations on possibility of extraterrestrial life. Author estimates there are numerous planets supporting countless other intelligent societies, many of which are much more developed than earth's. Book simultaneously published in Toronto by Ambassador Books, Ltd.

Anderson, Poul. Is there life on other worlds? With an introd. by Isaac Asimov. New York, Crowell-Collier Press, 1963. 223 p.

Speculative consideration of what we can be sure does not exist anywhere in space, what probably does exist, and some of the imaginative possibilities inherent in space travel.

Arrhenius, Svante. The life of the universe. London and New York, Harper & Bros. , 1909. 2v.

Conceptions by man of life in the universe from the earliest ages to the present time (1909). Translation of Manniskan infor varldsgatan (Stockhom, Geber, 1907).

Ball, Robert. The possibility of life on other worlds. The fortnightly review, v. 62, Nov. 1894: 718-729.

Noting that there was as yet no definite answer to the question of whether life can exist on any of the other worlds, the author gives a state-of-the-art summary of current hypotheses.

Barnes, Sam. Life on other planets. Machine design, v. 35, June 6, 1963: 118-123.

Overview of current exobiological research in the U.S.

Bauchau, A. Les météorites sont-elles chargées d'un message biologique? La revue nouvelle, v. 38, Sept. 15, 1963: 240-243.

Information surrounding discovery of the Orgueil meteorite is given. Controversy surrounding the biological and physico-chemical origin of organic matter found on it is discussed as well as significance of the discovery.

Bergamini, David. Fossils that say life may really be out of this world. Life, v. 51, Dec. 8, 1961: 45.

Identification of microscopic particles in a fragment of the Orgueil meteorite which resemble fossilized one-celled organisms strongly suggest that early steps of evolution probably took place elsewhere.

-----. Wax and wigglers: life in space? Life, v. 50, May 5, 1961: 57, 59-60, 62.

Complex waxlike hydrocarbons similar to those found in butter and living things in general were found in a fragment of the Orgueil meteorite by scientists Bartholomew Nagy, Warren Meinschein, and Douglas Hennessy. Walter Newton and Frederick Sisler revealed that when a pulverized specimen of a meteorite that fell in Murray, Ky. , in 1950, was placed in sterile solution for several months to see if anything would grow, droplets of it under a microscope revealed tiny, wiggling sausagelike particles about the size of bacteria but unlike terrestrial bacteria.

Berger, Rainer. The solar system and extraterrestrial life. In Advances in the astronautical sciences. v. 13. North Hollywood, Calif. , 1963. p. 649-665.

Discusses current experimental results, opinion, and speculation in research on problem of extraterrestrial life. Theories on chemical and prebiological evolution in space are examined in connection with theories on origin of life.

Berget, Alphonse. The appearance of life on worlds and the hypothesis of Arrhenius. In The Smithsonian Institution. Annual report of the board of regents for the year ending June 30, 1912. Washington, U.S. Govt. Print. Off., 1913. p. 543-551.

Conception of Svante Arrhenius that life can be carried from one planet to another: Germs swept away by ascending air currents which carry them to the limits of the atmosphere are repelled by the electrically charged dust that has penetrated there, coming from suns that have driven it away by the repelling pressure of their radiation. After they have arrived in space they attach themselves to some straying grains of dust of greater dimensions than theirs and which are consequently capable of obeying the attraction of a neighboring planet rather than the repelling force of radiation; they then penetrate into the atmosphere of this new planet and bring life to it. if life has not yet developed there.

Berland, Theodore. Meteorites: proof of life on other planets? Popular mechanics, v. 116, Aug. 1961: 108-112, 208, 210.

Report on research into whether meteors come from life-bearing planets.

Bernal, J. D. Is there life elsewhere in the universe? Science and culture, v. 28, Aug. 1962: 356-357.

Berrill, Norman John. Worlds without end: a reflection on planets, life, and time. New York, Macmillan, 1964. 240 p.

Speculative investigation of possibilities of life on other planets: nearest and best-known planets are compared with earth; hypothetical planets similar to earth but with one or another feature altered in some manner are examined in order to predict how familiar living things might be affected; life on earth is evaluated to determine which characteristics may be regarded as universal under certain circumstances and which are special; and imaginative efforts of speculative writers to conceive and describe creatures different from those known to us on earth are presented.

Blum, Harold F. Perspectives in evolution. American scientist, v. 43, Oct. 1955: 595-610.

Assuming life to exist on other planets of the billion solar systems now thought to comprise the known universe, the author says the next easy step is to assume that our own evolution here on earth has been paralleled elsewhere.

Bok, B. J. Life on other worlds. Australian science teacher's journal, v. 9, Nov. 1963: 4.

Bowman, Norman J. Silicon as a base for life forms. Journal of space flight, v. 3, Mar. 1951: 1-6.

Possibility of life forms in the universe based on silicon is considered and it
is concluded there are two favorable possibilities with a life form based on an
Si-O-Si bonding. The first is with an atmosphere of NH_3 with the body functions
carried out through changes in pH, temperature, and concentration of an
alkaline solution of silicates. The second case is with an atmosphere of HF
where digestion is carried out through aqueous HF and respiration would involve
exhalation of Si F_4 and water.

Bracewell, R. N. Life in the galaxy. In Cameron, A. G. W., ed. Interstellar
communication. New York, W. A. Benjamin, Inc., 1963. p. 232-242.

Author establishes concept that the other stars and star systems have planets
and that some of these planets are inhabitable. He postulates that life thereon is
less advanced than that of earth. Radar communication in the "galactic club"
is a fact, but not from intelligent source; however, we should be alert for
signals. It is speculated that sufficiently highly developed stellar communities are
common but that contacting them, or its reverse, would be a matter of chance.

Bradbury, Ray. A serious search for weird worlds. Life, v. 49, Oct. 24, 1960:
116-118, 120, 123-124, 126-128, 130.

Sketches are shown of strange creatures who may represent what creatures on
other inhabited planets look like. Explanation is made that although grotesque
by earth standards, they could develop this way in response to different
environments of other worlds. Project Ozma, the radio-telescope search for
life on other worlds, is discussed.

Brewster, David. More worlds than one. New York, Robert Carter & Bros.,
1854. 265 p.

Author defends doctrine of plurality of inhabited worlds by citing current
astronomical discoveries and by analyzing and refuting objections.

Briggs, Michael H. The distribution of life in the solar system: an evaluation of
the present evidence. Journal of the British Interplanetary Society, v. 18,
Sept.-Dec. 1962: 431-437.

Indirect evidence indicative of the existence of extraterrestrial life is given.

-----. Terrestrial and extraterrestrial life. Spaceflight, v. 2, Oct. 1959:
120-121.

Hypothesis for origin of life on earth is given based on three assumptions:
(1) intelligent life existed somewhere in the universe prior to the beginning of
life on earth; (2) interplanetary flight is possible by these intelligences; and
(3) lifeless earth was visited by extraterrestrials who either deliberately or
accidentally left microbes behind when they departed. Variations of and
objections to hypothesis are given.

Bun, Thomas P. and Flavio A. Pereira. "Biospheric index," a contribution to the problem of determination of the existence of extra-solar planetary biospheres. In VIIIth International Astronautical Congress, Barcelona, 1957. Proceedings. Vienna, Springer-Verlag, 1958. p. 63.

Authors report that planets within the solar system may be classified into three groups based on probable existence of life by comparative examination of regions of the solar ecosphere. Biospheric index for classification of given planet within indicated scale of groups may be established by comparison of spectroscopic absorption lines.

Cade, C. Maxwell. Are we alone in space? Discovery, v. 24, Apr. 20, 1963: 27-29.

Various theories of origin of life on earth are reviewed with reference to possible development of similar life forms on other planets of other solar systems. Extraterrestrial origin of life on earth (panspermia hypothesis) is discussed critically from moment of a spore's escape from another planet to the arrival on earth's surface. Life on Mars, Venus, and other planets is briefly discussed. Conclusion of speculation is that intelligent life does exist in other parts of the universe.

-----. Other worlds than ours. London, Museum Press, 1966. 248 p.

Consideration of possibility and implications of other worlds in space and other worlds in time.

Calvin, Melvin. Chemical evolution. In Cameron, A. G. W., ed. Interstellar communication. New York, W. A. Benjamin, 1963. p. 33-77.

From questions on the nature and characteristics of life, the author proceeds through theories on chemical evolution with the establishment of an environment conducive to the origin of self-replicating macromolecules. Speculation on life on other planets life elsewhere in the solar system, and life in the galactic systems is followed by a discussion of man's place in the universe. Of the two hundred million inhabitable planets in the visible universe, two areas selected for attempt at interstellar communication (Project Ozma) are Tau Ceti and Epsilon Eridani.

-----. Communication: from molecules to Mars. In A. I. B.S. Bull., v. 12, Oct. 1962: 29-44.

Current knowledge of chemical evolution on earth and the generation of molecular communities which give rise to terrestrial organisms is reviewed. It is hypothesized that given a corresponding set of molecules, temperature, and environment anywhere else in the universe, a similar sequence of evolution might have occurred as on earth. Mars is considered the most likely possibility for organic life.

-----. Origin of life on earth and elsewhere. Annals of internal medicine, v. 54. May 1961: 954-976.

Traces chemical evolution to the point when a primitive organism is formed. Applies this reasoning to question of whether we are likely to find that similar events have occurred elsewhere than on earth.

Calvin, Melvin. Round trip from space. Evolution, v. 3, Sept. 8, 1959: 362-377.

Cameron, A. G. W. Stellar life zones. In Cameron, A. G. W., ed. Interstellar communication. New York, W. A. Benjamin, Inc. 1963. p. 107-110.

Conclusion is reached that all single stars in space (except those with very low heavy-element contents) have a life zone containing an average of about 1.4 planets of undetermined size.

Chaikin, G. L. A transitional hypothesis concerning life on other bodies. Popular astronomy, v. 59, Jan. 1951: 50-51.

It is postulated that the existence of life as we know it in planetary systems is a transitional phenomenon that tends to flourish most under conditions of least stress on the "habitable" bodies.

Chamberlin, Ralph V. Life on other worlds. Bulletin of the University of Utah, v. 22, Feb. 1932: 1-52.

A study in the history of opinion on life in other worlds from 600 B.C. to 1931 A.D.

Conniff, James G. Who's out there: meteorite evidence. Columbia, v. 41, Aug. 1961: 3-5, 35, 37.

Conway, J. If there is life on other planets wouldn't there have to be polygenesis? Catholic messenger, v. 82, Aug. 6, 1964: 10.

Copland, Alexander. The existence of other worlds, peopled with living and intelligent beings, deduced from the nature of the universe. London, J. G. & F. Rivington, 1834. 210 p.

Presents reasons for believing the fixed stars and the planets are habitations for living beings. Cites writings of men who have believed in a plurality of inhabited worlds and states grounds for their belief. in their own words.

Cramp, Leonard G. The cosmos--expanding or orbital? Flying saucer review, v. 7, May-June 1961: 8-12.

Author proposes an original and topical theory on how the universe began.

Creighton, Gordon W. What do the Russians know? Flying saucer review, v. 8, Jan.-Feb. 1962: 20-21.

Translations from Krasnaya Zvezda, Ekonomich Gazeta, and Komsomolskaya Pravda expressing Soviet views about possible life beyond the earth.

Demoulin, Maurice. La vie dans l'univers. La nature, v. 64, Part I, Apr. 15, 1936: 369-371.

Dethier, Vincent G. Life on other planets. Catholic world, v. 198, Jan. 1964: 245-250.

Drake, W.R. Mercury, Jupiter, and others: can life exist? Flying saucer review, v. 6, Sept.-Oct. 1960: 18-22.

Survey of facts and speculations on possibility of life on Mercury, Jupiter and lesser known bodies in earth's solar system.

Drawert, Friedrich. Estraterrestrisches Leben. Naturwissenschaftliche Rundschau, v. 14. Feb. 1961: 68-70.

Ecosphere may shape life on distant planets. Science newsletter, v. 80, Oct. 21, 1961: 272.

Edwards, Frank. Frank Edwards' report: you can break the UFO barrier. Fate, v. 11, Nov. 1958: 77-83.

Astronomical evidence is presented to support speculation that life exists in solar systems other than earth's. Readers are urged to write their Congressmen asking them to require the Government to end secrecy regarding UFOs.

Ewing, Ann. Life in all solar systems? Science newsletter, v. 86, Sept. 26, 1964: 199.

Fears, Francis R. Silicon and extraterrestrial life forms. Journal of space flight, v. 2, Nov. 1950: 5-6.

A life form based on silicon metabolism which would remotely resemble the life on our planet cannot exist under such environmental conditions as are found on earth. It might exist in an entirely alien set of circumstances which are at present beyond our conception.

Firsoff, V. A. An ammonia-based life. Discovery, v. 23, Jan. 1963: 36-42.

Development of inorganic polymers which bear a resemblance to organic compounds but have, wholly or partly, a different chemical basis has led to speculations on various alternative life schemes. When liquid ammonia replaces water as a universal solvent, ammonolysis of the analogue compounds in an ammono-organic chemistry can replace hydrolysis in the process of digestion. The same reactions of chemical degradation which yield energy by oxidation in our system would be performed in that of ammonia through the agency of nitrogen. Instead of water and carbon dioxide as final products, ammonia and cyanogen C_2N_2 which is the ammonia analogue of CO_2, would be produced. Equivalent organic compounds in a nitrogen-based life system are given.

Firsoff, Valdemar Axel. Life beyond the earth. New York, Basic Books, Inc., 1963. 320 p.

Origin of life on earth and elsewhere is discussed, its subsequent evolution and present condition, and such forms of it as deviate most from human standards and thereby promise insight into alien structures that may exist on other worlds. Range of environments are examined within which life as we know it is possible as well as organic chemistries that would be viable in environments where terrestrial life could not exist.

Fontenelle, Bernard le Bovier de. Entretiens sur la pluralité des mondes. Paris, Editions de la Nouvelle France, 1945. 201 p.

Combines a popular defense of Copernican astronomy and Cartesian physics with an amusing and fanciful discussion of the plurality of inhabited worlds.

Hayatsu, Ryoichi. Orgueil meteorite--organic nitrogen contents. Science, v. 146, Dec. 4, 1964: 1291-1293.

Analysis of Orgueil meteorite is described in detail. Purines, amino derivates of sym-triazine and substituted guanidines are isolated and identified by chromatographic, spectroscopic, and other techniques. Results are discussed in terms of value as evidence of extraterrestrial life.

Heintze, Carl. Search among the stars. Princeton, N. J., Van Nostrand, 1966. 175 p.

Non-technical speculative discussion of whether there is intelligent life in the universe.

Holmes, David C. The search for life on other worlds. New York, Sterling Publishing Co., 1966. 240 p.

Non-technical discussion of man's place in the cosmos and possibility of intelligent life throughout the universe.

Horowitz, Norman. Is there life on other planets? Engineering and science, v. 24, Mar. 1961: 11-15.

Possible existence on Mars and Venus of terrestrial form of living matter based on proteins and nucleic acids is discussed.

Huang, Su-Shu. Occurrence of life in the universe. American scientist, v. 47, Sept. 1959: 397-402.

Prerequisites for the occurrence of life, especially in an advanced form, are discussed in the light of current knowledge of the stars and their evolution.

Huang, Su-Shu. The problem of life in the universe and the mode of star formation. In Cameron, A.G.W., ed. Interstellar communication. New York, W. A. Benjamin, Inc., 1963. p. 89-92.

General conclusions concerning the occurence of life in the universe are presented. It is predicted that out of 42 known stars, (including the sun) within 5 parsecs from us, only three stars have a good chance of supporting advanced living beings on their planets, if such planets exist. Three arguments are presented for believing that the formation of planets around stars is a common phenomenon.

-----. Some astronomical aspects of life in the universe. Sky and telescope, v. 21, June 1961: 312-316.

Stellar life histories are briefly discussed as well as prerequisites for a life-supporting planet. It is suggested that most single stars of the main sequence between F5 and K5 could probably support life of an advanced form on the planets revolving around them. Temperature and atmosphere of Mars and Venus are discussed in detail and speculations made as to existence of life there.

Jackson, Francis L. and Patrick Moore. Life in the universe. New York, W. W. Norton, 1962. 140 p.

Applies current knowledge in astronomy, biology, botany, and chemistry to consideration of theories about extraterrestrial life. Concludes that in observable universe there must be millions of planets supporting carbon-based life similar in principle to terrestrial forms but greatly varied in detail.

Jones, Harold Spencer. Life on other worlds. London, English Universities Press, 1940. 259 p.

Summarizes evidence on probability of life on other worlds provided by astronomy: conditions necessary for birth of a planetary system may occur so rarely that among the vast number of stars in any one stellar universe we may expect to find only a very limited number that have a family of planets; and among these families of planets, there cannot be more than a small proportion where conditions are suitable for life to exist. Life elsewhere in the universe is therefore the exception and not the rule.

Kavanau, J. L. Some physico-chemical aspects of life and evolution in relation to the living state. American naturalist, v. 81, May 1947: 161-183.

Kind, S. S. Speculations on extraterrestrial life. Spaceflight, v. 1, July 1958: 288-289.

Author defines life in terrestrial terms and considers the possible existence of life, as we know it, on Mars and Venus.

Leonard, Frederick C. Life on other worlds. Popular astronomy, v. 41, May 1933: 260-263.

Life on other planets -- what are the possibilities? Flying saucers, Oct. 1966: 8-11.

Summary of current scientific data on the possibility of intelligent life on other planets in our solar system. Reprinted from the BUFORA (England) Journal and Bulletin.

Lighthall, W. D. The law of cosmic evolutionary adaptation: an interpretation of recent thought. Transactions of the Royal Society of Canada, ser. 3, v. 34, sec. 2, 1940: 135-141.

Like nothing on earth. Lamp, v. 44, Summer 1962: 16-21.

In 1961, scientists at Esso Research and Engineering Co. and at Fordham and New York universities, working in collaboration, found within a tiny fragment of the Orgueil meteorite chemical indications of the existence of life. They also found fragments which they believe are fossilized remnants of living things in fragments of this and three other carbonaceous meteorites that had fallen at different times and places. This is postulated as strong evidence that elsewhere in our solar system life exists or has existed.

Limits of organic life in our solar system. American review of reviews, v. 43, Feb. 1911: 242-243.

Lönnqvist, C. Människan på Världsteatern. Stockholm, Ljus, AB, 1947. 218 p.

Discussion of the possibility of intelligent life on other worlds.

McColley, Grant, and H. W. Miller Saint Bonaventure, Francis Mayron, William Vorilong and the doctrine of a plurality of worlds. Speculum, v. 12, July 1937: 386-389.

Menzel, Donald. The universe in action. Birmingham, Ala., The Rushton Lecture Foundation, 1962. 71 p.

Discussion of the universe as it was, is now, and will be in the far distant future through evolution. The belief is expressed that life, even human or superhuman, may exist in millions of places in the universe.

Moffat, Samuel and Elie A. Shneour. Life beyond the earth. Epilogue by Joshua Lederberg. New York, Scholastic Book Services, 1965. 156 p.

Non-technical discussion of role of exobiology in search for life in the universe and in first contact with extraterrestrial civilization.

Moore, Patrick. The worlds around us. New York, Abelard-Schuman, 1956. 157 p.

Outlines conditions under which carbon-based life can survive and applies them to sun, moon, planets, satellites, and asteroids in the solar system. Hypothesizing that this is the only kind of life possible in the universe, author concludes that men on earth are alone in the solar system. Asserts that reports about visits to earth by extraterrestrial spacecraft are only "good stories."

The mystery of other worlds revealed. Greenwich, Conn. , Fawcett Publications, 1952. 144 p.

Chapter headings include: life on other worlds; communication with other worlds; the expanding universe; possibilities for an invasion base on the moon; a case for flying saucers; investigation of the Carolina saucer; are the flying saucers Russian-owned?

Oparin, Aleksandr I. Life in the universe. New York, Twayne Publishers, Inc., 1961. 245 p.

On basis of most recent information in natural science, author discusses probability of universal existence of life-bearing planets, with special attention to Mars and Venus. Translation of Zhizn' vo vselennoĭ (Moscow, 1956).

Ordway, Frederick I. , III, James P. Gardner, and Mitchell R. Sharpe, Jr. Astrobiology. In Basic aeronautics. Englewood Cliffs, N. J., Prentice-Hall 1962. p. 244-305.

Discusses effects of space environment on terrestrial organisms, reviewing typical laboratory studies and then describing some of the more important "in-space" biological research. Means of remotely searching for life on other worlds are then considered, followed by a resumé of experience to date on the search for evidence of extraterrestrial life on earth.

Pendergast, R. Terrestrial and cosmic polygenism. Downside review, v. 82, July 1964: 189-198.

Posin, Daniel Q. Life beyond our planet. New York, McGraw-Hill, 1962. 128 p.

Non-technical discussion of planets of our solar system, consideration of whether life of any kind exists on them, and discussion of ways of communicating with these or planets of other solar systems.

-----. Other suns, other planets, but is there other life? Today's health, v. 42, Nov. 1964: 56-69.

Proctor, Richard A. Life in other worlds. Knowledge, v. 11, 1887-88: 230.

Quimby, Freeman H. Concepts for detection of extraterrestrial life. Washington, National Aeronautics and Space Administration, 1964. 53 p. (NASA SP-56)

Methods which have been considered for the detection of extraterrestrial life and life-related substances in the near reaches of space are presented.

Revelle, R. Sailing in new and old oceans. A.I.B.S. Bulletin, v. 12, Oct. 1962: 45-47.

If modern theories about the formation of stars are correct, probably the great majority of stars have planets around them. On at least some of these, life may have evolved in a beneficent realm of light and liquid water and in an atmosphere of oxygen and nitrogen to a level as high and perhaps much higher, than the highest life known on earth. Communication with intelligent beings in planets of other stars would be almost impossible because of the distance involved.

Ross, John C. A scientist looks at life on other worlds. Fate, v. 12, Apr. 1959: 86-89.

Nobel prize winner Dr. Melvin Calvin asserts that life is inevitable on other worlds throughout the universe and that we may expect to find life forms more intellectually developed than man.

Rublowsky, John. Is anybody out there? New York, Walker and Co., 1962. 118 p.

Surveys recent findings in biology, physics, and astronomy and focuses them on question of whether life exists in the universe.

Rush, Joseph H. Life the universe. In The dawn of life. Garden City, N.Y., Hanover House, 1957. p. 188-217.

Appraisal of the possibility of life on the solar planets and beyond the solar system.

Sagan, Carl. On the origin and planetary distribution of life. Radiation research, v. 15, Aug. 1961: 174-192.

Author discusses current opinion and speculation concerning the origin and early history of life on earth, with particular emphasis on the role that radiation may have played, and with application to the problem of extra-terrestrial life.

-----. The quest for life beyond the earth. In Smithsonian Institution. Annual report of the board of regents for the year ending June 30, 1964. Washington, D. C., U.S. Govt. Print. Off., 1965. p. 297-306.

Questions on the possibility of extraterrestrial life and the origin of life are discussed and alternative interpretations of available data given.

Shapley, Harlow. Extraterrestrial life. Astronautics, v. 5, Apr. 1960: 32-33, 50, 52.

It is postulated that homo sapiens as a species may be unique, but there is good reason to expect that there are habitable planets with higher forms of life in other solar systems.

Sharp, Peter F. The search for life beyond the earth. Flying saucer review, v. 7, Nov.-Dec. 1961: 12-15.

Arguments are advanced on the possibility of life existing throughout the galaxy; ways in which man can attempt to detect it positively are suggested. It is also mentioned that the Tunguska "meteorite" of 1908 may have been an exploded extraterrestrial spacecraft.

Shneour, Elie A. and Eric A. Ottesen, comp. Extraterrestrial life: an anthology and bibliography. Washington, National Academy of Sciences-- National Research Council, 1966. 478 p.

Supplement to "Biology and the Exploration of Mars," report of study under auspices of Space Science Board and published as NAS-NRC Publication 1296. Contains selected papers, including Mariner IV and sounding rocket observations of Mars made in 1965, and bibliography of 2,000 selected references to world literature published through mid-1964 with addendum of papers published from that date through late 1965.

Simpson, George G. The nonprevalence of humanoids. Science, v. 143, Feb. 21, 1964: 769-775.

States following conclusions: (1) there are certainly no humanoids elsewhere in the solar system of which earth is part; (2) there is probably no extra- terrestrial life in the solar system of which earth is part, but the possibility is not wholly excluded as regards Mars; (3) there probably are forms of life on other planetary systems somewhere in the universe, but if so it is unlikely that we can learn anything whatever about them, even as to the bare fact of their real existence; (4) it is extremely improbable that such forms of life include humanoids, and apparently nearly as impossible that we could ever communicate with them in a meaningful and useful way if they did exist.

Sytinskaia, N. N. Est' li zhizn' na drugikh planetakh [Is there life on other planets?] Moscow, Gosudarstvennoe izdatel 'stvo kul 'turnoprosvetitel' noi literatury, 1952. 64 p.

A lecture dealing primarily with life on Mars and other planets. The author concludes that it is quite probable that vegetation exists on other planets, citing the Russian astronomer, G. A. Tikhov, who has indicated that the color of polar caps on Mars is greenish, not white, possible evidence of vege- tation, and that the melting ice and snow produces the water necessary to sus- tain life.

Tsung, Thomas. Is there life beyond the earth? New York, Exposition Press, 1963. 71 p.

The type of mind that believes in life on other worlds. Current opinion, v. 71, Nov. 1921: 630-631.

Veit, Karl. Planeten-menschen. Wiesbaden-Schierstein, Ventla-Verlag, 1961. 223 p.

Author surveys scientific opinion on the possibility of life on other worlds and summarizes UFO sighting reports from 1947 to date. Details are given of "contactee" reports and the alleged appearance and behavior of beings from outer space.

Williams, Henry S. Are the planets inhabited? Hearst's magazine, v. 24, Aug. 1913: 284-286.

Young, Richard S. Exobiology. In NASA-University Conference on the Science and Technology of Space Exploration. Proceedings. v. 1. Chicago, 1962. p. 423-429.

Reports on NASA exobiology program, including laboratory studies on organic compound synthesis under primitive earth conditions, analysis of meteorites, and life detection apparatus.

-----. Extraterrestrial biology. New York, Holt, Rinehart and Winston, 1966. 119 p.

Text is a discussion of life as it is found on earth and of the properties of life which suggest it might exist in more than one place in the universe.

Younghusband, Francis. The living universe. London, John Murray, 1933. 252 p.

Author postulates that the universe is a living universe and that the primordial germ of life appeared as the result of the interaction of the earth with life in the universe as a whole. He suggests that there may be the same myriad forms of life on different planets as there are on earth. All life is "derived from the same original source, and informed by the same Spirit."

COMMUNICATION

Ascher, Robert and Marcia Ascher. Interstellar communication and human evolution. Nature, v. 193, Mar. 10, 1962: 940-941.

The authors postulate that the potential of a search for signals from other civilizations is largely dependent on the adequacy of guesses about the probability of the existence of extraterrestrial technical civilizations, the probable stage of development of a civilization which we might contact, the longevity of attempts at contact following success or failure, and the result of possible contact and exchange. Article indicates steps in increasing the reasonableness of the guesses.

Barton, Michael X. Secrets of higher contact. Los Angeles, Futura Press, 1959. 30 p.

Technique by which human beings may "reach up into the high consciousness of the Interplanetary Beings and contact them" is revealed. Information transmitted telepathically to author by "Space Brothers."

Barton, Michael X. The spacemasters speak. Los Angeles, Futura Press, 1960. 34 p.

Messages from beings on Mars, Venus, and Antares allegedly transmitted telepathically to author for delivery during the Harmony Grove (Escondido, Calif.) Spacecraft Convention, July 2-4, 1960.

Beller, William. How to contact people in space. Missiles and rockets, v. 7, July 25, 1960: 42-44.

Author observes that scientists who believe there is intelligent life on other planets are divided on the question of how to go about getting in touch. He presents the plans of the different factions for receiving or initiating communication.

Bergier, Jacques. A l'ecoute des planètes. Paris, Fayard, 1963. 182 p.

Postulating that there are intelligent beings throughout the universe, the author speculates on the kind of technological development necessary to enable us to detect their presence within our atmosphere and in their own communities and to establish communication with them.

Boehm, George A. E. Are we being hailed from interstellar space? Fortune, v. 63, Mar. 1961: 144-149.

Survey of current theories of formation of earth and planets and the evolution of life is presented. Radio-telescope listening programs are discussed and the information that might be transmitted hypothesized.

Bracewell, R. N. Communications from superior galactic communities. Nature, v. 186, May 28, 1960: 670-671.

Author suggests that space probes from extra-galactic civilizations may already be within earth's atmosphere. He points out that this type of attempt at communication may be more feasible than radio signals sent over interstellar distances since it eliminates the need for ingenuity in selecting a star and correct wavelength and can give a more powerful signal than a home-based transmitter.

-----. Life in the galaxy. In Cameron, A.G.W., ed. Interstellar communication. New York, W. A. Benjamin, Inc., 1963. p. 232-242.

Author establishes concept that the other stars and star systems have planets and that some of these planets are inhabitable. He postulates that life thereon is less advanced than that of earth. Radar communication in the "galactic club" is a fact, but not from intelligent source, however, we should be alert for signals. It is speculated that sufficiently highly developed stellar communities are common but that contacting them, or its reverse, would be a matter of chance.

Bracewell, Ronald N. Radio signals from other planets. In Cameron, A. G. W., ed. Interstellar communication. New York, W. A. Benjamin, Inc., 1963. p. 199-200.

The most suitable microwave frequency to be searched for intelligent signals from other planets is considered. There are, however, reasons for not using 1,420 Mc or other microwave frequencies, if the distance to the nearest community more advanced than our own is 100 light-years rather than the 10 light-years investigated by Project Ozma.

Bradbury, Ray. A serious search for weird worlds. Life, v. 49, Oct. 24, 1960: 116-118, 120, 123-124, 126-128, 130.

Sketches are shown on strange creatures who may represent what creatures on other inhabited planets look like. Explanation is made that although grotesque by earth standards, they could develop this way in response to different environments of other worlds. Project Ozma, the radio-telescope search for life on other worlds, is discussed.

Briggs, Michael H. Other astronomers in the universe? Southern stars, v. 18, Sept. 1960: 147-151.

Author considers problems raised by the hypothesis that some cosmic radio signals are intelligently produced.

----- Superior galactic communities. Spaceflight, v. 3, May 1961: 109-110.

Author suggests that if there are intelligent extraterrestrials on planets in this galaxy, they may be scientifically and technologically advanced enough to know of both earth and of man as an intelligent life form. Attempt by them to establish contact might be by radio transmissions, space probes, and emission of radiation in the far infrared.

Cade, C. Maxwell. Communicating with life in space. Discovery, v. 24, May 1963: 36-41.

Methods of communication with intelligent extraterrestrial life and the implications of contact are considered. Establishment of contact with a superior race could lead to extermination of the human race. It is probable that intelligent life would tend toward the center of the galaxy because of the higher probability of contacting life there.

----- A long, cool look at alien intelligences: Part II -- modes of communication. Flying saucer review, v. 13, July-Aug. 1967: 15-17.

Discussion of three principal ways in which alien intelligences could communicate with us: (1) direct visitation; (2) remote communications; (3) ambassadorial liaison.

Cade, C. Maxwell. A long, cool look at alien intelligence. Part IV -- Possible significance of parapsychology. Flying saucer review, v. 13, Nov.-Dec. 1967: 13-15.

Discussion of ways in which prosopesis (alternating personalities) and ideoplasty (an idea manifesting as a bodily change in the same person) are related to the subject of flying saucers. It is suggested that many of the strange mental disturbances which we put down to madness, genius, hysterical dissociation, or drunkedness, are the early stirrings of ideoplastic concepts induced by cosmic telepathy.

----- A long, cool look at alien intelligence: Part V -- It's all in the mind. Flying saucer review, v. 14, Mar.-Apr. 1968: 7-9.

Author suggests the possibility that UFOs and poltergeists are among phenomena which could be "experienced, " with completely convincing realism, due to effects of electromagnetic fields. He also suggests that this electromagnetic radiation could be either terrestrial or extraterrestrial in origin; it could be either a stochastic natural process or the planned product of an alien intelligence.

Calvin, Melvin. Chemical evolution. In Cameron, A. G. W., ed. Interstellar communication. New York, W. A. Benjamin, 1963. p. 33-77.

From questions on the nature and characteristics of life, the author proceeds through theories on chemical evolution with the establishment of an environment conducive to the origin of self-replicating macromolecules. Speculation on life on other planets, life elsewhere in the solar system, and life in the galactic systems is followed by a discussion of man's place in the universe. Of the two hundred million inhabitable planets in the visible universe two areas selected for attemt at interstellar communication (Project Ozma) are Tau Ceti and Epsilon Eridani. Reasons for selection are given.

----- Talking to life on other worlds. Excerpt from address, with deciphering of a coded message. Science digest, v. 53, Jan. 1963: 14-19.

Cameron, A. G. W. Future research on interstellar communication. In his Interstellar communication. New York, W. A. Benjamin, Inc., 1963. p. 309-315.

Fields of research that can contribute in a more direct way to guesses about the nature of extraterrestrial societies are discussed. Nearest communicative civilization should be expected to be about 87 parsecs away (284 light-years). For civilizations on planets near the very faint stars which have been proposed as likely to exist, the laser may be the obvious way of communication, since the signal-to-noise ratio of their optical transmissions should be orders of magnitude better than that calculated for the sun by Schwartz and Townes.

Cameron, A. G. W., ed. Interstellar communication. New York, W. A. Benjamin, Inc., 1963. 320 p.

Publication contains monographs and reprints on specialized aspects of interstellar communication with critical commentary.

----- Stellar life zones. In Cameron, A. G. W., ed. Interstellar communication.
New York, W. A. Benjamin, Inc. 1963. p. 107-110.

Conclusion is reached that all single stars in space (except those with very low
heavy-element contents) have a life zone containing an average of about 1.4
planets of undetermined size.

Cocconi, Guiseppe and Philip Morrison. Searching for interstellar communications.
Nature, v. 184, Sept. 19, 1959: 844-846.

Speculates on optimum channel that might be used by an intelligent extraterrestrial civilization to contact earth. Concludes that the most promising radio
emission line to search for would be at 1420 Mc/s (λ= 21cm) of neutral hydrogen.

Creighton, Gordon W. What the Soviets are saying. Flying saucer review, v. 10,
Sept.-Oct. 1964: 26.

Summary of articles in Soviet press 1960-1964 about probable existence of extraterrestrial civilizations and possible means of communicating with them.

Crenshaw, James. What can we expect of "civilization" in outer space? Fate,
v. 20, Jan. 1967: 79-89.

Thought-provoking views on what may happen when and if earth's scientists put
us in contact with an outer-space civilization superior, inferior, or equivalent
to ours.

Da Silva, Renato I. No espaco nao estamos sós. São Paulo, Edart, 1966. 213 p.

Theories relating to possibility of life on the moon and other planets are summarized. Parapsychological phenomena of mental telepathy, precognition,
ESP, premonition, and astral projection are discussed as they might relate to
contact with extraterrestrial entities or intelligences.

Drake, Frank D. Intelligent life in space. New York, Macmillan, 1962. 128 p.

Summary of facts that seem to indicate existence of many civilizations in space
and discussion of ways in which men on earth might contact such civilizations.

----- Project Ozma. In Cameron, A. G. W. Interstellar communication. New
York, W. A. Benjamin, Inc., 1963. p. 176-177.

First systematic, high sensitivity search for manifestations of extraterrestrial
intelligent life are described. Tau Ceti and Epsilon Eridani were chosen as
subjects because they are the nearest single sunlike stars observable from telescope site. Preliminary observations uncovered no signals of extraterrestrial origin, but radar frequencies still appear to offer the greatest hope for
success in the search.

Drake, Frank D. Project Ozma. Physics today, v. 14, Apr. 1961: 40-46.

Theory of the origin of life is given and possibilities of contact with intelligent extraterrestrial life discussed. Author hypothesizes that frequencies near 1420.405 Mc/sec may be used by an extraterrestrial civilization attempting to signal earth.

----- Radio emission from the planets. Physics today, v. 14, Apr. 1961: 30-34.

Predictions based on optical infrared studies of Venus, Mars, Jupiter, and Saturn are compared with radio emission data. Biological significance of infrared surface conditions--based on radio emission data--is assessed.

----- The radio search for intelligent extraterrestrial life. In Mamikunian, Gregg and M. H. Briggs. Current aspects of exobiology. Pasadena, Calif., Jet Propulsion Laboratory, 1965. p. 323-345.

It is concluded that microwave radio signals are the most common means of interstellar communication; that terrestrial technology is capable of carrying on a successful search for signals but that the project, if it is to cope with all the reasonable possibilities, must be one of very great expense, complexity, and duration. It is also suggested that there are many other possible ways in which manifestation of intelligent life might be found, but at present few, if any, appear to offer enough hope of success to justify their active pursuit.

Dreyer, H. R. The man who knows the languages of the stars. Fate, v. 12, Aug. 1959: 78-79.

An inmate in a psychiatric institute in Prague, Czechoslovakia, believes he is in continual contact with other planets and records their speech in fine detail.

Dye, Clarkson. Radio to other worlds. Fate, v. 8, Mar. 1955: 88-96.

Account of the experiments of David Henry Wilson (London, England, circa 1915) with a specially-constructed wireless set and of messages he received from entities that were not inhabitants of earth.

Dyson, F. J. Search for artificial stellar sources of infrared radiation. Science, v. 131, June 3, 1960: 1667.

If extraterrestrial intelligent beings exist and have reached a high level of technical development, one by-product of their energy metabolism is likely to be the large-scale conversions of star-light into infrared radiation. It is proposed that a search for sources of infrared radiation should accompany the search for interstellar communications.

Flammarion, Camille. Inter-astral communication. American review of reviews, v. 5, Feb. 1892: 90.

Fuller, Curtis. Porpoise research: exploring an alien intelligence. Fate, v. 16, Nov. 1963: 52-60.

273

Scientists have been investigating the porpoise as the representative of an alien intelligence, seeking to communicate with it, seeking to understand what alien intelligence can be like. The porpoise's deeply convoluted brain is larger than man's.

Golay, M. J. E. Coherence in interstellar signals. IRE Proceedings, v. 49, 1961: 958-959.

It is stated it would appear there are four likely spectral regions within which a search should be made for coherent signals before any intelligent messages can be received: at half or at twice the hydrogen frequency, and with or without correction for nebular drift. When factors such as easier power generation and greater space coverage are considered, the two half-frequency regions appear more favorable.

----- Note on the probable character of intelligent radio signals from other planetary systems. In Proceedings of the IRE, v. 49, May 1961: 959.

Discussed are the spectral location and the character of radio signals that might be aimed at the earth from other planets of other solar systems.

Golomb, Solomon W. Extraterrestrial linguistics. Astronautics, v. 6, May 1961: 46-47, 96.

Author discusses what space travelers from earth might say--if they can find a way to say it--to alien intelligent beings they might discover in the universe.

Handelsman, M. Considerations on communication with intelligent life in outer space. In Wescon convention record. Proceedings. v. 6, pt. 5; 1962. Los Angeles, Wescon, 1962. 15 p. (Paper no. 4.4.)

Estimate of the probability of communication with intelligence in outer space is beset with many unknown factors, the author postulates. Sifting through these, the probability that a communicating civilization has existed at some time is assigned a value of between 2×10^{-2} and 10^{-6} for any star. To receive a signal from at least one civilization within 1,000 light years, it is estimated that examination of some 2×10^5 likely stars in a field of about 10^7 stars is required, a longevity of 50,000 years, and no previous intercommunication. The recommended signal to search for is a high-intensity, narrow-band transmission at or near the 21 cm. hydrogen frequency.

Hicks, Clifford B. We're listening for other worlds. Popular mechanics, v. 114, Sept. 1960: 81-85.

Huang, Su-Shu. Problems of transmission in interstellar communication. In Cameron, A. G. W., ed. Interstellar communication. New York, W. A. Benjamin, Inc., 1963. p. 201-206.

It is stated that beings who are transmitting signals to other worlds, in order to increase their chances of contacting civilizations in other worlds, must divide the antenna time and beam the signals successively to all stars which are within reach and which are believed to be able to support life of an advanced form. Since our present technology is perhaps inferior to that of others who can communicate with us, it is suggested that our transmitting station be used solely, at least for the next hundred years or so, for responding to intelligent messages from outer space that have been detected.

Jackson, C. D. and R. E. Hohmann. An historic report on life in space. New York, American Rocket Society, 1962. 7 p. (ARS Paper no. 2730-62)

Investigations and experimental data of Nikola Tesla, Guglielmo Marconi, and David Todd are presented. During the years 1899-1924 these experimental scientists, working independently of each other, observed laboratory data and related phenomena which suggested they were monitoring interplanetary communications. During the same period, the Russian theorist Konstantin Tsiolkovsky deduced a model of an intelligence existing independently of terrestrial influence. Data are first brought together in an historical model (1899-1924) and then are shown to be the natural complement of a current theoretical model (1959-1962).

Krasovskiy, Iu. Astronautics and extraterrestrial civilizations. Flying saucer review, v. 7, Sept.-Oct. 1961: 3-5.

Author discusses earth's objectives in the conquest of extraterrestrial space; possibility of life in other worlds; possibility of communicating with extraterrestrial civilizations; and the possibility of receiving intelligent signals from other worlds.

Lamb, Peter. Pictures from outer space. Spacelink, v. 4, Summer 1967: 13-17.

Details are given of what may have been the first recorded reception of picture transmission between planets.

McClain, Edward F. The 600-foot radio telescope. Scientific American, v. 202, Jan. 1960: 45-51.

The world's largest steerable telescope, under construction near Sugar Grove, W. Va., provides power to gather radio waves and resolve celestial radio sources.

Miles, Max B. Scientists track space radio signals. Fate, v. 12, June 1959: 57-58.

Mysterious radio signals whose absence of Doppler effect indicated travel away from the earth were monitored on frequencies of 20 and 40 megacycles for three hours in late November, 1958, from an Air Force Missile Test Center installation at Cape Canaveral.

Miller, E. Conrad and J. L. Smith. Some considerations regarding the possibility of contact with intelligent extraterrestrial beings. BUFORA journal and bulletin, v. 1, Winter 1964: 4-7.

Article states it is possible that contact will be made in the relatively near future with extraterrestrial intelligences and that this contact may occur as a ship to ship meeting in interplanetary space. Earth's crews should be briefed to take no possible action that could be deemed hostile and to take defensive measures only in the last resort for self-preservation. An effort should be made to determine whether it is possible to develop messages suitable for initial contact with an alien intelligence.

Mysterious broadcast from space ship? Flying saucers, Feb. 1959: 35-37, 46.

A mysterious broadcast was allegedly received on Aug. 3, 1958, on 75 meter international band in which the voice of a man said he was "Necoma" from the planet Jupiter and was broadcasting from a space ship 50,000 miles from earth. Incident was reported in a southeast U. S. newspaper.

The mystery of other worlds revealed. Greenwich, Conn., Fawcett Publications, 1952. 144 p.

Chapter headings include: life on other worlds; communication with other worlds; the expanding universe; possibilities for an invasion base on the moon; a case for flying saucers; investigation of the Carolina saucer; are the flying saucers Russian-owned?

Oakley, C. O. Math, our link with space people. Science digest, v. 49, June 1961: 7-13.

Oberth, Hermann. Katechismus der Uranidem. Wiesbaden-Schierstein, Ventla-Verlag, 1966. 160 p.

Communication with an extraterrestrial being through a psychic medium has caused Oberth to adopt this view: there is a soul which outlives the body; this world serves as a training-ground for the soul; the soul will continue life (on a planet where conditions are in keeping with its degree of development) after death.

Pascalis, Bernardino. Werkelijkheid of fantasie? Panorama, Feb. 21-27, 1967: 31-38.

Feature article on UFO reports in which there was alleged communication with the occupants or crew of the objects.

Pearman, J. P. T. Extraterrestrial intelligent life and interstellar communication: an informal discussion. In Cameron, A. G. W., ed. Interstellar communication. New York, W. A. Benjamin, Inc., 1963. p. 287-293.

From consideration of the prospects for existence of other societies in our galaxy and the problems involved in establishing communication with them, it is concluded that, if the more optimistic values of communicative lifetime are chosen, the number of civilizations becomes 10^5 to 10^9 and the distance of the nearest civilization is estimated at ten to a few hundred light-years.

Pelley, William D. Earth comes...design for materialization. Indianapolis, Fellowship Press, 1941. 303 p.

Author postulates that "presiding spirits" were obstructed in their work of projecting a perfect earth by "mischievous spirits"; this accounts for the apparent dissimilarity in peoples, inadvertent cataclysms, interrupted or capricious harvests, and intermittent phenomena tending to displace terrain and change polar rotations. "Great Ministering Overlords" were appointed to minister the world and are doing so at this moment.

----- Star guests...design for mortality. Nobleville, Ind., Soulcraft Press, 1950. 318 p.

Description of experiments in clairaudient writing and psychical contact with beings "of the more harmonious planes...above the planes of earth."

Pi in the sky. Newsweek, v. 67, Apr. 4, 1966: 22, 27.

Details of UFO sightings in the area around Ann Arbor, Mich., during late March 1966. One night a University of Michigan scientist blinked the "pi" equation in code, explaining that this could be understood by extraterrestrial creatures.

Pierce, J. R. and C. C. Cutler. Interplanetary communications. In Advances in space science. v. 1. Edited by Frederick I. Ordway, III. New York and London, Academic Press, 1959. p. 55-109.

Suggests that a simple space probe, radiating a watt of RF power, could transmit about 3 bits/sec per watt of information when Mars comes within 50×10^6 miles of earth. This minimal probe would be capable of transmitting 65,000 bits/sec from the moon, which is enough for high quality speech.

Posin, Daniel Q. Life beyond our planet. New York, MacGraw-Hill, 1962. 128 p.

Non-technical discussion of planets of our solar system, consideration of whether life or any kind exists on them, and discussion of ways of communicating with these or planets of other solar systems.

Price, George R. U.S. begins search for beings in other worlds. Popular science, v. 176, Apr. 1960: 66-69, 209.

Detailed description is given of Project Ozma--U.S. attempt to establish radio contact with extraterrestrial civilizations. Scientific justification for the project is reviewed.

Purcell, E. Radioastronomy and communication through space. In Cameron, A. G. W., ed., Interstellar communication. New York, W. A. Benjamin, Inc., 1963. 121-143.

Contributions to knowledge of distant galaxies by radioastronomy are reviewed and followed by a discussion of modes of travel beyond the solar system. After postulating there are other habitable non-solar planets, author discusses transmission of coded messages and the analysis of messages received, and suggests that a sequence of prime numbers be both sent and listened for over the period of centuries, not fiscal years.

Reeve, Bryant. The advent of the cosmic viewpoint. Amherst, Wis., Amherst Press, 1967. 256 p.

Postulating that earth's traditional cosmic isolationism is ending, the author discusses the implications of changes that are portended. He speculates on the effect that the landing of extraterrestrial spacecraft will have on man's concept of reality, his civilization, institutions, way of life, and manner of thinking and acting.

Revelle, R. Sailing in new and old oceans. A. I. B. S. Bulletin, v. 12, Oct. 1962: 45-47.

If modern theories about the formation of stars are correct, probably the great majority of stars have planets around them. On at least some of these, life may have evolved in a beneficent realm of light and liquid water and in an atmosphere of oxygen and nitrogen to a level as high and perhaps much higher, than the highest life known on earth. Communication with intelligent beings of planets of other stars would be almost impossible because of the distance involved.

Richards, Sam. Some philosophical implications of UFOs. Spacelink, v. 4, Summer 1957: 4-11.

It is pointed out that once we can comprehend and admit that there could be an intelligence superior to our own, it requires very little further thought to appreciate the difficulty of communication. Of the various types of apparently extraterrestrial beings visiting earth, it could be significant that they appear not only incapable of contact with us but there is no evidence of their contacting each other.

Rodgers, Philip. Spacemen speaking. Flying saucer review, v. 4, Sept.-Oct. 1958: 20-21.

Author gives details of sounds and voices that he has recorded on tape and believes to be extraterrestrial.

Rosenberg, Paul. Communication with extraterrestrial intelligence. Aerospace engineering, v. 21, Aug. 1962: 68-69, 111.

Author states that prevailing cosmological theory and laboratory experiments support the hypothesis that life exists outside earth's solar system. Electromagnetic signaling seems to be the only means now at our disposal for attempting to communicate with any extraterrestrial intelligence that may exist. Methods for communicating and receiving such signals, and speculation as to the type of message an extraterrestrial might transmit are reviewed.

Rowe, Kelvin. A call at dawn. El Monte, Calif., Understanding Publishing Co., 1958. 198 p.

Author expounds ideas and principles allegedly transmitted to him telepathically by beings from the planets Pluto and Jupiter and describes his trip into outer space in a flying saucer.

Sanford, Ray. Contact with a flying saucer. Fate, v. 9, May 1956: 12-18.

An experiment on Nov. 6, 1954, to contact a flying saucer through mental concentration allegedly succeeds.

Saunders, Alex. Alien life contemplation. Flying saucers, Oct. 1966: 21-22.

Speculates on the possibility of sentient life on other planets and on the implications for man of contact with such beings.

Schwartz, R. N. and C. H. Townes. Interstellar and interplanetary communication by optical masers. Nature, v. 190, Apr. 15, 1961: 205-208.

Possibility is examined of broadcasting an optical beam from a planet associated with a star some few or some tens of light-years away at sufficient power levels to establish communications with earth.

Shklovskii, Iosef S. and Carl Sagan. Intelligent life in the universe. Authorized translation by Paula Fern. San Francisco, Holden-Day, 1966. 509 p.

Extension and revision by Sagan of Shklovskii's Vselennaia, zhizn', razum [Universe, Life, Mind] (Moscow, 1963). Includes study of earth's solar system, discussion of nature of life and its possible occurrence on other planets, treatment of possibility that advanced communicative technical civilizations exist on planets of other stars, and discussion of problems in establishing contact with civilizations separated from earth by interstellar distances.

Smith, Bernard. People from outer space contact earth man by radio. Flying saucer review, v. 4, July-Aug. 1958: 28-29.

Report that voices and sounds from either extraterrestrial spacecraft or beings have been recorded on tape by blind musician.

That prospective communication with another planet. Current opinion, v. 66, Mar. 1919: 170-171.

Three undiscovered planets. Los Angeles, DeVorss & Co., 1967. 15 p.

Telepathic communication from planets supposedly on the etheric plane is transmitted by their alleged rulers. Peace and love are postulated to be earth's most urgent needs.

Von Hoerner, Sebastian. The general limits of space travel. Science, v. 137, July 6, 1962: 18-23.

It is postulated that space travel, even in the most distant future, will be confined to our own planetary system; a similar conclusion is said to apply to any other civilization, no matter how advanced it may be. The only means of communication between different civilizations thus seems to be electromagnetic signals.

----- The search for signals from other civilizations. Science, v. 134, Dec. 8, 1961: 1839-1843.

The search for extraterrestrial signals from an intelligent source should be guided by two estimates, one of the probable nature of such signals and the other of the distance from which they might come. Three different types of signals are considered: local broadcast, long-distance calls, and contacting signals. The nature of the signals will be defined entirely by the purpose they serve and by the most economical way to achieve this purpose. Several sets of conclusions are drawn as to the type of civilizations sending signals, the longevity of a technical civilization, and the nature of signals transmitted.

Wickland, Carl A. Thirty years among the dead. Los Angeles, National Psychological Institute, 1924. 390 p.

Report on psychical research demonstrating intermingling and intercommunication between the spiritual (invisible) and physical (visible) worlds.

Whittington, George. What's true about the disc? The journal of spaceflight and the rocket news letter, Apr. 1950: 2-5.

Author speculates on whether U. S. armed forces have succeeded in contacting UFO crew members and whether representatives of U. S. armed forces and/or the State Department are now in communication with extraterrestrial beings.

Williamson, George Hunt and Alfred C. Bailey. The saucers speak. Los Angeles, New Age Pub. Co., 1954. 127 p.

Documentary report of communication by radiotelegraphy between August 1962 and mid-1953 with extraterrestrial spacecraft in earth's atmosphere.

IMPLICATIONS

Barton, Michel X. Flying saucer revelations. Los Angeles, Futura Press, 1957. 38 p.

Discusses role of interplanetary beings in man's origin and evolution. Considers stories of contact between extraterrestrials and earth men and implications. Reports on flying saucer sighting at Giant Rock Airport, Yucca Valley, Calif., on Mar. 12, 1955, during Interplanetary Spacecraft Convention.

Brookings Institution. Proposes studies on the implications of peaceful space activities. Washington, D. C., U. S. Govt. Print. Off., 1961. 272 p. (87th Cong., 1st Sess. House. Report no. 242)

"The implications of a discovery of extraterrestrial life, " p. 215-216, warns that the discovery of intelligent life in the universe could have profound consequences for earth attitudes and values. It is pointed out that many societies have disintegrated when they had to associate with previously unfamiliar societies espousing different ideas and different ways of life; others that survived such an experience usually did so by paying the price of changes in values and attitudes, and behavior. Continuing studies are recommended to determine emotional and intellectual understanding, and attitudes -- and successive alterations of them if any -- regarding the possibility and consequences of discovering intelligent extraterrestrial life. The report was prepared for the National Aeronautics and Space Administration.

Cade, C. Maxwell. Other worlds than ours. London, Museum Press, 1966. 248 p.

Consideration of possibility and implications of other worlds in space and other worlds in time.

Carrouges, Michel. Les apparitions de martiens. Paris, Fayard, 1963. 275 p.

Study of UFO sightings reported during September-October 1954 as a sociological phenomenon.

Cleary-Baker, John. The significance of the UFO era. BUFORA journal and bulletin, v. 1, Autumn 1966: 9-10.

Discussion of the implications of alien visitation in human affairs.

Crenshaw, James. What can we expect of "civilization" in outer sapce? Fate, v. 20, Jan. 1967: 79-89.

Thought-provoking views on what may happen when and if earth's scientists put us in contact with an outer-space civilization superior, inferior, or equivalent to ours.

Danger from the stars: a warning from the Space Administration. Flying saucer review, v. 7, Man-June 1961: 7.

Article summarizes report prepared by Brookings Institution, Washington, D.C., in 1961 for the National Aeronautics and Space Administration on ramifications of discovery of intelligent life on other planets.

Drake, W. R. Man on the threshold of space. Flying saucer review, v. 6, Nov.-Dec. 1960: 22-24.

The author considers the prospects that await man as he prepares to travel to other planets.

Fuller, B. A. G. Flying saucers. The journal of philosophy, v. 49, Aug. 14, 1952: 545-559.

Postulating that intelligent life exists in forms quite different from ours and is dispersed throughout the universe, the author speculates on proceedings of a "cosmic Congress" including all kinds of "Saucerians". Delegates of every imaginable aspect--"not to speak of others defying terrestrial biological classification"--would compare their religious, moral, social, economic, and political ways of life. He expresses hope that once the myth of a superior race was exploded, constants would appear in the various ways of life and points of view and all planetary thinking would become interplanetary in scope and scale.

Miller, E. Conrad and J. L. Smith. Some considerations regarding the possibility of contact with intelligent extraterrestrial beings. BUFORA journal and bulletin, v. 1, Winter 1964: 4-7.

Article states it is possible that contact will be made in the relatively near future with extraterrestrial intelligences and that this contact may occur as a ship to ship meeting in interplanetary space. Earth's crews should be briefed to take no possible action that could be deemed hostile and to take defensive measures only in the last resort for self-preservation. An effort should be made to determine whether it is possible to develop messages suitable for initial contact with an alien intelligence.

Reeve, Bryant. The advent of the cosmic viewpoint. Amherst, Wis., Amherst Press, 1967. 256 p.

Postulating that earth's traditional cosmic isolationism is ending, the author discusses the implications of changes that are portended. He speculates on the effect that the landing of extraterrestrial spacecraft will have on man's concept of reality, his civilization, institutions, way of life, and manner of thinking and acting.

Richards, Sam. Some philosophical implications of UFOs. Spacelink, v. 4, Summer 1967: 4-11.

It is pointed out that once we can comprehend and admit that there could be an intelligence superior to our own, it requires very little further thought to appreciate the difficulty of communication. Of the various types of apparently extraterrestrial beings visiting earth, it could be significant that they appear not only incapable of contact with us but there is no evidence of their contacting each other.

INTELLIGENCE

Aharon, Y. N. ibn. The recent literature of extraterrestrialism. Saucer news, v. 12, Mar. 1965: 11-12.

Evaluates works on extraterrestrialism by Desmond Leslie and Dr. M. K. Jessup.

Ascher, Robert and Marcia Ascher. Interstellar communication and human evolution. Nature, v. 193, Mar. 10, 1962: 940-941.

The authors postulate that the potential of a search for signals from other civilizations is largely dependent on the adequacy of guesses about the probability of the existence of extraterrestrial technical civilizations, the probable stage of development of a civilization which we might contact, the longevity of attempts at contact following success or failure, and the result of possible contact and exchange. Article indicates steps in increasing the reasonableness of the guesses.

Asimov, Isaac. Is anyone there? Garden City, N. Y., Doubleday & Co., 1967. 320 p.

Collection of articles on science, speculation and science fiction that have appeared in popular magazines. The probability of intelligent life on worlds other than ours is the general theme.

Berrill, Norman John. Worlds without end: a reflection on planets, life, and time. New York, Macmillan, 1964. 240 p.

Speculative investigation of possibilities of life on other planets: nearest and best-known planets are compared with earth; hypothetical planets similar to earth but with one or another feature altered in some manner are examined in order to predict how familiar living things might be affected; life on earth is evaluated to determine which characteristics may be regarded as universal under certain circumstances and which are special; and imaginative efforts of speculative writers to conceive and describe creatures different from those known to us on earth are presented.

Bieri, Robert. Humanoids on other planets? American scientist, v. 52, Dec. 1964: 542-458.

Arguments are presented to support the view that if life has evolved on other planets in other solar systems and if some population has reached the level of conceptual thought, it is highly probable that the organisms so endowed will bear a strong resemblance to homo sapiens.

Bradbury, Ray. A serious search for weird worlds. Life, v. 49, Oct. 24, 1960: 116-118, 120, 123-124, 126-128, 130.

Sketches are shown of strange creatures who may represent what creatures on other inhabited planets look like. Explanation is made that although grotesque by earth standards, they could develop this way in response to different environments of other worlds. Project Ozma, the radio-telescope search for life on other worlds, is discussed.

Breig, Joseph A. Are there rational beings on planets far away? Ave Maria, v. 89, Mar. 7, 1959: 19.

Brewster, David. More worlds than one. New York, Robert Carter & Bros., 1854. 265 p.

Author defends doctrine of plurality of inhabited worlds by citing current astronomical discoveries and by analyzing and refuting objections.

Briggs, Michael H. Other astronomers in the universe? Southern stars, v. 18, Sept. 1960: 147-151.

Author considers problems raised by the hypothesis that some cosmic radio signals are intelligently produced.

----- Superior galactic communities. Spaceflight, v. 3, May 1961: 109-110.

Author suggests that if there are intelligent extraterrestrials on planets in this galaxy, they may be scientifically and technologically advanced enough to know of both earth and of man as an intelligent life form. Attempt by them to establish contact might be by radio transmissions, space probes, and emission of radiation in the far infrared.

----- Terrestrial and extraterrestrial life. Spaceflight, v. 2, Oct. 1959: 120-121.

Hypothesis for origin of life on earth is given based on three assumptions: (1) intelligent life existed somewhere in the universe prior to the beginning of life on earth; (2) interplanetary flight is possible by these intelligences; and (3) lifeless earth was visited by extraterrestrials who either deliberately and accidentally left microbes behind when they departed. Variations of and objections to hypothesis are given.

Cade, C. Maxwell. Are we alone in space? Discovery, v. 24, Apr. 20, 1963: 27-29.

----- A long, cool look at alien intelligences: Part I -- the non-uniqueness of man. Flying saucer review, v. 13, Mar.-Apr. 1967: 24-25.

Author states that while there is a high probability for the existence of intelligences in other parts of the universe, it does not follow that they must bear any resemblance to ourselves. If man is non-unique, it is because he is one of many intelligent races, not because he is one of many humanoid, or even biological species.

----- A long, cool look at alien intelligences: Part II -- the forms of intelligent organisms. Flying saucer review, v. 13, May-June 1967: 13-15, 19.

Three classes of possible intelligent organism are considered in detail: (1) humanoid or non-humanoid biological organisms; (2) mechanical intelligences such as self-programming computers; and (3) stable intelligent plasmoids.

----- Other worlds than ours. London, Museum Press, 1966. 248 p.

Consideration of possibility and implications of other worlds in space and other worlds in time.

284

Can astronomy ever say positively that other planets are inhabited? Current literature, v. 52, Jan. 1912: 64-66.

Chamberlin, Ralph V. Life on other worlds. Bulletin of the University of Utah,
v. 22, Feb. 1932: 1-52.

A study in the history of opinion on life in other worlds from 600 B. C. to 1931
A. D.

Civilization on other planets? U. S. S. R. , v. 1, Jan. 1964: 46-47.

In a series of four articles, V. Fesenkov, I. Shklovskii, A. Pasinskii, and
B. Liapunov discuss current theories and Soviet research in the field of
exobiology.

Clarke, Arthur C. The planets are not enough. The Saturday review, v. 38, Nov.
26, 1955: 11-12, 34-36.

Postulating that the evidence seems to indicate earthmen are the only thinking
inhabitants of the solar system, the author speculates on how man could survive a journey which may last for several thousand years to the planets of other
suns.

Cooper, John. Cities in the sky. Science digest, v. 28, Nov. 1950: 78-80.

Copland, Alexander. The existence of other worlds, peopled with living and intelligent beings, deduced from the nature of the universe. London, J. G. & F.
Rivington, 1834. 210 p.

Presents reasons for believing the fixed stars and the planets are habitations
for living beings. Cites writings of men who have believed in a plurality of inhabited worlds and states grounds for their beliefs in their own words.

Coupe, Charles. Are the planets inhabited? American Catholic quarterly, v. 124,
Oct. 1906: 699-720.

Creighton, Gordon W. What do the Russians know? Flying saucer review, v. 8,
Jan. -Feb. 1962: 20-21.

Translations from Krasnaya Zvezda, Ekonomich Gazeta, and Komsomolskaya
Pravda expressing Soviet views about possible life beyond the earth.

----- What the Soviet press is saying. Flying saucer review, v. 7, Nov. -Dec.
1961: 18-19.

Translation of article from Krasnaya Zvezda by Vladimir Lvov stating that intelligent and even human life exists in outer space.

Creighton, Gordon W. What the Soviets are saying. Flying saucer review, v. 10, Sept.-Oct. 1964: 26.

Summary of articles in Soviet press 1960-1964 about probable existence of extraterrestrial civilizations and possible means of communicating with them.

Crenshaw, James. What can we expect of "civilization" in outer space? Fate, v. 20, Jan. 1967: 79-89.

Thought-provoking views on what may happen when and if earth's scientists put us in contact with an outer-space civilization superior, inferior, or equivalent to ours.

Cyr, Guy J. Are there humanoids in space? Flying saucers, Aug. 1967: 12-14.

Author hypothesizes that the moon's so-called "crust" is actually the filamentous, closely knitted, microphyllous foliage of various flourishing florae held up to the sun for energy and meteoritic fertilizer. This "crust" also serves as a global, protective roof for the super-intelligent sentient beings who live under it and who are among the various kinds of extraterrestrials exploring our world.

Da Silva, Renato I. No espaço não estamos sós. São Paulo, Edart, 1966. 213 p.

Theories relating to possibility of life on the moon and other planets are summarized. Parapsychological phenomena of mental telepathy, precognition, ESP, premonition, and astral projection are discussed as they might relate to contact with extraterrestrial entities or intelligences.

Do other humans live? Newsweek, v. 52, Nov. 17, 1958: 56.

Dole, Stephen H. Habitable planets for man. New York, Blaisdell Publishing Co., 1962. 158 p.

Outlines necessary requirements for planets on which human beings as biological species (Homo sapiens) can live, and essential properties required of stars that would provide heat and light to such planets. Suggests that probability of finding indigenous intelligent life on other habitable planets is remote.

Dole, Stephen and Isaac Asimov. Planets for man. New York, Random House, 1964. 242 p.

A less technical presentation of ideas detailed in Habitable Planets for Man by Dole. Predicts possible consequences of eventual interstellar trips by man.

Drake, Frank D. Intelligent life in space. New York, Macmillan, 1962. 128 p.

Summary of facts that seem to indicate existence of many civilizations in space and discussion of ways in which men on earth might contact such civilizations.

Drake, W. R. Man on the threshold of space. Flying saucer review, v. 6, Nov. - Dec. 1960: 22-24.

The author considers the prospects that await man as he prepares to travel to other planets.

----- Mercury, Jupiter, and others: can life exist? Flying saucer review, v. 6, Sept. -Oct. 1960: 18-22.

Survey of .fact and speculation on possiblilty of life on Mercury, Jupiter and lesser known bodies in earth's solar system.

Edwards, Frank. Arthur C. Clarke looks at the universe. Fate, v. 12, May 1959: 68-75.

Astronomer and science fiction writer Arthur C. Clarke expresses his belief that intelligent beings unquestionably exist in other parts of the universe and might visit our solar system.

Ehrensvard, Gösta C. Man on another world. Chicago and London, University of Chicago Press, 1965. 182 p.

Some common factors of life as a universal phenomenon are suggested, especially the expansive expression of life that involves a certain degree of awareness. Translation of Expansion: liv i universum (Stockhom, Aldus/Bonniers, 1961).

Eiseley, Loren C. Is man alone in space? Scientific American, v. 189, July 1953: 80-82, 84, 86.

The author, an anthropologist, considers whether--in the light of what we know about evolution--another genus Homo may have arisen on a planet similar to the earth.

Ewing, Ann. Life in all solar systems? Science newsletter, v. 86, Sept. 26, 1964: 199.

Fears, Francis R. Silicon and extraterrestrial life forms. Journal of space flight, v. 2, Nov. 1950: 5-6.

A life form based on silicon metabolism which would remotely resemble the life on our planet cannot exist under such environmental conditions as are found on earth. It might exist in an entirely alien set of circumstances which are at present beyond our conception.

Ferber, Adolph C. The secret of human life on other worlds. New York, Pageant Press, 1957. 105 p.

Spiritual origin and nature of life are explained, not only on our world but also on the other worlds in our solar system. Writings of Emanuel Swedenborg, who claimed to have visited the moon and planets of our solar system by astral projection, are freely quoted.

Firsoff, Valdemar A. An ammonia-based life. Discovery, v. 23, Jan. 1963: 36-42.

Development of inorganic polymers which bear a resemblance to organic compounds but have, wholly or partly, a different chemical basis has led to speculations on various alternative life schemes. When liquid ammonia replaces water as a universal solvent, ammonolysis of the analogue compounds in an ammono-organic chemistry can replace hydrolysis in the process of digestion. The same reactions of chemical degradation which yield energy by oxidation in our system would be performed in that of ammonia through the agency of nitrogen. Instead of water and carbon dioxide as final products, ammonia and cyanogen C_2N_2 which is the ammonia analogue of CO_2, would be produced. Equivalent organic compounds in a nitrogen-based life system are given.

----- Life beyond the earth. New York, Basic Books, Inc., 1963. 320 p.

Origin of life on earth and elsewhere is discussed, its subsequent evolution and present condition, and such forms of it as deviate most from human standards and thereby promise insight into alien structures that may exist on other worlds. Range of environments are examined within which life as we know it is possible as well as organic chemistries that would be viable in environments where terrestrial life could not exist.

----- Life, mind and galaxies. Edinburgh and London, Oliver & Boyd, 1967. 111 p.

Evidence is presented to show that life is not a freak occurrence in the universe of stars and nebulae, but an integral part of its general pattern, and will arise naturally from the inorganic substratum wherever and whenever conditions become suitable for it, and, that these may be suitable for life of a different chemical order even though unfit for our type of carbohydrate biology. It is postulated that no definite boundary can be fixed between the organic and the inorganic world, which shade into each other by imperceptible degrees. Nor can the emergence of mind be pinpointed in biological evolution. There is unity in nature -- one encompassing reality.

Flammarion, Camille. Stories of infinity: Lumen--history of a comet--in infinity. Boston, Roberts Brothers, 1873. 287 p.

Discourse on the possibility of living forms throughout the universe that are unknown on earth. The universe is postulated as an infinity and earthly life as but a phase of infinity. Translated from the French by S. R. Crocker.

Friedman, Bruno. Millions of inhabited planets. Flying saucer review, v. 10, May-June 1964: 7-10.

The following questions are considered: (1) What makes scientists so sure today that there is intelligent life in space? (2) Where do we locate such living beings? (3) Are they more intelligent, just as, or less intelligent than we are? (4) How can we communicate with them, considering that they are likely to be completely different from us, have a completely different kind of language, and even completely different patterns of thought?

Fuhs, Allen E. Visual sensitivity of residents of other planets. ARS Journal, v. 30, June 1960: 577.

Visual sensitivity of hypothesized intelligent beings outside our solar system is discussed.

Fuller, B. A. G. Flying saucers. The journal of philosophy, v. 49, Aug. 14, 1952: 545-559.

Postulating that intelligent life exists in forms quite different from ours and is dispersed throughout the universe, the author speculates on proceedings of a "cosmic Congress" including all kinds of "Saucerians." Delegates of every imaginable aspect--"not to speak of others defying terrestrial biological classification"--would compare their religious, moral, social, economic, and political ways of life. He expresses hope that once the myth of a superior race was exploded, constants would appear in the various ways of life and points of view and all planetary thinking would become interplanetary in scope and scale.

Gatland, Kenneth W. and Derek D. Dempster. The inhabited universe. London, Alan Wingate, 1957. 182 p.

The theme throughout the book is that evolution is constantly bringing new forms of life into existence and that creation is a continuous process. Man is depicted as the product, not merely of a limited biological development, but of an inherent facet of cosmic evolution.

Gauroy, Pierre. Les mondes du ciel: terres vivantes on cimetières? Paris, Librarie Arthème Fayard, 1960. 303 p.

Inquiry into whether intelligent life could exist on other planets in our solar system based on current scientific data.

Greenstein, Jesse L. Speculation on man and the universe. Pasadena, Calif., The Author, 1967. 11 p.

Speculating that organic evolution throughout the universe would lead to life first in the water and then on land, the author suggests the common later development of mind everywhere, because of the inevitable growth of organic complexity. We have to be ready to accept the emotional impact on our scheme of values of accepting an odd extraterrestrial form of life as brother or sister. The green, three-eyed creatures of some distant world may have lived civilized lives for billions of years longer than there has been life on earth. If all are part of the common, natural evolution which concentrates into mind, we must expect them to be probably like ourselves, yet unimaginably different.

Harford, J. Rational beings in other worlds. Jubilee, May 1962: 17-21.

Heintze, Carl. Search among the stars. Princeton, Van Nostrand, 1966. 175 p.

Non-technical speculative discussion of whether there is intelligent life in the universe.

Heuer, Kenneth. Men of other planets. London, Victor Gallancz, Ltd., 1951. 160 p.

Text combines science and fancy in speculation about plurality of inhabited worlds. Author hypothesizes that there are worlds without end of every conceivable description in the universe; they are inhabited by intelligent beings whose forms, organs, and number of senses are infinitely diverse as result of physical conditions peculiar to their particular worlds.

Holmes, David C. The search for life on other worlds. New York, Sterling Publishing Co., 1966. 240 p.

Non-technical discussion of man's place in the cosmos and possibility of intelligent life throughout the universe.

Howells, W. Would other humans look like us? In Mankind in the making, New York, Doubleday & Co., 1959. p. 53-58.

Speculations are made on the probable form of extraterrestrial intelligent life. This life would be similar to man in many respects: a supporting structure, a liquid nutrient system, a nervous system, a large brain. Two sexes seem likely; beings would be land dwelling. Symmetry and coordination dictate probability of two arms each with multiple fingers, but there may be four legs instead of two. If man were eradicated, it is likely that intelligent life would have to evolve all over again since present animals have passed the point of differentiation.

Hoyle, Fred. Man in the universe. New York and London, Columbia University Press, 1966. 81 p.

In astronomy, the author says, we are faced by contradictions. Not all the apparent data of the moment can be correct; we do not know which fragments are right and which are wrong. Because we cannot experiment with the universe, we live in a kind of shifting uncertainty, shifting because as the years pass the balance of certainty of a given piece of data changes.

Huang, Su-shu. Occurrence of life in the universe. American scientist, v. 47, Sept. 1959: 397-402.

Prerequisites for the occurrence of life, especially in an advanced form, are discussed in the light of current knowledge of the stars and their evolution.

Huang, Su-Shu and R. H. Wilson, Jr. Astronomical aspects of the emergence of intelligence. New York, Institute of the Aerospace Sciences, 1963. 15 p. (IAS Paper no. 63-48)

The astronomical background which makes possible the emergence and development of intelligence in the universe is discussed. Stellar populations are related to the occurrence of life, and criteria are given for the life-supporting ability of a star. Environmental conditions necessary for life on planets are presented.

Jackson, Francis L. and Patrick Moore. Life in the universe. New York, W. W. Norton, 1962. 140 p.

Applies current knowledge in astronomy, biology, botany, and chemistry to consideration of theories about extraterrestrial life. Concludes that in observable universe there must be millions of planets supporting carbon-based life similar in principle to terrestrial forms but greatly varied in detail.

King, George. Life on the planets. Hollywood, Calif., The Aetherius Society, 1958. 29 p.

Series of lectures dealing with life in general on the planets Mars, Venus, Jupiter, and Saturn. There is also a lecture dealing with the system of government--Interplanetary Parliament--adopted by residents of these planets. Information allegedly transmitted telepathically to author.

Last, Cecil E. Man in the universe. London, Werner Laurie, 1954. 166 p.

The universe is conceived as a non-mechanical reality. In association with such a universe, the idea is elaborated that mind is the supreme factor in the economy of the universe and that matter is derived from consciousness and not consciousness from matter, in accordance with the suggestions of Jean, de Broglie, and Planck, supported by Einstein and Schrodinger.

Leiber, Fritz. Homes for men in the stars. Science digest, v. 58, Sept. 1965: 53-57.

Lewellen, John. You and space neighbors. Chicago, Children's Press, 1953. 58 p.

Discussion for juveniles of probable conditions on planets in our solar system and whether these conditions would support intelligent life of the species homo sapiens.

Ley, Willy. The mighty invaders from outer space. Catholic digest, v. 22, Apr. 1958: 25-29.

"Portrait" of the man from planet X: (1) he breathes air; (2) he eats both plants and meat; (3) he is probably not much larger than the largest human being; (4) he weighs at least 40 pounds and probably more; (5) he has a skull of some kind; (6) he has two eyes and ears; (7) his eyes and ears are near the brain; and (8) he has hands and feet. Condensed from This Week, Nov. 10, 1957.

Life on other planets -- what are the possibilities? Flying saucers, Oct. 1966: 8-11.

Summary of current scientific data on the possibility of intelligent life on other planets in our solar system. Reprinted from the BUFORA (England) Journal and Bulletin.

Lönnqvist, C. Människan på Världsteatern. Stockholm, Ljus, AB, 1947. 218 p.

Discussion of the possibility of intelligent life on other worlds.

McColley, Grant and H. W. Miller. Saint Bonaventure, Francis Mayron, William Vorilong and the doctrine of a plurality of worlds. Speculum, v. 12, July 1937: 386-389.

MacGowan, Roger A. and Frederick I. Ordway, III. Intelligence in the universe. Englewood Cliffs, N. J., Prentice-Hall, 1966. 402 p.

Subject of extra-solar intelligence is analyzed by survey of the existing literature, original interpretations of established facts, and conjectures based on theory and observation.

McHugh, L. C. Others out yonder. America, v. 104, Nov. 26, 1960: 295-297.

Macvey, John W. Alone in the universe? New York, Macmillan, 1963. 273 p.

Author considers speculatively and at length the types of beings that may exist in space in extra-solar systems. Suggests that appearance of mankind on earth may have been result of colonization by another planet or star-system, and that appearance of UFOs could harbinger second coming of a race from outer space.

Margaria, Rodolfo. On the possible existence of intelligent living beings on other planets. In XIIth International Astronautical Congress, Washington, D.C., 1961. Proceedings. Edited by Robert M. L. Baker, Jr., and Maude W. Makemson. Vienna, Springer-Verlag, New York and London, Academic Press, 1963. p. 556-563.

On a statistical basis, the author rules out the possibility that superior forms of life have developed on other planets that would lead finally to living beings that have the same type of intelligence as man and with whom man might communicate.

Maunder, E. Walter. Are the planets inhabited? London and New York, Harper & Bros., 1913. 165 p.

Discussion of the controversy on the plurality of inhabited worlds.

Mugler, C. Deux thèmes de la cosmologie grecque: devenir cyclique pluralité des mondes. Paris, Librarie C. Klincksieck, 1953. 192 p.

Survey of Greek literature for indications of a belief in the extraterrestrial origin of man and the existence of intelligent life throughout the universe.

Munitz, Milton K. Theories of the universe from Babylonian myth to modern science. Glencoe, Ill., The Free Press, 1957. 437 p.

Survey of current trends in scientific cosmology against the background of earlier efforts and achievements. Beginning with one of the earliest ventures in the form of myth, materials are included exhibiting the principal stages of progress in cosmological inquiry from antiquity up to the present time.

The mystery of other worlds revealed. Greenwich, Conn., Fawcett Publications, 1952. 144 p.

Chapter headings include: life on other worlds; communication with other worlds; the expanding universe; possibilities of an invasion base on the moon; a case for flying saucers; investigation of the Carolina saucer; are the flying saucers Russian-owned?

Ordway, Frederick I., III. Life in other solar systems. New York, E. P. Dutton, Inc., 1965. 96 p.

Reviews growing indirect and direct evidence of life-supporting extra-solar planetary systems with intelligent communities and speculates on the nature of extra-solar beings.

Pearman, J. P. T. Extraterrestrial intelligent life and interstellar communication: an informal discussion. In Cameron, A. G. W., ed. Interstellar communication. New York, W. A. Benjamin, Inc., 1963. p 287-293.

From consideration of the prospects for existence of other societies in our galaxy and the problems involved in establishing communication with them, it is concluded that, if the more optimistic values of communicative lifetime are chosen, the number of civilizations becomes 10^5 to 10^9 and the distance of the nearest civilization is estimated at ten to a few hundred light-years.

Perego, Angelo. Rational life beyond the earth? Theology digest, v. 7, Fall 1959: 177-178.

Posin, Daniel Q. Life beyond our planet. New York, MacGraw-Hill, 1962. 128 p.

Non-technical discussion of planets of solar system, consideration of whether life of any kind exists on them, and discussion of ways of communicating with these or planets of other solar systems.

Quarnström, Gunnar. Dikten och den nya vetenskapen. Lund, Sweden, C. W. K. Gleerup, 1961. 300 p.

Menzel, Donald H. Life in the universe. [n.p., 1965] 219 p.

The chances of finding intelligent life within our own solar system are discussed and it is concluded that they appear "vanishingly small." It is suggested that the Milky Way might contain up to a million planets inhabited by intelligent life; however, the chances are that the nearest such inhabited planet is so far away that if we were to send out a radio signal, we should have to wait 2,000 years for the reply. Reprinted from The graduate journal, v. 7, Winter 1965: 195-219.

----- The universe in action. Birmingham, Ala., The Rushton Lectures Founda— tion, 1962. 71 p. (The Rushton lectures, 1957)

Discussion of the universe as it was, is now, and will be in the far distant future through evolution. The belief is expressed that life, even human or super-human, may exist in millions of places in the universe.

Moore, Patrick. The worlds around us. New York, Abelard-Schuman, 1956. 157 p.

Outlines conditions under which carbon-based life can survive and applies them to sun, moon, planets, satellites, and asteroids in the solar system. Hypothesizing that this is the only kind of life possible in the universe, author concludes that men on earth are alone in the solar system. Asserts that reports about visits to earth by extraterrestrial spacecraft are only good stories.

Moreux, Théophile. Les autres mondes, sont-ils habités? Paris, Éditions Scientifica, 1912. 134 p.

Analyzes current information and theories bearing on existence of human life forms on other planets of the solar system. New edition published in Paris (G. Doin) 1950.

Motz, Lloyd. Extra-terrestrial intelligence and stellar evolution. New York, Institute of the Aerospace Sciences, 1963. 16 p. (IAS Paper no. 63-49)

Author postulates that in view of modern theories on the origin of the solar system, it is reasonable to conclude that all stars like the sun that are not binary systems are the centers of planetary systems like our own. Analysis of the role that density distribution in the original solar nebula and the solar tidal action and turbulence played in the formation of the planets leads to the conclusion that in each of the stellar planetary systems there are planets like the earth, Mars, and Venus that are capable of supporting intelligent life.

Müller, Wolfgang D. Man among the stars. New York, Criterion Books, 1957. 307 p.

Mental tour of the solar system and speculation about the living beings that may reside in other worlds. Translation of Du wirst die Erde sehn als Stern (Stuttgart, Deutsche Verlags-Anstalt, 1955).

Question of inhabited planets and the plurality of worlds is reviewed in connection with the astronomical revolution. The idea and the wishful dream connected throughout the centuries with the conception of other celestial bodies are examined: the idea of a flying man, "homo volans," and the dream of reaching other planets, especially the moon.

Raible, D. C. Men from other planets? Catholic digest, v. 25, Dec. 1960: 104-108.

Revelle, R. Sailing in new and old oceans. A. I. B. S. Bulletin, v. 12, Oct. 1962: 45-47.

If modern theories about the formation of stars are correct, probably the great majority of stars have planets around them. On at least some of these, life may have evolved in a beneficent realm of light and liquid water and in an atmosphere of oxygen and nitrogen to a level as high and perhaps much higher, than the highest life known on earth. Communication with intelligent beings of planets of other stars would be almost impossible because of the distance involved.

Rich, Valentin and Mikhail Chernenko. Tracks that lead to space. Flying saucer review, v. 6, May-June 1960: 3-6.

Translation of article in Literaturnaya Gazeta of Moscow in which Soviet scientist M. A. Agrest advances hypothesis that intelligent life exists in outer space and earth has been visited by space travelers for aeons.

Robinson, Jack and Mary Robinson. The case for extraterrestrial little men. Saucer news, v. 13, Fall 1966: 7-9.

Presents scientifically feasible biological hypothesis for existence of humanoid extraterrestrial beings.

Robinson, Louis. Are there men in other worlds? Current literature, v. 44, June 1908: 672-677.

Rocha, Hugo. Outros mundos outras humanidades. Porto, Editora Educacão Nacional, 1958. 371 p.

First part of book presents arguments from the literature and from scientific, philosophical, and religious writings supporting and opposing the theory of a plurality of inhabited worlds. Second part gives reports of individuals claiming contact with extraterrestrials, including Adamski, Bethurum, Fry, Allingham, Jorge and Napy Duclout, Kraspedon, and Ramatis and de Freitas Guimarães.

Rosenberg, Paul. Communication with extraterrestrial intelligence. Aerospace engineering, v. 21, Aug. 1962: 68-69, 111.

Author states that prevailing cosmological theory and laboratory experiments support the hypothesis that life exists outside earth's solar system. Electromagnetic signaling seems to be the only means now at our disposal for attempting to communicate with any extraterrestrial intelligence that may exist. Methods for communicating and receiving such signals, and speculation as to the type of message an extraterrestrial might transmit are reviewed.

Ross, John C. A scientist looks at life on other worlds. Fate, v. 12, Apr. 1959: 86-89.

Nobel prize winner Dr. Melvin Calvin asserts that life is inevitable on other worlds throughout the universe and that we may expect to find life forms more intellectually developed than man.

Sagan, Carl. Direct contact among galactic civilizations by relativistic interstellar spaceflight. Planetary and space science, v. 11, May 1963: 485-498.

Author postulates that there exists in the galaxy a loosely integrated community of diverse civilizations, cooperating in the exploration and sampling of astronomical objects and their inhabitants. There is therefore the likelihood that earth was visited at least once during historical times by an advanced civilization.

----- The quest for life beyond the earth. In Smithsonian Institution. Annual report of the board of regents for the year ending June 30, 1964. Washington, D. C., U.S. Govt. Print. Off., 1965. p. 297-306.

Questions on the possibility of extraterrestrial life and the origin of life are discussed and alternative interpretations of available data given.

Saunders, Alex. Alien life contemplation. Flying saucers, Oct. 1966: 21-22.

Speculates on the possibility of sentient life on other planets and on the implications for man of contact with such beings.

Schatzman, Evry. La vie existe-t-elle sur les autres planetes? [Paris, Université de Paris, Palais de la Découverte, 1963] 15 p.

Argument favoring hypothesis of intelligent life on planets throughout the galaxy.

Schiaparelli, G. V. Mars den gådefulde planet. Randers [Oversat af E. Slej] Denmark, UFO-NYTs Forlag, 1965. 73 p.

Surface features of Mars, especially its "canals," are discussed as possible indications of intelligent life on that planet. Translation of article entitled "Ueber die beobachteten Erscheinungen auf der Oberfläche des Planeten Mars," in Himmel und Erde, v. 1, 1888: 85-102, 147-159.

Serviss, Garrett P. Curiosities of the sky. New York, Harper & Bros., 1909. 268 p.

A broad general view of the chief mysteries and problems of astronomy is given; possibility of life and intelligence on the moon and on Mars is discussed.

Sewall, Frank. Life on other planets as described by Swedenborg. Philadelphia, Swedenborg Scientific Association, 1911. 20 p.

Discussion of Swedenborg's description of planets in the solar system and their inhabitants which he claimed to have visited by astral projection.

Shapley, Harlow. Extraterrestrial life. Astronautics, v. 5, Apr. 1960: 32-33, 50, 52.

It is postulated that homo sapiens as a species may be unique, but there is good reason to expect that there are habitable planets with higher forms of life in other solar systems.

----- Riddle of God, man and outer space. Coronet, v. 49, Feb. 1961: 40-44.

Shklovskii, Iosef S. and Carl Sagan. Intelligent life in the universe. Authorized translation by Paula Fern. San Francisco, Holden-Day, 1966. 509 p.

Extension and revision by Sagan of Shklovskii's Vselennaîa, zhizn', razum [Universe, Life, Mind] (Moscow, 1963). Includes study of earth's solar system, discussion of nature of life and its possible occurrence on other planets, treatment of possibility that advanced communicative technical civilizations exist on planets of other stars, and discussion of problems in establishing contact with civilizations separated from earth by interstellar distances.

Simpson, George G. The nonprevalence of humanoids. Science, v. 143, Feb. 21, 1964: 769-775.

States following conclusions: (1) there are certainly no humanoids elsewhere in the solar system of which earth is part; (2) there is probably no extraterrestrial life in the solar system of which earth is part, but the possibility is not wholly excluded as regards Mars; (3) there probably are forms of life on other planetary systems somewhere in the universe, but if so it is unlikely that we can learn anything whatever about them, even as to the bare fact of their real existence; (4) it is extremely improbable that such forms of life include humanoids, and apparently as near impossible that we could ever communicate with them in a meaningful and useful way if they did exist.

Slater, Alan E. The probability of intelligent life evolving on a planet. In VIIIth International Astronautical Congress, Barcelona, 1957. Proceedings. Vienna, Springer-Verlag, 1958. p. 395-402.

Report traces briefly the evolution of the human species from primitive life forms and shows that the differentiation that eventually led to man was far from inevitable. Concludes that it seems improbable that other forms of intelligent life will be found by voyagers through space.

Sloan, Eugene A. Artificial biosphere. Science, v. 132, July 22, 1960: 252.

Author supports suggestion of investigating solar far-infrared radiations as one way to detect extraterrestrial intelligence and hypothesizes that intelligent beings most probably have detected us.

Smith, S. L. The problems of exobiology. Part I: the origin of life. BUFORA journal and bulletin, v. 1, Winter 1965: 13-16.

Examination of the possibility of life existing beyond earth at a level of development compatible with the possession of interplanetary spaceships.

----- The problems of exobiology. Part II: life in the solar system. BUFORA journal and bulletin, v. 1, Spring 1966: 13-18.

Article discusses whether the processes that led to the evolution of man could have occurred beyond the solar system.

----- The problems of exobiology. Part III: life beyond the solar system. BUFORA journal and bulletin, v. 1, Summer 1966: 10-14.

Considers whether a process similar to that which led to the evolution of man could have occurred beyond the solar system; and if not, are there any other possible chemical processes that could lead to an alien form of life.

Sullivan, Walter. We are not alone. New York, McGraw-Hill, 1964. 325 p.

Traces evolution of man's concept of the cosmos and his place in it and discusses possibility and implications of universality of intelligent life. Rev. ed. 1966.

Suspect human life on millions of planets. Science newsletter, v. 74, Nov. 22, 1958: 328.

Warder, George Woodward. The cities of the sun. New York, G. W. Dillingham, 1901. 320 p.

Argues that the suns of the universe are not hot or burning globes but are self-luminous perfected worlds--the personal residence of Deity and the future abode of man. Housed in the "heavenly mansions and beautiful cities" of the sun are the former citizens of the solar planets, including earth's departed spirits.

White, George S. A book of revelations: a true narrative of life on many planets. Los Angeles, The Author, 1945. 198 p.

History of the earth and planets from creation to the present time (1945) as recorded in the "Master Book of Life" and revealed by "cosmic teachers."

Williams, Henry S. Are the planets inhabited? Hearst's magazine, v. 24, Aug. 1913: 284-286.

Younghusband, Francis. Life in the stars. London, John Murray, 1927. 222 p.

An exposition of the view that on some planets of some stars exist beings that are higher on the evolutionary scale than man and that on one of them exists "the supreme embodiment of the eternal spirit which animates the whole."

PHILOSOPHY

Adamski, George. Cosmic philosophy. [San Diego, Calif.] The Author, 1961. 87 p.

Author expounds doctrine of man's unity with all life taught by extraterrestrial beings with whom he has allegedly been in contact.

----- Flying saucers farewell. London, New York, Abelard-Schuman, 1961. 190 p.

Adamski discusses the reasons spacecraft from other planets are visiting earth and man's place in the universe as reportedly revealed to him through contact with beings from Venus, Mars, and Saturn. Published also with title Behind the Flying Saucer Mystery by Paperback Library (53-439), New York.

Barton, Michael X. Release your cosmic power. Los Angeles, Futura Press, 1961. 33 p.

A "way of life" based on the "cosmic secret of balance" is described. Information allegedly transmitted to author telepathically by extraterrestrial beings.

----- Secrets of higher contact. Los Angeles, Futura Press, 1959. 30 p.

Technique by which human beings may "reach up into the high consciousness of the Interplanetary Beings and contact them" is revealed. Information transmitted telepathically to author by "space brothers."

----- The spacemasters speak. Los Angeles, Futura Press, 1960. 34 p.

Messages from beings on Mars, Venus, and Antares allegedly transmitted telepathically to author for delivery during the Harmony Grove (Escondido, Calif.) Spacecraft Convention, July 2-4, 1960.

----- Venusian health magic. Los Angeles, Futura Press, 1959. 59 p.

The "space brothers"--the Venusians--reveal how to use Lifetrons to rid the human body of its ills and assure radiant health and vitality.

Barton, Michael X. Venusian secret-science. Los Angeles, Futura Press, 1958. 76 p.

Seven-lesson course to reveal secret-science allegedly formulated on Venus 33 million years ago and designed to speed earth-man's evolution by stimulating "the total mind as well as the soul." Information transmitted to author telepathically.

----- World secret of Fatima. Los Angeles, Futura Press, 1962. 35 p.

Fatima message teaches that there exists in the universe one law in three parts: (1) be a life spirit; (2) do love all of life, and (3) have wisdom, knowingness and the truth. Law is fulfilled only by demonstrating affinity for all life.

----- Your part in the great plan. Los Angeles, Futura Press, 1960. 30 p.

Discusses what man's purpose is and how he may fulfill it. Suggests that we are now living at the end of an age and predicts that earth will undergo big geological changes.

Bethurum, Truman. The voice of the planet Clarion. Prescott, Ariz., The Author, [195-] 88 p.

Collection of poetry and prose written by Bethurum while he was allegedly under the telepathic control of Aura Rhanes, the female captain of a spacecraft from the planet Clarion.

The book of spaceships and their relationship with earth, by the god of a planet near the earth and others. Clarksburg, W. Va., Saucerian Publications, 1966. 70 p.

Alleged communications from rulers of Mars, Pluto, Neptune, Uranus, Saturn, Jupiter, Venus, Mercury, and three undiscovered planets describing their inhabitants, civilization, and philosophy. Messages reportedly received on earth through "psychic channeling."

Danger from the stars: a warning from the Space Administration. Flying saucer review, v. 7, May-June 1961: 7.

Article summarizes report prepared by Brookings Institution, Washington, D.C., in 1961 for the National Aeronautics and Space Administration on ramifications of discovery of intelligent life on other planets.

Dewey, Mark. A man from space speaks. Houston, Texas, The Author, 1966. 38 p.

A philosophy of life allegedly dictated to author by Amano, a teacher on the planet Mars, during direct contact over a five-year period. Postulates that Martians are the ancestors of terrestrials.

Ferguson, William. A message from outer space. Oak Park, Ill., Golden Age Press, 1955. 54 p.

300

A translation decoding the Book of Revelations allegedly given to author telepathically by "Khauga, the angel who gave it to St. John." Flying saucers are said to be the spacecraft of "perfected beings" who are "progressed to a four dimensional state of reality" and who are "preparing earth for the second coming of Jesus."

From Jupiter, planet of joy. Los Angeles, DeVorss & Co., 1967. 15 p.

Message from the alleged ruler of the planet Jupiter who gives the history of the planet, describes its inhabitants, and invites earth-men to visit that planet.

From planet Pluto with brotherly love. Los Angeles, DeVross & Co., 1967. 32 p.

Ways in which life on earth differs from that on other planets are described by alleged ruler of Pluto and method of effecting a reform suggested. Civilization of Pluto is discussed.

Fry, Daniel W. The curve of development. Lakemont, Ga., CSA Printers and Publishers, 1965. 75 p.

Outlines development of the human soul "through stages of increasing ability and manifestation." Speculates that there may be other planets where life, intelligence and spiritual development have progressed beyond the average level achieved on earth; the earth human may at some stage of his development take up residence on such an advanced planet where the environment is more conducive to rapid progress.

Golowin, Sergius. Götter der Atom-Zeit; moderne Sagenbildung um Raumschiffe und Sternenmenschen. Bern und München, Francke Verlag, 1967. 128 p.

The book represents a collection of the "new stories and fairy tales" of our age. By citing actual reports (references included) the author shows the results of an unscientific approach to the UFO question: fantastic stories describing spaceships, beings from other planets, interviews conducted with them, reports of their family and lovelife, their work, attempts to sabotage terrestrial atomic plants, attempts to better mankind, warnings of the harmful effects of foods, and other problems.

Halsey, Wallace C. Cosmic end-time secrets. Los Angeles, Futura Press, 1965. 102 p.

Contains collected writings, lectures, and charts of the author. UFOs, their origin and purpose, are discussed, as well as the story of creation; the Tower of Babel; our solar system's imbalance; functions of the Pyramids; the Infinite Light; squaring the body; pineal gland or "third eye" development; teleportation; the work of the Melchizedek Order; cosmic high noon; the transitor beam; the White Stone; and the Solar Tongue.

Howard, Dana. Over the threshold. Los Angeles, Llewellyn Publications, 1957. 140 p.

Subjective report of paranormal contact between author and a being from Venus who, in mission to "guide men in the ways of perfection, " discourses on such subjects as: The Intuitions; Disease and Destruction; Reincarnation; Religion; The Subworlds; The Alchemy of Finance; The Secret of Youth; and The Meaning of Consciousness.

Invitation from the planet Venus. Los Angeles, DeVorss & Co., 1967. 20 p.

Culture and philosophy of the inhabitants of the planet Venus are described and the mission of Venusian spacecraft to earth discussed. Material was allegedly dictated by the ruler of Venus.

King, George. A cosmic message of divine opportunity. Hollywood, Calif., The Aetherius Society, 1964. 9 p.

From a spaceship in earth's atmosphere, a message is allegedly delivered to author through telepathic communication with a "Cosmic Master": all right-thinking people must coordinate their efforts in such a manner that as much spiritual power and divine energy as possible can be radiated to the rest of mankind.

----- The day the gods came. Los Angeles, The Aetherius Society, 1965. 71 p.

Text is comprised of a move-by-move account of how on July 8, 1964, a "great Hierarchal Being manipulated tremendous energies in order to perform the Cosmic Initiation of Earth. " Earth is represented as the living, breathing goddess "Terra" who "must shortly take her rightful place in the cosmic scheme of evolution. " Information allegedly transmitted telepathically to author by "cosmic intelligences. "

----- Join your ship. Hollywood, Calif., The Aetherius Society, 1964. 16 p.

Details are given of a meeting of the Supreme Tribunal of cosmic intelligences allegedly held on the planet Saturn on May 29, 1964; decisions affecting earth are discussed. Author claims to have received transmissions telepathically.

----- Life on the planets. Hollywood, Calif., The Aetherius Society, 1958. 29 p.

Series of lectures dealing with life in general on the planets Mars, Venus, Jupiter, and Saturn. There is also a lecture dealing with system of government --Interplanetary Parliament--adopted by residents of these planets. Information allegedly transmitted telepathically to author.

----- The nine freedoms. Los Angeles, The Aetherius Society, 1963. 200 p.

Gives a concise account of man's coming to earth, why he is here, and why he is at the bottom of the evolutionary ladder in this solar system. Outlines the exact path through evolution that man must take in order to become a "God-man. " Reveals the way in which man will eventually attain the "glorious state of inter-planetary existence. " Information allegedly delivered to author telepathically in nine consecutive transmissions by "a prominent Master of unquestionable Cosmic Status. "

King, George. You are responsible. London, The Aetherius Press, 1961. 173 p.

Author claims to be in complete telepathic rapport with people living on other, more evolved planets and provides detailed information from these entities regarding the dangers of radioactivity in its uncontrolled state such as atomic bomb experimentation.

Macvey, John W. Journey to Alpha Centauri. New York, Macmillan, 1965. 256 p.

Speculative consideration of interstellar travel, its prospects, and implications. Study--in series of extracts from diaries--of human, moral, and sociological problems that could confront first stellar astronauts on 215-year expedition to Alpha Centauri during the seven generations the trip would take.

Menger, Howard. From outer space to you. Clarksburg, W. Va., Saucerian Books, 1959. 256 p.

Report of contacts with visitors from other planets and discussion of their philosophy.

Miller, Will and Evelyn Miller. We of the new dimension. Los Angeles, The Authors, [195-] 115 p.

Intelligences from other worlds and dimensions allegedly dictate the book telepathically to the authors. The role of the individual in the universe and how he can advance into a well-balanced, fuller life is discussed.

Mustapa, Margit. Book of brothers. New York, Vantage Press, 1963. 196 p.

Allegedly in telepathic contact with "brothers" from Venus, author communicates their messages to aid mankind "grow inwardly, spiritually, and mentally toward extraplanetary dimensions in thinking."

The mystery of other worlds revealed. Greenwich, Conn. Fawcett Publications, 1952. 144 p.

Chapter headings include: life on other worlds; communication with other worlds; the expanding universe; possibilities of an invasion base on the moon; a case for flying saucers; investigation of the Carolina saucer; are the flying saucers Russian-owned.

Neptune from experience gives advice. Los Angeles, DeVorss & Co., 1967. 16 p.

Manner in which Neptune has managed to rid itself of the manipulators of the money system and their following dark forces is described by the alleged ruler of that planet.

Pestalozzi, Rudolph H. Letters to you from Baloran. San Francisco, Kay Publishing Co., 1965. 154 p.

Baloran--an etheric being not confined to a single planet--allegedly transmits 22 letters telepathically through Pestalozzi. Subjects discussed are: (1) efforts to start, sustain, and develop civilization on the planet earth; (2) incidents described in the Bible; (3) cause of the tragedy that has befallen man in this age; (4) man's perverted and distorted doctrine of thought and conduct; and (5) end of the present age and what man should do to adjust to the new age.

Planet Mercury sends greetings. Los Angeles, DeVorss & Co., 1967. 32 p.

Description of the topography of the planet Mercury, its cities, and inhabitants by the alleged ruler of the planet. Mission of spacecraft sent from Mercury to earth is discussed.

Pritchett, E. Blanche. Transcripts of "44." Arlington, Va., Marcap Council, 1966. 66 p.

Transcribed calls by "44" to a Salt Lake City, Utah, radio station. Subjects discussed include solar and galactic government and the Solar and Galactic Councils; the twelve planets of this solar system; the principle of temporal harmonics and the principle of universal balance and their application to the concepts of reincarnation and Karma; concept resolution and the higher levels of existence; formation of the Planetary Council and the return of Christ; galactic zones; space ships and the Galactic Communication Center; and the galactic central sun.

Sumner, F. W. The coming golden age. Los Angeles, New Age Publishing Co., 1957. 206 p.

Five part treatise: (1) presentation of cosmic changes now in progress; (2) messages from the spirit world confirming these changes; (3) forces from other planets offered to assist man through this crisis; (4) beginning of the New Age; and (5) interpretation of New Age objectives.

Troxwell, Hope. The Mohada teachings. Independence, Calif., School of Thought, 1964. 43 p.

Messages to "elevate man on his path through this world" allegedly transmitted telepathically to author by an "intergalactic" being.

Uranus, lover of man, speaks. Los Angeles, DeVorss & Co., 1967. 29 p.

Invitation to earth men to visit the planet Uranus is issued by the alleged ruler of the planet and the history and explanation of astrology given.

White, George S. A book of revelations: a true narrative of life on many planets. Los Angeles, The Author, 1945. 198 p.

History of the earth and planets from creation to the present time (1945) as recorded in the "Master Book of Life" and revealed by "cosmic teachers."

Wilcox, Hal. Zemkla, interplanetary avatar. Los Angeles, Galaxy Press, 1966. 57 p.

Advanced metaphysical wisdom is allegedly transmitted to author personally by Zemkla--from the planet Celo--for enlightenment of mankind. Author describes trip to Celo aboard flying saucer.

Extraterrestrial Visitors

Adamski, George. How to know a spaceman, if you see one. Probe, v. 3,
Mar. -Apr. 1966: 5-6.

Author describes his rationale for recognizing "space people." Reprinted from September 1962 Cosmic Science News Letter.

Ancient records of UFO in Japan. Australian saucer record, v. 2, June
1962: 15-17.

Material in ancient Japanese history books that may be interpreted as
meaning tnat earth has had extraterrestrial visitors from the very
earliest times is listed in chronological order from 637-1714 A.D.
Reprinted from Flying Saucer News of Japan published by the Cosmic
Brotherhood Association.

Barker, Gray. The case for non-human space visitors. Flying saucers,
Feb. 1959: 18-23.

Cites landing/contact reports that would seem to indicate that some flying
saucers either contain or are piloted by non-humanoid entities. Mentions
speculation that alien animals might be deposited on earth, then taken up
again to undergo laboratory examination to determine how the atmosphere,
disease germs, and other environmental factors on earth had affected them.

Bible. Old Testament Apocryhal Books. Enoch. Transl. by R. H. Charles.
London, Society for Promoting Christian Knowledge, 1917. 154 p.

Book of Enoch, especially verses VI - XI, is often cited as an historical
account of extraterrestrial influences in man's origin.

Burr, Frank. Visitors from afar. Flying saucer review, v. 9,
Mar. -Apr. 1963: 19-20.

Commenting on the theory that we have persons from outer space living
amongst us, the author suggests that a port of entry by space people could
be through the mountains of the north of India and other territories of the
East where the people believe in the occult and where controls governing
the movement of individuals are not stringent.

Calvin, Melvin. Round trip from space. Evolution, v. 3, September 8, 1959:
362-377.

Carr, Aidan M. Take me to your leader. Homiletic and pastoral review, v. 65,
Dec. 1964: 255-256.

Crandall, L. The Venusians. Los Angeles, New Age Publishing Co. , 1955.
76 p.

Drake, W. Raymond. Gods or spacemen? Amherst, Wis. , Amherst Press,
1964. 176 p.

Author suggests that present theology may be based on false premises since
the experiences and visions of saints are phenomena that might be associated
with UFOs and their extraterrestrial crews. He reviews the mythological
and religious traditions of the countries of the world to demonstrate worldwide
"race memories" of spacemen visiting earth. He suggests that terrestrial
destruction in ages past may have been caused by interplanetary warfare rather
than by collision of celestial bodies with earth.

Drake, W. Raymond. Spacemen in antiquity. Sunderland, England, The Author,
[196-] 1 v.

Typescript is composed of the following monographs: Spacemen in Antiquity;
UFOs over Ancient Rome; Space Gods in Ancient Britain; Spacemen in
Saxon Times; UFOs Fought for Charlemagne; Spacemen in Norman Times; A
Bride from Space; Spacemen in the Middle Ages; Spacemen in Ancient India;
Spacement in Old Tibet; Spacemen in Old China; Spacemen in Old Japan;
Semiramis, Space-Queen of Babylon.

Drake, W. Raymond. Spacemen in the ancient East. London, Neville
Spearman, 1968.

Traditions are cited which tell of "supermen, " from the skies, "Divine
Dynasties, " who ruled on earth in India, Tibet, China, Japan, and Babylonia.

Drury, Neville. Flying ships in "Oahspe." Australian flying saucer review, no. 9, Nov. 1966: 40-41.

Author cites portions of Oahspe that provide details on space visitations.

Edwards, Allan W. An angel unawares? Flying saucer review, v. 7, Jan. - Feb. 1961: 7-10.

Description of contact with "extraordinary" beings that author suggests could be visitors from other planets who are living on earth among us.

Finch, Bernard. The ark of the Israelites was an electrical machine. Flying saucer review, v. 11, May-June 1965: 18-19.

On examination of the Ark of the Covenant in terms of modern physics, the author suggests that what is described is an electric storage machine resembles the Leyden jar of today. He says accounts in the Bible of the association of Moses, the high priests, and others with lightning bolts, balls of fire, and luminous clouds in the sky would make it seem that the secret of the electro-static machine was obtained from extraterrestrials; it was used as a method of terrorizing the people and diverting their worship from idols to higher ideals and philosphies.

Fouéré, René. Surhumains ou sous-humains, anges ou démons, que sont les extra-terrestres? Phénomènes spatiaux, Mar. 1966: 5-11.

Speculation on the nature of the extraterrestrial beings apparently visiting earth based in part on reports of "contactees. "

Golowin, Sergius. Götter der Atom-Zeit; moderne Sagenbildung um Raumschiffe und Sternenmenschen. Bern und München, Francke Verlag, 1967. 128 p.

The book represents a collection of the "new stories and fairy tales" of our age. By citing actual reports (references included) the author shows the results of an unscientific approach to the UFO question: fantastic stories describing spaceships, beings from other planets, interviews conducted with them, reports of their family and lovelife, their work, attempts to sabotage terrestrial atomic plants, attempts to better mankind, warnings of the harmful effects of foods, and other problems.

Hapgood, Charles H. The Piri Reis map of 1513. Keene, N. H. , The Author, 1962. 48 p.

The accuracy of both latitude and longitude throughout the Piri Reis map of 1513 is inexplicable in terms of our present ideas of the extent of geographical knowledge and cartographic science in ancient times or in the Renaissance, the author contends. It has been speculated that data used were from aerial survey by an extraterrestrial spacecraft.

Hunt, Douglas. The miracles of Apollonius of Tyana. Fate, v. 9, June 1956: 67-73.

Dematerialization of chains and instant transportation of the human body are "miracles" attributed to Apollonius--thought by some to be an extra-terrestrial being.

Le Poer Trench, Brinsley. Men among mankind. London, Neville Spearman, Ltd., 1962. 199 p.

The fact that the course of history has been changed abruptly by certain unusual men, extraordinary in their abilities, is discussed by author. Since these men demonstrated marked differences from ordinary people of any period in time, it is suggested they may have been extraterrestrials.

----- The sky people. London, N. Neville Spearman, 1960. 224 p.

Develops idea that a race of extraterrestrial beings with superior wisdom and technology have visited earth periodically through the ages to show humanity the way to realize its manhood and potential galactic status. Cites references in the Bible, ancient manuscripts, folklore, and other literature to support theory.

Misraki, Paul. Les extraterrestres, par Paul Thomas [pseud.] Paris, Plon, 1962. 224 p.

Develops hypothesis that from earliest antiquity to modern times, extra-terrestrial beings have kept earth under surveillance, have at times visited this planet, and have frequently modified the course of history by means of spectacular appearances. Cites biblical passages and ancient manuscripts.

Moseley, James W. Peruvian desert: map for saucers? Fate, v. 8, Oct. 1955: 28-33.

Describes complex markings recently discovered on the desert near Nasca, Peru, by airliners passing over the area. Markings may be 1,000 years old and are clearly visible and meaningful only from the air. It is speculated that they may have been constructed as signals to interplanetary visitors or to some advanced earth race that occasionally visited the peoples of the region.

Rich, Valentin and Mikhail Chernenko. Tracks that lead to space. Flying saucer review, v. 6, May-June 1960: 3-6.

Translation of article in Literaturnaya Gazeta of Moscow in which Soviet scientist M. A. Agrest advances hypothesis that intelligent life exists in outer space and earth has been visited by space travelers for aeons.

Sagan, Carl. Direct contact among galactic civilizations by relativistic interstellar spaceflight. Planetary and space science, v. 11, May 1963: 485-498.

Author postulates that there exists in the galaxy a loosely integrated community of diverse civilizations, cooperating in the exploration and sampling of astronomical objects and their inhabitants. There is therefore the likelihood that earth was visited at least once during historical times by an advanced civilization.

Sendy, Jean. Les dieux nous sont nés. Paris, Bernard Grasset, 1966. 343 p.

Citing the Bible as a prime authority, the author postulates that the "gods" were extraterrestrial beings who came to earth to create mankind and promote civilization and who continue to exercise manipulative influence. Flying saucers, the miracle of Fatima, evocations, premonition, precognition, and other psychic and hallucinatory experience are discussed in this context.

Space visitors: From which planets do they originate? Is there life on them? Newnes practical mechanics, v. 24, Jan. 1957: 203-204, 207.

Known information on the planetary atmospheres and physical conditions of the planets is summarized for the purpose of establishing whether or not life could be sustained on them. It is concluded that even the worst apparent location as an abode of life cannot be dismissed as entirely impossible.

Stranges, Frank E. Danger from the stars. Venice, Calif., International Evangelism Crusades, Inc., 1960. 14 p.

Author postulates that planet earth has been host to generations of interstellar visitors who can travel with or without what we call flying saucers and who fall into four classifications: ministering angels; guardian angels; angel reapers; and fallen angels. He discusses their characteristics and traits and then warns against "counterfeit" flying discs causing crashes, near collisions, near-havoc, and all manner of fear and superstition. He lists occurrences 1945-1960 that seem to indicate a pattern of violence and deliberate interference.

Stranges, Frank E. Stranger at the Pentagon. Van Nuys, Calif., International Evangelism Crusades, 1967. 201 p.

Account, as allegedly told to author, of visit to earth by Valiant Thor of Venus and his address to a special group at the United Nations and meeting with high officials at the Pentagon.

Sykes, Egerton. The extra terrestrials. London, Markham House Press, 1967. 20 p.

Postulating that although our planetary system is but one of hundreds of millions within our galaxy, the Milky Way, author says it is inevitable that on various occasions we have been visited by exploration teams from other planets whose technology is a few thousand years in advance of our own. Impact which these earlier visits had upon our culture may have been small, but in some cases it was just enough to enable one race to assume a technological supremacy over others and thus advance the course of history. These visitors from other planetary systems correspond to the Elohim of of the Old Testament. Also discussed in the context of the UFO phenomenon are the Taselli frescoes; Baalbek; the Book of Ezekiel; the Bayan Kara Ula discs; the Star of Bethlehem; the Honshu figurines; and Baba Yurga.

Vyner, J. The mystery of Springheel Jack. Flying saucer review, v. 7, May-June 1961: 3-6.

Author suggests that Springheel Jack, a notorious figure that terrorized the English countryside in 1838, may have been a visitor from outer space. Facts in article were taken from contemporary accounts and checked against all available records for accuracy.

Vyner, J. The mystery of Springheel Jack. Fate, v. 14, Oct. 1961: 27-33.

Account of a peculiarly costumed being, who could leap incredible distances, used a sort of "ray gun" on occasion, and terrorized many responsible citizens in Middlesex, England, 1837-1838. Reprinted from Flying Saucer Review.

Williamson, George Hunt. Road in the sky. London, N. Spearman, 1959. 248 p.

Develops hypothesis that there is a connection between the flying saucers of the past and present and the legends of mankind that attempt to explain God and the supernatural. Cites instances of past extraterrestrial visitations records in legends and myths of ancient civilizations and of the American Indians.

Williamson, George Hunt. Secret places of the lion. Amherst, Wis.,
Amherst Press, 1958. 230 p.

Autnor cites Biblical passages and material in ancient manuscripts
to support theory that many leaders of the past were men and women
from other worlds in time and space who had migrated to earth in what
today are called UFOs to assist mankind in its climb from beasthood
to manhood. He discloses discoveries suggesting that ancient civilizations in South America, especially, had continuing contact with extraterrestrial visitors.

Zeitsev, Vyacheslav. Visitors from outer space. Sputnik, v. 1, Jan.
1967: 162-179.

Author reports on thirty years research to substantiate theory that
intelligent beings from outer space have had contact with earth. Among
evidence cited are hieroglyphics deciphered by Chinese archeologist
revealing that extraterrestrial spacecraft landed on earth 12,000 years
ago; legends supporting information in the hieroglyphics and vestiges
of graves and skeletons that seem to confirm the legends; myths,
Biblical passages, and apocryphal legends; and frescoes dating from
1350 at Dechaney Monastery, Yugoslavia.

Ball Lightning and Fireballs

Arnold, Kenneth. Are space visitors here? Fate, Summer 1948: 4-21.

Reports of apparent meteor and fireball activity during 1948 are examined.
Author suggests that they are not aerial phenomena but extraterrestrial
spacecraft.

Benedicks, Carl. Theory of the lightning-balls and its application to the
atmosphere phenomenon called "flying saucers. " Arkiv för geofysik,
v. 2, no. 1, 1954: 1-11.

Author theorizes that reported UFO sightings are in reality ball lightning
and gives data supporting his position.

Brand, Walther. Der Kugelblitz. Hamburg, Henri Grand, 1923. 170 p.

Theories in explanation of ball lightning are given. Characteristics that
distinguish ball lightning from other meteorological phenomena (such as
line lightning and meteors) are noted.

Cade, C. Maxwell. Fireballs and flying saucers. Flying saucer review,
v. 13, Jan. -Feb. 1967: 10-12.

Case histories are given of sightings which very probably were due to
ball lightning. Author warns, however, that it is more "unscientific" to
try to dismiss all unexplained aerial phenomena than it is to hold the open-
minded view that some of them may be the artefacts of extraterrestrial
communities.

Constance, Arthur. The inexplicable sky. London, W. Laurie, 1956: 308 p.

Discusses sky phenomena, including meteors, fireballs, mirages, and things that fall from the heavens. Cites cases of reported extraterrestrial visitations and advances theory with supporting arguments that non-terrestrial intelligences are coming to, or emerging from other dimensions into, earth's atmosphere. American ed. (New York, Citadel Press) published 1957.

Creighton, Gordon W. Foo fighters. Flying saucer review, v. 8, Mar.-Apr. 1962: 11-15.

Author relates what is known about strange balls of fire that dogged the paths of allied pilots on operation over enemy territory during World War II.

Evenson, K. M. Ball lightning research at Highland Lookout, Montana. Santa Monica, Calif., Douglas Aircraft Co., 1968. 16 p.

Report on site survey of possible locations where ball lightning activity might be high enough to guarantee some success in making physical measurements.

Gaddis, Vincent H. Mysterious lights and fires. New York, David McKay Co., 1967. 280 p.

In three sections, "Earth's Glowing Ghosts," "Electro-Dynamic Man," and "Premature Cremations," the book deals with the enigmatic aspects of fires and lights. UFOs are treated in the first section. Agreeing that some of these objects appear to be metallic craft piloted by humanoid beings, the author points out that many reported sightings could be what he calls "electro-animals"-- a form of upper-atmospheric life perhaps feeding on pure energy. Firefalls, ball lightning, fireballs and similar phenomena are also treated in the first section.

Gaddis, Vincent H. UFO mystery: fire bolts from space. Saga, v. 34, May 1967: 25-27, 78-80; 82, 84, 86.

It is suggested that fireballs and fire falls that seemingly drop from unknown heights as spheroids or masses of illuminated gas or condensed energy regardless of weather conditions might be generated in the Van Allen radiation belts and might account for some of the world's most disastrous fires.

Galus, Henry S. The mystery of the crawling fireballs. Fate, v. 5, Feb.-Mar. 1952: 37-40.

Incidents in France involving "crawling fireballs" between 1898 and the early 1900's.

Hunt, Richard. Canadian fireballs. Flying saucer review, v. 12, Mar.-Apr. 1966: 33-34.

Summary of newspaper clippings relating to brilliant balls of fire that lit the skies and landscape across British Columbia and parts of the northwestern U.S. on Mar. 31, 1965.

Klass, Philip J. Many UFOs are identified as plasmas. Aviation week & space technology, v. 85, Oct. 3, 1966: 54-55, 57, 59, 61, 65, 67, 69, 71, 73.

Evidence is presented in support of theory that high-level UFOs could be created by electric discharge between clouds or between invisible layers of charged dust/ice particles. Occasional daylight sightings of what have been reported as well-structured or silhouetted objects are explainable as plasmas that give the illusion of metal structures possibly due to whirling dust or ice particles. Conclusions based on analysis of reports collected by National Investigations Committee on Aerial Phenomena.

Klass, Philip. Plasma theory may explain many UFOs. Aviation week & space technology, v. 85, Aug. 22, 1966: 48-50, 55-56, 60-61.

Theory is advanced that many low-altitude UFOs are a form of ball lightning (plasma), also called kugelblitz, that is generated by lightning or by corona discharge along high-voltage power lines under appropriate conditions. Idea was prompted by numerous UFO sightings observed on or near high-tension lines, especially at Exeter, N. H., during 1965, and the similarity of their characteristics to those reported for some kugelblitz sightings.

Klass, Philip J. UFOs -- identified. New York, Random House, 1968. 290 p.

Theory is advanced that most UFOs seem to be "natural plasmas of ionized air, sometimes containing charged dust particles or tiny charged ice particles." These plasmas may be closely related to St. Elmo's fire and ball lightning. They appear to whirl and float, sometimes maneuvering as though they were controlled by an intelligent being; they can also give off light. Hypothesis is applied to explain reported UFO sightings near Exeter, New Hampshire, and to an elleged saucer landing in Socorro, New Mexico.

Lauritzen, Hans. Flying saucers -- superconducting whirls of plasma. Flying saucers, Mar. 1967: 10-11.

Author hypothesizes that UFOs are super-conducting ring-shaped whirls of plasma trapped by earth's magnetic lines of force. Phenomena accompanying UFO sightings are explained in this context.

Miles, H. G. and A. J. Meadows. Fireballs associated with the Barwell meteorite. Nature, v. 210, June 4, 1966: 983-986.

On Dec. 24, 1965, meteoritic fragments fell in a restricted area in and about the village of Barwell, Leicestershire, England. Sighting of three bright fireballs and the associated sonic effects were recorded over the area. One of these resulted in the fall at Barwell. No evidence has yet been found for meteoritic falls associated with the other two fireballs.

Miles, H. G. and A. J. Meadows. Fireballs associated with the Barwell meteorite. Nature, v. 212, Dec. 17, 1966: 1339.

Article contains additional information on the fireballs associated with the meteorite fall at Barwell, Leicestershire, England, on December 24, 1965. Original report indicated existence of two fireballs; additional data imply existence of a third.

Rayle, Warren D. Ball lightning characteristics. Washington, D. C., NASA, 1966. 38 p. (NASA TN D-3188)

Surveys of NASA Lewis Research Center personnel were conducted to obtain information about ball lightning occurrences. Comparison of the frequency of observation of ball lightning with that of ordinary lightning impact points reveals that ball lightning is not a particularly rare phenomenon. Contrary to widely accepted ideas, the occurrence of ball lightning may be nearly as frequent as that of ordinary cloud-to-ground strokes.

Romig, Mary F. and Donald L. Lamar. Anomalous sounds and electromagnetic effects associated with fireball entry. Santa Monica, The Rand Corp., 1963. 60 p. (Rand Corp. Memorandum RM-3724-ARPA)

Memorandum describes nature of certain hissing sounds and electromagnetic effects associated with the passage of very bright meteors or fireballs and discusses their possible origin from the standpoint of atmospheric electricity and reentry physics. Study was motivated by possibility that a better understanding of these phenomena will lead to new techniques for determining the size, nature, and path of any large body entering earth's atmosphere.

Ruppelt, Edward J. Mystery of the green fireballs. Fate, v. 10, June 1957.

Fireball activity in New Mexico during winter 1954 is discussed and theories as to its possible nature outlined.

S'agissait-il de foudre globulaire? Phénomènes spatiaux, June 1969: 17-23.

Newspaper accounts of unusual atmospheric phenomena that may have been ball lightning.

Sykes, Egerton. Flying saucers and negative matter. Atlantis, v. 5, Sept. 1952: 49-51.

It has been established, asserts the author, that if heavy matter can be volatized instantaneously, it may under certain circumstances recombine on the negative side of the scale. This secondary stage will be shortlived, but will have characteristics similar to those of fireballs.

Teletov, G. S. Sharovaia molniia [Ball lightning]. Priroda, no. 9, 1966: 84-92.

Article reviews the nature and properties of ball lightning and discusses the hypotheses that have been advanced to explain them.

U. S. Library of Congress. Science and Technology Division. Ball lightning bibliography, 1950-1960. Prepared under the sponsorship of the USA Signal Missile Support Agency, Missile Electronic Warfare Division in cooperation with Technical Library Branch, White Sands Missile Range, N. M. Washington, 1961. 15 p.

Contains 43 annotated references, mostly foreign.

Wilkins, Harold T. The strange mystery of the foo fighters. Fate, v. 4, Aug. -Sept. 1951: 98-106.

Weird colored balls of fire of fantastic and variable speeds that were encountered by U.S. and British pilots over Truk Lagoon, Japan; the West Rhine area of Alsace Lorraine; and over the Bavarian Palatinate during World War II are described.

Disc—like Aircraft

Avro Canada's Omega. The aeroplane, v. 84, May 1, 1953: 568.

Article discusses the unusual aerodynamic, thermodynamic, and structural problems posed by the disc-type aircraft under construction by Avro Canada, Ltd.

Barker, Gray. Has man conquered gravity? Flying saucers, July-Aug. 1958: 8-11.

Discussion of Otis T. Carr's circular-foil design OTC-X1 aircraft designed for flight to within 1,000 miles away from earth and to be powered by "utron" energy derived from "natural environmental sources."

Barton, Michael X. We want you. Los Angeles, Futura Press, 1960. 34 p.

Author suggests that not all UFOs come from outside or inside the planet earth but that some of them are Nazi-built (from the blueprints of Vikton Schauberger) at an armed fortress in Patagonia (Argentina) to which Adolph Hitler fled in July 1945. He speculates that the story of Hitler's suicide was fraudulent and that Hitler is still alive. The unfulfilled predictions of Karl Michalek between 1958 and 1960 are also analyzed.

Canada builds a flying saucer. Fate, v. 6, Oct. 1953: 14-17.

A disc-like aircraft under development by Avro Canada, Ltd., is described.

Disc aircraft inadequate to explain UFOs. The UFO investigator, v. 2, Dec. - Jan. 1963-1964: 6-8.

Descriptions of disc-like aircraft: Couzinet "aerodyne", Adrian Phillips' "Saucercraft"; Chance Vought XF5U-1 "Flying Pancake"; Chance Vought V-173 "Flying Flapjack"; Otis T. Carr "OTC-X"; Hilton Re-entry Vehicle; Hiller "Flying Platform"; National Research Associates' "Flying Saucer Ride"; Weygers' "Discopter"; Swedenborg Saucer; Ryan Disc; General Dynamics' Lenticular Re-Entry Vehicle; V-7.

Du Soir, W. E. The saucer that didn't fly. Fate, v. 12, Aug. 1959: 32-34.

Account of Otis T. Carr's unsuccessful attempt in April 1958 to launch a prototype model of a saucer-shaped aircraft. Propulsion was to have been by "utron" energy.

Fry, Daniel W. Steps to the stars. Lakemont, Ga., CSA Publishers, 1956. 83 p.

The basic physical concepts underlying the construction and operation of a vehicle that could undertake interplanetary travel are discussed.

Fuller, Curtis. Canada builds a saucer. Fate, v. 12, Sept. 1959: 70-73.

Avro Canada, Ltd., is preparing to test-fly a saucer-shaped craft which reportedly can move sidewise, hover, or skim close to the ground to avoid radar detection.

Haggerty, James J. and Cornelius Ryan. The Navy comes up with a real flying saucer. Collier's, v. 135, Apr. 29, 1955: 30-35.

Description of a circular one-man aircraft that can hover, climb, and dart sideways using the "ducted fan" propulsion principle; a propeller operating in a shallow cylinder sucks air through the vehicle, generating a downward thrust force which supplies vertical lift. Aircraft was built by Hiller Helicopters, Palo Alto, Calif., under direction of the Office of Naval Research in 1954.

Is this the real flying saucer? Look, v. 19, June 14, 1955: 44-46.

Design study for a flying-saucer fighter prepared for Look by Republic Aviation Corp. engineer Thomas Turner. Sketches indicate appearance of a craft that would fulfill following requirements: (1) ability to take off and land vertically; (2) high speed of over Mach 2.; (3) high rate of climb; (4) excellent maneuverability; (5) heavy armament; (6) ability to operate at 60,000 ft.

Johns, Cornelius. Flying saucers swamp the Vietcong. Argosy, v. 366, Jan. 1968: 30-31, 66, 68-69.

Role of air-cushion vehicles in the Vietnam war is discussed.

Nollet, A. R.   Flying saucers...a hard look.   Marine corps gazette, v. 43, Dec. 1959: 20-25.

States that hopes for a U. S. scientific breakthrough based on Apr. 29, 1959, article in U. S. News and World Report entitled "Flying Saucer Age for the U. S. --It's Getting Nearer" were misplaced since the saucers turned out to be Ground Effect Vehicles.   Describes the different types of GEV's worldwide and suggests military uses.

One man's flying saucer.   Pace, v. 11, Aug. 1966: 62-63.

A flying-saucer-shaped personal commuter aircraft designed by Univ. of California aerodynamics professor Paul Moller is discussed.   Eight feet, in diameter, it weighs 400 lbs., will reach 5,000 ft. altitude, and attain speed of 150 mph.

Russia claims "flying saucer."   The UFO investigator, v. 2, Dec.-Jan. 1963-1964: 1-2.

Krasnaya Zvezda is cited in article as having reported early in 1963 that Soviet engineers had successfully tested a "flying saucer" aircraft.   Statements from U. S. S. R. on UFOs 1952-1961 are listed.

Saucer blue book.   Time, v. 66, Nov. 7, 1955: 52.

Secretary of the Air Force Donald A. Quarles released information about a vertically rising jet aircraft soon to be tested by Ryan Aeronautical Co. that might be mistaken for a flying saucer.   He also released a Project Blue Book analysis of 4,965 reported flying saucer sightings.

Saucer-eyed dragons.   Time, v. 55, Apr. 17, 1950: 52-54.

Discussion of controversy surrounding statement in U. S. News & World Report (Apr. 7, 1950) that the Navy had developed a revolutionary aircraft, a combination of helicopter and jet plane, capable of outflying any other.   This plane was said to be "the flying saucer."

Stine, G. Harry.   The prowling mind of Henri Coanda.   Flying, v. 80, Mar. 1967: 64-68.

Among inventions of Henri Coanda was a lenticular aerodyne (flying saucer) designed in 1935.   Coanda effect (tendency of a moving jet of air or water to adhere to an adjacent surface) would be used to create vertical lift without forward motion and to control aircraft.   Although aerodyne was never built, tests on critical portions of it were made in France and results indicate it is practical.

Taylor, Henry J. The "flying saucer" is good news. Reader's digest, v. 57, July 1950: 14-16.

Condensed from a radio broadcast. Author claims that so-called flying saucers are U.S. Navy experimental jet fighters and are a military secret. He says that Navy sources at Patuxent, Md., confirm his allegations.

Unidentified Submarine Objects

Binder, Otto O. The mystery of flying saucers at sea. Rudder, v. 84, Feb. 1968: 21-23, 75.

Account of UFOs observed at sea and suggestions of how boatmen can help solve the phenomenon.

Bowen, Charles. A South American trio. Flying saucer review, v. 11, Jan.-Feb. 1965: 19-21.

Three UFO sighting cases from South America: (1) In April 1957, a resident of Cordoba, Argentina, allegedly encountered a landed flying saucer and was invited by one of the crew members to enter for an inspection tour; (2) On Jan. 10, 1958, an unidentified floating object was viewed off the coast of São Paulo, Brazil, by several witnesses before sinking out of sight; (3) During a fire near São Bernado do Campo, Brazil, in 1963, a flying saucer landed amid the flames, and several tall, good-looking "people" emerged from it and picked up pieces of burnt material, stones, and other debris.

Fouéré, René. Existe-t-il des bases sous-marines de soucoupes volantes? Phénomènes spatiaux, Feb. 1965: 16-25.

Lists instances 1845-1960 where disc-like or wheel-like glowing objects were seen entering the oceans, in or on the oceans, or leaving the oceans. Gives reasons the ocean depths would be ideal flying saucer bases.

Galindez, Oscar A. Crew of Argentine ship see submarine UFO. Flying saucer review, v. 14, Mar.-Apr. 1968: 22.

A "submergible UFO with its own illumination" allegedly paced the Argentine steamer, Naviero, for 15 minutes on July 30, 1967. Article taken from press reports in the Argentine newspapers La Razon, Cordoba, and Los Principios.

Hinfelaar, H. J. Submarine craft in Australian waters. Flying saucer review, v. 12, July-Aug. 1966: 28-30.

Reports appearances of Unidentified Submarine Objects (USOs) in New Zealand and Australian waters in 1965.

Ley, Willy. The wheels of Poseidon; and Too much imagination. In For your information: on earth and in the sky. New York, Doubleday & Co., 1967. p. 69-88, 157-168.

A phenomenon is described that occurs in the Indian Ocean and that has been described by several eyewitnesses: a pulsating near-circular disturbance roughly 1,000-1,500 feet in diameter is seen with streaks of light like the beams of a searchlight radiating from its center and revolving counter-clockwise. Views are given supporting speculation that the Podkamennaya Tunguska Meteorite of Central Siberia (1908) was in fact an exploded extra-terrestrial spacecraft.

Lorenzen, Coral. Diving for lost UFO. Fate, v. 17, May 1964: 62-65.

Efforts are being made to salvage a flying saucer which seemed in mechanical difficulty when it allegedly sank in the Peropava River, Brazil, on October 31, 1963.

Luminous wheels puzzle seamen. New scientist, Mar. 9, 1967, v. 33: 447-448.

In March 1966, three merchant ships in the Gulf of Tnailand independently observed the apparently unexplained phenomenon known as the phosphorescent wheel: bands of luminosity skimming across the surface, apparently radiating from a central bright source. The wheels can rotate in either direction and there have been reports of two wheels, one above the other, rotating in opposite directions. Professor Kurt Kalle of Hamburg, authority on phosphorescent wheels, attributes the phenomenon to bioluminescence.

Luminous wheels puzzle seamen. Spacelink, v. 4, Summer 1967: 12-13.

In the Gulf of Thailand and waters to the south-east during March 1967, three merchant ships independently observed the unexplained phenomenon known as the phosphorescent wheel: bands of luminosity apparently radiating from a central bright source. Professor Kurt Kalle of Hamburg, authority on luminescent wheels, attributes them to bioluminescence. From New Scientist, March 9, 1967.

Ribera, Antonio. More about UFOs and the sea. Flying saucer review, v. 11, Nov.-Dec. 1965: 17-18.

Author summarizes events which may indicate underwater reconnaissance by UFOs of submarine bases.

Ribera, Antonio. UFOs and the sea. Flying saucer review, v. 10, Nov.-Dec. 1964: 8-10.

Account of strange happenings at sea that might support hypothesis that the bodies of water covering three-quarters of earth's surface are providing a hiding place for UFOs.

Robertson, W. S. UFOs and the Scottish seas. Flying saucer review, v. 11, May-June 1965: 36-37.

Account from newspaper sources of UFO sightings in the waters off the coast of Scotland, 1961-1965.

Steiger, Brad and Joan Whritenour. Unidentified underwater saucers. Saga, v. 36, June 1968: 34-37, 54-57.

Instances are cited in which UFOs seen hovering over oceans, lakes, and rivers have submerged in the water. It is suggested that the objects may have underwater "bases."

Turner, Richard. Some unfamiliar 'PSUFOs': the phosphorescent wheels. Flying saucer review, v. 13, Sept.-Oct. 1967: 7-9.

Account of unusual bioluminescent phenomena that may be mistaken for UFOs. Lists sightings by seamen (1875-1910) of "phosphorescent wheels" that may fall into this category.

Fortean Phenomena

Constance, Arthur. The inexplicable sky. London, W. Laurie, 1956. 308 p.

Discusses sky phenomena, including meteors, fireballs, mirages, and things that fall from the heavens. Cites cases of reported extraterrestrial visitations and advances theory with supporting arguments that non-terrestrial intelligences are coming to, or emerging from other dimensions into, earth's atmosphere. American ed. (New York, Citadel Press) published 1957.

Fort, Charles. The books of Charles Fort. Introd. by Tiffany Thayer. New York, Henry Holt, 1941. 1125 p.

Contents: The book of the damned; New lands; Lo!; Wild talents. Collection of mysterious and unexplained events gleaned from newspaper reports. Accounts of strange things falling from the sky, the appearance of unidentified flying objects, showers of frogs and various animals, teleportations, disappearing people, and other odd phenomena. It is stated that since these events fall within the province of no known science, they have never been properly investigated.

Gallegos, Faustin. The pulsing honeycomb from space. Fate, v. 11, Sept. 1958: 40-43.

A football-shaped object of cells resembling those of a honeycomb reportedly fell in a Miami, Fla., yard on Feb. 28, 1958. It pulsated, was translucent and intangible, and had completely vanished--by "melting"--within 45 minutes from the time it was seen to fall from the sky.

Gardner, Martin. In the name of science. New York, G. P. Putnam's Sons, 1952. 320 p.

Survey of "quasi-scientific" theories. Chapters are included on the flat and hollow earth theories; Fortean phenomena; Atlantis and Lemuria; flying saucers; poltergeist phenomena, extrasensory perception; and pneumokinesis.

Gould, Rupert T. Enigmas. New Hyde Park, N. Y., University Books, 1965. 248 p.

Information about mysteries which have not been resolved up to the present day. Evidence that there were once giants on the earth and relating to the probability of intelligent life on Mars is discussed.

----- Oddities. New Hyde Park, N. Y., University Books, 1965. 228 p.

Collection of facts relating to incidents and phenomena which have not at present been satisfactorily explained. Among the topics mentioned are "the devil's hoofmarks," Orffyreus's wheel, and the planet Vulcan.

Jessup, Morris K. The case for the UFO, unidentified flying objects. Introd. by Frank Edwards. New York, Citadel Press, 1955. 239 p.

Author analyzes and correlates many paranormal phenomena of scientific record and theorizes that objects such as stones, ice, water, colored rain, organic matter, living organisms, and vegetable matter that have fallen to earth from the heavens come from intelligently operated extraterrestrial spacecraft or are in some way formed, guided, or influenced by the operators of such spacecraft.

Splitter, Henry W. Wonders from the sky. Fate, v. 6, Oct. 1953: 33-40.

Typically "Fortean" phenomena of strange things that have fallen from the sky, including toads, green rain, mud, rocks, angleworms, fish, blood and meat are reported.

Towner, Cliff R. Silver chaff from the sky. Fate, v. 10, Mar. 1957: 94-98.

Apparent fall from the sky on Aug. 27, 1956, of metallic shreds concomitant with reports of strange lights in the sky. Chickens consuming the material died.

Weideman, June E. Mysterious foam in St. Louis. Fate, v. 9, Dec. 1956: 20-21.

Fall from the sky of a strange, warm, odorless, foamy, white substance is described. Incident allegedly occurred over St. Louis on Aug. 20, 1956.

Wilkins, Harold T. "Damned" phenomena--fire and monsters. Fate, v. 6, Dec. 1953: 68-73.

Descriptions of mysterious flames, phantom ships, and huge sea serpents given by pre-Fortean historians and annalists (209 B. C. -17th century) are listed.

----- Did ancients see flying saucers? Fate, v. 6, Oct. 1953: 28-32.

Mysterious aerial fire and similar phenomena on the earth and sea noted by old Roman authors (including Julius Obsequens, Pliny, and Titus Livius) and medieval writers (including Geoffrey Gaimer and Lycosthenes) are cited.

Wilkins, Harold T. Mystery of the falling ice. Fate, v. 4, May-June 1951: 22-27.

Summary of phenomena of ice falling from the skies since 1811. Author postulates concomitant UFO activity.

----- When the skies rained blood. Fate, v. 6, Apr. 1953: 58-63.

Reports cases of blood falling from the heavens that were noted by historians in the days of the Roman empire (265 B.C.-759 A.D.).

UFOs and Religion

Are "contact group" sightings metaphysical? Flying saucers, July-Aug. 1958: 12-15, 19.

Referring to the group of UFO investigators who place a mystical, religious, or metaphysical interpretation on the entire UFO phenomenon, author states these concepts cannot be rejected but must be considered. They could comprise a facet of the overall picture.

Blaher, Damian J. Is anybody there? Friar, Sept. 1963: 15-17.

Discussion of the theological implications of space travel and the discovery of extraterrestrial people.

Brandt, Ivan. The stumbling block of orthodoxy. Flying saucer review, v. 8, July-Aug. 1962: 26-29.

The fiercest opposition to hypotheses supporting the reality of flying saucers has always come from those who adopt a materialistic view of the universe, the author states. It would seem that those who have closed their minds against the mystery of religion have automatically rejected any other mystery, and this may explain both the conspiracy of silence and the policy of conventionalizing as many as possible of the otherwise inexplicable UFO sightings, he adds.

Brasington, Virginia F. Flying saucers in the Bible. Clarksburg, W. Va., Saucerian Books, 1963. 78 p.

Study of flying saucers and related phenomena in the Bible. Quotes passages from Genesis, Exodus, Leviticus, Numbers, Deuteronomy, Joshua, Books of Samuel, Books of Kings, Job, Psalms, Isaiah, Ezekiel, Daniel, Matthew, Mark, Luke, and Revelations.

Cassens, Kenneth H. UFOs and the modern Bible. Fate, v. 8, Aug. 1955: 51-53.

Cove, Gordon. Who pilots the flying saucers? London, The Author, 1955. 80 p.

Flying saucers, according to the author, are celestial warnings of an impending Divine interruption of the course of world events: they are to warn men of the coming judgement and to encourage the believer.

Dean, John W. Flying saucers and the Scriptures. New York, Vantage Press, 1964. 173 p.

Text is an amplification of illustrated lecture bearing same title; uses scriptural passages and recent documentation of reported UFO sightings to support theory that earth has received visitors from space since earliest times whose missions are peaceful and who are "messengers of God."

Downing, Barry H. The Bible and flying saucers. Philadelphia, J. B. Lippincott Co., 1967. 221 p.

Author, a minister and Biblical scholar, postulates that many of the phenomena in the skies which are described in the Bible were what we term as UFOs today.

Drake, W. R. Gods or spacemen? Amherst, Wis., Amherst Press, 1964. 176 p.

Author suggests that present theology may be based on false premises since the experiences and visions of saints are phenomena that might be associated with UFOs and their extraterrestrial crews. He reviews the mythological and religious traditions of the countries of the world to demonstrate worldwide "race memories" of spacemen visiting earth. He suggests that terrestrial destruction in ages past may have been caused by interplanetary warfare rather than by collision of celestial bodies with earth.

Easton, W. B. Space travel and space theology. Theology today, v. 17, Jan. 1961: 428-429.

Ferguson, William. A message from outer space. Oak Park, Ill., Golden Age Press, 1955. 54 p.

A translation decoding the Book of Revelations allegedly given to author telepathically by "Khauga, the angel who gave it to St. John." Flying saucers are said to be the spacecraft of "perfected beings" who are "progressed to a four dimensional state of reality" and who are "preparing earth for the second coming of Jesus."

Gaspa, Pietro, Monito all'umanita. Sassari, Italy, Arti Grafiche Editoriali S. p. A., 1962. 127 p.

Author relates the UFO phenomenon to the Thomistic concept of the nature and attributes of superior spiritual entities. Photographic illustrations of thesis included.

Goff, Kenneth. The flying saucers. Englewood, Colorado, The Author, 1955. 32 p.

Appearance of "flying saucers" in the heavens is said to be according to schedule and in line with God's divine plan: they are the battle chariots of God, destined to play an important part in the destruction of Godless alliances prophesied by Enoch to take place at the second coming of Christ.

Grant, W. V. Men from the moon in America. Dallas, Texas, The Author, [195-] 31 p.

"Space men" who have allegedly contacted certain humans are supernatural beings from an evil (anti-Christ) source and are not from the moon, other planets, or a Russian satellite, the author postulates. Their goal of ruling the world is to be accomplished by deceiving and thereby influencing mankind.

Grant, W. V. Men in the flying saucers identified. Dallas, Tex., The Author, [195-] 32 p.

Author postulates that flying saucers are real and that there are supernatural entities in them; however, he claims that these spirits are demoniac anti-Christ forces attempting to dupe man and take over our world.

Jack, Homer A. Religion and the saucers. Fate, v. 8, Mar. 1955: 20-23.

Discussing the religious implications of flying saucers if they should herald intelligent life on other planets of our sun or of other suns, Dr. Jack says that Christianity would be hardest hit: "... if Christ was born and crucified on these other planets so that those races also could know God..., Christ's life here would lose all divine meaning."

James, Trevor. Scientists, contactees and equilibrium. Flying saucer review, v. 6, Jan.-Feb. 1960: 19-21.

Author suggests that review of stories of persons allegedly contacted by extraterrestrial beings reveals a struggle between Christ and anti-Christ forces. Allegations should be evaluated not so much in the light of whether they are possible or valid but in the light of who contacted these people: were they forces of good or forces of evil?

Jessup, Morris K. UFO and the Bible. New York, Citadel Press, 1956. 126 p.

Book purports to show that (1) there is a causal common denominator for many of the Biblical wonders, and (2) that this common cause is related to the phenomenon of the UFO, both directly and indirectly.

Kleinz, John P. Theology of outer space. Columbia, v. 40, Oct. 1960: 27-28, 36-37.

Reeve, Bryant and Helen Reeve. Flying saucer pilgrimmage. Amherst, Wis., Amherst Press, 1957. 304 p.

Account of two-year private research by authors into UFO phenomenon which involved 23,000 miles of travel to interview individuals claiming contact with extraterrestrial beings. Religious, philosophic, and prophetic implications of UFO appearances are also discussed.

Ribera, Antonio. What happened at Fatima? Flying saucer review, v. 10, Mar. -Apr. 1964: 12-14.

Resumé of the miracle at Fatima, north of Lisbon, Portugal, which extended from May 13 to Oct. 7, 1917, in context of the UFO phenomenon. Author suggests that UFO occupants may present themselves in terms familiar to "contactees, " usually as divine manifestations.

The saucer question. The Catholic digest, v. 16, Oct. 1952: 121.

Father Francis J. Connell, dean of Catholic University's School of Sacred Theology, summarizes the Church's position on the question of invaders from outer space. Theologically speaking, outer space dwellers might fall into four principal classes: (1) they might have received a supernatural destiny from God; (2) God could have created them with a natural but eternal destiny; (3) they might be rational beings who sinned against God but were never given the chance to regain grace; and (4) they might have received supernatural gifts and kept them, leading the paradisical existence of Adam and Eve before they ate the forbidden fruit.

The theology of saucers. Time, v. 60, Aug. 18, 1952: 62.

Father Francis J. Connell, dean of Catholic University's School of Sacred Theology, summarized his church's position on the question of invaders from outer space. He noted that "the principles of [Catholic] faith are entirely reconcilable with even the most astounding possibilities regarding life on other planets. "

Viney, Basil. Invasion from space. The contemporary review, v. 188, Oct. 1955: 257-260.

After briefly reviewing what is known and what is speculated about flying saucers, the author says it does not appear that interplanetary or interstellar or inter-galaxial communication could have any effect on the genuine religious fundamentals. He believes the vision of the being of God would be magnified and that the prospect of human brotherhood on a cosmic scale never before conceived would uplift us from all petty world-parochial quarrels.

UFOs and Time

Another speech by Wilbert B. Smith. Flying saucer review, v. 9, Nov.-Dec. 1963: 11-14.

Author, head of Canadian Project Magnet, imparts information allegedly obtained from extraterrestrial sources that casts serious doubt on validity of some basic concepts of our science and on our ideas of time. He mentions having made "hardware that works" from information given him by extraterrestrial intelligences. Extracts from speech delivered to Vancouver (Canada) Flying Saucer Club in March 1961.

Cadman, A. G. A layman's time and space. Flying saucer review, v. 10, Nov.-Dec. 1964: 19-21.

Theories are advanced regarding time measurement. It is suggested that the penalty or advantage of exceeding the speed of light might be invisibility, and that UFOs could well be vehicles which only become visible when they decelerate from their conventional speed which is greater than the speed of light. Reprinted from June 13, 1964, Sphere.

Cox, Adrian R. A question of time. Flying saucer review, v. 10, Mar.-Apr. 1964: 18-21, 34.

Time is one of the two aspects of speed. Vast distances in space can be minimized by an increase in speed. Are there any limits to speed? This article attempts an answer, and has implications for interstellar flight.

Cox, Adrian. A question of time. Flying saucer review, v. 10, July-Aug. 1964: 7-9.

Time factor in covering interstellar distances is basic reason for unwillingness of scientists to accept existence of interplanetary spacecraft, author postulates. He suggests reasons an advanced extraterrestrial civilization may have surmounted this apparent difficulty.

De Arujo, Hernani Ebecken. Einstein, espaço-tempo. Rio de Janeiro, The Author, 1965. 89 p.

Einstein's "clock paradox" which suggests that at speeds approaching that of light man would travel into the past or into the future is confirmed, according to author, by existence of UFOs whose speed has been clocked on radar as thousands of kilometers an hour. He refers to 11,500 yr.-old cave inscriptions of flying saucers and mother ship discovered in Varzelandia, Brazil, in 1963, and suggests they prove man is travelling or will travel through space-time that is "continuous at four dimensions."

Fouêrê, Rene. Seraient-ils des revenants du futur? Phénomènes spatiaux, June 1966: 11-14.

Author speculates on an explanation for the fact that UFO occupants do not attempt widespread contact with humans: they might be time travelers returning to the past from the future.

Gravity and Anti-gravity

Barker, Gray. Has man conquered gravity? Flying saucers, July-Aug. 1958: 8-11.

Discussion of Otis T. Carr's circular-foil design OTC-X1 aircraft designed for flight to within 1, 000 miles away from earth and to be powered by "utron" energy derived from "natural environmental sources. "

Burridge, Gaston. Townsend Brown and his anti-gravity discs. Fate, v. 11, Nov. 1958: 40-48.

Propulsion principle based on the Biefeld-Brown effect was successfully used by Brown to fly saucer-like discs. Method has definite anti-gravitic potentials.

Cordonnier, Gerard. Polarization de la masse levitation et antigravitation. Phénomènes spatiaux, Sept . 1966: 21-24.

Author suggests that the phenomenon of levitation be investigated in depth for clues as to how the force of gravity is overcome.

Cramp, Leonard G. Space, gravity, and the flying saucer. Introd. by Desmond Leslie. London, T. Werner Laurie, Ltd., 1954. 182 p.

Postulating that UFOs are intelligently controlled extraterrestrial spacecraft, author introduces theory and supporting arguments that they are propelled by a controlled gravitational field.

Edwards, Frank. Frank Edwards' report. Fate, v. 10, Aug. 1957: 51-57.

Notes alleged discovery in 1926 by Dr. Charles F. Bush that the substance lintz basalt seemingly defies the laws of gravity by not accelerating in free fall. Notes that in April of 1957 five major aeronautical companies may have been engaged in anti-gravity research projects. Alleges that the Air Force has a multimillion dollar plant equipped especially for investigation of anti-gravity and counter-gravitational forces. Suggests that research activity relates to determining propulsion mode of UFOs.

Fedi, Remo. Un grande enigma: il mistero dell'attrazione. Clypeus, v. 5, Feb. 1968: 2-6.

Discussion of theories relating to gravitational attraction between celestial bodies.

Sharp, Peter F. A look at gravitation. Flying saucer review, v. 8, July-Aug. 1962: 29-31, 33.

Examination of theories and recent speculation about gravitation as it relates to the UFO phenomenon.

Sykes, Egerton. Negative or contra terrene matter. Atlantis, v. 5, July 1952: 25-29.

Article on the subject of negative mass and whether its properties will neutralize gravity.

Van As, I. A. Anti-gravity: the science of electrogravitics. Flying saucer review, v. 8, Jan.-Feb. 1962: 22-24.

Principle is proposed for an anti-gravity dia-magnetic spacecraft of aluminum and bismuth that would travel along the lines of force of the planets.

Van den Berg, Basil. My discovery will prove Adamski's claim. Flying saucer review, v. 8, Nov.-Dec. 1962: 3-5.

Author claims to have deciphered the hieroglyphics on a photographic plate allegedly given Adamski by Venusians and to have constructed an anti-gravity device based on them.

Veldman, James S. Saucers, gravity, and men. Flying saucers, July-Aug. 1958: 72-76.

Author speculates that the Government may be searching for means to control gravity in effort to develop aircraft whose performance can match the reported behavior of UFOs.

Hollow Earth Theory

Barton, Michael X. Rainbow City and the inner earth people. Los Angeles, Futura Press, 1960. 31 p.

Suggests that legendary Rainbow City--owned by a race of people living inside the earth and used as a base for their flying saucers--is in Antarctica near its eastern coast. Flying saucers in our skies may therefore be coming from inside the earth instead of from other planets.

Beckley, Timothy G. The Shaver mystery and the inner earth. Clarksburg, W. Va., Saucerian Publications, 1967. 118 p.

Review of the Shaver mystery and succinct overview of the whole tradition of underground races.

Bernard, Raymond. Flying saucers from the earth's interior. Joinville, Santa Catarina, Brazil, The Author, [1966?] 89 p.

Author presents evidence from Arctic explorers concerning the existence of a hollow earth with openings at the poles. Admiral Byrd reportedly penetrated this region for 2,300 miles, entering a land of mountains, forests, lakes, rivers, greenery, and animal life.

----- The hollow earth. Mokelumne Hill, Calif., Health Research, 1963. 105 p.

Book purports to present scientific evidence that the earth is hollow with openings at its poles rather than solid with a fiery center of molten metal. It also argues that in earth's interior exists an advanced civilization which is the creator of the flying saucers. Published also in 1964 edition (New York, Distributed by Fieldcrest Pub. Co., 1964).

"Byrd did make North Pole flight in Feb., 1947!"--Giannini. Flying saucers, Feb. 1961: 4-11.

Series of letters between Richard Ogden and Amadeo Giannini, author of
Worlds beyond the Poles discussing whether or not Admiral Byrd actually
flew over the North Pole in February 1947 and whether or not he "penetrated
1,700 miles beyond it."

Dickhoff, Robert E. Agharta. Boston, Bruce Humphries, Inc., 1951. 106 p.

Author asserts that Agharta in central China is one of seven underground cities
built by Martians who had come to colonize earth and later settled by them to
escape radioactivity following an atomic war between Atlantis and Lemuria.
Openings to subterranean tunnels giving access to these cities--and through
which Martian interplanetary spacecraft can still enter and exit--are in Tibet,
Siberia, North and South America, and some remote mountain peaks.

----- Homecoming of the Martians. Ghaziabad, India, Bharti Assn. Publications,
1958. 175 p.

Hidden "mystery cities," above and below the earth could well be the habitat
in which the original earth colonizers, the Martians, live a secluded, protected,
scientific existence, the author suggests. These cities may be Lhasa, Agharta
(Tzangpo Valley, Tibet), and Rainbow City, Antarctica. He believes that
flying saucers are Martian spaceships whose pilots manipulate a power principle
of planetary, magnetic currents. Mankind and its destiny is supervised by
these beings. Book also published by Health Research, Mokelumne Hill, Calif.,
1964.

Emerson, Willis George. The smoky god. New York, Fieldcrest Publishing Co.,
1964. 186 p.

Evidence is presented in support of the hollow earth theory and the existence of
a superior civilization in the earth's interior.

Gardner, Marshall B. A journey to the earth's interior. Aurora, Ill., The Author,
1913. 69 p.

Author expounds the theory of a central sun within the earth's interior.

Gardner, Martin. In the name of science. New York, G. P. Putnam's Sons, 1952.
320 p.

Survey of "quasi-scientific" theories. Chapters are included on the flat and
hollow earth theories, Fortean phenomena, Atlantis and Lemuria, flying
saucers, poltergeist phenomena, and ESP and PK.

Palmer, Ray, ed. The hidden world, No. A-1. Amherst, Wis., Palmer
Publications, 1961. 192 p.

Stories of Richard Shaver, who believes the earth is inhabited underground, in gigantic caves whose area is more extensive than the surface land area, by the "dero"--an idiot people governed by degenerate forces, and the "tero" --who are governed by constructive forces. Both groups are descendants of an immortal Titan-Atlan race that fled earth when the sun started giving off poisonous radiation that caused them to age and then die. Included are: A witch in the night; The tormenting voices; Flight into futility; I enter the caves; A taste of heaven; The living library; I remember Lemuria; Disaster and escape; The ancient alphabet; A dictionary of the Mantong language; Why the caves are secret.

----- Saucers from earth: a challenge to secrecy. Flying saucers, Dec. 1959: 8-21.

Author suggests that the most logical origin for flying saucers is our own earth and that the hollow earth theory, which suggests the interior of the earth is populated by a highly evolved race with great technological skill, merits serious attention.

Shaver, Richard S. The elder world. In Palmer, Ray, ed. The hidden world, No. A-6. Amherst, Wis., Palmer Publications, 1962. p. 964-977.

Lore of the Shaver mystery and life in earth's inner world.

----- Fiction-fact; theory-science. In Palmer, Ray, ed. The hidden world, No. A-5. Amherst, Wis., Palmer Publications, 1962. p. 884-911.

Author expands on his theory that the groups secretly manipulating mankind and world history are the evil "deros" and the beneficent "teros" who reside in caverns inside the earth.

----- How to make a portrait of dero activity. In Palmer, Ray, ed. The hidden world, no. A-8. Amherst, Wis., Palmer Publications, 1962. p. 1349-1353.

Step-by step instructions for obtaining photographic proof of dero activity.

----- In the beginning. In Palmer, Ray, ed. The hidden world, No. A-5. Amherst, Wis., Palmer Publications, 1962. p. 931-949.

Author writes that the first race to inhabit earth was very diverse in form and was the product of intermingling of many extraterrestrial races. This race perished when the sun sent out an unpredicted wave of heat that destroyed all life in our solar system. The second race to inhabit earth, also of extra-terrestrial origin, was the Titan-Atlan under whose rule Atlantis flourished. Destruction of this civilization was by flood.

----- The invisible interview, or, what do you know about flying saucers? In Palmer, Ray, ed. The hidden world, No. A-8. Amherst, Wis., Palmer Publications, 1962. p. 1526-1532.

Relationship between UFOs and their pilots and the "dero" and "tero" is discussed.

Shaver, Richard S. Lo, the wonder of the occult explanation! In Palmer, Ray, ed. The hidden world, No. A-5. Amherst, Wis., Palmer Publications, 1962. p. 912-928.

Article attempts to disprove the existence of spirits and poltergeists as living things of an interpenetrating or co-existent "etherean" world and postulates the existence in caverns within the earth of machines which can be used to produce phenomena similar in every way to spirit phenomena.

----- The lorelei. In Palmer, Ray, ed. The hidden world, No. A-6. Amherst, Wis., Palmer Publications, 1962. p. 978-992.

Greek and Roman myths are interpreted in modern terms. Author postulates that the "gods" existed and were the "front" the cavern people erected between themselves and discovery by the vigorous races that lived on earth's surface early in her history.

----- Mandark...postscript, 1948. In Palmer, Ray, ed. The hidden world, No. A-4. Amherst, Wis., Palmer Publications, 1961. p. 588-632.

Story about the caves under Jerusalem as they exist in modern times-- inhabited by the "deros" and "teros."

----- Return of Sathanas. In Palmer, Ray, ed. The hidden world, No. A-4. Amherst, Wis., Palmer Publications, 1961. p. 663-765.

Legend of Sathanas, generally called Satan, and much of the lore of the "deros" and "teros" and of their life inside the earth.

----- La sorcière. In Palmer, Ray, ed. The hidden world, No. A-5. Amherst, Wis., Palmer Publications, 1962. p. 839-883.

Tale of sorceresses living on the surface of the earth who find ways to be useful to the cavern-dwelling "dero" of the earth's inner world to the detriment of mankind.

----- What I am trying to say. In Palmer, Ray, ed. The hidden world, No. A-16. Amherst, Wis., Palmer Publications, 1964. p. 2695-2700.

Author summarizes what he has tried to accomplish in his writings: (1) explain all early history of man as being wrong deductions based on false premises and give a truer picture of man's past; (2) show what originated the God legend; (3) explain witchcraft; (4) explain spiritualism; (5) show that all religions have been used in the past, are still used, and will be used in the future towards ends of which we have no knowledge or understanding; (6) show that deep in the rock under nearly every nation of earth lie scientific secrets of an "Elder" race which would make "modern" science obsolete; (7) show that modern scientists are obstructed in their work by a class of people resident within the earth to an extent that robs us of 90% of the progress they would bring us; (8) show that our vast wars are started and kept going by these beings; (9) show that age is caused by radioactives thrown off from the sun; and (10) show that all the race called modern man is exploited, fooled, and destroyed, kept from all real progress, by a race that considers them enemies for the most part or cattle.

Wentworth, Jim. Clarifying the Shaver mystery. In Palmer, Ray, ed. The hidden world, No. A-13. Amherst, Wis., Palmer Publications, 1964. p. 2123-2149.

Article summarizes the basic principles of "Shaverism, " which postulates an inner world of evil "deros" and good "teros" who manipulate mankind and world events through use of machines in their possession.

----- Spiritualism and the Shaver mystery. In Palmer, Ray, ed. The hidden world, No. A-8. Amherst, Wis., Palmer Publications, 1962. p. 1404-1415.

Author questions whether all forms of occult or Fortean phenomena could indeed be caused by Shaver's material, flesh-and-blood cavern dwellers and suggests that it is unlikely.

Disappearances

Comella, Tom. Have UFOs "swallowed" our aircraft? Fate, v. 14, May 1961: 32-37.

Master Sergeant O. D. Hill of Project Bluebook allegedly related instances where aircraft being tracked on radar mysteriously disappeared after "merging" with UFOs also being tracked.

The deadly Bermuda triangle. Flying saucer review, v. 10, July-Aug. 1964: 14-17.

Summary of mysterious disappearances of aircraft between 1945 and 1963 in airspace over triangle formed by drawing a line from Florida to Bermuda, from Bermuda to Puerto Rico, and from Florida through the Bahamas.

Disappearances of aeroplanes. LUFORO bulletin, v. 3, Sept. -Oct. 1962: 5-6.

List of aircraft disappearances 1913-1955, giving pilot's name, point of departure, and region of disappearance.

Foss, William O. The missing crew of the airship L-8. Fate, v. 12, Nov. 1959: 74-78.

Two naval aviators disappeared from the USN blimp L-8 on Apr. 18, 1958, while on routine submarine patrol over the California coastline.

Gaddis, Vincent H. [Survey of mysterious disappearances] In his Invisible horizons. Philadelphia, Chilton Co., .1965, p. 161-225.

Describes disappearances of men and aircraft under circumstances that would suggest kidnapping by extraterrestrials.

Sanderson, Ivan T.   The spreading mystery of the Bermuda triangle.
Argosy, v. 367, Aug. 1968: 35-37, 71, 73.

Author discusses a pattern revealed in the disappearance of ships,
planes, and submarines.

Related Subjects

GENERAL REFERENCES

Baker, James. The exteriorization of the mental body. New York, The William-Frederick Press, 1954. 32 p.

A scientific interpretation of the out-of-the-body experience known as pneumakinesis.

Baroja, Julia C. The world of the witches. Chicago, University of Chicago Press, 1964. 313 p.

Examines the question of the nature of reality in a world where there are witches and sorceresses believed to have the power to perform certain acts connected with night, the moon, and nocturnal spirits.

Bessor, John P Mysterious lights of Australia. Fate, v. 6, Aug. 1953: 87-90.

The "min-min light" phenomenon of Australia is described. Characteristically visible only at night, "a huge globe of brilliant light soars up from the wooded horizon, travels rapidly over the treetops for some distance and then hovers, stationary for some time, giving the observer the eerie impression it is watching him."

Cade, Cecil Maxwell. Other worlds than ours. London, Museum Press, 1966. 248 p.

Consideration of possibility and implications of other worlds in space and other worlds in time.

Coates, James. Seeing the invisible. London, New York, Fowler & Co., 1909. 315 p.

Studies in psychometry, thought transference, telepathy, and allied phenomena that attest to reality of forces and powers that cannot be measured by physical means.

Corrall, Alice Enid. Witchcraft: the sixth sense and us, by Justine Glass [pseud.] London, Neville Spearman, 1966. 205 p.

Witches and witchcraft are evaluated in terms of extrasensory perception and as the reservoir of "Know-how" of the psychic faculties. Contact with forces beyond the world of form is suggested as axiomatic.

Da Silva, Renato I. No espaço não estamos sós. São Paulo, Edart, 1966. 213 p.

Theories relating to possibility of life on the moon and other planets are summarized. Parapsychological phenomena of mental telepathy, precognition, ESP, premonition, and astral projection are discussed as they might relate to contact with extraterrestrial entities or intelligences.

Donnelly, Joseph W. Diary of a psychic. Hollywood, Fla., The Author, 1966. 60 p.

Anecdotes and personal experiences of author in the development of extrasensory perception allegedly written under guidance of "spirit mentors." Includes discussion of psychic-occult-UFO matters.

Dunne, John W. An experiment with time. London, Faber and Faber, 1934. 288 p.

Analysis of the "time regress": author proves to his own satisfaction that the human mind, or memory, can move forward in time as well as backward.

Eddington, Arthur S. The nature of the physical world. London, J. M. Dent Sons, 1935. 345 p.

Summary of the philosophy of the new physics: (1) The symbolic nature of the entities of physics is generally recognized and the scheme of physics is formulated in such a way as to make it almost self-evident that it is a partial aspect of something wider; (2) Strict causality is abandoned in the material world; (3) Recognizing that the physical world is entirely abstract and without 'actuality' apart from its linkage to consciousness, we restore consciousness to the fundamental position instead of representing it as an inessential complication occasionally found in the midst of inorganic nature at a late stage of evolutionary history; (4) The sanction for correlating a 'real' physical world to certain feelings of which we are conscious does not seem to differ in any essential respect from the sanction for correlating a spiritual domain to another side of our personality.

Flammarion, Camille. Mysterious psychic forces. Boston, Small, Maynard and Co., 1907. 466 p.

Study of psychical phenomena. Author concludes that man has in himself a fluidic and psychic force whose nature is still unknown, but which is capable of acting at a distance upon matter and of moving the same. This force, the expression of our will, is both psychical and physical.

----- The unknown. New York and London, Harper & Bros., 1900. 487 p.

A collection of psychic facts that shows that we live in the midst of an invisible world in which forces are at work of which we know very little. There are mental transmissions, communications of thoughts, and psychic currents between human souls. We may see without eyes and hear without ears "not by unnatural excitement of our sense of vision or of hearing, ... but by some interior sense, psychic and mental."

Fuller, Curtis. A psychiatrist looks at psychic doubles. Fate, v. 12, Jan. 1959: 67-75.

The psychic double (autoscopic phenomenon) is defined in medical terms by Dr. Narcyz Lukianowicz of Barry Hospital, Bristol, England, as a "complex psycho-sensorial hallucinatory perception of one's own body image projected into external visual space." Detailed studies of phenomenon appeared in August 1958 issue of Archives of Neurology and Psychiatry.

Geier, Chester S. Ghost light of Hornet. Fate, v. 9, Apr. 1956: 58-61.

A strange luminous glow that appears each night in the Joplin-Neosho area of Missouri and that defies scientific explanation is described.

Geley, Gustave. From the unconscious to the conscious. New York and London, Harper & Bros., 1921. 327 p.

Interpretation of the evolution of the individual and the universe. Continuous development of the conscious is postulated as an evolutionary fact; this conscious, grown to its full stature, will be able to transcend all its limitations, to attain what is now inaccessible, to understand what is now incomprehensible.

Giannini, Amadeo. Worlds beyond the poles. New York, Vantage Press, 1959. 218 p.

Author attempts to prove his contention that there are no northern or southern limits to the earth; celestial land areas appearing "up" or out from the earth constitute physical land routes from the earth to every land area of the universe.

Hampton, Wade T. How to hypnotize by telepathy. Fate, v. 9, Nov. 1956: 88-94.

Tests indicate that a subject may be entranced by mental command.

----- Mystery of hypnotic "ecstacy." Fate, v. 10, Jan. 1957: 94-99.

Discussion of the "visions" of ecstatics and the bearing that the phenomenon might have on the existence of a "spirit world" and on communication with beings on another plane of existence.

Kapp, R. O. Toward a unified cosmology. New York, Basic Books, 1960. 303 p.

Hypothesis is defended that the laws of physics are not restrictive in the sense in which laws in statute books are. The laws of physics, it is claimed, neither require nor prohibit any specific number, event, condition, property, configuration, or other feature. They permit everything to occur that is logically consistent with all observable facts and that is, in this sense, logically possible. It is shown that our understanding of gravitation is more defective than that of most natural phenomena and eight questions of major significance are listed to which answers cannot yet be provided.

Krafft, Carl F. Ether and matter. Richmond, Va. Dietz Printing Co., 1945. 117 p.

Defending the dynamic ether and vortex atom theory, the author believes that all phenomena of the physical universe are only different manifestations of the various modes of motion of the all-pervading ether. He refers to the panpsychic doctrine that the consciousness has its origin in the ether. The ether would then be the common substrate of both mind and matter and would have psychical as well as physical attributes, both of which would be governed by similar or analogous laws and principles.

Last, Cecil E. Man in the universe. London, Werner Laurie, 1954. 166 p.

The universe is conceived as a non-mechanical reality. In association with such a universe, the idea is elaborated that mind is the supreme factor in the economy of the universe and that matter is derived from consciousness and not consciousness from matter, in accordance with the suggestions of Jean, de Broglie, and Planck, supported by Einstein and Schrodinger.

Lawrence, Lincoln. Were we controlled? New Hyde Park, N. Y., University Books, 1967. 173 p.

Evidence is presented indicating that Lee Harvey Oswald and Jack Ruby played the roles of mere robots and were manipulated without their knowledge through a new technique of mental programming called R.H.I.C. and E.D.O.M. (Radio-Hypnotic Intracerebral Control and Electronic Dissoultion of Memory).

Loftin, Bob. Spooksville's ghost lights. Tulsa, Okla., The Author, 1967. 28 p.

Compilation of stories, news items, and testimonials concerning strange "lights in the sky" seen at Spooksville, 11 miles southwest of Joplin, Mo.

Mamontoff, Nicholas. Can thoughts have form? Fate, v. 13, June 1960: 41-46.

Experiment is described in which a thought form (egrigor) - a red-haired cat wearing Russian boots - was created through intense concentration by psychic researchers. It is suggested that many cases of "visions" are actually egrigors.

Manning, Henry P. The fourth dimension simply explained. New York, Dover Publications, 1960. 251 p.

A collection of essays selected from those submitted in the Scientific American's prize competition.

Miller, E. C. Correspondence: ethics and space travel. Spaceflight, v. 4, July 1962: 139.

With the a priori assumption that intelligent extraterrestrial life may exist, three statements of ethical conduct are urged for discussion and adaptation: (1) no contact would be made with intelligent life not possessing spaceflight capability; (2) no sectarian or belligerent views or acts would be made without common understanding; (3) no artifact or specimen not within the technical competence of both parties would be exchanged.

O'Brien, Barbara. Operators and things: the inner life of a schizophrenic. Cambridge, Arlington Books, Inc. [1959] 166 p.

In her effort to understand how she suddenly entered a world of hallucinatory characters in which the reasoning mechanism had been fogged and the unconscious mind was in control, the author presents an account of our present state of knowledge and ignorance about schizophrenia. Account has same similarities to reports by UFO "contactees."

Oehler, Pauline. The psychic photography of Ted Serios. Fate, v. 15, Dec. 1962: 67-82.

Ted Serios has apparent ability to produce photographs of places he has never been, never seen, and of which he has no previous knowledge under strictly controlled conditions that preclude fraud.

Parkes, A. S. and A. U. Smith. Transport of life in the frozen or dried state. British medical journal, May 16, 1959: 1295-1297.

Pendergast, R. Terrestrial and cosmic polygenism. Downside review, v. 82, July 1964: 189-198.

Pierce, J. R. Relativity and space travel. Institute of Radio Engineers, Proceedings, v. 47, June 1959: 1053-1061.

Puri, Omananda. The boy and the brothers. London, Victor Gallancz Ltd., 1959. 303 p.

An allegedly factual account of a young man who, while in a trance state-- apparently "possessed" by superior "beings" or entities--performed miracles of healing and served as an evangelist.

Rampa, T. Lobsang. The third eye. Garden City, N. Y., Doubleday & Co., 1956. 256 p.

Case in which a Tibetan entity allegedly took possession of the body of Cyril Hoskin so that he lost all memory of his past life and had instead the full memory of a Tibetan from babyhood onwards. Novel is the account of the controlling entity's life in a lamasery and psychic powers imparted to him by opening of the "third eye."

Ross, John C. Dr. Hyden's psychic horror drug. Fate, v. 14, Aug. 1961: 25-27.

Dr. Holger Hyden, professor of histology at the University of Göteborg, Sweden, has discovered a tasteless drug--tricyano-amino-propene (TAP)--that can be

Rowland, John. Mysteries of science. London, Werner Laurie, 1955. 214 p.

The problem considered is whether science as a whole really has limitations which are inherent in the very nature of science itself and, if so, what these limitations actually are. Also discussed is the corollary problem of deciding what part of human life and thought can be expected to deal adequately with those things which lie well outside the scientific sphere. The UFO phenomenon is cited as an example of the real reluctance on the part of orthodox scientists to examine facts that lie outside the more or less arbitrary limits of ordinary scientific investigations.

Shirley, Ralph. The mystery of the human double: the case for astral projection. New Hyde Park, N. Y., University Book, 1965. 189 p.

Postulating that the physical body and the consciousness are separable, book deals with both the voluntary and involuntary exteriorization of the etheric body and treats the methods which have been adopted for the etheric body to leave the physical body at will and the value of the results so obtained.

Stumbough, Virginia. Fairies were real. Fate, v. 10, Nov. 1957: 83-90.

Author claims that fairies did live, that they were the last of the Neolithic peoples in Europe. Short, stocky, dark-skinned, they came from the region of the Mediterranean, were dominant in Europe for 500 years and had disappeared as a pure race by the end of the Middle Ages. Dr. Margaret Murray's The God of the Witches (London, Faber and Faber, 1952) is one of the sources.

Tassi, Dan. The mind and time and space. Philadelphia, Dorrance & Co., 1962. 114 p.

Proposes thesis that time and space are not limitations to extrasensory perception; all knowledge and information within the universe throughout eternity is therefore available to consciousness with proper prodding inside the mind. Discusses how these concepts were applied to the study of the planets and describes experiments in which the evolutionary history of a given planet was sought by the experimenter from a subject under hypnosis.

Thornton, Ronald C. The unified field: an extension of the general theory of relativity to date. Oxford, England, Vincent-Baxter Press, 1951. 23 p.

Explanation of how the unified field theory collates every single occurence of any type in one unitary conception. Author asserts that such a unity is the true nature of the universe.

Tyrrell, George N. Apparitions. London, Gerald Duckworth & Co., 1953. 172 p.

Reformulates in a concrete and detailed manner the theory that apparitions are telepathic hallucinations and attempts to meet the obvious objections to it.

Velikovsky, Immanuel. Worlds in collision. Garden City, N. Y., Doubleday & Co., 1950. 401 p.

Author's research among the ancient records of man ranging from unequivocal statements in written documents, through remembrances expressed in myth and legend, to archeological evidence in the form of obsolete calendars and sundials led him to a three-fold thesis: (1) there were global catastrophes in historical times; (2) these catastrophes were caused by extraterrestrial agents; and (3) these agents, in the most recent of catastrophes, can be identified as the planets Venus and Mars, Venus playing the dominant role.

Warder, George Woodward. The cities of the sun. New York, G. W. Dillingham, 1901. 320 p.

Argues that the suns of the universe are not hot or burning globes but are self-luminous perfected worlds--the personal residence of Diety and the future abode of man. Housed in the "heavenly mansions and beautiful cities" of the sun are the former citizens of the solar planets, including earth's departed spirits.

Wilkins, G. Hubert and Harold M. Sherman. Thoughts through space. New York, Creative Age Press, 1942. 421 p.

Authenticated record of the Wilkins-Sherman experiments in long-distance telepathy.

Young, John R. The negative universe. Fate, v. 11, Apr. 1958: 87-89.

Hypothesizes that intelligent beings may exist in a "negative universe" that interpenetrates and coexists with ours without our being conscious of it. Suggests that this might explain poltergeist manifestations and flying saucers.

Younghusband, Francis. Life in the stars. London, John Murray, 1927. 222 p.

An exposition of the view that on some planets of some stars exist beings that are higher on the evolutionary scale than man and that on one of them exists "the supreme embodiment of the eternal spirit which animates the whole."

Zubek, T. J. Theological questions on space creatures. American ecclesiastical review, v. 145, Dec. 1961: 393-399.

Churchward, James. Cosmic forces as they were taught in Mu. New York, The
   Author, 1934. 246 p.

   Translations of fragments of the "Sacred Inspired Writings--Scientific Section"
   written over 70,000 years ago on the lost continent of Mu.

----- The lost continent of Mu. New York, Ives Washburn, 1931. 335 p.

   Information about Mu based on translations of two sets of ancient tablets:
   (1) the Naacal tablets discovered in India, and (2) stone tablets discovered by
   William Niven in Mexico. Some of the subjects embodied are an account of
   the creation in minute detail; life and its origin; the origin and workings of
   the "four Great Cosmic Forces," and the creation of woman. Author asserts
   that both sets of tablets establish that at one time earth had an ancient civilization which was superior to our own and far in advance of us in important
   essentials.

----- The sacred symbols of Mu. New York, I. Washburn, 1939. 296 p.

   Evidence is presented that all religions have common origin in Lemuria's
   sacred writings: Moses condensed "The 42 Questions" of the Osirian religion
   into our Ten Commandments; the Lord's Prayer and our Proverbs are in
   the sacred writings of Mu.

De Camp, L. Sprague. Lost continents: the Atlantis theme in history, science, and
   literature. New York, Gnome Press, 1954. 362 p.

   Legends concerning Atlantis, Mu, and other "lost continents" are explored and
   the literature concerning the topic, including fiction, analyzed.

Donnelly, Ignatius. Atlantis: the antediluvian world. New York, Gramercy
   Publishing Co., 1949. 355 p.

   An attempt to demonstrate several propositions: (1) that there once existed in
   the Atlantic Ocean, opposite the mouth of the Mediterranean Sea, a large
   island--the remnant of an Atlantic continent--known to the ancient world as
   Atlantis; (2) that the description of this island given by Plato is not fable but
   history; (3) that Atlantis was the region where man first rose from a state of
   barbarism to civilization; (4) that the gods and goddesses of the ancient Greeks,
   the Phoenicians, the Hindus, and the Scandinavians were simply the kings,
   queens, and heroes of Atlantis--the acts attributed to them being a confused
   recollection of real historical events; (5) that the mythologies of Egypt and
   Peru represented the original religion of Atlantis, which was sun-worship;
   (6) that the oldest colony formed by the Atlanteans was probably Egypt, whose
   civilization was a reproduction of that of the Atlantic island; (7) that the
   implements of the Bronze Age were derived from Atlantis and that the
   Atlanteans were the first manufacturers of iron; (8) that the Phoenician alphabet,

parent of all the European alphabets, was derived from an Atlantis alphabet; (9) that Atlantis perished in a terrible convulsion of nature, in which the whole island was submerged by the ocean with nearly all its inhabitants; and (10) that a few persons escaped in ships and on rafts, and carried to the nations east and west the tidings of the catastrophe, which has survived to our own time in the Flood and Deluge legends of the different nations of the Old and New worlds.

Globe, H. C. Atlantis sank later than you think. Fate, v. 10, Aug. 1957: 19-24.

Records indicating that some remnants of the Atlantean continent may have existed near the Arctic Circle as late as the 16th century are cited by the author. He also suggests that the Greek navigator Pythias, the only man to sail to the North Country between 400 B. C. and 500 A. D., witnessed the final death throes of the sinking Atlantis.

Murray, Jacqueline. Flying saucers and Atlantis. Flying saucer review, v. 5, May-June 1959: 18-19, 25.

Author postulates that certain beings who had been incarnate on the planet Venus elected to reincarnate on earth to assist with its evolution and thus started the civilization of Atlantis. When Atlantis was destroyed by cataclysms, these Venusians may have been evacuated by flying saucers.

Oliver, Frederick S. A dweller on two planets, or The dividing of the way by Phylos the Tibetan. Los Angeles, Baumgardt Publishing Co., 1905. 423 p.

High attainments of the Atlanteans before engulfment of their continent are discussed. Rediscovery of Atlantean secrets is predicted and it is promised that mankind will surpass Atlantis' greatness. Phylos the Tibetan allegedly dictates manuscript telepathically to author.

Palmer, Ray, ed. The hidden world, No. A-1. Amherst, Wis., Palmer Publications, 1961. 192 p.

Stories of Richard Shaver, who believes the earth is inhabited underground, in gigantic caves whose area is more extensive than the surface land area, by the "dero"--an idiot people governed by degenerate forces, and the "tero"--who are governed by constructive forces. Both groups are descendants of an immortal Titan-Atlan race that fled earth when the sun starting giving off poisonous radiation that caused them to age and then die. Included are: A witch in the night; The tormenting voices; Flight into futility; I enter the caves; A taste of heaven; The living library; I remember Lemuria; Disaster and escape; The ancient alphabet; A dictionary of the Mantong language; Why the caves are secret.

MIRACLE AT FATIMA

Alexander, M. UFO - seen by 60,000 witnesses. Flying saucers from other worlds, May 1958: 83-85.

It is speculated that a silvery disc viewed by a crowd of 60,000 on October 13, 1917, at Fatima, Portugual, concomitant with appearance of a vision of the Virgin Mary, was a UFO. Reprinted from <u>Flying Saucer Review</u>.

Inglefield, Gilbert S. Fatima: the three alternatives. Flying saucer review, v. 10, May-June 1964: 5-6.

Events at Fatima, Portugal, on Oct. 13, 1917, must have one of three explanations, claims the author: (1) the dancing sun was a phenomenon that science can explain; (2) it was a pure miracle; or, (3) it was due to UFO intervention either on its own or with the liaison of Christian agency.

Ribera, Antonio. What happened at Fatima? Flying saucer review, v. 10, Mar.-Apr. 1964: 12-14.

Resumé of the miracle at Fatima, north of Lisbon, Portugal, which extended from May 13 to Oct. 13, 1917, in context of the UFO phenomenon. Author suggests that UFO occupants may present themselves in terms familiar to "contactees," usually as divine manifestations.

Stone, Fred P. The visions at Fatima and the flying saucers. Australian saucer record, v. 2, Second quarter, 1956: 7-11.

Author expresses his views of the remarkable similarity between the account of the miracle at Fatima, Portugal, on Oct. 13, 1917, and descriptions given by eye witnesses all over the world of flying saucer sightings.

Walsh, William T. Our Lady of Fatima. New York, Macmillan, 1947. 227 p.

Three shepherd children from Serra da Aire, Portugal, reported six times in 1917 that they had seen a circular globe of light descend from the heavens and had spoken with a lady--later thought to be the Virgin Mary--who had stepped from inside it.

POLTERGEISTS

Cade, C. Maxwell. A long, cool look at alien intelligence: It's all in the mind. Flying saucer review, v. 14, Mar.-Apr. 1968: 7-9.

Author suggests the possibility that UFOs and poltergeists are among phenomena which could be "experienced," with completely convincing realism, due to effects of electromagnetic fields. He also suggests that this electromagnetic radiation could be either terrestrial or extraterrestrial in origin; it could be either a stochastic natural process or the planned product of an alien intelligence.

Fodor, Nandor. On the trail of the poltergeist. New York, Citadel Press, 1958. 222 p.

Poltergeist manifestations are believed by author to be due to profound cleavage of personality in which part of the mental system is "torn loose, " like a disembodied entity, but is still capable of personality development, as any autonomous complex would be, though on a different, apparently fourth-dimentional plane of activity.

Owen, A. R. G. Can we explain the poltergeist? New York, Garrett Publications, 1964. 436 p.

Various mutually exclusive possible approaches to the ' supernatural" are discussed. The viewpoint adopted for poltergeist happenings is that of regular naturalism, which seeks to explain phenomena in terms of processes which operate in conjuction with, and without nullifying, known laws of nature. No evidence is found in poltergeist cases reviewed to support assumption that any role is played by a discarnate entity or "spirit" other than at most an extension of the personality of the "medium. " Data suggest that poltergeist activity is a "psychic" phenomenon in the sense of being associated with the higher human brain centers when these are not fully inhibited by sleep, nor deranged by epileptiform discharge, nor imperfectly developed as in mental defect. The association with adolescence may be psychological rather than directly physiological.

Windes, V. M. Flying rocks and bouncing lights in Llano, New Mexico. Fate, v. 20, Nov. 1967: 96-99.

Account of apparent poltergeist phenomena accompanied by bouncing bluish or grayish lights about the size of a golf ball.

PROPHESIES

Barton, Michael X. D-day seers speak. Los Angeles. Futura Press, 1959. 35 p.

Describes a "sudden, catastrophic cleansing" of earth due to take place before the end of the 20th century and marked by the shift of the earth upon its axis.

----- The seven golden prophesies. Los Angeles, Futura Press, 1960. 30 p.

Book is based on treatise Comte de Gabalis by French mystic Abbé de Villars. Interprets prophesies of world peace by (1) the Magi; (2) the Sibylline oracles; (3) Enoch; (4) Micah; (5) Elder Edda; (6) Isaiah; and (7) Merlin the Magician.

----- The weeping angel prediction. Los Angeles, Futura Press, 1964. 32 p.

An angel in a picture in Worthing, England is reported (1961) to "weep. " Author suggests that manifestation is a sign to humanity--comparable to sightings of flying saucers--that "the One who is presenting the phenomenon. . .will have revealed himself to the universe through a process of nuclear evolution" by 1967.

Barton, Michael X. Your part in the great plan. Los Angeles, Futura Press, 1960. 30 p.

Discusses what man's purpose is and how he may fulfill it. Suggests that we are now living at the end of an age and predicts that earth will undergo big geological changes.

Brown, Hugh A. The coming Antarctica disaster. Fate, v. 9, May 1956: 28-34.

Author believes that Antarctic ice, growing at the rate of seven trillion tons a year, may cause the earth to career on its axis, causing floods that will engulf the continents.

Cleary-Baker, John. UFOs and the Antarctic icecap. BUFORA journal and bulletin, v. 1, Summer 1965: 14-16.

Critique of theory that growth of the icecap at the South Pole will cause the axis of the earth to tilt, resulting in a worldwide flood. (UFOs are said by some to be in our skies to serve as a rescue squad during this catastrophe.)

Cleaver, A. V. Astronautics--its development during the second century of the RAeS (1966-2066). The aeronautical journal, v. 72, May 1968: 373-384.

Forecasting the course of astronautics in the next 100 years, the author predicts: "By AD 2066, I would expect to find many hundreds, and probably thousands, of men and women living semipermanently on the Moon, Mars... on the moons of Jupiter and Saturn, and in large orbiting space stations."

Stumbough, Virginia. The coming West Coast disaster. Fate, v. 16, June 1963: 40-47.

Psychics predict that catastrophic earthquakes and tidal waves are due on the West Coast, along the Andreas Fault, anytime from the present to 1999.

TELEPORTATION

Creighton, Gordon. Teleportations. Flying saucer review, v. 11, Mar.-Apr. 1965: 14-16.

Examination of some of the evidence in cases in which a UFO may have picked a person up in one place and set him down again elsewhere.

Fodor, Nador. Mind over space: the mystery of teleportation; apported through disintegration. Fate, v. 10, Feb. 1957: 87-93.

Fourth dimensional theory is advanced to explain the vanishing and reappearing of both living and inanimate objects with complete disregard for material and spatial barriers: aported objects are, by an act of will on the part of the operators, disintegrated into their molecular elements without altering form, then passed through the interstices of matter that would normally block penetration, and reintegrated by a second exercise of the power of the will.

Fodor, Nador. Mind over space: the mystery of teleportation; borne by the poltergeist. Fate, v. 9, Sept. 1956: 79-96.

Mysterious appearances and re-appearances attributed to poltergeists.

----- Mind over space: the mystery of teleportation; carried by the devil. Fate, v. 9, Aug. 1956: 89-96.

Account of medieval belief in the devil's role in teleportation.

----- Mind over space: the mystery of teleportation; conveyed by spirits. Fate, v. 9, Oct. 1956: 85-96.

The poltergeist as the agent in teleportation.

----- Mind over space: the mystery of teleportation; falling into the fourth dimension. Fate, v. 9, Dec. 1956: 84-95.

Instances are cited where individuals were apparently translated into another space-time dimension.

----- Mind over space: the mystery of teleportation. Fate, v. 9, Apr. 1956: 81-91.

Passages in the Bible are cited which might be considered accounts of teleportation.

----- Mind over space: the mystery of teleportation; kidnapped by fairies. Fate, v. 9, July 1956: 82-87.

Case of levitation and teleportation attributed to fairies.

----- Mind over space: the mystery of teleportation; Mrs. Guppy and the "apport post." Fate, v. 10, May 1957: 88-94.

Discussion of circumstances surrounding teleportation of Mrs. Guppy on June 23, 1871, over a three-mile distance in England.

----- Mind over space: the mystery of teleportation; shifted through dematerialization. Fate, v. 10, Mar. 1957: 82-91.

Cases of teleportation of the human body are cited.

Fodor, Nador. Mind over space: the mystery of teleportation; snatched up in the spirit net. Fate, v. 10, June 1957: 93-98.

Account of instances where psychic mediums were apparently carried from place to place by "beings from the spirit world. "

----- Mind over space: the mystery of teleportation; spirits--or the unconscious? Fate, v. 10, Aug. 1957: 89-108.

Discussion of whether a genuine mystery is concealed behind ancient and modern records of teleportation or whether all is myth, illusion, and fraud.

----- Mind over space: the mystery of teleportation; the flight of Mrs. Guppy. Fate, v. 10, Apr. 1957: 90-98.

A remarkable instance of human teleportation took place on June 23, 1871, in London, when a Mrs. Guppy was teleported over a distance of three miles.

----- Mind over space: the mystery of teleportation; the marquis vanishes. Fate, v. 10, July 1957: 89-98.

Teleportation of a medium during a seance is described.

----- Mind over space: the mystery of teleportation; transported by ecstacy. Fate, v. 9, June 1956: 89-96.

Records of teleportation in 14th-18th century historical documents are cited.

----- Mind over space: the mystery of teleportation; traveling by magic. Fate, v. 9, May 1956: 87-94.

References to teleportation in pre-Christian mythology are cited.

Sanderson, Ivan T. Atta the telepathic teleporting ant. Fate, v. 16, May 1963: 45-52.

Teleportation of the huge queen from one cell in the community to another in an emergency is apparently possible to the Atta ant. Experiments in which the queen was marked with dye sprayed on in an intricate pattern seem to confirm this.

TUNGUSKA METEORITE

Barker, Gray. Chasing the flying saucers. Flying saucers, Oct. 1959: 20-30.

Mentions theory of Prof. B. Liapunov of the U. S. S. R. Academy of Science that a "cosmic ship" intended to land in Mongolia crashed in Siberia because of mechanical difficulties. Statement was made after analysis of report by 1957 Russian expedition to site of devastating explosion (1908) previously thought to be caused by big meteor impact.

Dempster, Derek. Does Siberia hold the proof? Flying saucer review, v. 8, Jan.-Feb. 1962: 4-6.

Summarizes the history of the Tungus (Siberia) meteorite of June 30, 1908--widely thought to be a nuclear-powered spacecraft--and reports the latest news on the subject from the U. S. S. R.

Edwards, Frank. Did a space ship explode over Siberia? Fate, v. 12, Oct. 1959: 44-51.

On the basis of a 1958 scientific expedition to the Tunguska region of Siberia, Soviet scientist Alexander Kazantsev has developed the theory that the 1908 explosion there was an atomic-powered spacecraft which disintegrated at an altitude of 1.2 miles.

Kazantsev, Alexander. Gosti iz kosmosa [Guests from space] Moscow, Moskovskii Rabochii, 1963. 612 p.

A collection of science-fiction stories which present Kazantsev's ideas of purported invaders from other planets. A series of 23 photographs is included mostly of paintings on rocks found in the Sahara Desert, one from Delhi, and three from Siberia which show the fallen trees following the Tunguska catastrophe which the author claims was caused by a nuclear explosion or by an extraterrestrial space ship.

----- The Martian. In A visitor from outer space, science fiction stories by Soviet writers; Violet L. Dutt, translator. Moscow, Foreign Languages Publishing House, 1961, p. 149-162.

Fiction. An electronic computer deciphers the diary written on earth by a Martian left behind when his spacecraft exploded in the Tunga taiga, Siberia, on June 30, 1908.

----- A visitor from outer space. In A visitor from outer space, science fiction stories by Soviet writers; Violet L. Dutt, translator. Moscow, Foreign Languages Publishing House, 1961, p. 110-148.

Fiction. Exploits the hypothesis of an extraterrestrial spacecraft explosion in Tunga, Siberia, on June 30, 1908. While many scientists believe that devastation of a forest there over an area with a radius of about 50 kilometers was due to explosion of a bolide, the meteor was not recovered and no crater was discovered.

Ley, Willy. The wheels of Poseidon; and Too much imagination. In For your information: on earth and in the sky. New York, Doubleday & Co., 1967. p. 69-88, 157-168.

A phenomenon is described that occurs in the Indian Ocean and that has been described by several eyewitnesses: a pulsating near-circular disturbance roughly 1,000-1,500 feet in diameter is seen with streaks of light like the beams of a searchlight radiating from its center and revolving counter-clockwise. Views are given supporting speculation that the Podkamennaya Tunguska meteorite of Central Siberia (1908) was in fact an exploded extra-terrestrial spacecraft.

Plekanov, G. F. and others. O vliiamii vzryva tungusskogo meteorita na geomagni-tnoe pole. [The effect of the Tunguska meteorite explosion on the magnetic field]. Geologiya i geofizika, no. 6, 1961: 94-96.

Analysis of magnetograms shows that the fall of the Tunguska meteorite on June 30, 1908, produced magnetic effects similar to those that would be produced by a nuclear explosion. English translation published December 1961 by U. S. Joint Publications Research Service, its translation JPRS: 11608.

Report from the Soviet Union: Did the Tungus meteorite contain anti-matter? Flying saucers, Dec. 1966: 29-30.

Hypothesis to the effect that the Tungus meteorite "explosion" on the Siberian taiga in 1908 was the result of annihilation of anti-matter has been supported in article by Soviet specialists Konstantinov, Bredov, Beliavsky, and Sokolov, printed in the Cosmic Research Bulletin.

Sharp, P. F. The search for life beyond the earth. Flying saucer review, v. 7, Nov.-Dec. 1961: 12-15.

Arguments are advanced on the possibility of life existing throughout the galaxy; ways in which man can attempt to detect it positively are suggested. Mentions that the Tunguska meteorite of 1908 may have been an exploded extraterrestrial spacecraft.

Tungusskoe divo [Tunguska wonder]. Tekhnika molodezhni, no. 2, 1966: 10-13.

Summary of opinions expressed by reputable Russian scientists regarding the Tunguska explosion; a map shows the devasted area. The consensus is that the explosion was neither a meteorite nor a comet but an unknown phenomenon resembling a nuclear blast.

Zigel'. Felix Yu. Iadernii yzryv [Nuclear explosion over the taiga]. Znaniye-sila, Dec. 1961: 24-27.

Evidence is presented to support author's view that the cause of the explosion in the Tunguska taiga on June 30, 1908, could not have been a meteorite, not even one of very great mass.

Zigel', Felix Yu. Manevr tungusskogo tela [Maneuvering of the Tunguska object].
Smena, Feb. 1967: 30.

Summary of a lecture delivered by the author before the Sternberg State
Astronomical Institute's Section on Interstellar Communications. Author
cites testimony of a number of witnesses that shortly before the Tunguska
explosion, the object made a 90° turn, corroborating his theory that the
Tunguska body was artificial.

----- Pocherk tungsskogo vzryva [Handwriting of the Tunguska explosion]. Smena,
No. 10, May 1966: 22-25.

In the article the author shows and compares three microbarograms: one from
a chemical explosion, one from a nuclear explosion, and that from the
Tunguska explosion. He states that the microbarogram of the Tunguska
explosion is unlike that of the first two. He concludes that the Tunguska
explosion was not caused by a meteorite or by a comet. He speculates whether
the Tunguska object may be an artificial or man-made body, anti-matter, or a
spaceship from another planet.

Selected Fiction

Angelucci, Orfeo. Son of the sun. Los Angeles, DeVorss & Co., 1959. 211 p.

Imaginative account of experiences among Alpha Centaurians spiritually, morally, technologically superior to earthmen and of trip into sun's interior on one of their spacecraft.

Asimov, Isaac. The naked sun. New York, Doubleday & Co., 1957. 187 p.

Science-fiction detective mystery. Earth has come under the domination of underpopulated, roboticized, powerful "Outer Worlds." A member of the New York City police force becomes the first earthman to set foot on another planet when he is invited to help solve a political murder.

----- The stars, like dust. Garden City, New York, Doubleday & Co., 1951. 218 p.

Science fiction involving a plot to overthrow the race that has subjugated all planets in 50 galaxies, including earth.

----- Triangle. Garden City, New York, Doubleday & Co., 1952. 516 p.

Three science fiction stories: The currents of space; Pebble in the sky; and The stars. All concern the machinations of aggressive civilizations bent on conquering the planets inhabited by humans in all the galaxies.

Bott, Henry A. Is there life on earth? Fate, v. 15, Oct. 1962: 64-71.

Fiction. The Martian Academy of Science presents arguments on "The Improbability of Life on Earth."

Burroughs, Edgar Rice. At the earth's core; Pellucidar; Tanar of Pellucidar. New York, Dover Publications, 1963. 433 p.

Three science fiction novels based on the "hollow earth" theory and describing an inner world 500 miles beneath earth's crust--accessible through openings at the poles--where evolution of flora and fauna progressed somewhat differently than on earth's surface.

Burroughs, Edgar Rice. Carson of Venus. New York, Canaveral Press, 1963. 312 p.

Fiction. Adventures of an American, Carson Napier, on Venus as allegedly narrated telepathically to author. In a country called Korva, Carson helps depose a mad dictator. First published by Edgar Rice Burroughs, Inc., Tarzana, Calif., in 1938.

----- Escape on Venus. Tarzana, Calif., Edgar Rice Burroughs, Inc., 1946. 347 p.

Fiction. Further adventures of Carson Napier of California on Venus during which he and his mate are captured successively by several subhuman tribes.

----- The gods of Mars. New York, Canaveral Press, 1962. 348 p.

Science-fantasy adventure. Captain John Carter of Virginia, miraculously teleported to Mars, finds himself among peoples whose evolution passed by degrees from true plant life to a combination of plant and animal.

----- John Carter and the giant of Mars. New York, Canaveral Press, 1964. 208 p.

In final volume of Martian science-fantasy series, John Carter of Virginia, former Confederate officer, successfully copes with the wicked machinations of a synthetic man. In Skeleton Men of Jupiter, he foils the warlike race on that planet that is bent on conquering Mars and enslaving its population.

----- Llana of Gathol. Tarzana, Calif., Edgar Rice Burroughs, Inc., 1948. 317 p.

Four loosely intertwined science-fiction novelettes about Mars, a dying planet on which natural resources have almost vanished and where air and water are barely sufficient to meet the requirements of the population.

----- The master mind of Mars. New York, Grosset & Dunlap, 1929. 312 p.

Science fiction. Capt. Ulysses Paxton, U.S. Army, finds himself on Mars in his astral body. He is forced to serve a mad surgeon who has learned to transfer successfully the brain of one individual to the brain pan of another.

----- Pirates of Venus. New York, Canaveral Press, 1962. 314 p.

Science-fantasy adventure. Carson Napier, son of an English officer and his American wife, takes off from Guadalupe Island, Mexico, for Mars in a rocket ship he personally constructed. Through an error in calculation, he lands on Venus instead.

Burroughs, Edgar Rice. A princess of Mars. New York, Dover Publications, 1964. 356 p.

Science-fantasy adventure in which John Carter of Virginia, former Confederate officer, is miraculously transported to the planet Barsoom (Mars) and through a series of daring military exploits becomes a prince of the leading city and marries its princess.

----- Synthetic men of Mars. Tarzana, Calif., Edgar Rice Burroughs, Inc., 1940. 315 p.

A brilliant but mad Martian surgeon attempts to create artificial life. He succeeds, but produces only monsters, who revolt and attempt to take over the entire planet. John Carter of Virginia, who has been teleported to Mars, sees to it that "good" triumphs.

----- Tales of three planets. New York, Canaveral Press, 1964. 282 p.

Three science-fantasy adventure novelettes. Beyond the Farthest Star relates the adventures of Tangor, an American shot down behind the German lines in 1939, who awakens to find himself on the planet Poloda. A man from 50,000 B.C. is restored to life from a frozen condition and searches for his lost sweetheart in The Resurrection of Jimber-Jaw. The Wizard of Venus relates the adventures of Carson Napier who landed on that planet accidentally while enroute to Mars from the U.S. and outwits a sorcerer who allegedly turns Venusians into cattle.

----- Three Martian novels. New York, Dover Publications, 1962. 499 p.

Science-fantasy adventure. John Carter, a Confederate officer mustered out of service at the close of the Civil War, is miraculously tele-transported to the planet Mars where he encounters strange races of men and beasts, weird nations and weirder peoples.

Campbell, John W. The mightiest machine. Providence, R. I., Hadley Publishing Co., 1935. 228 p.

Mighty spaceships move at speeds faster than light from star system to star system, warping themselves through another dimension at the whim of Aarn Munro, a mental and physical superman, descendant of earthmen raised on the surface of the planet Jupiter.

Chipman, DeWitt C. Beyond the verge: home of the ten lost tribes of Israel. Part I. In Palmer, Ray, ed. The hidden world, No. A-6. Amherst, Wis., Palmer Publications, 1962. p. 993-1134.

Fiction. Taking with them the Ark of the covenant, the Ten Tribes of Israel enter the North Pole entrance to earth's inner world to await the time "when the Lord calls them all back to Jerusalem."

Chipman, Dewitt C. Beyond the verge: home of the ten lost tribes of Israel. Part II. In Palmer, Ray, ed. The hidden world, No. A-7. Amherst, Wis., Palmer Publications, 1962. p. 1154-1213.

Fiction. Earth's inner world is described as the Ten Lost Tribes of Israel make it their home "until God calls them back to Jeruslem in fulfillment of all his prophesies."

Clarke, Arthur C. Childhood's end. New York, Harcourt, Brace & World, Inc. 1953. 216 p.

Fiction. Omnipotent creatures from out of space stop all wars on earth and get mankind to behave. Mankind unifies into a single intelligence and ascends the next step of the ladder of evolution.

----- Prelude to Mars. New York, Harcourt, Brace & World, Inc., 1965. 497 p.

Two complete fiction novels. Prelude to Space relates preparation for the first trip to the moon. Sands of Mars concerns a science-fiction writer's trip to Mars and his efforts to win the confidence of the pioneers (from earth) there.

----- The sands of Mars. New York, Gnome Press, 1952. 216 p.

A science fiction journalist visits Mars and attempts to win the confidence of the colonists (from earth) there in order to acquire material for a novel.

Conklin, Groff, ed. Invaders of earth. New York, Vanguard Press, Inc., 1952. 333 p.

Science fiction anthology. Antareans planning to colonize earth's oceans conduct experiment in artifical ecological imbalance in This Star Shall be Free, by Murray Leinster. An extraterrestrial visitor to earth disguises his identity in Robert M. Williams' Castaway. A parasitical, intelligent virus from another galaxy seeks human bodies to inhabit and control in Impulse, by Eric F. Russell. In Allan Lang's An Eel by the Tail, a polymorphous, extra-galactic being materializes in a high school physics class. A Date to Remember, by William F. Temple, hypothesizes that wise extraterrestrials are leading earthmen forward subtly and almost imperceptably to an improved future. A gaseous extraterrestrial space animal functioning like a storm front attempts to take over earth in Storm Warning, by Donald Wollheim. In Margaret St. Clair's A Child of Void, immaterial aliens from another space-time continuum who can produce material phenomena, plan to colonize earth. A visiting extraterrestrial with no desire to be on earth, but in desperate need of a part for his spacecraft that is not manufactured here, finds a solution to his problem in Tiny and the Monster, by Theodore Sturgeon. Theme of The Discord Makers, by Mack Reynolds, is that extraterrestrials on the verge of taking over earth have already infiltrated key positions in governments and communications and education systems. An invader comes to earth for the sole purpose of being listened to and admired in Milton Lesser's Pen Pal. Saurian visitants are in trouble and land their spacecraft on earth near a whaling vessel peacefully pursuing its maritime affairs; the spacecraft is fleeing another alien--a true monster that is a threat to both human and saurian in Not only Dead Men, by A. E. Van Vogt. Enemies in Space, by Karl Grunert, is the tale of a planned invasion of earth that is affected by political conflict among the invaders. Invasion from Mars: radio script

version of H. G. Wells' novel, The War of the Worlds, adapted by Howard
Koch and presented by Orson Welles on Mercury Theater of the Air over CBS
on Oct. 30, 1938. A form of life resembling radio waves and dependent on
the movement of the ether, invades earth in The Waveries, by Frederic Brown.
Extraterrestrials hoping to meet earthmen as equals and colleagues conclude
that earth's life class is too primitive and full of hostilities and aggressions
for contact to be feasible in Edward Grendon's Crisis. Creatures from a
highly-advanced planet are eager to help promote advancement of earth's
civilization in Angel's Egg, by Edgar Panghorn. In William Tenn's Will You
Walk a Little Faster? an alien civilization assigned to inhabit earth after
humanity extinguishes itself makes a proposition designed to expedite matters.
A polymorphous creature from Mercury that devours metal invades first the
earth and then the moon in Henry Norton's The Man in the Moon. In Pictures
Don't Lie, by Katherine McLean, submicroscopic aliens evolved on a high-
gravity planet with thin atmosphere that is situated near a blue-white star,
can only see objects in the ultra-violet range. The Greatest Tertian is Anthony
Boucher's burlesque on the scholarly efforts of a posthuman race to understand
earth's vanished civilization.

Craigie, Dorothy. The voyage of the Luna I, by David Craigie [pseud] London,
Eyre & Spottiswoode, 1948. 272 p.

Science fiction. Twin teenagers -- stowaways on a rocket launched to the moon--
explore the lurain. They encounter half-bat, half-fish creatures and uncover
evidence there was once human life on the moon with technological capability.

Cyrano de Bergerac, Savinien. Other worlds. London, New York, Toronto,
Oxford University Press, 1965. 232 p.

Author is the hero of two vayages in space, first to the moon and then to the
sun. Original French edition with title Histoire Comique published in 1950.

De Camp, L. Sprague. Divide and rule. Reading, Pa. Fantasy Press, 1948.
231 p.

Rodent-like oviparous invaders from outer space conquer earth and maintain
their supremacy by keeping men ignorant and split into small, quarreling,
feudal states.

Derleth, August W., ed. Beachheads in space. New York, Pellegrini & Cudahy,
1952. 320 p.

Science fiction anthology on theme of interplanetary exploration. In The Star,
by David Keller, citizens of a nearby star receive information that earth is
planning an invasion and find a means to save their nation. Earth is under
surveillance from a vantage point on the moon in Jack Williamson's The Man
from Outside. In Beachhead, by Clifford Simak, an intergalactic scientific
mission discovers that although they were protected against the obvious and
imaginable, they were defenseless against the unknowable and unimaginable.
The Years Draw Nigh by Lester del Rey, depicts a dying cosmos. A vast

interlocking system of interplanetary systems is described by Eric F. Russell in Metamorphosite. L. Sprague de Camp in The Ordeal of Professor Klein and A. E. Van Vogt in Repetition ironically postulate that interplanetary worlds might duplicate the pattern of human civilization. In Breeds There a Man, Isaac Asimov suggests that extraterrestrial beings whose life span might be thousands of years are studying the life cycle of Homo sapiens as they might bacteria in a test tube. Invasion by extraterrestrials in various physical forms, from multi-dimensional worlds, with differing motives is foreseen in John B. Harris' Meteor; John Wyndham's And the Walls Came Tumbling Down; and and Donald Wandrei's The Blinding Shadows.

----- The other side of the moon. New York, Pellegrini & Cudahy, 1949. 461 p.

Science fiction anthology. The effect that outer stars have on earth is theme of The Star, by H. G. Wells. The Thing on Outer Shoal, by P. Schuyler Miller, is a tale of animal mutations. A sorcerer from another planet -- exploring the mysteries of time, space, and other dimensions -- comes to earth in Frank B. Long's The World of Wulkins. Mysterious monoliths form the gateway between three-dimensional earth and a civilization on a higher plane of vibration -- The City of the Singing Flame, by Clark A. Smith. A cosmic entity attempts to make the adjustment between ethereal life and planet life in H. P. Lovecraft's Beyond the Wall of Sleep. An extraterrestrial creature is encountered by a bum in The Devil of East Lupton, by Murray Leinster. Existence on earth today of a race of mutants representing the next step in man's evolution beyond Homo sapiens is postulated in Nelson Bond's Conqueror's Isle. Attempted invasion of earth by plant-animal-mineral creatures from another world is the theme of Something from Above, by Donald Wandrei. An invading force is killed off by an organism living in a symbiotic relationship with the planet's native population in Will F. Jenkins' Symbiosis. As part of an invasion scheme, an android is sent to earth from Mars in The Vault of the Beast, by A. E. Van Vogt. The Earth Men, by Ray Bradbury, speculates that Martians are so much like earthlings that they have completely satisfied themselves there is no life on any sister planet and have evolved a comprehensive plan for dealing with all self-styled visitors from other planets. Spiro, by Eric F. Russell, concerns a spy by that name from Mars who is able to assume any plant, animal, or mineral form at will. In Resurrection, by A. E. Van Vogt, invaders from another galaxy seeking to colonize earth, find no surviving life on the planet and are destroyed by a human they revive in attempt to discover nature of catastrophe that had occurred.

Dikty, T. E., ed. Great science fiction stories about Mars. New York, Frederick Fell, Inc., 1966. 187 p.

Science fiction based on hypothesis that life exists on Mars. Development of an extra brain lobe enables Martians to manipulate matter in The Sound of Bugles, by Robert M. Williams. Invaders from Mars are robbing earth of its atmosphere for use on their own planet in Nonstop to Mars, by Jack Williamson. The First Martians, by A. E. Van Vogt is based on the adaptability of Indians from the Andes Mountains to the Martian environment. Martian animal life is reported as an admixture of mamilian and insect attributes in Via Etherlin by Eando Binder. Interstellar expedition in Tin Lizzie, by Randall Garrett, discovers that a microscopic life form, akin to bacteria and thriving on hydrocarbon compounds, was responsible for converting Mars' atmosphere to N2O3 and its seas to nitric acid, thereby making the planet uninhabitable for carbon-based life forms. Scientific expedition to is assaulted by a semi-intelligent form of life resembling prairie tumbleweed in Under the Sand Seas, by Oliver E. Saari. Key to the language of vanished Martian civilization is discovered in Omnilingual, by H. Beam Piper.

Drake, W. Raymond. I come from tomorrow. Sunderland, England, The Author, [196-] 272 p.

Typescript. Fiction. Tallus, a young priest-scientist from the year 4168 A.D., travels back through time to the year 1980 A.D. He makes an intensive study of the philosophy and way of life of the twentieth century to try to discover why this civilization deserved destruction. Late in 1980, earth was to be struck by a comet: the Soviet Union, the United States, and China would be engulfed; Atlantis would arise; the earth's axis would be displaced; Great Britain would become an archipelago in the tropics.

----- Miss Venus. Sunderland, England, The Author, [196-] 69 p.

Typescript. Three-act comedy. An exhilarating blonde from Venus lands on earth to help the women of Great Britain persuade the government to outlaw the hydrogen bomb.

----- The stolen bride. Sunderland, England, The Author, [196-] 5 p.

Typescript of a love poem. A flying saucer is the vehicle used by a lover killed in an accident to rescue his beloved from a loveless marriage.

French, Paul. David Starr, Space ranger. Garden City, N. Y., Doubleday & Co., 1952. 186 p.

Science fiction. Organisms on Mars as intelligent as men attempt to gain control of earth through a unique form of bacteriological warfare.

----- Lucky Starr and the big sun of Mercury. Garden City, Doubleday & Co., N. Y., 1956. 191 p.

Science fiction. A project based on Mercury to intercept sunlight, push it through hyperspace, and distribute it evenly over earth so that earth's seasons could be rearranged at will is sabotaged by a raiding party from another galaxy.

----- Lucky Starr and the oceans of Venus. Garden City, N. Y., Doubleday & Co., 1954. 186 p.

Science fiction. Creatures possessing power of complete mental domination over others exert this power under control of invaders from Sirius in effort to subjugate planets of earth's solar system.

----- Lucky Starr and the rings of Saturn. Garden City, N. Y., Doubleday & Co., 1958. 179 p.

Science fiction and interstellar political intrigue. Invaders from Sirius attempt take-over of inhabited planets in earth's solar system.

Garver, Ronald G. The saucer people. Boston, Meador Publishing Co., 1957. 132 p.

Fiction. Extraterrestrial beings impart supernatural powers to an earthman on condition that he use them to advance mankind but not to destroy it.

Garvin, Richard M. and Edmond Addeo. The FORTEC conspiracy. Los Angeles, Sherbourne Press, 1968. 181 p.

UFO "thriller" based on "clasic" UFO sighting cases.

Gibson, Edmund H. A.D. 2018: recollections of the chaplain of a space ship. New York, Greenwich Book Publishers, 1958. 62 p.

Fiction. A trip to Venus is the means through which the crew gains knowledge of intelligent life throughout the universe and of cosmic Christianity.

Guttridge, Len. The biggest news in the world. Flying saucers from another world, June 1957: 70-75.

Fiction. Invasion by UFOs and benevolent crew.

Harris, John B. The Midwich cuckoos, by John Wyndham [pseud.] New York, Ballantine Books, 1957. 247 p.

Fiction. A flying saucer lands on the British town of Midwich and twenty-four hours are blotted from the memories of everyone in the community. As of the following day, every woman in town turns out to be pregnant. When the children are born, they are distinguished by great golden eyes. By the time they are nine they have developed a community mind and a community will, special powers which they admit will untimately doom mankind. They are destroyed through ther trust in the man who educated them.

Harris, John B. Out of the deeps, by John Wyndham   pseud.   New York,
Ballantine Books, 1953. 182 p.

Fiction. Chronicles in detail the attempts of an alien race who have settled
in earth's ocean depths to destroy mankind.

Heinlein, Robert A.   The menace from earth.   London, Dobson, Books Ltd.,
1959. 255 p.

Science fiction stories. Flying saucer landings in The Year of the Jackpot
harbinger worldwide catastrophes and ultimately the end of the world. In
By His Bootstraps, a man comes back from the future to meet himself, fights
himself, while himself stands by and watches; a man from 30,000 years hence
is sent back to obtain certain itmes for a resident of the future who also
turns out to be himself.

----- The puppet masters. Garden City, N. Y., Doubleday & Co., 1951. 219 p.

Fiction. Each member of a race of slugs from out of space takes complete
physical and mental control of a human being.

Hoyle, Fred and John Elliot. A for andromeda. New York, Harper & Bros.,
1962. 206 p.

Fiction. Radio signals are received containing assembly instructions for a
human being. They were transmitted from a now dead world in our nearest
neighboring galaxy, the Andromeda nebula, two million light years distant.

Jenkins, William F. Sidewise in Time, by Murray Leinster [pseud]. Chicago,
Shasta Publishers, 1950. 211 p.

Collection of fiction stories. Sidewise in time suggests that the past, future
and present travel not in a straight line, but like a curving river; not only
are events of the actual past, present, and future blended, but also time
tracks that never happened. Proxima Centauri is the tale of an interstellar
spaceship that is a world in itself as well as one presenting a civilization of
carnivorous plants. A Logic Named Joe deals with the time when a device
would be present in every home, linked in with a central univac-type "tank, "
which would contain all man's knowledge and would dispense information to
subscribers. De Profundis relates the inability of intelligent life inhabiting
the ocean depths to comprehend that intelligent life can exist on earth's surface. In The Fourth Dimensional Demonstrator, a machine is built which,
by moving back in time, will bring into being a replica of an object placed
upon it. The Power is the story of the member of an extraterrestrial race,
stranded on earth, who wishes to impart his wisdom to mankind but is instead killed because of their incomprehension.

Kazantsev, Alexander. A visitor from outer space. In A Visitor from outer
space, science fiction stories by Soviet writers; Violet L. Dutt, translator.
Moscow, Foreign Languages Publishing House, 1961. p. 110-148.

Fiction. Exploits the hypothesis of an extraterrestrial sapcecraft explosion in Tunga, Siberia, on June 30, 1908. While many scientists believe that devastation of a forest there over an area with a radius of about 50 kilometers was due to explosion of a bolide, the meteor was not recovered and no crater was discovered.

Kim-Nicklasson, Lars. Erotikvisslarna. Vänersborg, Vänerforlaget, 1967. 123 p.

Fictional account of the landing of a spaceship carrying space creatures whose primary concern seems to be with sex and who proceed to investigate the sexual habits of humans. The sexual habits of both are described in detail. Based in part on the experiences of a Brazilian farmer, Antonio Villas Boas, and the Americans, Barney and Betty Hill, as reported in James G. Fuller's The Interrupted Journey: Two Lost Hours "Aboard a Flying Saucer" (New York, Dial Press, 1966).

Knight, Damon. Three novels. Garden City, N. Y., Doubleday & Co., 1967. 189 p.

Three stories dealing with invasion of earth by alien beings: Rule Golden, Natural State, and The Dying Man.

Lewis, Clive S. Out of the silent planet. London, John Lane, 1938. 182 p.

Fiction. Hero is accidentally involved in a trip to Malacandra (Mars) and learns that the universe -- except for earth -- exists in harmony and peace, having a common language and a common interplanetary religion and government.

----- Perelandra. London, John Lane, 1943. 256 p.

Fiction. Temptation comes to an unfallen world, Perelandra (the planet Venus), through a demon-possessed visitor from earth; through the good offices of another visitor from earth, however, it remains unfallen.

----- That hideous strength. London, John Lane, 1945. 474 p.

Fiction. Earth is the scene of a cosmic struggle between the dominant forces of darkness and the struggling forces of good.

Lindsay, David. A voyage to Arcturus. New York, Macmillan, 1963. 244 p.

Interplanetary fiction. Main character journeys via spaceship to a planet circling around the star Arcturus. He has a series of adventures, usually involving spiritual temptation and most often culminating in murder. God is represented as a vulgar, selfish being who creates life for the sensual pleasure it gives Him, and by His act inflicts untold misery on spirit thus imprisoned in flesh.

Lovecraft, Howard P. The call of Cthulhu. In his The Dunwich horror and others.
Sauk City, Wis., Arkham House, 1963. p. 130-159.

Tale of a cult that worships the "Great Old ones" who lived ages before there
were any men, who "came to the young world out of the sky, " and who are now
inside the earth and under the sea. The mode of speech of these beings is
transmitted thought and they "speak to the sensitive among mankind by mold-
ing their dreams. "

----- The colour out of space. In his The Dunwich Horror and others. Sauk
City, Wis., Arkham House, 1963. p. 60-88.

An amorphous globule of color from another world or plane of existence sub-
sists on terrestrial life forms.

----- The Dunwich horror. In his The Dunwich horror and others. Sauk City,
Wis., Arkham House, 1963. p. 160-202.

A creature partly resembling man but from another plane of existence plans
extirpation of entire human race and all animal and vegetable life from earth
to a dimension outside the material universe.

----- The shadow out of time. In his The Dunwich horror and others. Sauk City,
Wis., Arkham House, 1963. p. 370-431.

Fantasy based on the premise that mankind is only one -- perhaps the least --
of the highly evolved and dominant races of this planet's long and largely
unknown career.

----- The whisperer in darkness. In his The Dunwich horror and others. Sauk
City, Wis., Arkham House, 1963. p. 212-277.

Tale of "outer space beings" more vegetable than animal that traverse interstellar space in corporeal form to obtain metals from mines on earth and
then transport them to their own worlds.

Macvey, John W. Journey to Alpha Centauri. New York, Macmillan, 1965.
256 p.

Speculative consideration of interstellar travel, its prospects, and implications.
Study -- in series of extracts from diaries -- of human, moral, and sociological problems that could confront first stellar astronauts on 215-year expedition to Alpha Centauri during the seven generations the trip would take.

Newman, Bernard. The flying saucer. New York, Macmillan, 1950. 250 p.

----- The Dunwich horor. In his The Dunwich horror and others. Sauk City, Wis., Arkham House, 1963. p. 160-202.

A creature partly resembling man but from another plane of existence plans extirpation of entire human race and all animal and vegetable life from earth to a dimension outside the material universe.

----- The shadow out of time. In his The Dunwich horror and others. Sauk City, Wis., Arkham House, 1963. p. 370-431.

Fantasy based on the premise that mankind is only one -- perhaps the least -- of the highly evolved and dominant races of this planet's long and largely unknown career.

----- The whisperer in darkness. In his The Dunwich horror and others. Sauk City, Wis., Arkham House, 1963. p. 212-277.

Tale of "outer space beings" more vegetable than animal that traverse interstellar space in corporeal form to obtain metals from mines on earth and then transport them to their own worlds.

Macvey, John W. Journey to Alpha Centauri. New York, Macmillan, 1965. 256 p.

Speculative consideration of interstellar travel, its prospects, and implications. Study -- in series of extracts from diaries -- of human, moral, and sociological problems that could confront first stellar astronauts on 215-year expedition to Alpha Centauri during the seven generations the trip would take.

Newman, Bernard. The flying saucer. New York, Macmillan, 1950. 250 p.

Fictitious account of effectiveness of a hoax in uniting nations of the world against threat of invasion by Martians.

Russell, Eric F. Sinister barrier. Reading, Pa., Fantasy Press, 1948. 253 p.

Fiction. Humans come to the realization that the planet earth is "owned" by alien globes of light called Vitons who "breed" us like cattle and influence our history for their own purposes.

Santesson, Hans S., ed. Flying saucers in fact and fiction. New York, Lancer Books, 1968. 224 p.

Anthology of science fiction stories in which the central themes revolve
around "flying saucers" and imaginative solutions to the mystery. Two
non-fiction essays, one pro-UFO by Ivan T. Sanderson, and one anti-
UFO by Lester Del Rey, are included. Other outstanding science
fiction writers such as Robert Bloch, Judith Merril, Theodore Sturgeon,
John Stephens, Miriam Allen de Ford, Bertram Chandler, Edward D. Hoch,
Aidan van Alm, John Nicholson, and Richard Wilson are represented.

Short, Gertrude. A visitor from Venus. New York, William-Frederick Press,
1949. 43 p.

Fiction. A woman from Venus indicates the possibility of world peace
based on organized action by women everywhere.

Smith, Edward E. The first lensman. Reading, Pa., Fantasy Press, 1950.
306 p.

Fiction. The lensman are a group of men and women from many worlds,
trained to mental and physical attainment so high as to mark them
as beginning of a superior race. Ultimately, through selective mating,
they will achieve a point of development where they can become guardians of
the galaxy. The lens itself is a communication device worn on the wrist of a
lensman; if worn by anyone but its owner it proves deadly.

----- Galactic patrol. Reading, Pa., Fantasy Press, 1950. 273 p.

Fiction. The Galactic Patrol is an interstellar police force organized
to combat the piracy and lawlessness threatening the structure of galactic
civilization. Behind the scenes are prime movers. The Arisians, whose spores,
projected through the galaxy, caused life to form in their image on many
worlds, manipulate events for good. The Eddorians, creatures from another
space continuum, in their lust for power are the cause of most ills.

Van Vogt, Alfred E. Slan. New York, Simon and Schuster, 1951. 247 p.

Fiction. Slan is the story of a nine-year-old boy who is a member of
a superhuman race. His people possess both mental and physical
superiority, being capable of reading minds through the aid of
antenna-like tendrils in their hair; two hearts invest them with extraordinary stamina. His parents killed, the boy fights to survive in a
society where organized hunts are conducted against slans by the humans
and where tendrilless slans -- born without the ability to read minds --
are even more dangerous enemies.

----- The voyage of the space beagle. New York, Simon and Schuster, 1950, 240 p.

Interplanetary fiction. During colonization of a galactic-wide system, interstellar scientific expedition encounters creatures whose drives and needs are based on nonhuman metabolism and who have ability to control energy fields and the minds of humans. New science of nexialism, providing techniques for speeding up processes of absorbing knowledge and of using effectively what has been learned, is applied to same humans in the expedition from annihilation.

----- The world of Ā. New York, Simon and Schuster, 1948. 246 p.

Fiction. The protagonist, a mutant with a double mind, doesn't know who he is and tries to find out. Selected as one of the most advanced intellects on earth, he goes to Venus for special training and is told the secret of immortality.

Vasse, Cornelie (Wouters) [baronne de]. Le char volant ou voyage dans la lune. Paris, Veuve Ballard & Fils, 1783. 203 p.

Fictitious account of trip by philosopher Erastus to the moon, the sun, and other planets, with descriptions of their climates, customs, and inhabitants.

Verne, Jules. A journey to the center of the earth. London, New York, G. Routledge, 1887. 254 p.

Fiction. Finding instructions on a piece of parchment for reaching the center of the earth through an Icelandic volcano, Professor Hardwigg of Hamburg goes on the journey, taking along his nephew, Henry Lawson, and an Icelander names Hans Bjelke.

Wells, Herbert George. The first men on the moon. Longdon, G. Newnes, Ltd., 1901. 342 p.

Fictitious account of discovery of substance opaque to gravity and its use in constructing spacecraft which lands first men on the moon. Voyage, landing, and exploration of moon described in detail; human society criticized through depiction of a non-human culture.

Wilhelm, Kate. The killer thing. Garden City, New York, 1967. 190 p.

Fiction. A malfunctioning robot programed to kill with the laser becomes a threat to the galaxy.

MIRAGES

The first four references are among the most useful standard texts on physical meteorology. All contain adequately detailed treatment of the general theory of mirages.

Fleagle, Robert G. and Joost A. Businger. An introduction to atmospheric physics. New York, Academic Press, 1963, pp. 272-302.

Humphreys, W.J. Physics of the air. New York, McGraw-Hill Book Co., 3rd edition, 1940, pp. 455-475.

Johnson, John C. Physical meteorology. New York, The Technology Press of M.I.T. and John Wiley & Sons, 1954, pp. 1-30.

Tverskoi, P.N. Physics of the atmosphere. Jerusalem, Israel Program for Scientific Translations, 1965, pp. 457-478.

Durst, C.S. and G.A. Bull. An unusual refraction phenomenon seen from a high-flying aircraft. Meteorological Magazine, London, 85 (1010), August 1956: 237-242.

Discusses the rarely seen mirage caused by refraction of light through an elevated layer of warm air. The optical effects of such layers have often been invoked to explain UFO sightings. This article clarifies the severe restrictions on elevation angle at which such mirages are possible.

Fleagle, Robert G. The optical measurement of lapse rate. Bulletin of the American Meteorological Society, 31(2), February 1950: 51-55.

The author develops a method to measure the change of temperature with height by optically measuring the apparent change in elevation of a light source. Nomograms are provided which show the difference between apparent and true elevations as a function of lapse rate and length of optical path.

Gordon, J.H. Mirages. Washington, D.C., Smithsonian Institution Publication 4398, 1959, published 1960.

A non-technical article that describes mirage formation as depending on a lens of air similar in function to lenses in cameras.

Haug, Odd. On the theory of superior mirages. Meteorologiske Annaler, Oslo, 3(12), 1953: 295-310.

A full discussion of light passing through a strong inversion.

ten Kate, H. Luchtspiegelingen. Hemel en Dampkring, 49(5), 1951: 91-94.

Clear explanations, with good illustrations, of the theory of mirages.

Kohl, G. Erklärung einer luftspiegelung nach oben aus radiosondierungen. Zeitschrift fur Meteorologie, 6(11), November 1952: 344-348.

A mirage in Fichtelgebirge is explained quantitatively from radiosonde data.

Minnaert, M. Light and colour in the open air. New York, Dover Publication, 1954.

A superb example of non-technical exposition covering not only mirages but also nearly every other aspect of visual and optical phenomena in the sky and the landscape, from rainbows to the spoke-patterns in bicycle wheels.

Ozorai, Zoltán. Légkröi tükröződések nullámgelüteken (Mirages on wave surfaces) Időjárás, 58(3), May-June 1954: 143-153.

Classical mirage theory only handles the formation of three images. The author proposes to handle more than three images by considering reflections from wave surfaces on inversions.

Pernter, J.M. and F.M. Exner. Meteorologische optik. Leipzig and Vienna, Wilhelm Braumuller, 2nd edition, 1922, pp. 57-238.

The classical work on meteorological optics. The theory of mirages is developed in great detail and a number of striking cases are carefully examined.

375

Raman, Sir C.V. The optics of mirages. Current science, Bangalore, 29(8),
August 1959: 309-313.

The author explains the basic concepts of inferior and superior mirages.

Wood, Robert W. Physical optics. New York, Dover Publications, 3rd edition,
1961, pp. 64-98.

A classical work in the field. Wood, a gifted experimentalist, produced
mirages in the laboratory by heating sand-covered iron plates. His careful
measurements are witness to the essential validity of present-day mirage
theory.

Menkello, Frederick. Quantitative aspects of mirages. ETAC Report 6112,
Environmental Technical Applications Center, Military Air Command,
USAF, Washington, D.C., March 1969. 15 p.

Even under unusual meteorological conditions, mirages only take place at
angles very near the horizon. This report presents graphs and nomograms for
determining the angles under which mirages can be seen. Drawings and graphs
are given to scale.

ADDENDA

U.S. Air Force officers' briefing on UFOs. Proceedings. Boulder, University of Colorado, 1967. 36 p.

Summary of discussions and presentations that were tape recorded during June 12-13, 1967 meeting. Included are: The UFO Problem by Robert J. Low; Identification of Flying Objects by Franklin E. Roach; Problems of Human Perception as Related to the UFO Phenomenon by Michael A. Wertheimer; Investigating Sightings by David R. Saunders; and Instrumentation by Joseph H. Rush.

Barry, J. Dale. Ball lightning. Journal of atmospheric and terrestrial physics, v. 29, 1967: 1095-1101.

Results are presented of extensive survey of reported ball lightning observations during the last 300 years. A statistical description of the phenomenon was obtained in terms of its properties and characteristics. The description is discussed and various relationships between the properties and characteristics of the phenomenon are established. In addition, several properties previously attributed to ball lightning are shown to be erroneous.

Boffey, Philip M. UFO project: trouble on the ground. Science, v. 161, July 26, 1968: 339-342.

Discussion of problems and controversy surrounding the University of Colorado study of UFOs directed by Edward U. Condon.

Calkins, Ken. America has closed the credulity gap. Boeing magazine, v. 38, May 1968: 15.

Postulating that the public has become accustomed to readily accepting the incredible, the author says it is difficult to find a scientist who will publicly dispute what appears to be patently ridiculous. He discusses in this context circumstances surrounding the death of the horse, Snippy, in Colorado during September 1967.

Capparella, Angelo, III. Letters: French UFOs. Science, v. 161, August 16, 1968: 631.

Author challenges statement by Thornton Page of Wesleyan University (Science, v. 160, June 14, 1968: 1258) that no telescope or observatory has taken a picture of a UFO. He notes that Jacques Vallee mentions in Challenge to Science (Chicago, Henry Regnery, 1966) that two images were recorded by the trajectory analyzers at Forcalquier Observatory, France, May 3-4, 1957.

U.S. Congress. House. Committee on Science and Astronautics. Symposium on unidentified flying objects. /Washington, U.S. Govt. Printing Office, 1968/ 247 p. (90th Congress, 2d session. House. Report no. 7).

Contains statements by Dr. J. Allen Hynek, Dr. James E. McDonald, Dr. Carl Sagan, Dr. Robert L. Hall, Dr. James A. Harder and Dr. Robert M. L. Baker. Prepared papers are included by Dr. Donald H. Menzel, Dr. R. Leo Sprinkle, Dr. Garry C. Henderson, Dr. Stanton T. Friedman, Dr. Roger N. Shepard and Dr. Frank B. Salisbury.

Cote, Alfred J. UFO study credibility cloud? Industrial research, June 1968: 26-28.

Following conclusions emerged as the result of Industrial Research inquiry into status of University of Colorado UFO study: (1) the project does not stress investigation of the people doing the observing, rather than of physical phenomena; (2) there appears to be no effort in the study directed at a serious evaluation of extraterrestrial hypotheses; (3) a follow-on investigation apparently will be proposed in the final report, in a chapter that treats future government handling of UFOs.

Fowler, Raymond E. Engineer involvement in UFO investigations. American engineer, May 1968: 29-31.

The Massachusetts Investigating Subcommittee of the National Investigations Committee on Aerial Phenomena (NICAP) has enlisted engineering talent to assist in solving the UFO phenomenon. During 1967, approximately 100 UFO sightings were investigated in Massachusetts under engineer supervision.

(U.S.) GAO investigating contract on UFOs. Scientific research, June 10, 1968: 18.

Details are given of U.S. General Accounting Office scrutiny of the University of Colorado contract requested by Congressman J. Edward Roush (D-Ind.).

Hynek, J. Allen. UFOs and the numbers game. Natural history, v. 77, March 1968: 24, 25, 66, 70.

Two UFO books are reviewed: Uninvited Visitors, by Ivan T. Sanderson and Flying Saucers -- Here and Now! by Frank Edwards.

Jones, R. V. The natural philosophy of flying saucers. Physics bulletin, July 1968: 225-230.

Author reviews the "character of the evidence regarding flying saucers," and concludes that if known natural phenomena are insufficient to explain everything that has been genuinely seen, the alternative to the intelligently controlled vehicles hypothesis is an as yet unrecognized phenomenon.

Keel, John A. New flying saucer crime wave they can't cover up. Male, v. 18, December 1968: 28, 54, 56.

Cases throughout the world are reported (1953-1967) in which people have allegedly been pursued, injured, kidnapped and killed by UFOs.

Konecci, Eugene B. Bioastronautics review - 1963. Washington, D.C., National Aeronautics and Space Administration, 1963. 82 p.

Author notes interest of both U.S. and U.S.S.R. in phenomenon of electro-magnetic communication between living organisms and possible applications in space. He says: "To the Soviets, these applications mean a 'thought register,' an 'electronic hypnotizer,' and 'thought transfer over distance'; and to Western scientists and engineers the results of valid experimentation in energy and information transfer could lend to new communications media and advanced emergency techniques ... Presented at the 14th International Astronautics Federation meeting in Paris, September 26-October 1, 1963. /Some alleged "contactees have claimed that communication with UFO occupants was by thought transfer.7

Langmuir, Irving. Pathological science. Transcribed and edited by R. N. Hall. Schenectady, N. Y., General Electric Research and Development Center, 1968. 13 p. /Report no. 68-C-035/.

Transcript of talk given by author at G.E. Research Laboratory, Schenectady, N.Y., on December 18, 1953. Examples are given of cases in which there was no dishonesty involved, but where false conclusions were reached because the researchers did not understand the extent to which human beings can delude themselves due to subjective effects, wishful thinking, or threshold interactions. The Davis-Barnes experiment, Blondlot's N-rays, and Gurwitsch's mitogenetic rays are discussed in this context.

McDonald, James E. Does Congress have a responsibility to investigate the UFO problem? Tucson, Arizona, The Author, 1968. 4 p.

In talk to the Burro Club luncheon meeting on June 3, 1968, Rayburn Building, Washington, D.C., author asks for a Congressional inquiry into the UFO phenomenon. He emphasizes that the inquiry should be assigned to a committee primarily concerned with matters of science and technology.

Mayfield, Melburn R. The rise of gravity in the 17th century; or a life in the day of Isaac Newton. Physics today, June 1968: 42-46.

Satirical verse purporting to "bring a powerful new insight into some of the long-standing mysteries concerning the personal and professional life of Sir Isaac Newton": the source of his "philosophical innovations" and "mathematical elegancies" was a beautiful female flying saucer occupant.

Moller, P.S. Engineering professor teaches UFO course at the University of California. American engineer, May 1968: 32-34.

Students discuss social and technical implications of worldwide UFO sightings in an experimental course, "Flying Saucers: The Social and Technological Implications," given at the University of California at Davis.

Morse, Robert F. UFOs and the technological community. American engineer, May 1968: 24-28.

Noting that reports of unidentified flying objects have been with us for at least two decades, the author says the time has come to enlist the full resources of the technological community, worldwide, in an examination of these persistent and as yet unexplained sighting reports.

Natural lasers cause UFOs? The laser weekly, v. 1, no. 25: 2.

According to Victor T. Tomberg of the Biophysics Research Lab at New York Medical College, natural laser action in space may be responsible for UFO phenomena. Tomberg maintains that natural laser and maser action should exist in outer space. He also claims that this concentrated radiation may be aimed at our sky and might explain some of the unidentified flying objects that have been reported.

Page, Thorton. Letters: French UFOs. Science, v. 161, August 16, 1968: 631.

Author insists on the accuracy of his claim that no telescope or observatory has taken a picture of a UFO. He says that photographs taken at Forcalquier Observatory, France, May 3-4, 1957, described by Jacques Vallee in Challenge to Science (Chicago, Henry Regnery, 1966) do not fit the hypothesis of extra-terrestrial bodies entering our atmosphere at 5 to 7 miles per second.

-------------. Photographic sky coverage for the detection of UFOs? Science, v. 160, June 14, 1968: 1258-1260.

Author says that in connection with a course on flying saucers that he taught at Wesleyan University, it was determined that over a period of 20 years, during which there were at least 11,000 visual sightings of UFOs, no astronomical photograph has recorded one, even though artifical satellites, meteors, and asteroids are frequently noted. Article speculates on what frequency of random UFO tracks could be missed by astronimical telescopes now in use.

Powers, William T. UFO in 1800: meteor? Science, v. 160, June 14, 1968: 1260.

Article contains reprint of William Dunbar's report in Transactions of the American Philosopical Society (v. 6, no. 25, 1804) of an aerial object that was never positively identified. Powers comments that Dunbar's drawing of the object was not very different in shape from some of the phenomena reported currently.

Review of the University of Colorado report on unidentified flying objects by a panel of the National Academy of Sciences. NAS, 1969. 6 p.

NAS panel headed by Dr. Gerald M. Clemence, Yale University, concurs with scope, methodology and findings of the Colorado Project (Condon) report. Concludes "On the basis of present knowledge the least likely explanation of UFOs is the hypothesis of extraterrestrial visitations by intelligent beings." Reprinted in News Report, National Research Council (NAS-NAE), XIX(2), Feb. 1969: 6-8. Also printed by the Clearinghouse for Federal Scientific and Technical Information in hard copy and microform.

Salisbury, Frank B. Exobiology. Fort Collins, Colorado, The Author, 1964. 9 p.

Author outlines the kinds of evidence for extraterrestrial life and comments briefly on some of the more pertinent points. He cites testimony of witnesses who claim to have experienced or seen a visitation by an extraterrestrial intelligent being. Paper delivered at the First Annual Rocky Mountain Bio-engineering Symposium held at the U.S. Air Force Academy, Colorado, May 4-5, 1964, sponsored by the USAF Academy and the Committee on Electrical Techniques in Medicine and Biology of the Institute of Electrical and Electronic Engineers.

Saunders, David R. and R. Roger Harkins. UFOs? yes!, where the Condon Committee went wrong. New York, Signet Books, 1968. 256 p.

Bias and mis-direction of the Condon investigation at the University of Colorado is alleged by an ex-member of the group and collaborator, with introduction by John Fuller.

Scientific Study of unidentified flying objects, conducted by the University of Colorado under contract No. F44620-67-C-0035. Dr. Edward U. Condon, scientific director. Daniel S. Gillmore, editor. Boulder, 1968, three volumes, 1,465 p. 80 plates.

Final report of the University of Colorado project studying UFOs under support provided by the Air Force Office of Scientific Research, OAR, at the direction of the Secretary of the Air Force. Two-year project concluded (a) that about 90 percent of all UFO reports prove to be quite plausibly related to ordinary phenomena, (b) that little if anything has come from the study of UFOs in the past 21 years that has added to scientific knowledge, and (c) that further extensive study of UFO sighting is not justified in the expectation that science will be advanced thereby. At the same time it is emphasized that (c) is an opinion based on evidence now available. Also printed in hard copy and microform by Clearinghouse for Federal Scientific and Technical Information, vol. 1, AD 680 975; vol. 2, AD 680 976; vol. 3, AD 680 977. Also printed complete by Bantam Books, New York, 1969, with introduction by Walter Sullivan, New York Times. Also printed by E. P. Dutton, New York, 1969.

Syiem, S. Sand. A flying saucer? Hindustan standard, November 12, 1967: 5.

Two eyewitness report sighting a whirling cylindrically-shaped UFO 200-300 feet high near Dympep Village, India, on October 18, 1967.

Walker, Sydney, III. Establishing observer creditability: a proposed method. Journal of the astronautical sciences, v. 15, March-April 1968: 92-96.

Brief review of critical chain of linked processes -- anatomic, phipiologic, and psychological -- which operate to determine the nature of the observations made by an individual, whether of an accident, a planned experiment, or a phenomenon such as a UFO. Purpose of review is to demonstrate how, through the use of proper medical examination, the integrity of the observer system can be established in such a way that eye witness creditability does not have to be left to the kind of speculation that is so frequent.

Wertheimer, Michael. A case of "autostasis" or reverse autokinesis. Perceptual and motor skills, 26, 1968: 417-418.

Three of five observers of a light in the night sky that was actually moving continuously along a linear course reported it as stationary as long as the light was on. The phenomenon, "autostatis," seems to be opposite to the well-known phenomenon of autokinesis, or apparent motion of an actually stationary light in an undifferentiated field.

Communication with extraterrestrial intelligence. IEEE Spectrum, v. 3, no. 3, March 1966: 153-163.

A condensation of Session 1-5 of the 1965 IEEE Military Electronics Conference (MIL-E-CON 9), Washington, D. C., Sept. 22-24, 1965, based on the questions of recognizing and communicating with extraterrestrial intelligence. Harold Wooster, moderator, Paul L. Garvin, Lambros D. Callimahos, John C. Lilly, William O. Davis and Francis J. Heyden.

AUTHOR INDEX

383

Leonard, Frederick C.   263
Le Poer Trench, Brinsley   10, 29,
   118, 119, 309
Leroy, Gerard   173, 180
Leslie, Desmond   10, 51, 68, 83, 138
Levin, Gilbert V.   242
Lewellen, John   291
Lewis, Clive S.   370
Ley, Willy   105, 242, 291, 323, 358
Liddel, Urner   119
Lighthall, W. D.   264
Lindsay, David   369
Lindsay, Gordon   68, 95, 119
Liss, Jeffrey G.   204, 242
Lloyd, Dan   75, 105, 204
Loftin, Robert   10, 119, 346
Lonnqvist, C.   264, 292
Lore, Gordon   10, 171
Lorenzen, Coral E.   11, 39, 68, 83,
   106, 119
Lovecraft, Howard P.   370
Lovitch, A.   51
Lowell, Percival   242
Luciano, Galli   68
Luckiesh, Matthew   136
Luna, Walter F.   95, 186
Lyustiberg, Villen   29

-M-

MacGowan, Roger A.   292
Macvey, John W.   292, 303, 370, 371
Magee, Judith   204
Mallan, Lloyd   29, 157, 162
Mamontoff, Nicholas   346
Manas, John H.   120
Mandel, Siegfried   30
Maney, Charles A.   12, 30, 42, 77,
   121, 132, 162, 186, 205, 253
Mann, Mary   186
Manning, Henry P.   347
Marais, D.   30, 96
Margaria, Rodolfo   292
Margolis, Howard   30, 162, 219
Markowitz, William   30, 216
Marshall, James S.   242
Martin, D. M.   69
Martin, Mitch   154
Mauer, Edgar F.   121
Maunder, E. W.   292
Mayher, Ralph   142
McClain, Edward F.   275
McColley, Grant   264, 292
McCoy, John   18, 99
McDonald, James E.   11, 12, 29, 95,
   119, 120, 162, 215, 216
McHugh, L. C.   292

Meadows, A. J.   315, 316
Meerloo, Joost A.   121, 155
Menger, Howard   69, 303
Menzel, Donald H.   55, 121, 122, 133,
   264, 294
Merker, Donald   221
Mesnard, Joel   205
Michael, Cecil   69, 155
Michel, Aime   12, 78, 83, 84, 106,
   122, 133, 134, 162, 175, 186, 187,
   242
Michell, John F.   51
Miles, H. G.   315, 316
Miles, Max B.   275
Miller, Evelyn   155, 303
Miller, E. C.   275, 282, 347
Miller, H. W.   264, 292
Miller, Max B.   30, 43, 51, 70, 106,
   162, 187
Miller, R. DeWitt   122
Miller, Robert W.   12, 171
Miller, Stewart   30, 163
Miller, Will   155, 303
Misraki, Paul   51, 96, 309
Mitchell, Betty   69
Mitchell, Helen   69
Moffat, Samuel   264
Mollohan, Hank   187
Moore, Patrick   236, 241, 251, 263,
   264, 291, 294
Moorehouse, Frederick G.   31, 122,
   149
Moreux, Theophile   294
Morgan, Dean   187
Morrison, Philip   272
Moseley, James W.   12, 52, 122, 309
Motz, Lloyd   294
Mugler, C.   232, 293
Mulholland, John   123
Muller, Hermann J.   230
Muller, Wolfgang D.   294
Munday, John C.   163
Mundo, Laura   70, 242
Munitz, Milton K.   226, 236, 293
Murray, Jacqueline   232, 351
Mustapa, Margit   303

-N-

National Investigations Committe on
   Aerial Phenomena   13, 175, 188,
   205
Nebel, Long John   13, 70
Needham, A. E.   226
Nelson, Albert F.   243
Nelson, Buck   70, 85
Newman, Bernard   370, 371
Nicolson, Majorie H.   251

Winder, R. H. B.   74, 75, 79, 109,
    151, 212
Windes, V. M.   353
Wolk, George   40
Wood, Robert H.   131
Woodley, Morris   194
Wright, Eric   222
Wylie, C. C.   131
Wylie, Philip   131

-Y-

Young, John R.   131, 349
Young, Mort   58, 158
Young, Richard S.   268
Younghusband, Francis   227, 268, 299,
    349

-Z-

Zaitsev, Vyacheslav   53, 312
Zenabi, J.   18, 73, 249
Zigel, Felix   38, 168, 212, 359
Zinsstag, Lou   38, 139, 178, 194
Zubek, T. J.   349
Zully, Alphones   87

Unidentified Flying Objects

A Selected Bibliography

Compiled by
Kay Rodgers

Reference Section
Science and Technology Division

Library of Congress   Washington   1976

Library of Congress Cataloging in Publication Data

Rodgers, Kay.
  Unidentified flying objects.

    1. Flying saucers—Bibliography. I. United States. Library of
Congress. Science and Technology Division. Reference Section.
II. Title.
Z5064.F5R63   [TL789]   016.0019′42   76-608275
ISBN 0-8444-0212-5

PREFACE

In 1969, the U.S. Air Force published Lynn Catoe's comprehensive *UFO's And Related Subjects; An Annotated Bibliography,* which was prepared in the Library's Science and Technology Division under contract to the Air Force Office of Scientific Research in support of a project at the University of Colorado led by the late noted scientist Edward U. Condon.

The present bibliography, intended for the more general reader, provides selective coverage of the UFO literature that has appeared since that time, including some of the lively published debate that followed issuance of the "Condon report." The coverage is limited to English-language works but does include translations and materials published abroad. Other bibliographies are listed, as are books, congressional and other government reports, articles from journals and magazines (but not the daily press), and proceedings of conferences and symposia. In some cases, more than one edition of a book is listed (such as American and British editions) to assist interested readers whose access may be limited.

BIBLIOGRAPHIES

Beard, Robert Brookes. Flying saucers, U.F.O.'s and extraterrestrial life: a bibliography of British books, 1950-1970. Swindon, 1971. 5 p.   Z5064.F5

Brennan, Norman. Flying saucer books and pamphlets in English; a bibliographical checklist. Buffalo? 1971?   94 p.   Z5064.F5B74

Catoe, Lynn E. UFOs and related subjects; an annotated bibliography. Washington, U.S. Govt. Print. Off., 1969.   401 p.
                                         Z5064.F5C37
     This was compiled by the Science and Technology Division of the Library of Congress for the Air Force Office of Scientific Research in support of its scientific research project at the University of Colorado on unidentified flying objects under the direction of Dr. Edward U. Condon. It is available from the National Technical Information Service, 5285 Port Royal Road, Springfield, Va. 22161, as AD-688 332.

DeVoe, Barbara M. Unidentified flying objects: a selected annotated bibliography. Washington, Congressional Research Service, Library of Congress, 1969.   49 p.

Jain, Sushil Kumar, *and* Christine Horswell. Twenty years of flying saucers; a select list of interesting books and periodical articles published during 1947-1966. Tenderden (Kent.), Sushil Jain Publications, 1967-. v.   Z5064.F5J3

Page, Henrietta M. Flying saucers; a bibliography. Aiken, S.C., Page, 1975.   18 p.   Z5064.F5P3 1975

Sable, Martin Howard. UFO guide: 1947-1967; containing international lists of books and magazine articles on UFO's, flying saucers, and about life on other planets; world-wide directories of flying saucer organizations, professional groups and research centers concerned with space research and astronautics, a partial list of sightings, and an international directory of flying saucer magazines. Beverly Hills, Calif., Rainbow Press, 1967.   100 p.
                                         Z5064.F5S3

BOOKS

Adamski, George. Flying saucers farewell. London, New York, Abelard-Schuman, 1961. 190 p. TL789.A29

Adler, Bill, *comp.* Flying saucers have arrived! New York, World, 1970. 352 p. TL789.A334 1970

————, *comp.* Letters to the Air Force on UFOs. New York, Dell, 1967. 157 p. TL789.A34
From the files of the U.S. Air Force "Project blue book."

Aggen, Erich. UFOs: the unknown factor. Kitchener, Ont., Galaxy Press, 1970. 45 p. TL789.A46

Anchor. Transvaal episode; a UFO lands in Africa. Corpus Christi, Tex., Essene Press, 1958. 48 p. TL789.3.A48

Anderson, Carl Arthur. Two nights to remember! Los Angeles, Calif., New Age, 1956. 55 p. TL789.3.A5

Barker, Gray, *comp.* Book of Adamski. Clarksburg, W. Va., Saucerian Books, 196-? 78 p. TL789.B28

———— Book of saucers. Clarksburg, W. Va., Saucerian Books, 1965. 77 p. TL789.B29

Barton, Michael X. Educational and inspirational courses of study. Los Angeles, Futura Press, 1957-64. 13 v. TL789.3.B36

———— The German saucer story. Los Angeles, Futura Press, 1968. 88 p. TL789.B33

Beere, D. Chessman. USP—a physics for flying saucers; an interpretation from memory of a communication from Atos Xetrov, visitor. Del Mar, Calif., USP Press, 1973. 54 p. QC6.B424

Benham, Wilfrid Earnshaw. Biometric analysis of the "flying saucer" photographs. 1st ed. reprinted with illustrations. Hastings (Sussex), Metaphysical Research Group, 1968. 29 p. TL789.B47 1968

Bergrun, Norman R. Tomorrow's technology today. Campbell, Calif., Academy Press, 1972. 65 p. TL789.B48

Bernard, Raymond W. Flying saucers from the Earth's interior. Mokelumne Hill, Calif., Health Research, 196-? 89 p. QE509.B465
Includes bibliographical references.

—————— The hollow earth, the greatest geographical discovery in history made by Admiral Richard E. Byrd in the mysterious land beyond the poles, the true origin of the flying saucers. New York, University Books, 1969.   254 p.   QE509.B47 1969
Bibliography: p. 16-17.

Binder, Otto Oscar.   What we really know about flying saucers. Greenwich, Conn., Fawcett Publications, 1967.   224 p.
TL789.B55

Blum, Ralph, and Judy Blum.   Beyond earth: man's contact with UFOs. New York, Bantam, 1974.   248 p.   TL789.B59
Bibliography: p. 235-236.

Bray, Arthur R.   Science, the public and the UFO. Ottawa, Bray Book Service, 1967.   193 p.   TL789.B7
Bibliography: p. 166-182.

British Unidentified Flying Object Research Association. A guide to the UFO phenomenon. London, B.U.F.O.R.A., 1972.   178 p.
TL789.B74

Buckle, Eileen.   The Scoriton mystery. London, Spearman, 1967. 303 p.   TL789.B8

Burt, Eugene H.   UFO's and diamagnetism; correlations of UFO and scientific observations. New York, Exposition Press, 1970.   134 p.
TL789.B9

Campione, Michael J.   U.F.O.s . . . 20th century's greatest mystery. Cinnaminson, N.J., 1968.   129 p.   TL789.C32

Carter, Joan Frances.   Fourteen footsteps from outer space. Dallas, Tex., Royal, 1966.   168 p.   TL789.3.C37

Cathie, Bruce Leonard.   Harmonic 33. Wellington, Auckland, etc., Reed, 1968.   207 p.   TL789.C39

Cathie, Bruce Leonard, and P. N. Temm.   Harmonic 695; the UFO and anti-gravity. Wellington, Reed, 1971.   201 p.   TL789.C38

Chapman, Robert.   Unidentified flying objects. London, Mayflower, 1970.   160 p.   TL789.C49 1970

Chase, Frank Martin.   Document 96; a rationale for flying saucers. Clarksburg, W. Va., Saucerian Publications, 1968.   123 p.
TL789.C5

Clark, Jerome, and Loren Coleman.   The unidentified: notes toward solving the UFO mystery. New York, Warner Paperback Library, 1975.   272 p.   TL789.C56
Bibliography: p. 251-262.

Colorado. *University*. Final report of the scientific study of unidentified flying objects. Edward U. Condon, scientific director. Daniel
S. Gillmore, editor. Introd. by Walter Sullivan. New York, Dutton,
1969. 967 p.   TL789.C658 1969
    Commonly known as the Condon report or Project Bluebook
report.

———— Final report of the scientific study of unidentified flying
objects conducted by the University of Colorado. Edward U.
Condon, scientific director. Daniel S. Gillmore, editor. Boulder,
Colo., 1968. 3 v. (1465 p.)   TL789.C658
    Commonly known as the Condon report or Project Bluebook
report.

Cox, Donald William. America's explorers of space, including a
special report on UFO's. Illus. by Dwight Dobbins. Maplewood,
N.J., Hammond, 1967. 93 p.   TL789.85.A1C65

Davidson, Leon. Flying saucers: an analysis of the Air Force
project blue book special report no. 14. 3d ed. Ramsey, N.J.,
Ramsey-Wallace Corp., 1966. 128 p.   TL789.D3 1966

———— Flying saucers: an analysis of the Air Force project blue
book special report no. 14. 4th ed. Clarksburg, W. Va., Saucerian
Books, 1971. 1 v.   TL789.D3 1971

Dean, John W. Flying saucers closeup. Clarksburg, W. Va., G.
Barker, 1969, c1970. 224 p.   TL789.3.D42

Derenberger, Woodrow W. Visitors from Lanulos. As related by
Woodrow W. Derenberger to the author, Harold W. Hubbard. New
York, Vantage Press, 1971. 111 p.   TL789.3.D47

Downing, Barry H. The Bible and flying saucers. Philadelphia,
Lippincott, 1968. 221 p.   TL789.D68

Dutta, Rex. Flying saucer message. London, Pelham, 1972. 117 p.
                                                   TL789.D89

———— Flying saucer viewpoint. London, Pelham, 1970. 115 p.
                                                    TL789.D9

Eden, Jerome. Planet in trouble; the UFO assault on Earth. New
York, Exposition Press, 1973. 214 p.   TL789.E26
    Bibliography: p. 211-214.

Edwards, Frank. Flying saucers, here and now! New York,
L. Stuart, 1967. 261 p.   TL789.3.E38

———— Flying saucers, serious business. New York, L. Stuart, 1966. 319 p. TL789.E3

Emenegger, Robert. UFO's, past, present, and future. New York, Ballantine, 1974. 180 p. TL789.E43

Ferguson, William. My trip to Mars. Clarksburg, W. Va., Saucerian Publications, 196-? 14 p. TL789.3.F47

Flammonde, Paris. The age of flying saucers; notes on a projected history of unidentified flying objects. New York, Hawthorn Books, 1971. 288 p. TL789.F5
    Bibliography: p. 269-274.

Flying saucers illustrated. Compiled by the editors of Real magazine. Studio City, Calif., Kling House, 1967. 79 p. TL789.F57

Flying saucers; twenty-one years of UFO's, the great mystery of our time. New York, Cowles Education Corp., 1968. 157 p.
    TL789.F59

Ford, Brian John. The earth watchers. London, Frewin, 1973. 211 p. TL789.F63

Fort, Charles. New lands. New York, Garland, 1975, c1941. 222 p.
    QB54.F78 1975

Fowler, Raymond E. UFOs: interplanetary visitors; a UFO investigator reports on the facts, fables, and fantasies of the flying saucer conspiracy. Jericho, N.Y., Exposition Press, 1974. 365 p.
    TL789.F64

Fry, Daniel W. The White Sands incident. Louisville, Ky., Best Books, 1966. 120 p. TL789.F7 1966

Fuller, John Grant. Incident at Exeter; the story of unidentified flying objects over America today. New York, Putnam, 1966. 251 p. TL789.F8

———— The interrupted journey; two lost hours "aboard a flying saucer." New York, Dial Press, 1966. 301 p. TL789.F82

Girvin, Calvin C. The night has a thousand saucers. El Monte, Calif., Understanding, 1958. 168 p. TL789.G57

Glemser, Kurt. Men in black: startling new evidence. Kitchener, Ont., 1970. 45 p. TL789.3.G5

———— U.F.O. report, 1969. Kitchener, Ont., 1970. 44 p.
    TL789.G58
    Bibliography: p. 34-44.

5

Glemser, Kurt. UFOs: menace from the skies. Kitchener, Ont., Galaxy Press, 1972. 36 p. TL789.G59

Grant, Walter V. Men from the moon in America: did they come in a Russian satellite? Dallas, Faith Clinic, 195-? 31 p. TL789.G7

———— Men in the flying saucers identified: not a mystery! Dallas, Faith Clinic, 195-? 32 p. TL789.3.G68

Green, Gabriel, *and* Warren Smith. Let's face the facts about flying saucers. New York, Popular Library, 1967. 127 p. TL789.3.G7

Gross, Loren E. The UFO wave of 1896. Fremont, Calif., Loren E. Gross, 1974. 30 p. TL789.G76

Hervey, Michael. UFOs over the southern hemisphere. London, Hale, 1975. 250 p. TL789.H44 1975

Hobana, Ion, *and* Julien Weverbergh. UFO's from behind the Iron Curtain. Translated from the Dutch. London, Souvenir Press, 1974. 309 p. TL789.H57 1974
  Bibliography: p. 289-303.

The Humanoids by Aimé Michel and others. Edited by Charles Bowen. Chicago, Regnery, 1969. 256 p. TL789.H85 1969

Hynek, J. Allen. The UFO experience; a scientific inquiry. Chicago, Regnery, 1972. 276 p. TL789.H9

Hynek, J. Allen, *and* Jacques Vallee. The edge of reality: a progress report on unidentified flying objects. Chicago, Regnery, 1975. 228 p. TL789.H89 1975

Jacobs, David Michael. The UFO controversy in America. Bloomington, Indiana University Press, 1975. 362 p. TL789.J26 1975

Kachur, Victor. Space scientists and the UFO phenomenon: an informal survey prepared by V. Kachur. Bedford, Mass., Biospace Associates, 1967. (Biospace Associates. Report 672) TL789.K33

Keel, John A. The Mothman prophecies. New York, Saturday Review Press, 1975. 269 p. TL789.K37 1975

———— Strange creatures from time and space. London, Spearman, 1975. 288 p. QL89.K43 1975

———— UFO's: Operation Trojan Horse. New York, Putnam, 1970. 320 p. TL789.K36 1970
  Bibliography: p. 308-312.

Keyhoe, Donald Edward. Aliens from space: the real story of un-identified flying objects. Garden City, N.Y., Doubleday, 1973. 322 p.   TL789.K386

Klass, Philip J. UFOs explained. New York, Random House, 1975, c1974. 369 p.   TL789.K56 1975

Knaggs, Oliver. Let the people know. Cape Town, H. Timmins, 1966. 113 p.   TL789.K59

Layne, Meade. The coming of the guardians; an interpretation of the "flying saucers" as given from the other side of life. 5th ed. Vista, Calif., Borderland Sciences Research Associates Foundation, 1964. 72 p.   TL789.L36 1964

Le Poer Trench, Brinsley, *Hon.* The eternal subject. London, Souvenir Press, 1973. 216 p.   TL789.L38 1973

———— The flying saucer story. London, Spearman, 1966. 208 p.   TL789.L4
     Bibliography: p. 197-202.

———— Mysterious visitors: the UFO story. London, Pan Books, 1975. 175 p.   TL789.L38 1975

———— Mysterious visitors: the UFO story. New York, Stein and Day, 1973, c1971. 192 p.   TL789.L415 1973

———— Operation earth. London, Spearman, 1969. 128 p.   TL789.L42 1969
     Bibliography: p. 117-123.

———— Secret of the ages: UFOs from inside the earth. London, Souvenir Press, 1974. 192 p.   TL789.L44 1974

Leslie, Desmond, *and* George Adamski. Flying saucers have landed. Rev. and enl. ed., with a special commentary on George Adamski by Desmond Leslie. London, Spearman, 1970. 281 p.   TL789.L46 1970
     Bibliography: p. 279-281.

Lobsang Rampa, Tuesday. My visit to Venus. Illus. by Gene Duplantier. Clarksburg, W. Va., Saucerian Books, 1966? 42 p.   TL789.3.L6

Loftin, Robert. Identified flying saucers. New York, D. McKay, 1968. 245 p.   TL789.L54
     Bibliography: p. 239-245.

Lore, Gordon I. R., *and* Harold H. Deneault. Mysteries of the skies; UFOs in perspective. Englewood Cliffs, N.J., Prentice-Hall, 1968. 237 p.   TL789.L58

Lorenzen, Coral E., *and* Jim Lorenzen. Flying saucer occupants. Introd. by Frank B. Salisbury. New York, New American Library, 1967. 215 p.   TL789.L59

———— UFOs: the whole story. New York, New American Library, 1969. 301 p.   TL789.L67

Lorenzen, Jim, *and* Coral Lorenzen. UFO's over the Americas. New York, New American Library, 1968. 254 p.   TL789.L65

McCampbell, James M. UFOlogy: new insights from science and common sense. Belmont, Calif., Jaymac, 1973. 153 p. TL789.M15

McCoy, John. They shall be gathered together. Corpus Christi, Tex., 1957. 74 p.   TL789.3.M28

McCoy, John, Ray Stanford, *and* Rex Stanford. From out of this world. Corpus Christi, Tex., 1957. 66 p.   TL789.3.M27

Mallan, Lloyd. The official guide to UFOs. New York, Science & Mechanics, 1967. 96 p.   TL789.M24

Martin, Dan. Seven hours aboard a space ship. Clarksburg, W. Va., Saucerian Publications, 1968. 17 p.   TL789.3.M36

Mitchell, Helen, *and* Betty Mitchell. We met the space people; the story of the Mitchell sisters. Clarksburg, W. Va., Saucerian Books, 1959. 15 p.   TL789.3.M57

Moseley, James W. The Wright Field story. Clarksburg, W. Va., Saucerian Books, 1971. 80 p.   TL789.M65

Moyer, Ernest P. The day of celestial visitation. 2d ed. Hicksville, N.Y., Exposition Press, 1975. 304 p.   TL789.M68 1975
Includes bibliographical references.

National Investigations Committee on Aerial Phenomena. UFOs: a new look; a special report. Edited by Donald E. Keyhoe and Gordon I. R. Lore. Washington, 1969. 46 p.   TL789.N33

Nelson, Buck. My trip to Mars, the Moon, and Venus. Mountain View, Mo., 1966, c1956. 44 p.   TL789.3.N44 1966

Owens, Ted. Flying saucer intelligences speak. 2d ed. Kitchener, Ont., Galaxy Press, 1972. 32 p.   TL789.3.O87 1972

———— How to contact space people. Clarksburg, W. Va., Saucerian Books, 1969. 96 p.   TL789.3.O9

Pallman, Ludwig F.   Cancer planet mission. London, Foster, 1970.
216 p.   BF1999.P24

Phillips, Ted, *comp.* Physical traces associated with UFO sightings:
a preliminary catalog. Northfield, Ill., Center for UFO Studies,
1975.   144 p.   TL789.P44
Bibliography: p. 139-141.

Prytz, John M.   Ufology and the UFO; an anthology of selected
papers on UFOs, exo-biology and astronomy. Kitchener, Ont.,
Galaxy Press, 1970.   47 p.   TL789.P75

Rehn, K. Gösta.   UFOs here and now. Translated from the Swedish
by Patricia Crampton. London, Abelard, 1974.   198 p.
                                                    TL789.R45 1974
Bibliography: p. 196-198.

Salisbury, Frank B.   The Utah UFO display: a biologist's report, with
data from the files of Joseph Junior Hicks. Old Greenwich, Conn.,
Devin-Adair, 1974.   286 p.   TL789.S18
Bibliography: p. 231-238.

Sanderson, Ivan Terence.   Invisible residents; a disquisition upon
certain matters maritime, and the possibility of intelligent life
under the waters of this earth. New York, World, 1970.   248 p.
                                                          GC28.S25

———— Uninvited visitors: a biologist looks at UFO's. London,
Spearman, 1969.   245 p.   TL789.S2 1969
Bibliography: p. 242-244.

The Saucerian review.   Edited by Gray Barker. Clarksburg, W. Va.,
1956.   98 p.   TL789.S24

Saunders, David Robertson, *and* R. Roger Harkins.   UFOs? Yes!
Where the Condon committee went wrong. Introd. by John G.
Fuller. New York, World, 1969, c1968.   256 p.   TL789.S25
Bibliography: p. 253-256.

Segraves, Kelly L.   Sons of God return. New York, Pyramid Books,
1975.   191 p.   TL789.S32

Shuttlewood, Arthur.   UFOs, key to the new age. London, New
York, Regency Press, 1971.   218 p.   TL789.S515

———— The Warminster mystery. London, Spearman, 1967.   207 p.
                                                        TL789.S516

Smith, Wilbert B.   The boys from Topside. Edited by Timothy Green
Beckley. Clarksburg, W. Va., Saucerian Books, 1969.   96 p.
                                                       TL789.3.S57

Soule, Gardner.   UFOs and IFOs; a factual report on flying saucers.
New York, Putnam, 1967.   192 p.   TL789.3.S6 1967

Spencer, John Wallace.   No earthly explanation: mankind, a space
experiment. Springfield, Mass., Phillips, 1974.   240 p.   TL789.S67

Stamey, Dennis.   U.F.O.s—realm of the fantastic. Kitchener, Ont.,
Galaxy Press, 1970.   47 p.   TL789.S72

Stanford, Ray, and Rex Stanford.   Look up. Corpus Christi, Tex.,
Essene Press, 1958.   66 p.   TL789.S74

Stanton, L. Jerome.   Flying saucers: hoax or reality? New York,
Belmont Books, 1966.   157 p.   TL789.S75

Stanway, Roger Howard, and Anthony R. Pace.   Flying saucer
report: UFO's unidentified, undeniable. Stoke-on-Trent (Staffs.),
Newchapel Observatory, 1968.   91 p.   TL789.S753

Steckling, Fred.   Why are they here? Spaceships from other worlds.
Introd. by Charlotte Blob. New York, Vantage Press, 1969.   148 p.
                                                   TL789.S756

Steiger, Brad.   Mysteries of time & space. Special archeological
research by Ron Calais. Englewood Cliffs, N.J., Prentice-Hall,
1974.   232 p.   GN741.S83
     Bibliography: p. 211-225.

Steiger, Brad, and Joan Whritenour.   Flying saucers are hostile.
New York, Award Books, 1967.   160 p.   TL789.S76

Stewart, Edward A.   The Apollyon; a guide in the observation and
reporting of the unidentified flying objects (U.F.O.). Rev. ed.
Bordentown, N.J., 1973.   17 p.   TL789.3.S73

Stranges, Frank E.   Danger from the stars; a warning from Frank
E. Stranges. Van Nuys, Calif., I.E.C., 196-?   14 p.   TL789.S77

———— My friend from beyond earth. Kitchener, Ont., Galaxy Press,
1972.   24 p.   TL789.3.S76

———— New flying saucerama. 4th ed. Glendale, N.Y., International
Evangelism Crusades, 1966.   117 p.   TL789.S78 1966

The True report on flying saucers, by leading UFO authorities,
including Donald E. Keyhoe. Exclusive project blue book sighting,
photos from U.S. Air Force files. Compiled by the editors of True.
Greenwich, Conn., Fawcett Publications, 1967.   96 p.   TL789.T7

Twitchell, Cleve. The UFO saga. Lakemont, Ga., CSA Press, 1966. 94 p.   TL789.T94

Unidentified Flying Objects Research Committee. The Fitzgerald report; a complete and detailed account of the sighting of an unidentified flying object, Sheffield Lake, Ohio, September 21, 1958. Akron? Ohio, 1959. 19 p.   TL789.3.U54

United States. *Air Force.* Aids to identification of flying objects. Washington, U.S. Govt. Print. Off., 1968. 36 p.   TL789.U5345
Bibliography: p. 35-36.

United States. *Congress. House. Committee on Science and Astronautics.* Aliens in the skies; the scientific rebuttal to the Condon Committee report. Testimony by six leading scientists before the House Committee on Science and Astronautics, July 29, 1968. Edited and with an introd. and commentary by John G. Fuller. New York, Putnam, 1969. 217 p.   TL789.U56
Commonly known as the Fuller report.

Vallee, Jacques. Anatomy of a phenomenon: unidentified objects in space—a scientific appraisal. Chicago, Regnery, 1965. 210 p.   TL789.V33
Bibliography: p. 193-200.

———— Passport to Magonia: from folklore to flying saucers. Chicago, Regnery, 1969. 372 p.   TL789.V338
Includes bibliographical references.

Vallee, Jacques, *and* Janine Vallee. Challenge to science; the UFO enigma. Chicago, Regnery, 1966. 268 p.   TL789.V335
Bibliography: p. 241-258.

Vesco, Renato. Intercept—but don't shoot; the true story of the flying saucers. Translated by D. D. Paige. New York, Grove Press, 1971. 338 p.   TL789.V4213

Webb, David F. 1973, year of the humanoids: an analysis of the fall 1973 UFO/humanoid wave. Webb, 1974. 62 p.   TL789.W38
Includes bibliographical references.

Wilkins, Harold Tom. Flying saucers uncensored. New York, Citadel Press, 1955. 255 p.   TL789.W49

Williamson, George Hunt. The saucers speak; a documentary report of interstellar communication and radiotelegraphy. Rev. ed. London, Spearman, 1963. 160 p.   TL789.W5 1963

Wilson, Clifford A. UFOs . . . and their mission impossible. New York, New American Library, 1975, c1974. 225 p.   TL789.W53
Bibliography: p. 223-225.

JOURNAL ARTICLES

Air Force conclusion; spacemen don't fly saucers. Senior scholastic, v. 95, Jan. 12, 1970: 2.   AP2.S477

Are flying saucers real? latest on an old mystery. U.S. news & world report, v. 75, Nov. 5, 1973: 75-76.   JK1.U65

Armagnac, A. P. Condon report on UFO's, should you believe it? Popular science, v. 194, Apr. 1969: 72-76.   AP2.P8

Binder, O. O. How flying saucers can injure you. Mechanix illustrated, v. 64, Jan. 1968: 64-66+   T1.M46

Blob, meet UFO. Newsweek, v. 81, June 11, 1973: 32.   AP2.N6772

Blum, R. Are UFOs for real? Reader's digest, v. 104, June 1974: 89-93.   AP2.R255

Boffey, P. M. UFO project; trouble on the ground. Science, v. 161, July 26, 1968: 339-342.   Q1.S35

———— UFO study: Condon group finds no evidence of visits from outer space. Science, v. 163, Jan. 17, 1967: 260-262.   Q1.S35

Carlson, David R. The Air Force and the UFO. Aerospace historian, v. 22, winter 1974: 210-217.   UG633.A1A515

Clarke, A. C. Whatever happened to flying saucers? Saturday evening post, v. 243, summer 1971: 10.   AP2.S22

Closing the Blue Book; Air Force to call off UFO investigations due to Condon report. Time, v. 94, Dec. 26, 1969: 28.   AP2.T37

Condon, E. U. Scientific study of UFOs; University of Colorado report; excerpts. Saturday review, v. 52, Feb. 1, 1969: 53-55.   Z1219.S25

———— UFOs I have loved and lost; adaptation of address, April 1969. Bulletin of the Atomic Scientists, v. 25, Dec. 1969: 6-8.   TK9145.A84

Condon study rebuts UFOs; critics offer own version. Physics today, v. 22, Mar. 1969: 67+   QC1.P658

Edward Condon: a physicist never afraid of a fight. Physics today, v. 22, Mar. 1969: 66-67.   QC1.P658

Flying saucers: not real, but—. U.S. news & world report, v. 66, Jan. 20, 1969: 6. JK1.U65

Fuller, J. G. Flying saucer fiasco. Look, v. 32, May 14, 1968: 58+ AP2.L79

Heiserman, D. Now, a do-it-yourself UFO. Popular science, v. 196, May 1970: 109. AP2.P8

Hooven, F. J. UFOs and the evidence; Condon report. Saturday review, v. 52, Mar. 29, 1969: 16-17+ Z1219.S25

Hynek, J. A. How to photograph a UFO. Popular photography, v. 62, Mar. 1968: 69+ TR1.P885

——— A review of E. U. Condon's Scientific study of unidentified flying objects. Bulletin of the Atomic Scientists, v. 25, Apr. 1969: 39-42. TK9145.A84

——— UFO's and the numbers game. Natural history, v. 77, Mar. 1968: 24-25+ QH1.N13

Hynek, J. A., and B. Ford. Science takes another look at UFO's. Science digest, v. 73, June 1973: 9-13. Q1.S383

Krutch, J. W. If you don't mind my saying so; inexplicable saucer reports. American scholar, v. 38, summer 1969: 370+ AP2.A4572

Lights in the sky; letters. Physics today, v. 28, Oct. 1975: 9+ QC1.P658

Lost cause; Condon report. Nation, v. 208, Jan. 27, 1969: 100. AP2.N2

Mead, M. UFOs—visitors from outer space? Redbook, v. 143, Sept. 1974: 57-58+ AP2.R28

New flying saucer story. Mechanix illustrated, v. 70, Feb. 1974: 34-35+ T1.M46

New turn for flying saucers. U.S. news & world report, v. 67, Dec. 29, 1969: 7. JK1.U65

Nixon, Stuart. How to report things that go bump in the night. Quill, v. 62, July 1974: 19-23. PN4700.Q5

Noonan, A. Man who saw Venus; interview, edited by L. Mallan. Mechanix illustrated, v. 64, May 1968: 58-60+ T1.M46

Page, T. Photographic sky coverage for the detection of UFO's. Science, v. 160, June 14, 1968: 1258-1260.   Q1.S35

Prescott, P. S. A review of J. A. Keel's Mothman prophecies. Newsweek, v. 85, Mar. 24, 1975: 84.   AP2.N6772

Salisbury, F. B. Recent developments in the scientific study of UFO's. BioScience, v. 25, Aug. 1975: 505-512.   QH1.A277

Saucer diehards. Time, v. 97, June 28, 1971: 49.   AP2.T37

Saucers' end; Condon report. Time, v. 93, Jan. 17, 1969: 44-45.   AP2.T37

Shooting down the UFO's; Condon report. Newsweek, v. 73, Jan. 20, 1969: 54.   AP2.N6772

Stardust and moonshine; UFO sightings. Newsweek, v. 82, Oct. 29, 1973: 31.   AP2.N6772

Study grounds flying saucers. Senior scholastic, v. 94, Jan. 31, 1969: 21-22.   AP2.S477

UFO clans gather. Time, v. 106, Nov. 3, 1975: 64.   AP2.T37

UFO report rejects nonterrestrial origin. Aviation week and space technology, v. 90, Jan. 27, 1969: 85.   TL501.A8

UFO's over Washington; call for renewed scientific and governmental saucer research. Newsweek, v. 72, Aug. 12, 1968: 72.   AP2.N6772

Vallee, J. A review of J. A. Hynek's UFO experience. Bulletin of the Atomic Scientists, v. 29, Apr. 1973: 49-52.   TK9145.A84

Warren, D. I. Status inconsistency theory and flying saucer sightings. Science, v. 170, Nov. 6, 1970: 599-603.   Q1.S35

Whatever happened to UFO's? Science news, v. 99, June 26, 1971: 435-436.   Q1.S76

Who sees flying saucers? Science digest, v. 69, Feb. 1971: 34-35.   Q1.S383

PROCEEDINGS

Apro UFO Symposium, *5th, Pottstown, Pa., 1974.* Proceedings of the 5th APRO UFO Symposium, June 15, 1974, Pottstown, Pennsylvania, sponsored by Aerial Phenomena Research Organization. Tucson, Ariz., Aerial Phenomena Research Organization, 1974. 22 p. TL789.A1A67 1974

Congress of Scientific UFOlogists, *New York, 1967.* New York's first flying saucer convention. Reported by Bessie J. Gibbs and Opal Smith. Winchester, Va., B. J. Gibbs, 1967? 106 p.
TL789.A1C6 1967

Eastern UFO Symposium, *Baltimore, 1971.* Proceedings. Edited by Coral E. Lorenzen. Tucson, Ariz., Aerial Phenomena Research Organization, 1971. 40 p. TL789.A1E37 1971

Friedman, Stanton T. UFOs—myths & mystery; 1971 Midwest UFO Conference sponsored by Midwest UFO Network (MUFON), n.p., 1971. 1 v. TL789.A1F73

Midwest UFO Conference, *2d, St. Louis, 1971.* UFO's—defiance to science; conference proceedings. O'Fallon, Mo., UFO Study Group of Greater St. Louis, 1971. 115 p. TL789.M498 1971
Bibliography: p. 112-115.

Midwest UFO Conference, *3d, Quincy, Ill., 1972.* MUFON '72, conference proceedings, June 17, 1972. Quincy, Ill., Midwest UFO Network (MUFON), 1972. 145 p. TL789.A1M5 1972

Mufon UFO Symposium, *5th, Akron, Ohio, 1974.* MUFON 1974: UFO symposium proceedings, Akron, Ohio, June 22, 1974. Edited by Walter H. Andrus. Quincy, Ill., Mutual UFO Network, 1974. 162 p.
TL789.A1M83 1974

UFO's—a scientific debate. Edited by Carl Sagan and Thornton Page. New York, Norton, 1974, c1972. 310 p. TL789.A1U23 1974
Papers presented at a symposium sponsored by the American Association for the Advancement of Science, held in Boston on Dec. 26-27, 1969.

United States. *Congress. House. Committee on Science and Astronautics.* Symposium on unidentified flying objects. Hearings, Ninetieth Congress, second session. July 29, 1968. Washington, U.S. Govt. Print. Off., 1968. 247 p. TL789.U57